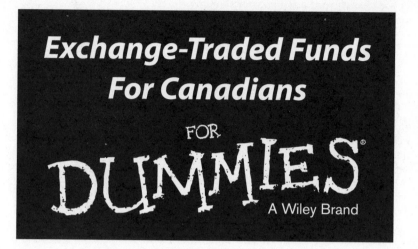

Exchange-Traded Funds For Canadians

FOR DUMMIES
A Wiley Brand

by Russell Wild, MBA, and Bryan Borzykowski

FOR DUMMIES
A Wiley Brand

Exchange-Traded Funds For Canadians For Dummies®

Published by: **John Wiley & Sons Canada, Ltd.,** 6045 Freemont Blvd., Mississauga, ON L5R 4J3, www.wiley.com

Copyright © 2013 by John Wiley & Sons Canada, Ltd.

For general information on John Wiley & Sons Canada, Ltd., including all books published by John Wiley & Sons, Inc., please call our distribution centre at 1-800-567-4797. For reseller information, including discounts and premium sales, please call our sales department at 416-646-7992. For press review copies, author interviews, or other publicity information, please contact our publicity department, Tel. 416-646-4582, Fax 416-236-4448. For technical support, please visit www.wiley.com/techsupport.

Wiley publishes in a variety of print and electronic formats and by print-on-demand. Some material included with standard print versions of this book may not be included in e-books or in print-on-demand. If this book refers to media such as a CD or DVD that is not included in the version you purchased, you may download this material at http://booksupport.wiley.com. For more information about Wiley products, visit www.wiley.com.

Library and Archives Canada Cataloguing in Publication Data

Wild, Russell, author

    Exchange-traded funds for Canadians for dummies / Russell Wild,
Bryan Borzykowski.

(For dummies)

Includes index.

Canadian edition of Exchange-traded funds for dummies, c2012.

Issued in print and electronic formats.

ISBN 978-1-118-52457-2 (pbk.).—ISBN 978-1-118-52463-3 (epub).—
ISBN 978-1-118-52464-0 (mobi).—ISBN 978-1-118-52462-6 (pdf)

    1. Exchange traded funds. 2. Stock index futures.

I. Borzykowski, Bryan, author II. Title. III. Series: —For dummies

HG6043.W44 2013   332.63'27   C2013-903237-1

                                                 C2013-903238-X

Printed in the United States of America

10 9 8 7 6 5 4 3 2 1

Contents at a Glance

Table of Contents

Part II: Building the Stock (Equity) Side of Your Portfolio

Introduction

· ·

*E*very month, it seems, Bay Street comes up with some newfangled invest-ment idea. The array of financial products (replete with 164-page prospec-tuses) is now so dizzying that the old lumpy mattress is starting to look like a more comfortable place to stash the cash. But one relatively new product out there is definitely worth looking at. It's something of a cross between an index mutual fund and a stock, and it's called an *exchange-traded fund,* or ETF.

Just as computers and fax machines were used by big institutions before they caught on with individual consumers, so it was with ETFs. This made-in-Canada product (it's true!) was first embraced by institutional traders — investment banks, hedge funds, and insurance firms — because, among other things, ETFs allow for the quick juggling of massive holdings. Big traders like that sort of thing. During the past several years, millions of North American investors have poured their savings into ETFs — mostly U.S.-based ones, but the Canadian market has been gaining steam too.

We like and use ETFs too. They have grown exponentially in the past few years, and they will surely continue to grow and gain influence. While we can't claim that our purchases and recommendations of ETFs account for much of the growing $1 trillion-plus ETF market, we're happy to be a (very) small part of it. After you've read *Exchange-Traded Funds For Canadians For Dummies,* you may decide to become part of it as well, if you haven't already.

During the last few years, most of the financial world has been focused on imploding hedge funds, mutual fund redemptions, and Bernie Madoff–like swindlers. But one story that should be getting more attention is the rising popularity of ETFs. Thanks to the recession and today's slow-moving market, many folks have ditched their advisors and are now buying these low-cost products. ETFs are almost always cheaper than mutual funds, and they serve as solid building blocks for a diversified portfolio.

But ETFs have gotten a bad rap, too, especially for the role they played in the infamous "flash crash" of May 6, 2010 (see Chapter 2), and for the ongoing role they are playing in the increasingly nauseating volatility of the markets. According to one 2010 report from the Ewing Marion Kauffman Foundation, "ETFs are choking the recovery and may pose unrecognized risks to the financial markets."

Well, we're not so sure about that (especially given that the stock market shot up 10 percent in the six months immediately following the Kauffman report, and the S&P 500 continues to climb today). We discuss the overall effect that ETFs have had on financial markets, but what we concentrate on most in this book is how changes in the ETF market affect *you* — the individual investor. And in that arena, without question, there have been many changes both positive and negative.

One very positive change in the past several years is that investors now have access to ETFs that cover most areas of the market. Half a decade ago, you couldn't buy an ETF that would give you exposure to high-yield bonds. Or international bonds. Or international real estate investment trusts (REITs). All that has changed. ETFs that represent all those asset classes, and many more, now exist. Building an entire well-diversified portfolio out of ETFs was not humanly possible several years ago; it is very possible today.

Another very positive development: ETFs are being used more and more in Registered Retirement Savings Plans (RRSPs) and Tax-Free Savings Accounts (TFSAs), where many of Canada's hard-working people store the bulk of their savings. And they've been appearing in Registered Education Savings Plans (RESPs), too. Insurance companies have also jumped into the fray, offering ETFs in some of their annuity plans (which, unfortunately, are still often overpriced).

Although having more products to choose from is great, many new ETFs are actually bad investments, pure and simple. They were introduced to take advantage of the popularity of ETFs. They are overly expensive, and they represent foolish indexes (extremely small segments of the market, or indexes constructed using highly questionable methodologies). Much of this book is designed to help you tell the good from the bad.

Many of the newer ETFs are also specifically designed for short-term trading — which you would know if you read the really small print at the bottom of the advertisements — and short-term trading usually gets small investors into big trouble.

A scary number of the newer ETFs are based on back-tested models: They track whatever indexes, or invest in whatever kinds of assets, have done the best in recent months or years. These ETFs (or the indexes they track) have shining short-term performance records, which induce people to buy. But past short-term performance is a very, very poor indicator of future performance.

Actively managed ETFs have been slower to take off than Bay Street had hoped but have made inroads during the past couple of years. These ETFs differ radically from the original index ETFs. Actively managed ETFs don't track any indexes at all but instead have portfolios built and regularly traded by managers attempting to beat the indexes. Active management, study after study has shown, usually doesn't work all that well for investors, even though the managers themselves often get very rich (more in Chapter 2).

And finally, many of the newer exchange-traded products aren't ETFs at all but very different financial instruments called *exchange-traded notes* (ETNs). ETNs aren't bad, per se, but they represent risks that ETFs do not . . . and that too few people understand (see our discussion in Chapters 14 and 15).

About This Book

As with any other investment, you're looking for a certain payoff in reading this book. In an abstract sense, the payoff will come in your achieving a thorough understanding and appreciation of a powerful financial tool called an exchange-traded fund. The more concrete payoff will come when you apply this understanding to improve your investment results.

What makes us think ETFs can help you make money?

- ✔ **ETFs are intelligent.** Most financial experts agree that playing with individual stocks can be hazardous to one's wealth. Anything from an accounting scandal to the CEO's sudden angina attack can send a single stock spiralling downward. That's why owning lots of stocks — or bonds — through ETFs or mutual funds makes sense for the average investor.

- ✔ **ETFs are cheap.** At least 150 ETFs charge annual management expenses of 0.20 percent or lower, and a few charge as little as 0.06 percent a year. The average Canadian actively managed mutual fund, in contrast, charges 2.5 percent a year. Index mutual funds generally cost a tad more than their ETF cousins. Such cost differences, while appearing small on paper, can make a huge impact on your returns over time. We crunch some appropriate numbers in Chapter 2.

- ✔ **ETFs are open books.** Quite unlike mutual funds, an ETF's holdings are readily visible. If this afternoon, for example, we were to buy 100 shares of the iShares S&P/TSX 60 Index Fund, we would know that exactly 7.83 percent of our money was invested in Royal Bank, 6.77 percent was invested in TD Bank, and 4.04 percent was invested in Suncor Energy. You don't get that kind of detail when you buy most mutual funds. Mutual fund managers, like stage magicians, are often reluctant to reveal their secrets. In the investment game, the more you know, the lower the odds you will get sawed in half.

  (News flash: North American regulators are still debating just how open the portfolios of the newer actively managed ETFs will have to be. For the time being, however, most ETFs track indexes and the components of any index are readily visible.)

And speaking of open books, if the one you're now reading were like some (but certainly not all) mutual funds, it would be largely unintelligible and expensive. (It might be doubly expensive if you tried to resell the book within 90 days!) Luckily, this book is more like an ETF. Here's how:

- ✓ *Exchange-Traded Funds For Canadians For Dummies* **is intelligent.** We don't try to convince you that ETFs are your best investment choice, and we certainly don't tell you that ETFs will make you rich. Instead, we lay out facts and figures and summarize some hard academic findings, and we let you draw your own conclusions.

- ✓ *Exchange-Traded Funds For Canadians For Dummies* **is cheap.** Hey, top-notch investment advice for only $29.99 (plus or minus any discounts, shipping, and tax). . . . Where else are you going to get that kind of deal? *And* if you come to the conclusion after reading this book that ETFs belong in your portfolio, you'll likely get your $29.99 (plus any shipping costs and tax) back — in the form of lower fees and tax efficiency — in no time at all.

- ✓ *Exchange-Traded Funds For Canadians For Dummies* **is an open book.** We've already established that!

If you've ever read a *For Dummies* book before, you have an idea of what you're about to embark on. This is not a book you need to read from front to back. Feel free to jump about and glean whatever information you think will be of most use. You won't have to take a quiz at the end. You don't have to commit it all to memory.

Keep in mind that when this book was printed, some web addresses may have needed to break across two lines of text. If that happened, rest assured that we haven't put in any extra characters (such as hyphens) to indicate the break. So, when using one of these web addresses, just type in exactly what you see in this book, pretending as though the line break doesn't exist. If you're reading this as an e-book, you've got it easy – just click the web address to be taken directly to the web page.

Throughout this book, you usually find the heavy technical matter tucked neatly into sidebars (those grey-shaded boxes). But if any technicalities make it into the main text, we give you a heads up with a Technical Stuff icon so you can skip over that section, or just speed-read it if you wish.

Foolish Assumptions

We assume that most of the people reading this book know a fair amount about the financial world. We think that's a fairly safe assumption. Why else would you have bought an entire book about exchange-traded funds?

If you think that convertible bonds are bonds with removable tops and that the futures market is a place where fortune tellers purchase crystal balls, we help you along the best we can by letting you know how to find out more about certain topics. However, you may be better off picking up and reading a copy of the basic nuts-'n-bolts *Investing For Canadians For Dummies* by Eric Tyson and Tony Martin (Wiley). After you spend some time with that title, c'mon back to this book. You'll be more than welcome!

Icons Used in This Book

Throughout the book, you find little globular pieces of art in the margins called *icons*. These admittedly cutesy but handy tools give you a heads-up that certain types of information are in the neighbourhood.

Although this is a how-to book, you also find plenty of whys and wherefores. Any paragraph accompanied by this icon, however, is guaranteed pure, 100 percent, unadulterated how-to.

The world of investments offers pitfalls galore. Wherever you see the bomb, know that there is a risk of your losing money — maybe even Big Money — if you skip the passage.

Read twice! This icon indicates that something important is being said and is really worth putting to memory.

If you don't really care about the difference between standard deviation and beta, or the historical correlation between value stocks and REITs, feel free to skip or skim the paragraphs with this icon.

The world of Bay Street (and Wall Street) is full of people who make money at other people's expense. Where you see the pig face, know that we're about to point out an instance where someone will likely be sticking a hand deep in your pocket.

Beyond the Book

In addition to the material in the print or e-book you're reading right now, this product also comes with some access-anywhere goodies on the web. Check out the free Cheat Sheet at www.dummies.com/cheatsheet/exchange tradedfundsforcanadians for articles on Canadian brokerages offering ETFs, Top Canadian websites on ETF advice, and a whole lot more.

Where to Go from Here

Where would you like to go from here? If you wish, start at the beginning. If you're interested only in stock ETFs, hey, no one says that you can't jump right to Part II. Bond ETFs? Go ahead and jump to Part III. It's entirely your call.

Part I

The ABCs of ETFs

The 5th Wave   By Rich Tennant

"Thank goodness it's not his investment portfolio."

In this part . . .

In these first few ground-laying chapters you find out what makes exchange-traded funds different from other investment vehicles. You discover the rationale for their being, why they are popular with institutional investors, why they are rapidly becoming so popular with non-institutional folk, and why the authors of this book like them almost as much as they like milk chocolate.

Although the art and science of building an ETF portfolio come later in the book, this first part introduces you to how ETFs are bought and sold and helps you ponder whether you should even be thinking about buying them.

Chapter 1

The (Sort of Still) New Kid on the Block

· ·

In This Chapter

▶ Discovering the origins of ETFs

▶ Understanding their role in today's world of investing

▶ Tallying their phenomenal growth

▶ Looking at the biggest names in ETFs

· ·

*N*o doubt, a good number of pinstriped ladies and gentlemen in and around Bay Street exist who froth heavily at the mouth when they hear the words *exchange-traded fund*. In a world of very pricey investment products and very well paid investment-product salespeople, ETFs are the ultimate killjoys.

Since their arrival on the investment scene in the early 1990s, more than 1,500 ETFs have been created — including about 250 in Canada — and ETF assets have grown faster than those of any other investment product. That's a good thing. ETFs enable the average investor to avoid shelling out fat commissions or paying layers of ongoing, unnecessary fees. And they've saved investors oodles and oodles in taxes.

Hallelujah.

In the Beginning

What do basketball, snowmobiles, insulin, and ETFs have in common? They were all invented in Canada. Yes, you read that correctly. Though our southern neighbours created the stock market, the mutual fund, and many other investment products, the Toronto Stock Exchange developed the first exchange-traded fund. The Toronto 35 Index Participation fund — the first ETF — was listed in March 1990. It tracked the TSE 35 Composite Index, an index made up of the 35 largest and most liquid stocks on the TSX.

As important as the ETF has become, the story behind its development isn't quite as exciting as, say, the story behind the gas mask or hockey, two other Canadian inventions. As one Toronto Stock Exchange insider explained, "We saw it as a way of making money by generating more trading." Thus was born the original ETF, best known as TIP. The TSE 35 Composite Index was then the closest thing that we had to America's Dow Jones Industrial Average index. Some of the companies on the index included Bell Canada, the Royal Bank, and the now-defunct Nortel.

Enter the traders

TIP was an instant success with large institutional stock traders who could now trade an entire index in a flash. The Toronto Stock Exchange got what it wanted — more trading. And the ETF got its start.

TIP has since morphed to track a larger index, the so-called S&P/TSX 60 Index, which — you probably guessed — tracks 60 of Canada's largest and most liquid companies. The fund also has a different name, the iShares S&P/TSX 60 Index Fund, and it trades under the ticker XIU. It is now managed by BlackRock, Inc., which, upon taking over the iShares lineup of ETFs from Barclays in 2009 (part of a juicy $13.5 billion deal), has come to be the biggest player in ETFs in the world. We introduce you to BlackRock and other ETF suppliers in Chapter 3. (A completely different BlackRock-managed U.S. ETF now uses the ticker TIP, but that fund has nothing to do with the original TIP; the present-day TIP invests in U.S. Treasury Inflation-Protected Securities.)

Moving south of the border

As much as we may not want to admit it, Canadians have invented a lot of things that Americans have then perfected. Think about the BlackBerry and the iPhone. While the ETF was born in Canada, and was popular, this index-tracking product is as widespread as it is thanks to the U.S. market. The ETF took three years to get to the States, but like most things American, when it launched, it launched big.

The mother of all U.S. ETFs was born on January 22, 1993, and listed on the American Stock Exchange (which, in January 2009, became part of NYSE Euronext). The first U.S.-based ETF was called the S&P Depositary Receipts Trust Series 1, commonly known as the SPDR (or Spider) S&P 500, and it traded (and still does) under the ticker symbol SPY.

SPDRs, DIAMONDS, Qubes . . . why the plurals?

Many ETFs have names that end in an *s*. We don't refer to ETFs this way in this book because doing so can be confusing, but you will often hear people talk about the DIAMONDS and the Qubes. Why is that? After all, you would never refer to Fidelity's Canadian Disciplined Equity Fund as *Disciplines*. So why the plural when talking about a single ETF? The convention refers not just to the fund but also to the components of the fund. Thus, *DIAMONDS* refers to the 30 companies that make up the Dow Jones Industrial Average index. *Qubes* refers to the 100 companies that make up the NASDAQ-100 Index. But rest assured that when brokers talk about DIAMONDS and Qubes, they're talking about a single ETF.

The SPDR S&P 500, which tracks the S&P 500 index, an index of the 500 largest U.S. companies, was an instant darling of institutional traders. It has since branched out to become a major holding in the portfolios of many individual and institutional investors — and a favourite of favourites among day traders.

Fulfilling a Dream

ETFs were first embraced by institutions, and they continue to be used, big time, by banks and insurance companies and such. Institutions sometimes buy and hold ETFs, but they're also constantly buying and selling ETFs and options on ETFs for various purposes, some of which we touch on in Chapter 18. For us noninstitutional types, the creation and expansion of ETFs has allowed for similar juggling (usually a mistake for individuals); but more important, ETFs allow for the construction of portfolios possessing institutional-like sleekness and economy.

Goodbye, ridiculously high mutual fund fees

The average mutual fund investor with a $150,000 portfolio filled with actively managed funds likely spends $3,750 (2.5 percent) or so in annual expenses. By switching to an ETF portfolio, that investor may incur trading costs (because trading ETFs generally costs the same as trading stocks) of perhaps $100 or so to set up the portfolio, and maybe $50 or so a year thereafter. But now his ongoing annual expenses will be about $375 (0.25 percent). That's a difference, ladies and gentlemen of the jury, of big bucks. We're looking at an overall yearly savings of $3,375, which is compounded every year the money is invested.

Hello, building blocks for a better portfolio

In terms of diversification, portfolios should include large stocks; small stocks; micro cap stocks; Canadian, U.S., European, and Chinese stocks; intermediate-term bonds; short-term bonds; and real estate investment trusts (REITs) — all held in low-cost ETFs. We discuss diversification and how to use ETFs as building blocks for a class A portfolio in Part II.

Yes, you can use other investment vehicles, such as mutual funds, to create a well-diversified portfolio. But ETFs make diversifying much easier because they tend to track very specific indexes. They are, by and large, much more "pure" investments than mutual funds. An ETF that bills itself as an investment in, say, small growth stocks is going to give you an investment in small growth stocks, plain and simple. A mutual fund that bills itself as an investment vehicle for small growth stocks may include everything from cash to bonds to shares of General Electric (no kidding, and we give other examples in the next chapter).

Will you miss the court papers?

While scandals of various sorts — hidden fees, "soft-money" arrangements, after-hours sweetheart deals, and executive kickbacks — have plagued the world of mutual funds and hedge funds, the ETF industry has far fewer court dates to make. That's because the vast majority of ETFs' managers, forced to follow existing indexes, have very little leeway in their investment choices. Unlike many investment vehicles, ETFs are closely regulated and they trade during the day, in plain view of millions of traders — not after hours, as mutual funds do, which can allow for sweetheart deals when no one is looking. Of course, anything can happen and there has been legal action around leveraged ETFs, but, for the most part, these funds haven't been "judged" nearly as much as other securities.

In Chapter 2, we discuss in greater detail the transparency and cleanliness of ETFs.

Not Quite as Popular as the Latest Teen Idol, but Getting There

ETFs have a lot going for them, so we're not surprised that they have spread like a Justin Bieber video on YouTube. (Fun fact: Bieber also was created in Canada.) From the beginning of 2000, when there were only 80 ETFs on the

U.S. market, to the end of 2012, when there were about 1,300 ETFs, the total assets invested in ETFs rose from $52 billion to just about $1.3 trillion. In Canada, the ETF industry had just $3 billion in assets under management in 2000; that's climbed to $54 billion in 2012.

Certainly, $54 billion pales in comparison to the $811 billion or so invested in Canadian mutual funds. But if current trends continue, ETFs may indeed become as popular as the Biebs.

Part of ETFs' popularity stems from the growly bearish market of the first decade of this millennium. Investors who had been riding the double-digit annual returns of the 1990s suddenly realized that their portfolios weren't going to keep growing in leaps and bounds, and perhaps it was time to start watching investment costs. There has also been a greater awareness of the triumph of *indexing* — investing in entire markets or market segments — over trying to cherry-pick stocks. Much more on that topic in Chapter 2.

Moving from Bay Street to Main Street

In the world of fashion, trendsetters — movie stars or British royals — wander out into public wearing something that most people consider ridiculous, and the next thing you know, everyone is wearing that same item. Investment trends work sort of like fashion trends, but a bit slower. It took from 1990 until 2001 or so for this newfangled investment vehicle to really start moving. By about 2003, insiders say, the majority of ETFs were being purchased by individual investors, not institutions or investment professionals.

BlackRock, Inc., which controls about 45 percent of the U.S. market and about 75 percent of the Canadian market for ETFs, estimates that approximately 60 percent of all the trading in ETFs is done by individual investors. The other 40 percent is institutions and fee-only financial advisors.

Fee-only, by the way, signifies that a financial advisor takes no commissions of any sort. It's a very confusing term because *fee-based* is often used to mean the opposite. Check out Chapter 20, where we talk about what kind of financial professional can help you to build and manage an ETF portfolio, or whether you need one at all.

Actually, individual investors — especially the buy-and-hold kind of investors — benefit much more from ETFs than do institutional traders. That's because institutional traders have always enjoyed the benefits of the very best deals on investment vehicles. That hasn't changed. For example, institutions often pay much less in management fees than do individual investors for shares in the same mutual fund. (Fund companies often refer to *institutional class* versus *investor class* shares. All that really means is "wholesale/low price" versus "retail/higher price.")

The little kid is growing fast: ETFs' phenomenal growth

Following are a few facts and figures that indicate how the ETF market compares with the mutual fund market and how rapidly ETFs are gaining in popularity.

The amount of money invested in Canada-based ETFs and mutual funds as of September 2012:

- ✔ **ETFs:** $54 billion
- ✔ **Mutual funds:** $811 billion

The total number of Canadian-based ETFs and mutual funds as of September 2012:

- ✔ **ETFs:** 250
- ✔ **Mutual funds:** About 5,000

Increase in Canada-based ETFs since 2006:

- ✔ **2006:** 32
- ✔ **2012:** 250
- ✔ **Percentage change increase:** 681%

Increase in Canada ETF providers since 2006:

- ✔ **ETF providers in 2006:** 2
- ✔ **ETF providers in 2012:** 7
- ✔ **Percentage change increase:** 250%

Total net assets growth in ETFs between 2006 and 2012:

- ✔ **2006:** $15 billion
- ✔ **2012:** $54 billion
- ✔ **Percentage change increase:** 250%

Mutual funds versus ETFs

You may think we sound like we're pushing ETFs as not only the best thing since sliced bread but also a replacement for sliced bread. Well, not quite. As much as we like ETFs, good old mutual funds still enjoy their place in the sun. That's especially true of inexpensive index mutual funds, such as the ones offered by TD Canada Trust or CIBC. Mutual funds, for example, are clearly the better option when you're investing in dribs and drabs and don't want to have to pay for each trade you make . . . although some Canadian brokerage houses, such as Scotia iTrade and Qtrade, allow customers to trade certain ETFs for free.

One of the largest purveyors of ETFs is The Vanguard Group, the very same people who pioneered index mutual funds. While the company doesn't offer its mutual funds in Canada, it did start selling ETFs at the end of 2011. Still, because it offers both index funds and ETFs, making an apples-to-apples comparison of ETFs and index mutual funds by looking at Vanguard's American offerings is easy. But rest assured — a point we make over and over in this book — this ain't rocket science. For most buy-and-hold investors, ETFs are almost always the better choice, at least in the long run. We look more closely at the ETFs-versus-mutual funds question when we design specific portfolios and give actual portfolio examples in Chapters 15 and 16.

Ready for Prime Time

Although most investors are now familiar with ETFs, mutual funds remain the investment vehicle of choice by a margin of 15:1. The reasons for the dominance of mutual funds are several. First, mutual funds have been around a lot longer and so got a good head start. Second, largely as a corollary to the first reason, most company retirement plans and pension funds still use mutual funds rather than ETFs; as a participant, you have no choice but to go with mutual funds. And finally, the vast majority of ETFs are index funds, and index funds aren't going to become the nation's favourite investment vehicle anytime soon. They should, but they won't. People just aren't that logical.

Index mutual funds, which most closely resemble ETFs, have been in existence since 1976 when Vanguard first rolled out the Index Investment Trust fund. Since that time, Vanguard and other mutual fund companies have created hundreds of index funds tracking every conceivable index. (TD Canada introduced its popular e-Series index funds in 1999.) Yet index funds remain relatively obscure. According to figures from the Investment Company Institute, index mutual funds in the U.S. hold less than 8 percent of all money invested in mutual funds.

Why would anyone want to invest in index funds or index ETFs? After all, the financial professionals who run actively managed mutual funds spend many years and tens of thousands of dollars educating themselves at places with real ivy on the walls, like Harvard and the University of Toronto. They know all about the economy, the stock market, business trends, and so on. Shouldn't we cash in on their knowledge by letting them pick the best basket of investments for us?

The ripple effect: Forcing down prices on other investment vehicles

You don't need to invest in ETFs to profit from them. They are doing to the world of investing what Chinese labour has done to global manufacturing wages. That is, ETFs are driving prices down. Thanks to the competition that ETFs are giving to mutual funds, fund providers have been lowering their charges. Many companies have cut their management expense ratios (MERs) over the years to help keep mutual funds attractive. Investors Group, one of Canada's largest fund companies, said in May 2012 that it would start reducing its MERs by 0.4 percent per year on two-thirds of its funds, which is about $4 per $1,000 of assets. Part of the reason for the reduction, said the company's CEO, was that Canadians are simply more aware of fund costs these days. Thanks to the ETFs, people know that they can fork over less for fees.

Can you pick next year's winners?

Okay, study after study shows that most actively managed mutual funds don't do as well in the long run as the indexes. But certainly some do much better, at least for a few years. And any number of magazine articles will tell you exactly how to pick next year's winners.

Alas, if only it was that easy. Sorry, but studies show rather conclusively that it is anything but easy. Morningstar, on a great number of occasions, has earmarked the top-performing mutual funds and mutual fund managers over a given period of time and tracked their performance moving forward. In one representative study, the top 30 mutual funds for sequential five-year periods were evaluated for their performance. In each and every five-year period, the "30 top funds," as a group, did worse than the S&P 500 in subsequent years.

Good question! Here's the problem with hiring these financial whizzes, and the reason that index funds or ETFs generally kick their ivy-league butts: When these whizzes from Harvard and the University of Toronto go to market to buy and sell stocks, they are usually buying and selling stocks (not directly, but through the markets) from *other* whizzes who graduated from Harvard and the U of T. One whiz bets that ABC stock is going down, so he sells. His former classmate bets that ABC stock is going up, so she buys. Which whiz is right? Half the time, it's the buyer; half the time, it's the seller. Meanwhile, you pay for all the trading, not to mention the whiz's handsome salary while all this buying and selling is going on.

Economists have a name for such a market; they call it *efficient*. It means, in general, that so many smart people are analyzing and dissecting and studying the market that the chances are slim that any one whiz — no matter how whizzical — is going to be able to beat the pack.

That, in a nutshell, is why actively managed mutual funds tend to lag behind the indexes, usually by a considerable margin. If you want to read more about why stock pickers and market timers almost never beat the indexes, pick up a copy of the seminal *A Random Walk Down Wall Street* by Princeton economist Burton G. Malkiel (W. W. Norton). Or check out this website — www.indexfunds.com — that's run by something of an indexing fanatic (hey, there are worse things to be) that is packed with articles and studies on the subject. You could spend days reading!

The proof of the pudding

One study, done in 2010 by Wharton finance professor Robert F. Stambaugh and University of Chicago finance professor Lubos Pastor, looked back at 23 years of data. The conclusion: Actively managed funds have trailed, and will likely continue to trail, their indexed counterparts (whether mutual funds or ETFs) by nearly 1 percent a year. That may not seem like a big deal, but compounded over time, 1 percent a year can be *huge*.

To show you how only 1 percent can make a big difference over time, we'll plug in a few numbers: An initial investment of $100,000 earning, say, 7 percent a year, would be worth $386,968 after 20 years. An initial investment of $100,000 earning 8 percent for 20 years would be worth $466,096. That's $79,128 extra in your pocket, all things being equal, if you invest in index funds.

Moving from the world of academia and theory to the real world, we now look at that very first ETF introduced in the United States, the SPDR S&P 500 (SPY). Since its inception in January 1993, that fund has enjoyed an average annual return of 8.53 percent — not bad, considering that it survived two very serious bear markets (2000–2002 and 2008–2009). Very few actively managed funds can match that record. (You can find some performance specifics in the next chapter.)

By the way, SPY, as well as it has performed, has several flaws that make it far from our first choice of ETF for most portfolios; we will divulge these in Chapter 5. But despite its flaws, SPY remains by far the largest ETF on the market, with total assets of $131 billion. (The largest fund of any kind is the PIMCO Total Return mutual fund (PTTRX), with total net assets of $288 billion.) In terms of number of shares traded daily, nothing even comes close to SPY.

The major players

In Parts II and III of this book, we provide details about many of the ETFs on the market. Here, we want to introduce you to just a handful of the biggies. You will likely recognize a few of the names.

In Table 1-1, we list the six largest Canadian ETFs on the market as of mid-October 2012, as calculated by assets under management.

Table 1-1	The Six Largest Canadian ETFs by Assets	
Name	*Ticker*	*Assets (in billions of dollars)*
iShares S&P/TSX 60 Index	XIU	$11.50
iShares DEX Short Term Bond Index	XSB	$2.24
iShares DEX All Corporate Bond Index	XCB	$2.02
iShares DEX Universe Bond Index	XBB	$1.92
iShares S&P 500 Index C$-Hedged	XSP	$1.77
iShares S&P/TSX Capped Composite Index	XIC	$1.42

In Table 1-2, we list the six largest U.S. ETFs based on their assets.

Table 1-2	The Six Largest American ETFs by Assets	
Name	*Ticker*	*Assets (in billions of dollars)*
SPDR S&P 500	SPY	$131.1
SPDR Gold Shares	GLD	$60.7
Vanguard MSCI Emerging Markets ETF	VWO	$57.1
iShares MSCI Emerging Markets Index	EEM	$44.9
iShares Core S&P 500	IVV	$40.9
iShares MSCI EAFE Index	EFA	$40.6

Commercialization is tainting a good thing

Innovation is a great thing. Usually. In the world of ETFs, a few big players (BlackRock, State Street Global Advisors, Vanguard) jumped in early when the going was hot. Now, in order to get their share of the pie, a number of new players have entered the fray with some pretty wild ETFs. "Let's invest in all companies whose CEO is named Fred!" Okay, no Fred portfolio exists, but the way things are going, it could happen.

RIP these ETFs

New ETFs are being born every week, but at the same time, others are dying. Hundreds of products during the past several years have been zipped up, closed down, folded, and sent to that Great Brokerage in the Sky. No need to shed tears for the investors; they are okay.

If you're holding shares in a particular ETF that closes down, you will usually be given at least several weeks' notice. You can sell, or you can wait till the final day and receive whatever is the value of the securities held by the ETF at that point. It isn't like holding a bond that goes belly up. You may have a bit of a hassle redoing your portfolio, and you may face sudden tax consequences. If the ETF tracks a very small segment of the market, a bit of investor panic may depress prices. But you won't go broke.

As for the purveyors of the ETFs that have closed, we may shed only a crocodile tear or two. Most of the ETFs that have gone under are exactly the kinds of ETFs that we try to steer you away from in this book: They tracked narrow segments of the market (companies based in Oklahoma, for example); or they tracked somewhat silly and complex indexes (dividend rotation); or they were highly leveraged, exposing investors to excessive risk; or they were overpriced; or all of the above! The public simply would not buy. Bravo, public.

Here is just a small sampling from 2012's ETF graveyard:

- Horizons GMP Junior Oil and Gas Index ETF (HJE)
- Horizons BetaPro NYMEX Crude Oil Inverse ETF (HIO)
- Horizons BetaPro NYMEX Long Natural Gas/Short Crude Oil Spread ETF (HNO)
- Horizons BetaPro NYMEX Long Crude Oil/ Short Natural Gas Spread ETF (HON)
- Horizons BetaPro COMEX Gold Inverse ETF (HIB)
- Horizons BetaPro U.S. 30-year Bond Bull Plus ETF (HTU)
- Global X Fishing Industry ETF (FISN)
- Global X Waste Management ETF (WSTE)
- FocusShares ISE-Reverse Wal-Mart Supplier ETF (WSI)
- Russell 2000 Low Beta ETF (SLBT)

On the Internet, a blog exists for anything and everything, including potential ETF closures. ETF Deathwatch lists any U.S. ETF that is at least six months old and has an "average daily value traded" of less than $100,000 for three consecutive months — or has assets under management of less than $5 million for three consecutive months. You should probably not get overly attached to these ETFs. To find the Deathwatch blog, go to www.investwithanedge.com, and type "deathwatch" in the search box.

We tend to like our ETFs vanilla plain, maybe with a few sprinkles. They should follow indexes that make sense. And, above all, their expense ratios should be looooow. At present, plenty of ETFs carry expense ratios of 0.20 percent or less. Some of the newer, more complicated ETFs, however, have expense ratios edging up into the ballpark of what you usually see for mutual funds. Several dozen ETFs that charge 0.75 percent a year or higher now exist, and some even carry net expense ratios of 1 percent or more.

Not all ETFs must follow traditional indexes — the ETF format allows for more variety than that. (Actually, when we think about it, some of the traditional indexes, like the Dow, are darn dumb. We explain why in Chapter 3.) But the ETF industry has lost some of its integrity over the past few years with higher expenses and some awfully silly investment schemes.

The rest of this book can help you to sidestep the greed and the silliness — to take only the best parts of ETF investing and put them to their best use.

Chapter 2

What the Heck Is an ETF, Anyway?

*B*anking your retirement on stocks is risky enough; banking your retirement on any individual stock, or even a handful of stocks, is Evel Knievel-jumping-the-Snake River-style investing. Banking on individual bonds is typically less risky (maybe Evel Knievel jumping a creek), but the same general principle holds. There is safety in numbers. That's why teenage boys and girls huddle together in corners at school dances. That's why gnus graze in groups. That's why smart stock and bond investors grab onto ETFs.

In this chapter, we explain not only the safety features of ETFs but also the ways in which they differ from their cousins, mutual funds. By the time you're done with this chapter, you'll have a pretty good idea of what ETFs can do for your portfolio.

The Nature of the Beast

Just as a deed shows that you have ownership of a house, and a share of common stock certifies ownership in a company, a share of an ETF represents ownership (most typically) in a basket of company stocks. To buy or sell an ETF, you place an order with a broker, generally (and preferably, for cost reasons) online, although you can also place an order by phone. The price of an ETF changes throughout the trading day, which is to say from 9:30 a.m. to 4:00 p.m. Toronto time, going up or going down with the market value of the securities it holds. (Sometimes there can be a little sway — times when the price of an ETF doesn't exactly track the value of the securities it holds — but that situation is rarely serious, at least not with ETFs from the better purveyors.)

Originally, ETFs were developed to mirror various indexes:

- ✔ The Toronto 35 Index Participation fund, the first ETF ever invented, was set up to track the TSE 35 Composite Index. The TSE 35 followed Canada's largest and most liquid companies.

- ✔ Canada's largest ETF, the iShares S&P/TSX 60 Index Fund (XIU), was created in 1999 and tracks the performance of the S&P/TSX 60. Like the TSE 35 did, this index follows the 60 largest Canadian companies.

- ✔ The SPDR S&P 500 (SPY), American's first and largest ETF, represents stocks from the S&P (Standard & Poor's) 500, an index of the 500 largest companies in the United States.

Since ETFs were first introduced, many others, tracking all kinds of things, including some rather strange things that we dare not even call investments, have emerged.

The component companies in an ETF's portfolio usually represent a certain index or segment of the market, such as large Canadian value stocks, small growth stocks, or micro cap stocks. (If you're not 100 percent clear on the difference between *value* and *growth,* or what a micro cap is, rest assured that we define these and other key terms in Part II.)

Sometimes, the stock market is broken up into industry sectors, such as financials, energy, and technology. ETFs exist that mirror each sector.

Regardless of what securities an ETF represents, and regardless of what index those securities are a part of, your fortunes as an ETF holder are tied, either directly or in some leveraged fashion, to the value of the underlying securities. If the price of TD bank stock, ten-year Government of Canada bonds, gold bullion, or oil futures goes up, so does the value of your ETF. If the price of gold tumbles, your portfolio (if you hold a gold ETF) may lose some glitter. If Suncor's stock pays a dividend, you are due a certain amount of that dividend — *unless* you happen to have bought into a leveraged or inverse ETF.

As we discuss in Chapter 11, some ETFs allow for leveraging, so that if the underlying security rises in value, your ETF shares rise doubly or triply. If the security falls in value, well, you lose according to the same multiple. Other ETFs allow you not only to leverage but also to *reverse leverage,* so that you stand to make money if the underlying security falls in value (and of course lose if the underlying security increases in value). We're not big fans of leveraged and inverse ETFs, for reasons we make clear in Chapter 11.

Choosing between the Classic and the New Indexes

Some of the ETF providers (iShares, Vanguard) tend to use traditional indexes, such as those we mention in the previous section. Others (PowerShares, BMO, RBC) tend to develop their own indexes.

For example, if you were to buy 100 shares of the iShares S&P/TSX 60 Index Fund (XIU), you'd be buying into a traditional index (large Canadian companies). At about $17.8 a share (at this writing), you'd plunk down $1,780 for a portfolio of stocks that would include shares of Royal Bank of Canada, TD Bank, Scotiabank, Suncor Energy, Barrick Gold, Canadian National Railway, and BCE. If you wanted to know the exact breakdown, the iShares prospectus found on the iShares website (or any number of financial websites, such as `finance.yahoo.com`) would tell you specific percentages: RBC, 7.48 percent; TD Bank, 6.76 percent; Scotiabank, 5.75 percent; Suncor, 4.58 percent; and so on.

Many ETFs represent shares in companies that form foreign indexes. If, for example, you were to own 100 shares of the iShares MSCI Brazil Index Fund (XBZ), with a market value of about $15 per share as of this writing, your $1,500 would buy you a stake in a number of large Brazilian financial, energy, and consumer staples companies. Chapter 9 is devoted entirely to international ETFs.

Both XIU and XBZ mirror standard indexes: XIU mirrors the S&P/TSX 60 Index, and XBZ mirrors the MSCI Brazil Index. If, however, you were to purchase 100 shares of the Invesco PowerShares Canadian Dividend Index ETF (PDC), you'd buy roughly $2,000 worth of a portfolio of stocks that mirror an index created by Indxis, a South Carolina-based company that creates indexes specifically for ETF providers.

A big controversy in the world of ETFs is whether the newfangled, customized indexes offered by companies like Invesco PowerShares make any sense. Most financial professionals are skeptical of anything that's new. They are a conservative lot. Those of us who have been around for a while have seen too many "exciting" new investment ideas crash and burn. But try to keep an open mind. For now, we continue with our introduction to ETFs, but rest assured that we address this controversy in Chapter 3 and throughout Part II.

Another big controversy is whether you may be better off with an even newer style of ETFs — those that follow no indexes at all but rather are supposedly actively managed. As we make clear in Chapter 1, we prefer index investing to active investing, but that's not to say that active investing, carefully pursued, has no role to play. More on that topic later in this chapter and throughout the book.

Other ETFs — a distinct but growing minority — represent holdings in assets other than stocks, most notably bonds and commodities (gold, silver, oil, and such). And then there are exchange-traded notes (ETNs), which allow you to venture even further into the world of alternative investments — or speculations — such as currency futures. We discuss these products in Part III of the book.

Preferring ETFs over Individual Stocks

Okay, why buy a basket of stocks rather than an individual stock? Quick answer: You'll sleep better.

You may recall that in 2000, Nortel Networks accounted for more than a third of the TSX's total valuation. The stock price was flying high, trading at about $124 a share, and the company made a lot of Canadians wealthy. Then, two years later, fuzzy accounting coupled with a bursting tech bubble sent Nortel's stock plummeting to about 50 cents a share. In 2009 the company was delisted from the TSX, and in 2012 it was in bankruptcy proceedings. Many Canadians saw their retirement savings disappear as the company went south.

Unfortunately, these sorts of things happen all the time in the world of stocks.

A company we'll call ABC Pharmaceutical sees its stock shoot up by 68 percent because the firm just earned an important patent for a new diet pill. A month later, the stock falls by 84 percent because a study in the *Canadian Medical Association Journal* found that the new diet pill causes people to hallucinate and think they are Genghis Khan.

Compared to the world of individual stocks, the stock market as a whole is as smooth as a morning lake. Heck, a daily rise or fall in the TSX of more than a percent or two (well, maybe 2 or 3 percent these days) is generally considered a pretty big deal.

If you're not especially keen on roller coasters, then you're advised to put your nest egg into not one stock, not two, but many. If you have a few million sitting around, hey, you'll have no problem diversifying — maybe individual stocks are for you. But for most of us commoners, the only way to effectively diversify is with ETFs or mutual funds.

Distinguishing ETFs from Mutual Funds

So what is the difference between an ETF and a mutual fund? After all, mutual funds also represent baskets of stocks or bonds. The two, however, are not twins. They're not even siblings. Cousins are more like it. Here are some of the big differences between ETFs and mutual funds:

- ✔ ETFs are bought and sold just like stocks (through a brokerage house, either by phone or online), and their prices change throughout the trading day. Mutual fund orders can be made during the day, but the actual trading doesn't occur until after the markets close.

- ✔ ETFs tend to represent indexes — market segments — and the managers of the ETFs tend to do very little trading of securities in the ETFs. (The ETFs are *passively* managed.) Most mutual funds are actively managed.

- ✔ Although they may require you to pay small trading fees, ETFs usually wind up costing you much less than mutual funds because the ongoing management fees are typically much less, and you're never charged a *load* (an entrance and/or exit fee, sometimes an exorbitant one) as you find with many mutual funds.

Table 2-1 provides a quick look at some ways that investing in ETFs differs from investing in mutual funds and individual stocks.

Table 2-1 ETFs versus Mutual Funds versus Individual Stocks			
	ETFs	*Mutual Funds*	*Individual Stocks*
Priced, bought, and sold throughout the day?	Yes	No	Yes
Offer some investment diversification?	Yes	Yes	No
Minimum investment?	No	Yes	No
Purchased through a broker or online brokerage?	Yes	Yes	Yes
Do you pay a fee or commission to make a trade?	Typically	Sometimes	Yes
Can that fee or commission be more than a few dollars?	No	Yes	No
Can you buy/sell options?	Sometimes	No	Sometimes
Indexed (passively managed)?	Typically	Atypically	No
Can you make money or lose money?	Yes	Yes	You bet

Your basic trading choices (for ETFs or stocks)

Buying and selling an ETF is just like buying and selling a stock; there really is no difference. Although you can trade in all sorts of ways, the vast majority of trades fall into these categories:

✔ **Market order:** This is as simple as it gets. You place an order with your broker or online to buy, say, 100 shares of a certain ETF. Your order goes to the stock exchange, and you get the best available price.

✔ **Limit order:** More exact than a market order, you place an order to buy, say, 100 shares of an ETF at $23 a share. That is the maximum price you will pay. If no sellers are willing to sell at $23 a share, your order won't go through. If you place a limit order to sell at $23, you'll get your sale if someone is willing to pay that price. If not, there will be no sale. You can specify whether an order is good for the day or until cancelled (if you don't mind waiting to see if the market moves in your favour).

✔ **Stop-loss (or stop) order:** Designed to protect you if the price of your ETF or stock takes a tumble, a stop-loss order automatically becomes a market order if and when the price falls below a certain point (say, 10 percent below the current price). Stop-loss orders are used to limit investors' exposure to a falling market, but they can (and often do) backfire, especially in very turbulent markets. Proceed with caution.

✔ **Short sale:** You sell shares of an ETF that you have borrowed from the broker. If the price of the ETF then falls, you can buy replacement shares at a lower price and pocket the difference. If, however, the price rises, you are stuck holding a security that is worth less than its market price, so you pay the difference, which can sometimes be huge.

For more information on different kinds of trading options, visit the TMX Money website at www.tmxmoney.com.

Why the Big Boys Prefer ETFs

When ETFs were first introduced, they were primarily of interest to institutional traders — insurance companies, hedge fund people, banks — who often have investment needs considerably more complicated than yours and ours. In this section, we explain why ETFs appeal to the largest investors.

Trading in large lots

Prior to the introduction of ETFs, a trader had no way to buy or sell instantaneously, in one fell swoop, hundreds of stocks or bonds. Because they trade both during market hours and, in some cases, after market hours, ETFs made that possible.

Institutional investors also found other things to like about ETFs. For example, ETFs are often used to put cash to productive use quickly or to fill gaps in a portfolio by allowing immediate exposure to an industry sector or geographic region.

Savouring the versatility

Unlike mutual funds, ETFs can also be purchased with limit, market, or stop-loss orders, taking away the uncertainty involved with placing a buy order for a mutual fund and not knowing what price you're going to get until several hours after the market closes. See the sidebar "Your basic trading choices (for ETFs or stocks)" if you're not certain what limit, market, and stop-loss orders are.

And because many ETFs can be sold short, they provide an important means of risk management. If, for example, the stock market takes a dive, *shorting* ETFs — selling them now at a locked-in price with an agreement to purchase them back (cheaper, you hope) later on — may help keep a portfolio afloat. For that reason, ETFs have become a darling of hedge fund managers who offer the promise of investments that won't tank if the stock market tanks. See Chapter 18 for more on this topic.

Why Individual Investors Are Learning to Love ETFs

Investors are often amazed to find out they can buy a financial product that will cost them a fraction in expenses compared to what they're currently paying. Low costs are the best part about ETFs. But their transparency (you know what you're buying) and the long track record of success for indexed investments are also good reasons to buy these products.

The cost advantage: How low can you go?

In the world of actively managed mutual funds (which is to say most mutual funds), the average annual management fee, according to Morningstar, is about 2.5 percent of the account balance. That may not sound like a lot, but don't be misled. A well-balanced portfolio with both stocks and bonds may return, say, 7 percent over time. In that case, paying 2.5 percent to a third party means that you've just lowered your total investment returns by about one-third. In a bad year, when your investments earn, say, 2.5 percent, you've just lowered your investment returns to *zero*. And in a *very* bad year . . . you don't need us to do the math.

The fees some mutual funds charge are astounding. Whereas the average is about 2.5 percent, some funds exist that charge a lot more than that. Investing in such a fund is tossing money to the wind. Yet people do it. The chances of your winding up ahead after paying such high fees are next to nil. Paying a *load* (an entrance and/or exit fee) that can total as much as 8.5 percent is just as nutty. Yet people do it.

In the world of index funds, the expenses are much lower, with index mutual funds averaging 0.64 percent and ETFs averaging 0.50 percent, although many of the more traditional domestic indexed ETFs cost no more than 0.20 percent a year in management fees. A handful are under 0.10 percent.

Some fees, as you can see in Table 2-2, are so low as to be negligible. Each ETF in this table has a yearly management expense of 0.17 percent or less.

Table 2-2	The Rock-Bottom Canadian ETFs	
ETF	*Ticker*	*Total Annual Management Expense*
Vanguard MSCI Canada Index	VCE	0.09%
Vanguard Canadian Short-Term Bond Index	VSB	0.15%
iShares S&P/TSX 60 Index	XIU	0.17%
Horizons S&P/TSX 60 Index	HXT	0.07%
Horizons S&P 500 Index	HXS	0.15%
BMO S&P/TSX Capped Composite Index	ZCN	0.17%

Numerous studies have shown that low-cost funds have a huge advantage over higher-cost funds. One study by Morningstar looked at stock returns over a five-year period. In almost every category of stock mutual fund, low-cost funds beat the pants off high-cost funds. Do you think that by paying high fees you're getting better fund management? Hardly. The Morningstar study found, for example, that among mutual funds that hold large blend stocks (*blend* means a combination of value and growth — an S&P 500 fund would be a blend fund, for example), the annualized gain was 8.75 percent for those funds in the costliest quartile of funds; the gain for the least costly quartile was 9.89 percent.

Why ETFs are cheaper

The management companies that bring us ETFs, such as BlackRock, Inc. and Invesco PowerShares, are presumably not doing so for their health. No, they're making a good profit. One reason they can offer ETFs so cheaply compared to mutual funds is that their expenses are much less. When you buy an ETF, you go through a brokerage house, not BlackRock or Invesco PowerShares. That brokerage house (Scotia iTrade, Qtrade, BMO InvestorLine) does all the necessary paperwork and bookkeeping on the purchase. If you have any questions about your money, you'll likely call TD Waterhouse, not BlackRock. So unlike a mutual fund company, which must maintain telephone operators, bookkeepers, and a mailroom, the providers of ETFs can operate almost entirely in cyberspace.

ETFs that are linked to indexes do have to pay some kind of fee to whoever created the index. But that fee is *nothing* compared to the exorbitant salaries that mutual funds pay their stock pickers, er, market analysts.

An unfair race

Active mutual funds really don't have much chance of beating passive index funds — whether mutual funds or ETFs — over the long run, at least not as a group. (Individual exceptions exist, but identifying them before the fact is virtually impossible.) Someone once described the contest as a race in which the active mutual funds are "running with lead boots." Why? In addition to the management fees that eat up much of any gains, there are also the trading costs. Yes, when mutual funds trade stocks or bonds, they pay a spread and a small cut to the stock exchange, just like everyone does. That cost is passed on to you, and it's on top of the annual management fees previously discussed.

Annual turnover costs for active mutual funds typically run about 0.8 percent. And active mutual fund managers must constantly keep some cash on hand for all those trades. Having cash on hand costs money, too: The opportunity cost is estimated to be in the neighbourhood of 0.4 percent.

So you take the 2.5 percent average management fee, and the 0.8 percent hidden trading costs, and the 0.4 percent opportunity cost, and you can see where the lead boots come in. Add taxes to the equation, and while some actively managed mutual funds may do better than ETFs for a few years, over the long haul we wouldn't bank on many of them coming out ahead.

The CRA's loss, your gain

Alas, unless your money is in a tax-advantaged retirement account, making money in the markets means that you have to fork something over to the

Canada Revenue Agency at year's end. That's true, of course, whether you invest in individual securities or funds. But before ETFs came along, individual securities had a big advantage over funds in that you were required to pay capital gains taxes only when you actually enjoyed a capital gain. With mutual funds, that isn't so. The fund itself may realize a capital gain by selling off an appreciated stock. You pay the capital gains tax regardless of whether you sell anything and regardless of whether the share price of the mutual fund increased or decreased since the time you bought it.

There have been times (pick a bad year for the market — 2000, 2008 . . .) when many mutual fund investors lost a considerable amount in the market yet had to pay capital gains taxes at the end of the year. Talk about adding insult to injury! One study found that over the course of time, taxes have wiped out approximately 2 full percentage points in returns for investors in the highest tax brackets.

In the world of ETFs, such losses are very unlikely to happen. Because most ETFs are index based, they generally have little turnover to create capital gains. To boot, ETFs are structured in a way that largely insulates shareholders from capital gains that result when mutual funds are forced to sell in order to free up cash to pay off shareholders who cash in their chips.

No tax calories

The structure of ETFs makes them different than mutual funds. Unlike with a mutual fund, you don't have to worry about paying taxes on distributions or gains made in the fund itself. You pay capital gains only if the price goes up and you sell — then you're taxed on the cash you made. If you lose money, you're able to claim a capital loss.

Market makers and croupiers

In the world of ETFs, we don't have croupiers, but we have market makers. *Market makers* are people who work at the stock exchanges and create (like magic!) ETF shares. Each ETF share represents a portion of a portfolio of stocks, sort of like how poker chips represent a pile of cash. As an ETF grows, so does the number of shares. Concurrently (once a day), new stocks are added to a portfolio that mirrors the ETF. See Figure 2-1, which may help you envision the structure of ETFs and what makes them such tax wonders.

When an ETF investor sells shares, those shares are bought by a market maker who turns around and sells them to another ETF investor. By contrast, with mutual funds, if one person sells, the mutual fund must sell off shares of the underlying stock to pay off the shareholder. If stocks sold in the mutual fund are being sold for more than the original purchase price, the shareholders left behind are stuck paying a capital gains tax. In some years, that amount can be substantial.

In the world of ETFs, no such thing has happened or is likely to happen, at least not with the vast majority of ETFs, which are index funds. Because index funds trade infrequently, and because of ETFs' poker-chip structure, ETF investors rarely see a bill from the CRA for any capital gains tax. That's not a guarantee that there will never be capital gains on any index ETF, but if there ever are, they are sure to be minor.

The actively managed ETFs — currently a very small fraction of the ETF market, but almost certain to grow — may present a somewhat different story. They are going to be, no doubt, less tax friendly than index ETFs but more tax friendly than actively managed mutual funds. Exactly where will they fall on the spectrum? It may take another year or two (or three) before we really know.

Tax efficient does not mean tax free. Although you won't pay capital gains taxes until you sell, you will pay taxes on any dividends issued by your stock ETFs, and stock ETFs are just as likely to issue dividends as are mutual funds.

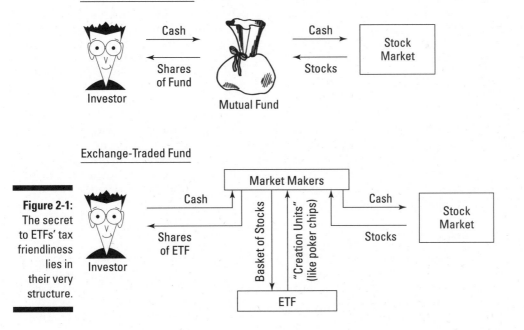

Figure 2-1: The secret to ETFs' tax friendliness lies in their very structure.

What you see is what you get

A key to building a successful portfolio, right up there with low costs and tax efficiency, is diversification, a subject we discuss more in Chapter 4. You cannot diversify optimally unless you know exactly what's in your portfolio. In a rather infamous American example, when tech stocks (some more than others) started to go belly up in 2000, holders of Janus mutual funds got clobbered. That's because they learned after the fact that their three or four Janus mutual funds, which gave the illusion of diversification, were actually holding many of the same stocks.

Style drift: An epidemic

With a mutual fund, you often have little idea of what stocks the fund manager is holding. In fact, you may not even know what *kinds* of stocks he is holding. Or even if he is holding stocks! We're talking here about *style drift,* which occurs when a mutual fund manager advertises his fund as aggressive but over time it becomes conservative, and vice versa. We're talking about the mutual fund manager who says he loves large value but invests in large growth or small value.

One classic case of style drift cost investors in the all-popular Fidelity Magellan Fund. The year was 1996, and then-fund manager Jeffrey Vinik reduced the stock holdings in his so-called stock mutual fund to 70 percent. He had 30 percent of the fund's assets in either bonds or short-term securities. He was betting that the market was going to sour, and he was planning to fully invest in stocks after that happened. He was dead wrong. Instead, the market continued to soar, bonds took a dive, Fidelity Magellan seriously underperformed, and Vinik was out.

One study by the Association of Investment Management concluded that a full 40 percent of actively managed mutual funds are not what they say they are. Some funds bounce around in style so much that an investor would have almost no idea where her money was. The Parnassus Fund, for example, was once placed by Morningstar in the small cap blend category. Then it moved to small cap value. Later it moved to mid cap blend. Later still, the fund was reclassified as mid cap growth.

ETFs are the cure

When you buy an indexed ETF, you get complete transparency. You know exactly what you are buying. No matter what the ETF, you can see in the prospectus or on the ETF provider's website (or on any number of independent financial websites) a complete picture of the ETF's holdings. See, for example, finance.yahoo.com. If you go to the website and type the letters "XFN" (the ticker symbol for the iShares S&P/TSX Capped Financials Index ETF) in the box in the upper left of the screen, you can see in an instant what your holdings are. You can see too, in Table 2-3.

Table 2-3	Holdings of the iShares S&P/TSX Capped Financials Index as of 10/05/2012
Name	**% Net Assets**
Royal Bank of Canada	20.36
TD Bank	17.62
Bank of Nova Scotia	16.01
Bank of Montreal	9.56
Canadian Imperial Bank of Commerce	7.49
Manulife Financial Corp.	6.08
Sun Life Financial Inc.	3.76
National Bank of Canada	2.83
Power Corporation of Canada	2.12
Intact Financial Corp.	1.98

You simply can't get that information on most actively managed mutual funds. Or if you can, the information is both stale and subject to change without notice.

Transparency also discourages dishonesty

The scandals that have rocked the mutual fund world over the years have left the world of ETFs nearly untouched. A fund manager can't do a lot of manipulating when his picks are tied to an index. And because ETFs trade throughout the day, with the price flashing across thousands of computer screens worldwide, no room exists to take advantage of the stale pricing that occurs after the markets close and mutual fund orders are settled. All in all, ETF investors are much less likely ever to get bamboozled than are investors in active mutual funds.

Getting the Professional Edge

We don't know about you, but when we go bowling and — as happens on very rare occasion — we bowl a strike, it's as if a miracle of biblical proportions has occurred. And then we turn on the television, stumble upon a professional bowling tournament, and see guys for whom *not* bowling a strike is a rare occurrence. The difference between amateur and professional bowlers is huge. The difference between investment amateurs and investment professionals can be just as huge. But you can close much of that gap with ETFs.

Consider a few impressive numbers

By investment professionals, goodness knows we're not talking about stockbrokers or variable-annuity salespeople, or our barbers, who always have stock recommendations. We're talking about the managers of foundations, endowments, and pension funds with $1 billion or more in invested assets. By amateurs, we're talking about the average Canadian investor with a few assorted and sundry mutual funds in an RRSP.

We compare the two using U.S. data. (A lot more Americans are studying these things, but the point is the same. Also, Canadians can invest in U.S. stocks and ETFs.) During the 20-year period 1990 through 2009, the U.S. stock market, as measured by the S&P 500 Index, provided an annual rate of return of 8.2 percent. Yet the average stock mutual fund investor, according to a study by Dalbar, earned an annual rate of 3.2 percent over that same period, just barely keeping up with the inflation rate of 2.8 percent a year. Bond-fund investors did much worse. Why the pitiful returns? Several reasons exist, but here are two main ones:

- Mutual fund investors pay too much for their investments.
- They jump into hot funds in hot sectors when they're hot and then jump out when those funds or sectors turn cold. (In other words, they are constantly buying high and selling low.)

Professionals tend not to do either of those things. To give you an idea of the difference between amateurs and professionals, consider this: For that very same 20-year period in which the average stock mutual fund investor earned 3.2 percent, and the average bond mutual fund investor earned 1 percent, the multibillion-dollar stock-and-bond-and-real-estate California Public Employees' Retirement System (CalPERS) pension fund, the largest in the U.S., earned nearly 8 percent a year.

You can do what they do!

Professional managers, you see, don't pay high expenses. They don't jump in and out of funds. They know that they need to diversify. They tend to buy indexes. They know exactly what they own. And they know that asset allocation, not stock picking, is what drives long-term investment results. In short, they do all the things that an ETF portfolio can do for you. So do it. Well, maybe . . . but first read the rest of this chapter!

Passive versus Active Investing: Your Choice

Surely, you've sensed by now our preference for index funds over actively managed funds. Until recently, all ETFs were index funds. And in the past few years, most index funds have been ETFs.

On March 25, 2008, Bear Stearns introduced an actively managed ETF: the Current Yield Fund ETF (YYY). As fate would have it, Bear Stearns was just about to go under, and when it did, the first actively managed ETF went with it. Prophetic? Perhaps. In the four years since, many actively managed ETFs have hit the street, with very little commercial success. In Canada, Horizons Exchange Traded Funds is the biggest purveyor of actively managed ETFs, with about 30 of them for sale. Other companies will likely follow suit at some point.

This development isn't necessarily a bad thing, but no one should be frothing at the mouth to invest in actively managed ETFs, either.

In the following sections, we look at a few of the pros and cons of passive and active investing.

The index advantage

The superior returns of indexed mutual funds and ETFs over actively managed funds have had much to do with the popularity of ETFs to date. Index funds (which buy and hold a fixed collection of stocks or bonds) consistently outperform actively managed funds. One study done by personal finance website NerdWallet (don't get thrown off by the name, it's a great site!) tracked mutual fund performance between 2002 and 2012 and found that only 24 percent of active managers outperformed the index. As well, the site found that asset-weighted return for actively managed products was 6.5%, while the return for passively managed index products was 7.3%. And that is just one of many, many studies that present similar results.

Here are some reasons that index funds (both mutual funds and ETFs) are hard to beat:

✔ They typically carry much lower management fees, sales loads, or redemption charges.

✔ Hidden costs — trading costs and spread costs — are much lower when turnover is low.

✔ They don't have cash sitting around idle (as the manager waits for what she thinks is the right time to enter the market).

✔ They are usually more tax efficient.

✔ They are more transparent — you know exactly what securities you are investing in.

Perhaps the greatest testament to the success of index funds is how many allegedly actively managed funds are actually index funds in (a very expensive) disguise. We're talking about closet index funds. According to a report in *InvestmentNews,* a newspaper for financial advisors, the number of actively managed stock funds that are closet index funds has tripled over the past several years. As a result, many investors are paying high (active) management fees for investment results that can be achieved with low-cost ETFs.

R-squared is a measurement of how much of a fund's performance can be attributed to the performance of an index. It can range from 0.00 to 1.00. An R-squared of 1.00 indicates *perfect correlation*: When a fund goes up, it's because the index was up — every time; when the fund falls, it's because the index fell — every time. An R-squared of 0.00 indicates no such correlation. This measurement is used to assess tracking errors and to identify closet index funds.

According to Morningstar data as interpreted by *InvestmentNews,* nearly 28 percent of all large cap funds carry a three-year R-squared of 0.95 or higher relative to the S&P 500 stock index. That kind of number makes them closet index funds. And if you look at the entire mutual fund industry, it is apparent that the triumph of indexing is becoming well known. Recently, the average large cap fund had an R-squared of almost 0.90. That number is up from 0.74 only a decade or so ago.

The allure of active management

Speaking in broad generalities, actively managed mutual funds have been no friend to the small investor. Their dominance remains a testament to people's ignorance of the facts and the enormous amount of money spent on (often deceptive) advertising and PR that give investors the false impression that buying this fund or that fund will lead to instant wealth. The media often plays into this nonsense with splashy headlines, designed to sell magazine copies or attract viewers, that promise to reveal which funds or managers are currently the best.

Still, active management can make sense — and that may be especially true when some of the best aspects of active management are brought to the ETF market. Some managers actually do have the ability to "beat the markets" — they are just few and far between, and the increased costs of active management often nullify any and all advantages these market-beaters have. If those costs can be minimized, and if you can find such a manager, you may wind up ahead of the game. Active management in ETF form may also be both more efficient and more transparent than it is in mutual fund form.

And finally, with some kinds of investments, such as commodities and possibly bonds, active management may simply make better sense in certain cases. We talk about these scenarios in Part III.

Why the race is getting harder to measure . . . and what to do about it

Unfortunately, the old-style "active versus passive" studies that consistently gave passive (index) investing two thumbs up are getting harder and harder to do. What exactly qualifies as an "index" fund anymore, now that many ETFs are set up to track indexes that, in and of themselves, were created to outperform "the market" (traditional indexes)? And whereas index investing once promised a very solid cost savings, some of the newer ETFs, with their newfangled indexes, are charging more than some actively managed funds. Future studies are likely to become muddier and muddier.

Here's our advice: Give a big benefit of the doubt to index funds as the ones that will serve you the best in the long run. If you want to go with an actively managed fund, follow these guidelines:

- Keep your costs low.
- Don't believe that a manager can beat the market unless that manager has done so consistently for years, and for reasons that you can understand. (That is, avoid "Madoff risk"!)
- Pick a fund company that you trust.
- Don't go overboard! Mix an index fund or two in with your active fund(s).
- All things being equal, you may want to choose an ETF over a mutual fund. But the last section of this chapter can help you to determine that. Ready?

Do ETFs Belong in Your Life?

Okay, so on the plus side of ETFs, we have ultra-low management expenses, better tax efficiency, transparency, and a lot of fancy trading opportunities, such as shorting, if you are so inclined. What about the negatives? In the sections that follow, we walk you through some other facts about ETFs that you should consider before parting with your precious dollars.

Calculating commissions

We talk a lot more about commissions when we compare and contrast various brokerage houses in Chapter 3, but we give you a heads-up here: You may have to pay a commission every time you buy and sell an ETF.

The infamous "flash crash" of 2010

On the afternoon of May 6, 2010, the stock market, if you'll indulge us for a moment and allow for the use of a highly technical term, went kablooey. No terrorist attacks occurred that day — no earthquakes or tsunamis or heart attacks in the White House either. With no real reason to explain it, the U.S. stock market suddenly plunged by nearly 10 percent. Some ETFs had fallen in value to mere pennies on the dollar. It seemed like the start of another Great Depression.

Oops.

The "flash crash" of 2010 was just a big mistake — a few computer glitches, essentially — and within 10 minutes, the market nearly recovered. Trades made in those 10 minutes were corrected, and life went on as normal. Sort of. For months that followed, market authorities scratched their collective chins, trying to figure out what exactly had gone wrong and how to make sure that it wouldn't happen again. They've since, they assure us, instituted circuit breakers so that the same kind of swift movement will result in the temporary shutting down of the market, allowing troublesome computer glitches to be addressed.

So now you're safe. Maybe.

Still, if you feel nervous about another "flash crash," perhaps one in which trades won't be corrected, exercise caution when trading your ETF holdings. A *stop order* tells your broker to sell your ETF if it drops below a certain price — say, for example, below $10 a share. In theory, that protects you from a market crash. But in reality, it may actually subject you to a crash. If, say, the price of your ETF shares drops precipitously enough, as prices did on May 6, 2010, your order to sell if the price dips below $10 may kick in at 10 *cents* a share. Solution: Instead of a stop order, use a *stop-limit order,* which tells the broker to sell your ETF if the price drops below, say, $10 a share, but not to sell if you can't get, say, at least $9 a share.

Or — perhaps a better solution — don't use stop orders at all. Rather, be prepared for some bumps in the road, and invest in the stock market only the money that you or your family won't need for a good time to come. (More on risk control in Chapter 4.)

Here's the good news: Trading commissions for stocks and ETFs (it's the same commission for either) have been dropping faster than the price of desktop computers. What once would have cost you a bundle, now — if you trade online, which you definitely should — is really pin money, perhaps as low as $6.95 a trade, and sometimes nothing at all. However, you can't simply ignore trading commissions. They aren't always that low, and even $6.95 a pop can add up. In most cases, you shouldn't agonize over the cost of trading ETFs; merely keep an eye on them.

Moving money in a flash

The fact that ETFs can be traded throughout the day like stocks makes them, unlike mutual funds, fair game for day traders and institutional wheeler-dealers. For the rest of us common folk, there isn't much about the way that ETFs are bought and sold that makes them especially valuable. Indeed, the ability to trade throughout the day may make you more apt to do so, perhaps selling or buying on impulse. As we discuss in detail in Chapter 17, impulsive investing, although it can get your endorphins pumping, is generally not a profitable way to proceed.

Understanding tracking error

At times, the value of the securities held by the ETF may trade above or below the index it follows. This situation is called *tracking error*. At times, an ETF may also sell at a price that is a tad higher or lower than what that price should be given the prices of all the securities held by the ETF. This situation is called selling at a *premium* (when the price of the ETF rides above the value of the securities) or selling at a *discount* (when the price of the ETF drops below the value of the securities). Both foreign-stock funds and bond funds are more likely to run off track, either experiencing tracking error or selling at a premium or discount. But the better funds do not run off track to any alarming degree.

In Chapter 3, we offer a few trading tricks for minimizing "off track" ETF investing, but for now, assume that it isn't something to worry about if you're a buy-and-hold ETF investor — the kind of investor we want you to become.

Making a sometimes tricky choice

In Parts II, III, and IV of this book, we give you lots of detailed information about how to construct a portfolio that meets your needs. Here, we just want to whet your appetite with a couple of very basic examples of decisions you may be facing.

The index mutual fund trap

Some companies, such as TD Bank, offer wonderful low-cost index mutual funds. But a problem with them is that either you can't buy them at other financial supermarkets (such as BMO InvestorLine or Scotia iTrade) or you have to pay a substantial fee to get into them. So building an entire portfolio of index mutual funds can be tough. If you want TD's e-Series index funds, you may be forced to pay high fees or to open up separate accounts at different supermarkets, which means extra paperwork and hassle. With ETFs, you can buy them anywhere, sell them anywhere, and keep them — even if they are ETFs from several different providers — all parked in the same brokerage house.

Say you have a choice between investing in an index mutual fund that charges 0.17 percent a year and an ETF that tracks the same index and charges the same amount. Or say you are trying to choose between an actively managed mutual fund and an ETF with the very same manager managing the very same kind of investment, with the same costs. What should you invest in?

If your money is in a taxable account, go with the ETF, provided you are investing at least a few thousand dollars and you plan to keep your money invested for at least several years. If you're investing less, or if you think you may need to tap the money anytime soon, you may be better off with the index mutual fund that won't charge you commissions to buy and sell shares.

But say you have, oh, $5,000 to invest in your RRSP. (All RRSP money is taxed as income when you withdraw it in retirement, and therefore the tax efficiency of securities held within an RRSP isn't an issue.) An ETF charges you a management fee of 0.15 percent a year, and a comparable index mutual fund charges 0.35 percent, but buying and selling the ETF will cost you $9.99 at either end. Now what should you do?

The math isn't difficult. The difference between 0.15 and 0.35 (0.20 percent) of $5,000 is $10. Recouping your trading fee of $9.99 will take you about a year. If you factor in the cost of selling (another $9.99), recouping your trading costs will take you nearly two years. At that point, the ETF will be your lower-cost tortoise, and the mutual fund your higher-cost hare.

In general, building an entire portfolio out of ETFs usually makes sense starting in the ballpark of $50,000. Anything less than that, and you're most likely better off with mutual funds or a mix of mutual funds and ETFs. The exception is if you're buying ETFs using Scotia iTrade or Qtrade, where many ETFs can be traded for free. In that case, the ETF portfolio may make sense for even the smallest of accounts.

Warning: If you have a trigger finger, and you're the kind of person who is likely to jump to trade every time there's a blip in the market, you would be well advised to go with mutual funds (that don't impose short-term redemption fees). You're less likely to shoot yourself in the foot!

Chapter 3

Getting to Know the Players

*E*ven the most novice of investors have heard of mutual funds. Countless commercials talk about mutual funds, advisors are always pushing funds, and it's likely you or your parents have owned mutual funds in the past. Mutual funds have been around for decades, so it's no surprise that often when you mention the letters *E, T,* and *F* to someone they look at you with a blank stare. Some may even shudder at the thought of giving up their beloved mutual funds.

Part of the problem is that people simply don't know where or how to purchase an ETF. Advisors often shy away from them because often they can't make as much money selling them as they can mutual funds. If you don't know how to buy an ETF, then you probably won't look into what they are and you'll end up forking over high fees to the mutual fund industry forever.

This chapter is something of a shopper's guide to ETFs — a mall directory, if you will. We don't suggest which specific ETFs to buy (we will, we will — but that's for later chapters). Instead, we show you where to find the brokerage houses that allow you to buy and sell ETFs; the financial institutions that create ETFs; the indexes on which the financial institutions base their ETFs; and the exchanges where millions of ETF shares are bought, sold, and borrowed each day.

Creating an Account for Your ETFs

You — you personally — can't just buy a share of an ETF as you would buy, say, a Tim Hortons coffee. You need someone to actually buy it for you and hold it for you. That someone is a broker, sometimes referred to as a *broker-age house* or a *broker-dealer.* Some broker-dealers, the really big ones, are sort of like financial department stores or supermarkets where you can buy ETFs, mutual funds, individual stocks and bonds, or fancier investment products like puts and calls. You'll recognize, we're sure, the names of such financial department stores: TD Waterhouse, Qtrade, BMO InvestorLine, and Scotia iTrade.

ETFs are usually traded just as stocks are traded. Same commissions. Mostly the same rules. Same hours (generally 9:30 a.m. to 4:00 p.m., Bay Street time). Through your brokerage house, you can buy 1 share, 2 shares, or 10,000 shares. Here's one difference between ETFs and stocks: Although people today rarely do it, you can sometimes purchase stocks directly from a company, and you may even get a pretty certificate saying you own the stock. (We *think* some companies still do that!) Not so with ETFs. Call BlackRock or Horizons and ask to buy a share of an ETF, and they will tell you to go find yourself a broker. Ask for a certificate, and . . . well, don't even bother.

The first step, then, prior to beginning your ETF shopping expedition, is to find a brokerage house, preferably a financial department store where you can keep all your various investments. It makes life a lot easier to have everything in one place, to get one statement every month, and to see all your investments on one computer screen.

Answering a zillion questions

The first question you have to answer when opening an account is whether it will be a registered or a non-registered account. If you want a registered account, you need to specify what kind (RRSP? TFSA?). We cover the ins and outs of retirement accounts — and how ETFs can fit snugly into the picture — in Chapter 19.

The next question you have to answer is whether you want to open a *margin* account or a *cash* account. A margin account is somewhat similar to a chequing account with overdraft protection. It means that you can borrow from the account or make purchases of securities (such as ETFs, but generally not mutual funds) without actually having any cash to pay for them on the spot. Cool, huh?

Unless you have a gambling addiction, go with margin. You never know when you may need a quick (and, compared to credit cards, inexpensive) loan. If you think you may have a gambling addiction, however, read the sidebar "Don't margin your house away!"

Don't margin your house away!

Russell once knew a woman whose husband handled all of the finances. Then they divorced. Divorcing couples usually split the family assets, but they also split the liabilities. This woman had no idea, until she divorced, that her hubby had been playing with stocks and ETFs, buying them on margin. Suddenly, she inherited a rather enormous debt. *Buying on margin* means that the brokerage house is lending you money, and charging you interest, so you can purchase securities. Ouch. One of the often-touted advantages of ETFs is that you can buy them on margin — something you often can't do with mutual funds. Margin buying can be very dangerous business. The fact that you can buy an ETF on margin is *not* an advantage as we see it. The stock market is risky enough. Don't ever compound that risk by borrowing money to invest. You may wind up losing not only your nest egg but also your home. This woman was able to save hers; not everyone is so lucky.

Two things about margin you should know:

- ✔ The brokerage house can usually change the rate of interest you're paying without notice.

- ✔ If your investments dip below a certain percentage of your margin loan, the brokerage house can sell your stocks and bonds right out from under you.

It can be dangerous business. Margin only with great caution.

You're also asked questions about beneficiaries and titling (or registration), such as whether you want your joint account set up with rights of survivorship. We'll just say one quick word about naming your beneficiaries: Be certain that who you name is who you want to receive your money if you die.

Beneficiary designations supersede your will. In other words, if your will says that all your ETFs go to your spouse, and your beneficiary designation on your account names someone else, your spouse loses; all the ETFs in your account will go to someone else.

For more information on what happens to your assets when you die, we recommend *Wills and Estate Planning For Canadians For Dummies* by JoAnn Kurtz and Margaret Kerr (Wiley).

Finally, you're asked all kinds of personal questions about your employment, your wealth, and your risk tolerance. Don't sweat them! Regulations require brokerage houses to know something about their clients. Honestly, we don't think anyone ever looks at the personal section of the forms. We've never heard any representative of any brokerage house so much as whisper any of the information included in those personal questions.

Placing an order to buy

After your account is in place, which should take only a few days, you're ready to buy your first ETF. Most brokerage houses give you a choice: Call in your order, or do it yourself online. Calling is typically more expensive because it requires the direct assistance of an actual person. Being the savvy investor that you are, you're not going to throw money away, so place all your orders online! If you need help, a representative of the brokerage house will walk you through the process step by step — for free!

Keep in mind when trading ETFs that the trading fees charged by the brokerage, although usually not all that much, can nibble seriously into your holdings. Even if you work with a brokerage house that waives charges for trading particular ETFs, there will still be a small cost called the *spread* that you don't readily see. Spreads can nibble at your portfolio just as the more visible fees do. Here's how to prevent getting nibbled:

- **Don't trade often.** Buy and hold, more or less (see Chapter 17). Yes, we know that a number of headlines since 2008 have declared that "buy and hold is dead." That's nonsense. Don't believe it. "Buy and hold," by the way, doesn't mean you *never* trade. But if you're making more than a few trades every few months, that's too much.

- **Know your percentages.** In general, don't bother with ETFs if the trade is going to cost you anything more than one-half of 1 percent. In other words, if making the trade is going to cost you $29 (an average amount for an online trade), you want to invest at least $5,500 at a pop. If you have, say, $1,000 to invest, you're often better off purchasing a no-load mutual fund, preferably an index fund, or waiting until you've accumulated enough cash to make a larger investment. Alternatively, you might choose a no-commission ETF, even if it's slightly less attractive than the ETF you'd have to pay a commission for. You may swap for the better alternative down the road, especially if you are funding a retirement account where swapping will have no tax consequences.

- **Be a savvy shopper.** Keep the cost of your individual trades to a minimum by shopping brokerage houses for the lowest fees, placing all your orders online, and arguing for the best deals. Yes, you can often negotiate with these people for better deals, especially if you have substantial bucks. Also know that many brokerage houses offer special incentives for new clients: Move more than $100,000 in assets and get your first 50 trades for free, or that sort of thing. Always ask.

But wait just a moment!

Please don't be so enthralled by anything you read in this book that you rush out, open a brokerage account, and sell your existing mutual funds or stocks and bonds to buy ETFs. Rash investment decisions almost always wind up being mistakes. Remember that whenever you sell a security, you may face serious tax consequences. If you decide to sell certain mutual funds, annuities, or life insurance policies, you may have to pay nasty surrender charges. If you're unsure whether selling your present holdings will make for a financial hit on the chin, talk to your accountant or financial planner.

Trading ETFs like a pro

If you're familiar with trading stocks, you already know how to trade ETFs. If you aren't, don't sweat it. Although there are all kinds of fancy trades you can make, and we'll touch on a few later, we're going to ask you now to familiarize yourself with only the two most basic kinds of trades: market orders and limit orders.

A *market order* to buy tells the broker that you want to buy. Period. After the order is placed, you will have bought your ETF shares . . . at whatever price someone out there was willing to sell you those shares.

A *limit order* to buy asks you to name a price above which you walk away and go home. No purchase will be made. (A limit order to sell asks you to name a price below which you will not sell. No sale will be made.)

Market orders are fairly easy. As long as you are buying a domestic ETF that isn't too exotic (the kind of ETFs we'll be recommending throughout this book); as long as you aren't trading when the market is going crazy; as long as you aren't trading right when the market opens or closes (9:30 a.m. and 4:00 p.m. EST on weekdays); you should be just fine.

A limit order may be a better option if you are placing a purchase for an ETF where the "bid" and the "ask" price may differ by more than a few pennies (this typically happens when an ETF's trading volumes are thin), or where there may be more than a negligible difference between the market price of the ETF and the net asset value of the securities it is holding. This would include foreign-stock ETFs, junk-bond ETFs, and any other ETFs that trade not that many shares — especially on a day when the market seems jumpy. The risk with limit orders is that you may not get your price, and so the order may not go through.

To execute a limit order without risk that you'll miss out on your purchase, place the order slightly above the last sale. If your ETF's last sale was for $10 a share, you may offer $10.01. If you're buying 100 shares, you may have just blown a whole dollar, but you'll have your purchase in hand.

Introducing the Shops

These days, loyalty is hard to come by. People often switch brands faster than they change their socks. It's a different story in the world of brokerage houses, though. After someone has a portfolio in place at a house such as TD Waterhouse, RBC Direct Investing, or Desjardins Securities' Disnat, that client is often very hesitant to switch. Figuring out why isn't difficult: Moving your account can sometimes be a big, costly, and time-consuming hassle. So, if you have money to invest, it behooves you to spend some serious time researching brokerage houses and to choose the one that will work best for you. It's likely you'll be stuck in that house for life.

What to look for

Here's what you want from any broker who is going to be holding your ETFs:

- Reasonable prices
- Good service, meaning they answer the phone without putting you through answering-system hell
- A user-friendly website
- Good advice, if you think you're going to need advice
- A service centre near you, if you like doing business with real people
- Incentives for opening an account, which can run the gamut from a certain number of fee-free trades to laptop computers
- Financial strength

Financial strength really isn't as important as the others because all brokerage houses carry insurance. Still, a brokerage house that collapses under you can be a problem, and it may take time to recoup your money. See the sidebar "Can you lose your ETFs if your brokerage house collapses?"

We give you our take on some of the major brokerage houses in just a moment, but we first want to talk a bit about prices, which can be downright devilish to compare and contrast.

A price structure like none other

Shopping for shoes? Beer? Pickled herring? Go to one store. Go to another. Or open up an issue of *Consumer Reports*. Compare the prices. Easy business.

Can you lose your ETFs if your brokerage house collapses?

Brokerage houses are insured through the Canadian Investor Protection Fund (CIPF). Each individual investor's securities are protected for up to $1 million should the brokerage house go belly up. Many larger brokerage houses carry supplemental insurance that protects customers' account balances beyond what the CIPF covers.

Note: Neither CIPF coverage nor any kind of supplemental insurance will protect the value of your account from a market downfall! For additional information on CIPF, check out its website at `www.cipf.ca`.

Comparing the prices at brokerage houses is anything but easy. At TD Waterhouse, for example, you'll pay from $7 to $29 per ETF trade, depending on how frequently you trade and how many assets you have in your account. At Scotia iTrade, you can buy 50 ETFs for free — no commission at all — but if you want to buy something else, then you'll have to cough up somewhere between $7 and $25. Then there's Questrade, which has no buying commissions or fees on its ETFs; you're charged only if you sell them. And even then, you're asked to pay only between $4.95 and $9.95. We lose you yet?

Relaying the complicated price structures of the various brokerage houses to you would take us many pages. We'll pass. Instead, in the following sections, we give you a short summary of the pricing, starting with the bank brokerages, and then leave you to do some legwork. Always look at the entire brokerage package, which includes not only the price of trades but also the total account fees. You need to do some comparing and contrasting on your own, but with the tools we give you, it shouldn't take an eternity. Please turn to Appendix A for the websites and phone numbers of the financial supermarkets listed next.

TD Waterhouse

There's a good chance you're a TD Waterhouse client. Why? Because it's the largest online brokerage firm in the country. A lot of people have a lot of assets with the bank, and it makes reviewing account balances — chequing, savings, and investments — easy.

Although its fees are competitive, they're not the cheapest of the bunch. If your household assets are more than $50,000, you'll be dinged a $9.99 flat-rate trading fee. If you make more than 150 trades a quarter, that fee will drop to $7 a trade. If you don't trade frequently or have less than $50,000 in house-hold assets, you'll have to fork over $29 for trades of up to 1,000 shares.

One reason why TD Waterhouse is popular is that it has a ton of investment research information. It's also got a nicely designed website that's fairly easy to navigate. The bank is also about to launch U.S.-dollar RRSP accounts, which is a boon for buyers of American-based ETFs.

BMO InvestorLine

We have a lot of good things to say about this popular bank brokerage firm. It's got an attractive interface; easy-to-access research from Globe Investor, Morningstar, and MarketWatch; and two model ETF portfolios that will help newbie investors get off to a quick start. Its fees are similar to other firms, but only two price points are offered — $9.99 for the frequent trader or the person with a large account and $29 for everyone else.

BMO InvestorLine has one feature that other brokerage houses don't have: real-life advice. This may seem counterintuitive — after all, you're using a dis-count brokerage so that you don't have to hear an advisor yammer on — but the company found that even do-it-yourselfers can use a little advice from time to time. The service, called adviceDirect, gives people stock and ETF picks and can answer investing-related questions on the phone, via e-mail, or through special tools on the website.

There's one catch, and — you can probably see where this is going — it's fees. You have to have at least $100,000 in your account to use the service, and then you have to pay a fee equal to 1 percent of your assets to get access to that live advice. The percentage of assets does go down when you have more money in your account, but be sure to keep costs in mind when using this program.

Scotia iTrade

The brokerage house formally known as E-Trade Canada has been given a fancy makeover and has plenty of great tools and research to help you make money.

The main advantage it has over its rivals, though, is that it offers 50 fee-free ETF purchases. Although that's fantastic — American brokerages have been offering no-commission ETFs for years — it's not quite as great a deal as it may seem. The freebies are mostly old Claymore funds, which are now owned by iTrade. You can't purchase stalwarts like XIC and XIU; most of the freebies are sector or country funds. You can buy the two popular iShares-laddered bond funds, but most people won't want to create a portfolio just out of these options.

If you want to buy something not on the list, then you'll have to pay between $6.99 and $24.99 in trading fees.

RBC Direct Investing

This site from RBC is similar to the others. Its fees range from $6.95 to $28.95, and it's partnered with Morningstar to offer stock, mutual fund, and ETF research. It also has several useful tools, including its Community tab, which allows Direct Investing clients to share ideas with one another.

CIBC Investor's Edge

Again, much like the others, though not as good. It doesn't offer U.S.-dollar registered accounts, and it lacks some of the tools that other brokerages have. Fees are comparable, ranging from $6.95 to $28.95.

Virtual Brokers

Now we get into some of the non-bank brokerage firms. Virtual Brokers is a relative newcomer on the scene; it launched in 2009. It was recently ranked the top brokerage firm in Canada by the *Globe and Mail*, and it's winning praises from investors across the country.

Although the *Globe* lists several different reasons why this topped its 2012 discount brokerage ranking, for our purposes there's one main reason to consider this site: All ETF purchases are free. Yes, you read that right. Any ETF you buy, Canadian or American, will cost you nothing.

Virtual Brokers does charge a fee to sell, but it's dirt cheap. You're dinged $0.01 per share of anything that's more than $1. The minimum commission is $0.99, and the maximum is $9.99. That's well below what the banks charge.

Qtrade

It's probably the most critically acclaimed non-bank brokerage of the bunch, and for good reason — Qtrade is user friendly, it's got great investment tools, and its fees are comparable to, if not better than, the competition's (prices range from $9.95 to $19).

Best of all, it has 60 commission-free ETFs. Like iTrade's freebie funds, most of the offerings are of the bond, sector, or international variety — the main domestic equity ETFs aren't on the list — but it also offers 20 U.S.-based funds, such as the Vanguard Consumer Discretionary ETF and the SPDR S&P International Financial Sector ETF.

Questrade

The only broker that can beat Questrade's cheap fees — stock commissions are between $4.95 and $9.95 — is . . . Questrade. In February 2013, the company announced that it would waive fees on every ETF purchased. It still charges its inexpensive commission on the sale of ETFs, but, like with Virtual Brokers, every North America-listed fund will cost you nothing to buy. Nada. Zilch.

To top it off, Questrade also offers U.S.-dollar RRSPs, and it doesn't charge annual fees on registered accounts.

Other online brokers

- **Credential Direct** (www.credentialdirect.com): Only one thing to note here: Investors with $50,000 or more in assets have to pay a $19 flat rate. Everyone else offers $9.99 or less.
- **Disnat** (www.disnat.com): The online brokerage arm of Desjardins Securities. Fees range from $9.95 to $29.
- **HSBC InvestDirect** (www.investdirect.hsbc.ca): Not much to write home about, other than its oddly numbered fees that range from $6.88 to $28.88. (The reason for the unusual fees is that 88 is considered lucky by Chinese investors, and this British company has roots in Hong Kong and Shanghai.)
- **National Bank Direct Brokerage** (w3.nbdb.ca): Similar to other bank brokerage firms' fees and features.

Presenting the Suppliers

Dozens and dozens of mutual fund providers are out there. Some of the firms may offer just one fund, and they sometimes give the impression that the entire business is run out of someone's garage. Not so with ETFs. Fewer providers exist (currently 7 in Canada and about 50 in the U.S.), they tend to be larger companies, and the top three providers (BlackRock, BMO, and Horizons) control the vast majority of the market. Why is that? Mostly it's because ETFs' management fees are so low that a company can't profit unless it enjoys the economies of scale and multiple income streams that come from offering a bevy of ETFs.

It's okay to mix and match — with caution

We want to emphasize that although picking a single brokerage house to manage your accounts makes enormous sense, there's no reason you can't own ETFs from different sources. Like your favourite professional sports team or clothing store, each supplier of ETFs has its own personality. A portfolio with a combination of iShares, Bank of Montreal, and Vanguard ETFs can work just fine. In fact, we would recommend *not* wedding yourself to a single ETF supplier but being flexible and picking the best ETFs to meet your needs in each area of your portfolio.

Note: Brokerage houses typically don't sell every available mutual fund. But we've never heard of a brokerage house limiting which ETFs it will sell. This includes U.S.- and foreign-listed ETFs. Because ETFs are listed on exchanges, Canadians can buy almost any ETF on the market, regardless of where it was made. Here's the reason you're allowed to do this: brokers who have a "seat" at an exchange have access to all stocks and ETFs traded there. So the broker isn't exactly offering investors every ETF. What he is offering is access to various exchanges, and that brings with it every listing on that exchange.

When mixing and matching ETFs we would just caution that you don't want holes in your portfolio, and you don't want overlap. Mixing and matching, say, a broad Canadian stock fund from one ETF provider with a European stock fund of another provider would be just fine because there's virtually no chance for either overlap or gaps. However, we would recommend that in putting together, say, a U.S. value and a U.S. growth fund, or a U.S. large cap and a U.S. small cap fund, in the hopes of building a well-rounded foreign portfolio, you may want to choose ETFs from the same ETF provider using the same index providers (Russell, Morningstar, S&P, and so on). That's because each indexer uses slightly (and sometimes not so slightly) different definitions of "value," "growth, "large," and "small." So mixing and matching funds from different providers may be less than ideal. More on this topic in Chapter 16.

Table 3-1 offers a handy reference to the Canadian ETF providers, which we introduce you to in a moment. Note that we list the companies in order of the total assets each has in all its ETFs.

Table 3-1	Canadian ETF Providers	
Company	*Number of ETFs*	*Claim to Fame*
BlackRock iShares	88	Biggest variety of funds
BMO ETFs	49	Healthy selection of bond funds
Vanguard Investments Canada	11	Cheap Canadian funds from a leading U.S. firm
RBC Global Asset Management	11	Offers target-date bond ETFs
First Asset Capital	16	Several Morningstar-made indexes to choose from
Horizons Exchange Traded Funds	76	Actively managed and inverse funds
Invesco PowerShares	14	Quirky indexes and alternative strategies

BlackRock iShares

With 88 ETFs in Canada, and many more in the U.S., iShares is the undisputed market leader. The firm behind iShares, BlackRock Inc., merged in 2009 with Barclays Global Investors, the mega-corporation that is now one of the largest investment banks in the world (it has more than $3.5 trillion in assets under management). In 2012 iShares Canada bought Claymore Investments, one of the more popular Canadian ETF providers, which only made it bigger. Through its iShares, BlackRock offers by far the broadest selection of any ETF provider. You can buy iShares that track the major S&P/TSX indexes for growth and value, large cap, and small cap stocks. Other iShares equity ETFs track the major MSCI indexes and, in the U.S., Russell and Morningstar indexes. You can also find industry-sector iShares ETFs from financials and energy to real estate services and agriculture.

In the U.S. and international arena, you can buy an iShares ETF to track almost anything from the American health care sector to ETFs that hold stock in Europe, Australia, and the Far East (MSCI EAFE). You can also own ETFs in narrower markets, such as the Malaysian or Brazilian stock markets. iShares also offers a broad array of fixed-income (bond) ETFs, with 16 Canadian-focused offerings ranging from government and corporate bonds to real-return and money market funds.

Management fees vary from a low of around 0.15 percent for the plain-vanilla large cap Canadian funds, such as the iShares S&P/TSX 60 Index Fund (XIU), to around 0.98 percent for the much more exotically flavoured iShares S&P CNX India Nifty 50 Index (XID).

Our review: You can't go too wrong with iShares. Our only beef is with the price of some of the international funds where BlackRock has enjoyed a monopoly thus far. On the other hand, the firm has done an outstanding job of tracking indexes and offering variety. We caution you, however, not to get sucked into the iShares candy store. Some of the ETFs track very small markets and market segments and clearly don't belong in most people's portfolios. We suggest that you think twice, for example, before making the American-based iShares MSCI All Peru Capped Index Fund (EPU) a major part of your portfolio.

For more information, call 866-474-2737 or visit www.ca.ishares.com.

BMO ETFs

Bank of Montreal launched its first slate of ETFs in 2009, and it's quickly become a favourite among many investors. It now has more than $5 billion in assets under management, and that number is growing every year.

BMO has made inroads in two areas — fixed-income funds and broad-based equities. It offers a solid suite of bond options that cover everything from short federal issues and provincial bonds to long corporate and high-yield U.S. fixed-income bonds.

It recently threw down the gauntlet for iShares when it changed the index that ZCN, BMO's broad-based stock offering, tracks. It used to follow the Dow Jones Canada Titans 60 Index, but it's now pegged to the S&P/TSX Capped Composite Index, which XIC, one of iShares more popular funds, also tracks.

For more aggressive investors, the company also offers *covered call* ETFs, such as the BMO Covered Call Canadian Banks ETF (ZWB), which are funds that use options to, theoretically, boost returns. Studies have shown that covered call strategies, where investors earn additional income by selling options on their holdings, does reduce volatility but also limits the upside gains. These instruments can be useful for people who are seeking extra income, but buy them only if you know what you're doing. (Most people don't.)

Our review: BMO is quickly becoming a force to be reckoned with in the ETF world. It has some interesting equity and fixed income options, but because it's still fairly new, some of the funds aren't quite as liquid as their iShares counterparts. They do make up for that on price in some cases — ZCN has an expense ratio of 0.15 percent versus XIC's 0.25 percent — but if you think you need to get out of something in a hurry, you may want to go with the larger player. Still, if you're buying and holding, and most people are, some of their cheaper-than-iShares options would do a portfolio good.

For more information, call 800-361-1392 or visit www.etfs.bmo.com.

Vanguard Investments Canada

It goes without saying that these people know something about index investing. Vanguard is a powerhouse provider in the U.S. — it launched the first index-based mutual fund for retail investors in 1976 with the Vanguard Index Trust 500 Portfolio. In 2001, Vanguard launched its first ETF. Although Canadians have been able to buy Vanguard's U.S. funds for years, in late 2011 it entered the Canadian market with a few domestic-focused funds.

Vanguard's main competitive differentiator is that it offers funds at extremely low costs. Some of its U.S.-based funds have a 0.06 percent expense ratio. That's almost stealing! Some Canadian funds are also extremely cheap; the MSCI Canada Index ETF (VCE) costs a mere 0.09 percent.

It will still take a few years before Vanguard comes even close to having the assets iShares has — VCE has just $102 million in net assets; XIU has more than $11 billion — but make no mistake, it will give the other Canadian companies a run for their money.

Our review: It's hard to beat cheap fees. If Vanguard can come out with more products — it has only 11 now — increase its assets, and continue to compete on price, then there's no reason why its funds can't make up a substantial part of a portfolio. The company has an excellent reputation and should be given a close look.

For more information, call 888-293-6728 or visit www.vanguardcanada.ca.

RBC Global Asset Management

The Royal Bank of Canada joined the Canadian ETF market in 2011, which makes it one of the youngest players. It's not like the other providers, though. It has only nine options, and they're all target-date corporate bond funds.

Each ETF matures in its given year — so, for example, the RBC Target 2013 Corporate Bond Index ETF comes "due" in 2013. You're paid interest throughout the lifetime of the fund, and at the maturity date the fund will be liquidated and you'll get your money back. It's a lot like owning an individual bond, but the ETF structure makes it much easier to own. The funds also hold between 20 and 50 investment-grade Canadian bonds, which is good for diversification. At the time of writing, you can buy target-date ETFs with maturity dates from 2013 to 2021.

Our review: Really only one reason exists to own one of these funds: if you know that you need money in a specific year. Say you plan to buy a house in 2016. The RBC Target 2016 Corporate Bond Index ETF (RQD) may be a good place to park your money for a couple years, and the interest will give your savings a bit of a boost. Otherwise, it's better to hold the far more liquid bond ETFs offered by iShares and BMO.

For more information, call 855-722-3837 or visit www.funds.rbcgam.com/etfs.

First Asset Capital

It's clear from its products that this relatively new entrant on the ETF scene — it launched in mid-2011 — is targeting the savvier ETF investor. It has a number of covered call ETFs and a convertible bond fund, and perhaps most unusual is its First Asset Morningstar National Bank Quebec Index ETF (QXM), which holds only companies with headquarters in *la belle province*.

It also has a momentum and value fund, which may be useful for people who want to get a bit more detailed with their portfolios. Its two dividend-focused funds — it has a Canadian and a U.S. one — are probably be the most mainstream of the bunch.

One interesting strategy the company has employed is a barbell approach to its bond funds. The bond funds will hold about 50 percent of their assets in short-term bonds with maturities of one to two years and the rest in long-term fixed-income bonds that come due in 10 to 20 years. The short-term bonds are supposed to protect investors against interest rate movements — shorter duration bonds are better in rising-interest environments — while the long-term investments add some extra yield.

Our review: There's no question that First Asset has an interesting array of funds, and its barbell bond funds are particularly intriguing. One problem with many of its funds is that they're not yet proven. "Backtested" data gives investors an idea of the types of returns the fund would have had if it had been around during the last few years, but it's impossible to say if it really would have performed as the data says. We need more numbers before we can say that these are worth owning. Plus, some of its funds, like its momentum and Quebec-focused ETFs, should be used only by a specific type of investor.

For more information, call 877-642-1289 or visit www.firstasset.com.

Horizons Exchange Traded Funds

When Horizons jumped into the ETF game in 2007, it sold mostly inverse and leveraged products. The company saw the other offerings on the market and felt that Canadians might want to try something different. A lot has been made about inverse and leveraged products over the years — mostly that average investors should stay away — so the company shifted focus and is now more heavily promoting its actively managed ETFs.

The company, which was bought in 2011 by Seoul, Korea-based Mirae Asset Global Investment, does have passive investments too, like the popular Horizons S&P/TSX 60 Index ETF (HXT). Unlike the iShares S&P/TSX 60 fund, though, this one is created using derivatives, which involves a third party, like a bank. Some people think derivative-based ETFs — these funds don't actually hold any stocks — are riskier, but others say that owners of Canadian-based derivative ETFs have nothing to worry about.

Consider Horizon if you're looking for something a little different from the plain funds that other companies offer. It's still debatable just how useful actively managed ETFs are, but it's possible that some may provide a little extra kick to returns. Be sure to do your homework before buying.

For more information, call 866-641-5739 or visit www.horizonsetfs.com.

Invesco PowerShares

PowerShares holds the distinction of being the third most popular ETF provider in Canada and the fourth most popular ETF shop in the U.S. It has some interesting products, such as the S&P/TSX Composite High Beta Index ETF (THB), which tracks the 50 stocks with the highest beta on the exchange.

Its main draws are its fixed-income funds — it has a high-yield corporate bond fund, a long-term government bond fund, and more — but it also has about $80 million in assets in its two fundamental index ETFs. Some experts like fundamental indexes because they're based on fundamental factors, such as book value cash flow, dividends, and other metrics. These indexes tend to have a value bent.

Most investors will likely want plain-vanilla funds for their portfolios, but if you want to be a bit more strategic, then consider this company.

A few U.S. ETF providers

Because Canadians can buy U.S. ETFs, it's a good idea to know at least a few of the American players. You've already been introduced to Vanguard and PowerShares — their approach is similar stateside, but they have a lot more to offer — but here are a few more.

State Street Global Advisors (SSgA) SPDRs

State Street's flagship ETF, the first ETF on the U.S. market, is the SPDR S&P 500 (SPY). It boasts more than $100 billion in net assets, which makes SSgA the second-largest provider of ETFs (behind BlackRock). State Street's ETFs follow traditional indexes, carry reasonable fees, and are varied enough to allow for a very well-diversified portfolio, at least on the domestic equity side. All told, SSgA's 100 U.S.-based ETFs hold more than $245 billion in assets.

Our review: The management expenses — 0.35 percent on average — are reasonable, and we like the variety of funds, from which, if you were so inclined, you could build an entire U.S. portfolio. The Select Sector SPDRs offer a very efficient way of investing in various industry sectors (if that's your thing). The websites are top-notch, and the SPDRs website in particular — www.spdrs.com — offers some fabulous portfolio-construction tools, such as the Correlation Tracker, which allows you to find ETFs that best complement your existing portfolio.

For more information, call 866-787-2257 or visit www.streettracks.net or www.spdrs.com.

ProShares

ProShares offers nearly the same number of ETFs as PowerShares. The Short QQQ ProShares (PSQ) allows you to *short* the NASDAQ 100: If the NASDAQ goes down 5 percent tomorrow, your ETF will go up (more or less) 5 percent. Of course, the inverse is true, as well. Other ProShares offerings allow you to short the Dow, the S&P 500, or the S&P MidCap 400, among other indexes. The Ultra ProShares lineup of ETFs allows you to move with the market at double the speed. Ultra QQQ ProShares (QLD), for example, is designed to rise 10 percent when the NASDAQ 100 goes up 5 percent (and, of course, to fall 10 percent when the NASDAQ 100 goes down 5 percent). All these percentages are rough approximations. In the real world, you're going to profit less and risk more than you hoped for. We should also note that the price relationships are only good for a one-day move. The returns aren't as easy to calculate if you hold these in investments for a longer time period. We talk more about inverse and leveraged ETFs in Chapter 11.

Our review: We're not too hot on shorting and leveraging strategies, especially as these ETFs employ them, which is to say on a daily returns basis. In short, selling short is akin to market timing, and market timing, while loads of fun, isn't often profitable. As for the less-than-double-your-money, more-than-double-your-risk ProShares Ultra ETFs, well . . . excuse us while we take a minute to scratch our heads and try to figure out the logic in that. See our discussion of both strategies in Chapter 11.

For more information, call 866-776-5125 or visit www.proshares.com.

Guggenheim

With its takeover of Rydex SGI in 2011, Guggenheim — which owned Claymore Investments until it sold it to BlackRock in 2012 — became eighth among U.S.-based ETF providers, with about $12 billion in assets. It is an interesting company with an unusual mix of products. Many of its ETFs are largely designed for people who are unhappy buying the usual indexes and want to take something of a gamble on a particular equity style, such as large growth stocks. For such an investor, Guggenheim offers its customized S&P 500/Citigroup Pure Growth ETF. Using a proprietary seven factors to determine which stocks among the S&P 500 are the most "growthy," the firm bundles them into a package that promises purity for the gung-ho growth investor. The company does the same for you on the other side if you are a gung-ho value investor. Yeeeehaaaaa!

If you want to gamble that the euro is about to go on a tear, you can buy the firm's Euro Currency Trust exchange-traded *product* — not quite an ETF, but almost. And perhaps most intriguing of all of Guggenheim's investment products, the firm offers an innovative S&P Equal Weight ETF (RSP), which, just like it sounds, offers you an opportunity to invest in the S&P 500 with all company stocks represented in equal allocations (as opposed to the more traditional market capitalization-weighted method of allocation).

Our review: With an average annual management fee of about 0.50 percent, Guggenheim funds are a bit pricey. As for the currency funds, we don't like gambling in currencies; there is simply no way to know which way the euro is going *vis-à-vis* the dollar. As for the "pure" funds, we find them intriguing, but in their first few years of existence, they haven't exactly lit the world on fire.

For more information, call 800-345-7999 or visit guggenheiminvestments.com.

Familiarizing Yourself with the Indexers

At the core of every ETF is an index. The index is the blueprint on which the ETF is based. Some ETF providers use old, established indexes. Others create their own, often in conjunction with seasoned indexers. As a rule, for an ETF to be any good, it has to be based on a solid index. On the other hand, a solid index doesn't guarantee a good ETF because other things, like costs and tax efficiency, matter as well. That being said, we turn now to the five indexers that create and re-create the indexes on which most ETFs are based.

Standard & Poor's

Owned by publishing powerhouse McGraw-Hill, Standard & Poor's is perhaps best known for its credit-rating services. The company also maintains hundreds of indexes, including the S&P/TSX Composite Index and the S&P 500 (the two you're most likely to see flashed across your television screen on the business channel). More than $1 trillion in investors' assets are directly tied to S&P indexes — more than all other indexes combined.

More ETFs are based on S&P indexes than any other, by far. Those include the iShares broad-based domestic and international ETFs, leveraged Horizons that track various market segments, and several BMO ETFs. For more information, visit www.standardandpoors.com.

PC Bond Analytics

Canada's major bond indexes, such as the DEX Universe Bond Index, were developed by this company. It's been in the bond index business since 1947, and most of the Canadian fixed-income ETFs are based on its creations. PC Bond has created all sorts of indexes, including laddered, target-date, real return, convertible, and maple bond indexes.

Most of the Canadian providers have at least some bonds based on PC Bond's DEX indexes, including iShares, BMO, First Asset, and RBC. For more information, go to www.canadianbondindices.com.

Dow Jones

If there were an index for the price of unsalted peanuts in Portugal, Dow Jones would be its purveyor. The company, aside from publishing *The Wall Street Journal* and *Barron's,* develops, maintains, and licenses more than 3,000 market indexes. Those indexes include the world's best-known stock indicator, the Dow Jones Industrial Average, which, in Russell's opinion, should have long ago gone the way of the Edsel. (He explains why in Chapter 5.)

The iShares value and growth ETFs are based on Dow Jones indexes, as are at least some of the ETFs issued by BMO. For more information, visit www.djindexes.com.

MSCI

With indexes of all kinds — stocks, bonds, hedge funds, Canadian, U.S., and international securities — MSCI (formerly Morgan Stanley Capital International), although not quite a household name, has been gaining ground as the indexer of choice for many ETF providers.

MSCI indexes are the backbone of the international Vanguard ETFs — its broad-based Canadian ETF follows an MSCI Index — as well as many of the iShares global-industry funds and single-country ETFs. For more information, visit www.msci.com.

Russell

The largest 1,000 U.S. stocks make up the Russell 1000 index, although it remains relatively obscure because the Dow Industrial and the S&P 500 hog the spotlight when it comes to measuring large cap performance. Then there's the Russell 2,000, which tracks the country's small cap stocks.. The Russell 1000 plus the Russell 2000 make up the Russell 3000. Those are Russell's more popular indexes, but it has plenty of others as well.

A dozen of the iShares U.S. ETFs are based on Russell indexes, as are several of Vanguard's U.S. offerings. ProShares and Direxion also use Russell indexes. For more information, visit `www.russell.com`.

Morningstar

Morningstar is best known for its mutual fund research, but it's recently gotten into the indexing game. First Asset is the only company that's using Morningstar's Canada-made indexes, though other companies, like iShares U.S., have ETFs that track indexes created by Morningstar's American shop. The company's Canadian indexes are more strategy-based — momentum, value, income, and so on — and less about following the broad market. For more information, visit `www.morningstar.ca`.

Meeting the Middlemen

In Canada, every ETF is listed on the Toronto Stock Exchange. There's nothing more to it than that. The States, though, has a more colourful history regarding its ETFs and exchanges.

In the beginning, most ETFs were traded on the American Stock Exchange. In July 2005, however, iShares decided to move its primary listings for 81 of its ETFs to the New York Stock Exchange, citing superior technology. Then, in 2008, the American Stock Exchange was gobbled up by the New York Stock Exchange, which today goes by the name NYSE Arca. As a result, more than 90 percent of all U.S.-based ETFs today are listed on the NYSE Arca, with the remainder listed on the NASDAQ.

Toronto Stock Exchange

The Toronto Stock Exchange was born in 1861, when 24 men got together at Toronto's Masonic Hall and traded stocks. There were only 18 listed securities back then, and trading was limited to one 30-minute session a day. The exchange has undergone major changes over the years, the most recent being the sale of the TMX Group, the company that owned the exchange, to the Maple Group, an organization made up of Canadian bankers and pension plan managers.

More than 1,400 companies and ETFs are listed on the TSX, with a total market cap of more than $1.8 trillion. The website for the TSX is at www.tmx.com.

NYSE Arca

Tracing its origins to 1792, the New York Stock Exchange (NYSE) Arca today lists about 8,000 securities, has about 3,000 member companies, and trades about 3.5 billion shares a day. Almost all U.S. ETFs are listed on the NYSE Arca. We list the exceptions in the next section on the NASDAQ. The website for NYSE Arca is www.nyse.com.

NASDAQ

No bricks and mortar here — the NASDAQ is a uniquely electronic exchange. ETFs listed on the NASDAQ include a handful or two of the foreign iShares ETFs, a dozen of the PowerShares industry-sector ETFs, and the PowerShares QQQ Trust, which tracks the 100 biggest stocks on the NASDAQ and is one of the most beloved ETFs among day-traders.

The acronym NASDAQ, by the way, stands for National Association of Securities Dealers Automatic Quotation. If you go to www.nasdaq.com and click on the link for ETFs, you'll find a number of very useful tools, including the ETF screener and (awesome, indeed) the ETF Heatmap, which allows you to see how 100 of the largest ETFs are faring on that particular day. We wouldn't say that the feature has great practical value, but for investment-world junkies like us, it offers a good rush.

Meeting the Wannabe Middlemen

On January 24, 1848, James Marshall found gold at Sutter's Mill, touching off the California gold rush. About 150 years later, ETFs were the hottest investment product in the land, and so began the ETF rush. Everyone wants in on the game. So we have our ETF providers, the brokerage houses where ETFs are bought and sold, the exchanges where they are listed, and the indexes on which they are based. Who else is there? Ah, the wannabe middlemen: They are about as necessary as forks in a soup kitchen, but be assured that they will continue to try to muscle in on the money.

Commissioned brokers

Most often they call themselves "financial planners," and some may actually do some financial planning. Many, however, are merely salespeople in poor disguise, marketing pricey and otherwise inferior investment products and living off the load. The *load* — or entrance fee — to buying certain investment products, such as some mutual funds, most annuities, and virtually all life insurance products, can be ridiculously high. Thank goodness they don't exist in the world of ETFs — yet.

Separately managed accounts (SMAs)

SMAs have traditionally been aimed at the well-to-do. Instead of buying into mutual funds, the wealthy hire a private manager with Persian rugs in his lobby to do essentially what a mutual fund manager does: pick stocks. But now some SMAs are billing themselves as "ETF SMAs." Instead of picking stocks, they pick ETFs — at a price.

ETF SMAs that promise to beat the market through exceptional ETF selection or market timing are unlikely to do any better than stock SMAs. You should not hold your breath waiting for these guys to make you rich. Some SMA managers may be very good at what they do, but much of what they do can be learned in this book. If you want to hire someone to manage your ETFs, that's fine, but if he starts talking about skimming 2 percent a year off your assets . . . heck, you'll do better on your own.

Annuities and life insurance products

We've seen ads lately from a variable annuity company that features ETFs in its portfolio. Great! That's better than high-priced mutual funds. But still, most variable annuities are way overpriced, carry nasty penalties for early withdrawal, and prove to be lousy investments. The same is true for many life insurance products other than simple term life. Investments in ETFs can make these products better, but that's a relative thing. As a rule, it's best to keep your investment products apart from your insurance products. And never buy an annuity unless you are absolutely sure you know what you are buying.

Mutual funds of ETFs

The term is "closet index funds," and there's an increasing number of them out there, just eager to take your money and invest it in "hand-picked" portfolios of stocks that strangely resemble the entire stock market. In the old days, closet index fund managers would actually have to wake up on Monday morning to make sure their high-priced portfolios were in line with the indexes. Today, they can sleep late because they've socked an indexed ETF or two into their portfolios. You, the investor, get to invest in the ETF or two, and the alleged manager of the mutual fund gets to milk you for much more than you would be charged as a direct ETF shareholder.

Question the purchase of any mutual fund that features ETFs among its top holdings. Ask yourself if there's a good reason for you to be paying two layers of management fees. And if those two layers add up to, say, more than a percentage point, you need to *really* start to question your purchase.

Part II

Building the Stock (Equity) Side of Your Portfolio

The 5th Wave · · · · · · · · · By Rich Tennant

"He's proposing an Alberta-style ETF — energy, cattle, and hairspray futures."

In this part . . .

Over the past 82 years, the S&P 500 (an index of large U.S. stocks) has enjoyed an average annual return of nearly 10 percent before inflation and 7 percent after inflation — a substantially greater return rate than bonds, CDs, gold, silver, or even real estate. Most foreign stocks have done equally as well. Small stocks have done even better. Although history doesn't always repeat, it does often echo. And for that reason, most investment advisors recommend that a good parcel of your long-term investments be put into stocks — and so do we.

As fate would have it, the majority of ETFs represent stock holdings. So it's appropriate that we now ask you to turn your attention to how to use ETFs to invest in the stock market. In the first chapter of this section, we look at some basic concepts of equity investing, most notably diversification and risk control. In the seven chapters that follow, we guide you through a step-by-step exploration of the world of stock ETFs. We examine which ETFs may belong in your portfolio and how to best mix and match them.

Chapter 4

Risk Control, Diversification, and Some Other Things You Need to Know

> *October. This is one of the peculiarly dangerous months to speculate in stocks. The others are July, January, September, April, November, May, March, June, December, August, and February.*
>
> — Mark Twain

A peculiarly good writer, but also a peculiarly bad money manager, Twain sent his entire fortune down the river on a few bad investments. A century and a half later, investing, especially in stocks, can still be a peculiarly dangerous game. But today we have low-cost indexed ETFs and a lot more knowledge about the power of diversification. Together, these two things can help lessen the dangers and heighten the rewards of the stock market. In this chapter, we hope to make you a better stock investor — at least better than Mark Twain.

Risk Is Not Just a Board Game

Well, okay, actually Risk *is* a board game, but we're not talking about *that* Risk. Rather, we're talking about investment risk. And in the world of investments, risk means only one thing: volatility. Volatility is what takes people's nest eggs, scrambles them, and serves them up with humble pie. Volatility is what causes investors insomnia and heartburn. Volatility is the potential for financially crippling losses.

Ask people who had most of their money invested in stocks in 2008. For five years before that, the stock market had done pretty darned well. Investors were just starting to feel good again. The last market downfall of 2000–2002 was thankfully fading into memory. And then . . . *POW* . . . the U.S. and Canadian stock markets tanked by nearly 40 percent between September and December 2008. Foreign markets fell just as much. Billions and billions were lost. Some portfolios (which may have dipped more than 40 percent, depending on what kind of stocks they held) were crushed. Many who had planned for retirement had to readjust their plans.

There was nothing pretty about 2008.

Is risk to be avoided at all costs? Well, no. Not at all. Risk is to be mitigated, for sure, but risk within reason can actually be *a good thing.* That is because risk and return, much like Romeo and Juliet or Corona beer and lime, go hand in hand. Volatility means that an investment can go way down or way up. . . . You hope it goes way up. Without some volatility, you resign yourself to a portfolio that isn't poised for any great growth. And in the process, you open yourself up to another kind of risk: the risk that your money will slowly be eaten away by inflation.

If you are ever offered the opportunity to partake in any investment scheme that promises you oodles and oodles of money with "absolutely no risk," run! You are in the presence of a con artist or a fool. Such investments do not exist.

The trade-off of all trade-offs (safety versus return)

To get to the Holy Grail — a big, fat payoff from your investments — you need to take on the Black Knight and the fire-breathing dragon. There simply is no way to make any sizeable amount of money from your investments without accepting some volatility. The Holy Grail isn't handed out to people who stuff money in their mattresses or carry their pennies to the local savings bank.

If you look at different investments over the course of time, you find an uncanny correlation between risk (volatility risk, not inflation risk) and return. Safe investments — those that really do carry genuine guarantees, such as Government of Canada bonds, guaranteed investment certificates (GICs), and, in many cases, but not all, money market funds — tend to offer very modest returns (or often negative returns, after accounting for inflation). Volatile investments — like stocks and junk bonds, the kinds of investments that cause people to lose sleep — tend to offer handsome returns if you give them enough time.

Time, then, is an essential ingredient in determining appropriate levels of risk. You would be wise to keep any cash you are going to need within the next six months to a year in a savings bank, or possibly in an ETF such as the iShares DEX Short Term Bond Index Fund (XSB), a short-term bond fund that yields a modest return but is very unlikely to lose value. You should *not* invest that portion of your money in any ETF that is made up of company stocks, such as the popular XIU. True, XIU can (and should), over time, yield much more than XSB, but it is also much more susceptible to sharp price swings. Unless you aren't going to need your cash for at least a couple of years, you are best off avoiding any investment in the stock market, whether it be through ETFs or otherwise.

So just how risky are ETFs?

Asking how risky, or how lucrative, ETFs are is like trying to judge a soup knowing nothing about the soup itself, only that it is served in a blue china bowl. The bowl — or the ETF — doesn't create the risk; what's inside it does. Thus stock and real estate ETFs tend to be more volatile than bond ETFs. Short-term bond ETFs are less volatile than long-term bond ETFs (we explain why in Part III). Small-stock ETFs are more volatile than large-stock ETFs. International ETFs often see more volatility than Canadian ETFs. And international "emerging-market" ETFs see more volatility than international developed-nation ETFs.

Figure 4-1 shows some examples of various ETFs and where they fit on the risk-return continuum. Note that it starts with bond ETFs at the bottom (maximum safety, minimum volatility) and nearer the top features the MSCI Emerging Markets Index and the China Index Fund. (An investment in Chinese stocks not only involves all the normal risks of business but also includes currency risk, as well as political risk. Buyer beware.)

High Risk

100

90   iShares China Index Fund (XCH)

80
70   Vanguard MSCI Emerging Markets Index ETF (VEE)

60
50   iShares Dow Jones Canada Select Value Index Fund (XCV)

40   iShares S&P/TSX 60 Index Fund (XIU)

30
Figure 4-1: 20   BMO Long Federal Bond Index ETF (ZFL)
The risk
levels of a 10   BMO Short Federal Bond Index ETF (ZFS)
sampling of
ETFs. **Low Risk**

Keep in mind when looking at Figure 4-1 that we are segregating these ETFs — treating them as stand-alone assets — for illustration purposes. As we discuss later in this chapter (when we discuss something called Modern Portfolio Theory), stand-alone risk measurements are of limited value. The true risk of adding any particular ETF to your portfolio depends on what is already in the portfolio. (That statement will make sense by the end of this chapter. We promise!)

Smart Risk, Foolish Risk

There is safety in numbers, which is why teenage boys and girls huddle together in corners at school dances. In the case of the teenagers, the safety is afforded by anonymity and distance. In the case of indexed ETFs and mutual funds, safety is provided (to a limited degree only!) by diversification in that they represent ownership in many different securities. Owning many stocks, rather than a few, provides some safety by eliminating something that investment professionals, when they're trying to impress, call *nonsystemic risk*.

Nonsystemic risk is involved when you invest in any individual security, such as shares of Telus, Encana, Scotiabank, Nortel, or RIM. It's the risk that the CEO of the company will be strangled by his pet python, that the national headquarters will be destroyed by a falling asteroid, or that the company's stock will take a sudden nosedive simply because of some Internet rumour started by an 11th-grader in the wilds of Manitoba. Those kinds of risks (and more serious ones) can be effectively eliminated by investing in ETFs or mutual funds rather than individual securities.

Nonsystemic risk contrasts with *systemic risk,* which, unfortunately, ETFs and mutual funds can't eliminate. Systemic risks, as a group, simply can't be avoided, not even by keeping your portfolio in cash. Examples of systemic risk include the following:

- ✔ **Market risk:** The market goes up, the market goes down, and whatever stocks or stock ETFs you own will generally (though not always) move in the same direction.

- ✔ **Interest rate risk:** If interest rates go up, the value of your bonds or bond ETFs (especially long-term bond ETFs such as ZFL, the BMO Long Federal Bond Index) will fall.

- ✔ **Inflation risk:** When inflation picks up, any fixed-income investments that you own (such as any of the conventional bond ETFs) will suffer. And any cash you hold will start to dwindle in value, buying less and less than it used to.

- ✔ **Political risk:** If you invest your money in Canada, England, the U.S., or Japan, there's little chance that revolutionaries will overthrow the government anytime soon. When you invest in the stock or bond ETFs of certain other countries (or when you hold currencies from those countries), you'd better keep a sharp eye on the nightly news.

- ✔ **Grand-scale risk:** The government of Japan wasn't overthrown, but that didn't stop an earthquake and ensuing tsunami and nuclear disaster from sending the Tokyo stock market reeling in early 2011.

Although ETFs can't eliminate systemic risks, don't despair. Although nonsystemic risks are a bad thing, systemic risks are a decidedly mixed bag. Nonsystemic risks, you see, offer no compensation. A company is not bound to pay higher dividends, nor is its stock price bound to rise simply because the CEO has taken up mountain climbing or hang gliding.

Systemic risks, on the other hand, do offer compensation. Invest in small stocks (which are more volatile and therefore incorporate more market risk), and you can expect (over the very long term) higher returns. Invest in a country with a history of political instability, and (especially if that instability doesn't occur) you'll probably be rewarded with high returns in compensation for taking added risk. Invest in long-term bonds (or long-term bond ETFs) rather than short-term bonds (or ETFs), and you are taking on more interest-rate risk. That's why the yield on long-term bonds is almost always greater.

In other words,

Higher systemic risk = higher historical returns

Higher nonsystemic risk = zilch

That's the way markets tend to work. Segments of the market with higher risks *must* offer higher returns or else they wouldn't be able to attract capital. If the potential returns on emerging-market stocks (or ETFs) were no higher than the potential returns on short-term bond ETFs or Canada Deposit Insurance Corporation-insured savings accounts, would anyone but a complete nutcase invest in emerging-market stocks?

How Risk Is Measured

In the world of investments, risk means volatility, and volatility (unlike angels or love) can be seen, measured, and plotted. People in the investment world use different tools to measure volatility, such as standard deviation, beta, and certain ratios such as the Sharpe ratio. Most of these tools are not very hard to get a handle on, and they can help you better follow discussions on portfolio building that come later in this book. Ready to dig in?

Standard deviation: The king of all risk measurement tools

So, you want to know how much an investment is likely to bounce? The first thing you do is look to see how much it has bounced in the past. Standard deviation measures the degree of past bounce and, from that measurement, gives us some notion of future bounce. To put it another way, standard deviation shows the degree to which a stock/bond/mutual fund/ETF's actual returns vary from its average returns over a certain time period.

Table 4-1 presents two hypothetical ETFs and their returns over the last six years. Note that both portfolios start with $1,000 and end with $1,101. But note, too, the great difference in how much they bounce. ETF A's yearly returns range from –3 percent to 5 percent, while ETF B's range from –15 percent to 15 percent. The standard deviation of the six years for ETF A is 3.09. For ETF B, the standard deviation is 10.38.

Table 4-1	Standard Deviation of Two Hypothetical ETFs	
Balance, Beginning of Year	**Return (% Increase or Decrease)**	**Balance, End of Year**
ETF A		
1,000	5	1,050
1,050	–2	1,029

Balance, Beginning of Year	Return (% Increase or Decrease)	Balance, End of Year
ETF A		
1,029	4	1,070
1,070	–3	1,038
1,038	2	1,059
1,059	4	1,101
ETF B		
1,000	10	1,100
1,100	6	1,166
1,166	–15	991
991	-8	912
912	15	1,048
1,048	5	1,101

Predicting a range of returns

What does the standard deviation number tell us? Let's take ETF A as an example. The standard deviation of 3.09 tells us that in about two-thirds of the months to come, we can expect the return of ETF A to fall within 3.09 percentage points of the mean return, which was 1.66. In other words, about 68 percent of the time returns should fall somewhere between 4.75 percent (1.66 + 3.09) and –1.43 percent (1.66 – 3.09). As for the other one-third of the time, anything can happen.

The standard deviation number also tells us that in about 95 percent of the months to come, the returns should fall within two standard deviations of the mean. In other words, 95 percent of the time you should see a return of between 7.84 percent [1.66 + (3.09 × 2)] and –4.52 percent [1.66 – (3.09 × 2)]. The other 5 percent of the time is anybody's guess.

Making side-by-side comparisons

The ultimate purpose of standard deviation, and the reason we're describing it, is that it gives you a way to judge the relative risks of two ETFs. If one ETF has a 3-year standard deviation of 12, you know that it is roughly twice as volatile as another ETF with a standard deviation of 6 and half as risky as an ETF with a standard deviation of 24. A real-world example: The standard deviation for most short-term bond funds falls somewhere around 0.7. The standard deviation for most precious-metals funds is somewhere around 26.0.

Important caveat: Don't assume that combining one ETF with a standard deviation of 10 with another that has a standard deviation of 20 will give you a portfolio with an average standard deviation of 15. It doesn't work that way at all, as you will see in a few pages when we introduce Modern Portfolio Theory. The combined standard deviation won't be any greater than 15, but it may (if you do your homework and put together two of the right ETFs) be much less.

Beta: Assessing price swings in relation to the market

Unlike standard deviation, which gives you a stand-alone picture of volatility, beta is a relative measure. It is used to measure the volatility of something in relation to something else. Most commonly that "something else" is the S&P 500 or the S&P/TSX Composite Index. Very simply, beta tells you that if the S&P rises or falls by x percent, then your investment, whatever that investment is, will likely rise or fall by y percent.

The S&P is considered the baseline, and it is assigned a beta of 1. So if you know that Humongous Software Corporation has a beta of 2, and the S&P shoots up 10 percent, Jimmy the Greek (if he were still with us) would bet that shares of Humongous are going to rise 20 percent. If you know that the Sedate Utility Company has a beta of 0.5, and the S&P shoots up 10 percent, Jimmy would bet that shares of Sedate are going to rise by 5 percent. Conversely, shares of Humongous would likely fall four times harder than shares of Sedate in response to a fall in the S&P.

In a way, beta is easier to understand than standard deviation; it's also easier to misinterpret. Beta's usefulness is greater for individual stocks than it is for ETFs, but nonetheless it can be helpful, especially when gauging the volatility of industry-sector ETFs. It is much less useful for any ETF that has international holdings. For example, an ETF that holds stocks of emerging-market nations is going to be volatile, trust us, yet it may have a low beta. How so? Because its movements, no matter how swooping, don't generally happen in response to movement in North American markets. (Emerging-market stocks tend to be more tied to currency flux, commodity prices, interest rates, and political climate.)

Also, if an ETF's beta looks suspiciously low, check to see what relative benchmark is being used. Some ETF providers use the index the ETF is supposed to replicate so, naturally, the beta will be near 1. They should use a standard benchmark, such as the S&P 500 or the S&P/TSX Composite Index instead.

Real-life examples of standard deviation and beta

Following are the (three-year) standard deviations and betas of several diverse ETFs. Note that iShares MSCI Hong Kong (EWH) is more volatile than iShares MSCI U.K. Index (EWU) as measured by its standard deviation, but EWH has a lower beta. That tells us that the volatility of the Hong Kong market, however great it is, seems to be less tied to the fortunes of the S&P 500 than is the volatility of the U.K. market. We're measuring the beta on the Canadian ETFs against the S&P/TSX Composite Index.

ETF	Ticker	Standard Deviation	Beta
iShares S&P/TSX 60	XIU	12.26	1.04
SPDR S&P 500	SPY	15.59	1.00
iShares S&P/TSX Capped Financials	XFN	13.86	0.86
iShares MSCI U.K. Index	EWU	19.57	1.28
PowerShares QQQ	QQQ	18.12	1.13
iShares MSCI Hong Kong	EWH	21.08	1.11

The Sharpe, Treynor, and Sortino ratios: Measures of what you get for your risk

Back in 1966, a goateed Stanford professor named Bill Sharpe developed a formula that has since become as common in investment-speak as RBIs are in baseball-speak. The formula looks like this:

$$\frac{\text{Total portfolio return} - \text{Risk-free rate of return}}{\text{Portfolio standard deviation}} = \text{Sharpe measure (or Sharpe ratio)}$$

The risk-free rate of return generally refers to the return you could get on a short-term Treasury bill. If you subtract that from the total portfolio return, it tells you how much your portfolio earned above the rate you could have achieved without risking your principal. You take that number and divide it by the standard deviation (discussed earlier in this section). And what *that* result gives you is the Sharpe ratio, which essentially indicates how much money has been made in relation to how much risk was taken to make that money.

Suppose Portfolio A, under manager Bubba Bucks, returned 7 percent last year, and during that year Government of Canada Treasury bills were paying

5 percent. Portfolio A also had a standard deviation of 8 percent. Okay, applying the formula,

$$\frac{7\% - 5\%}{8\%} = \frac{2\%}{8\%} = 0.25$$

That result isn't good enough for Bubba's manager, so he fires Bubba and hires Donny Dollar. Donny, who just read *Exchange-Traded Funds For Canadians For Dummies,* takes the portfolio and dumps all its high-cost active mutual funds. In their place, he buys ETFs. In his first year managing the portfolio, Donny achieves a total return of 10 percent with a standard deviation of 7.5. But the interest rate on Treasury bills has gone up to 7 percent. Applying the formula,

$$\frac{10\% - 7\%}{7.5\%} = \frac{3\%}{7.5\%} = 0.40$$

The higher the Sharpe measure, the better. Donny Dollar does his job much better than Bubba Bucks.

The Treynor approach was first used by — you guessed it — a guy named Jack Treynor in 1965. Instead of using standard deviation in the denominator, it uses beta. The Treynor measure shows the amount of money that a portfolio is making in relation to the risk it carries relative to the market. To put that another way, the Treynor measure uses only systemic risk, or beta, while the Sharpe ratio uses total risk.

Suppose that Donny Dollar's portfolio, with its 10 percent return, had a beta of 0.9. In that case, the Treynor measure would be

$$\frac{10\% - 7\%}{0.9} = \frac{3\%}{0.9} = \frac{.03}{0.9} = 0.033$$

Is 0.033 good? That depends. It's a relative number. Suppose that the market, as measured by the S&P/TSX Composite Index, also returned 10 percent that same year. It may seem like Donny isn't a very good manager. But when we apply the Treynor measure (recalling that the beta for the market is always 1.0),

$$\frac{10\% - 7\%}{1.0} = \frac{3\%}{1.0} = \frac{.03}{1.0} = 0.03$$

we get a lower number. That result indicates that while Donny earned a return that was similar to the market's, he took on less risk. Put another way, he achieved greater returns per unit of risk. Donny's boss will likely keep him.

Another variation on the Sharpe ratio is the Sortino ratio, which basically uses the same formula:

$$\frac{\text{Total portfolio return} - \text{Risk-free rate of return}}{\text{Portfolio standard deviation (downside only)}} = \text{Sortino ratio}$$

Note that instead of looking at historical ups and downs, it focuses only on the downs. After all, say members of the Sortino-ratio fan club, you don't lose sleep fretting about your portfolio rising in value. You want to know what your downside risk is. The Sortino-ratio fan club has been growing in size, but as yet, finding Sortino-ratio calculations for any given security, including ETFs, is difficult. We're sure it will get easier over time, because comparing downside risk among various ETFs can be a helpful tool.

Meet Modern Portfolio Theory

For simplicity's sake, we discuss the choice of one ETF over another (XSB or XIU?) based on risk and potential return. In the real world, however, few people, if any, come to a financial planner asking for a recommendation on a single ETF. More commonly, advisors are asked to help build a portfolio of ETFs. And when looking at an entire portfolio, the riskiness of each individual ETF, although important, takes a back seat to the riskiness of the entire portfolio.

In other words, advisors would rarely recommend or rule out any specific ETF because it is too volatile. How well any specific ETF fits into a portfolio — and to what degree it affects the risk of a portfolio — depends on what else is in the portfolio. What we're alluding to here is something called *Modern Portfolio Theory:* the tool most often used to help determine a proper ETF mix for a client's portfolio. We use this tool throughout this book to help you determine a proper mix for your portfolio.

Tasting the extreme positivity of negative correlation

Modern Portfolio Theory is to investing what the discovery of gravity was to physics. Almost. What the theory says is that the volatility/risk of a portfolio may differ dramatically from the volatility/risk of the portfolio's components. In other words, you can have two assets with both high standard deviations and high potential returns, but when combined they give you a portfolio with modest standard deviation but the same high potential return. Modern

Portfolio Theory says that you can have a slew of risky ingredients, but if you throw them together into a big bowl, the entire soup may actually splash around very little.

The key to whipping up such pleasant combinations is to find two or more holdings that do not move in synch: One tends to go up while the other goes down (although both holdings, in the long run, will see an upward trajectory). In the figures that follow, we show how you'd create the fantasy ETF portfolio consisting of two high-risk/high-return ETFs with perfect negative correlation. It is a fantasy portfolio because perfect negative correlations don't exist; they simply serve as a target.

Figure 4-2 represents hypothetical ETF A and hypothetical ETF B, each of which has high return and high volatility. Notice that even though both are volatile assets, they move up and down at different times. This fact is crucial because combining them can give you a nonvolatile portfolio.

Figure 4-3 shows what happens when you invest in both ETF A and ETF B. You end up with the perfect ETF portfolio — one made up of two ETFs with perfect negative correlation. (If only such a portfolio existed in the real world!)

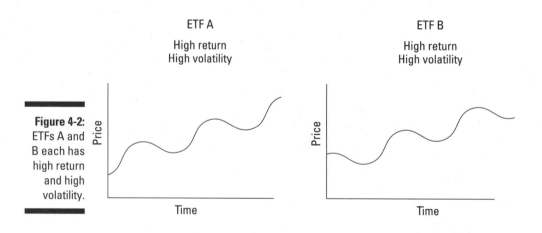

Figure 4-2: ETFs A and B each has high return and high volatility.

Settling for limited correlation

When stock markets take a punch, which happens on average every three years or so, most stocks fall. When the markets fly, most stocks fly. Not many investments regularly move in opposite directions. We do, however, find investments that tend to move independently of each other much of the time, or at least they don't move in the same direction all the time. In investment-speak, we're talking about investments that have *limited* or *low correlation*.

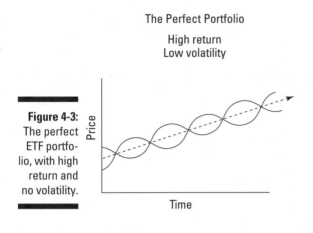

The Perfect Portfolio

High return
Low volatility

Figure 4-3:
The perfect
ETF portfo-
lio, with high
return and
no volatility.

Different kinds of stocks — large, small, value, and growth — tend to have limited correlation. Canadian stocks and foreign stocks tend to have even less correlation (see the sidebar "Investing around the world"). But the lowest correlation around is between stocks and bonds, which historically have had almost no correlation.

Say, for example, you had a basket of large stocks in 1929, at the onset of the Great Depression. You would have seen your portfolio lose nearly a quarter of its value every year for the next four years. Ouch! If, however, you were holding high-quality, long-term bonds during that same period, at least that side of your portfolio would have grown by a respectable 5 percent a year. A portfolio of long-term U.S. bonds held throughout the growling bear market in stocks of 2000 through 2003 would have returned a hale and hearty 13 percent a year. (That's an unusually high return for bonds, but at the time the stars were in seemingly perfect alignment.)

During the market spiral of 2008, there was an unprecedented chorus-line effect in which nearly all stocks — value, growth, large, small, Canadian, U.S., and foreign — moved in the same direction: down . . . depressingly down. At the same time, all but the highest quality bonds took a beating as well. But once again, portfolio protection came in the form of long-term U.S. government bonds, which rose by about 26 percent in value.

In August 2011, as S&P downgraded U.S. Treasuries (fortunately, Canada's still got their AAA rating), the stock markets again took a tumble. And — guess what? — Treasuries, despite their downgrade by S&P (but none of the other raters), spiked upward!

Investing around the world

You can see in this table of annual returns how correlated certain markets are. In 2008 everything went down, while almost every market went back up a year later. Markets seem to be moving less in unison the farther we get from the recession, but they're actually far more correlated than they were decades ago. About 15 years ago, Canadian stocks were 60 percent correlated to international equities; today's are 90 percent correlated.

	2008	2009	2010	2011	2012
Canadian Stock Market (S&P/TSX Composite)	−39.9	41.3	14.5	−11.1	4
U.S. Stock Market (S&P 500)	−41.0	27.8	12.8	0.0	11.5
Europe (S&P Europe 350)	−47.42	25.9	−1.6	−17.4	13.7
Japan (MSCI Japan)	−30.5	−4.4	13.4	−16.2	5.8
Emerging Markets (MSCI Emerging Markets)	−54.4	74.5	16.4	−20.4	15

Reaching for the elusive Efficient Frontier

Correlation is a measurable thing, represented in the world of investments by something called the *correlation coefficient.* This number indicates the degree to which two investments move in the same or different directions. A correlation coefficient can range from –1 to 1.

A correlation of 1 indicates that the two securities are like the Rockettes: When one kicks a leg, so does the other. Having both in your portfolio offers no diversification benefit. On the other hand, if investment A and investment B have a correlation coefficient of –1, that means they have a perfect negative relationship: They always move in the opposite directions. Having both in your portfolio is a wonderful diversifier. Such polar-opposite investments are, alas, very hard to find.

A correlation coefficient of zero means that the two investments have no relationship to each other. When one moves, the other may move in the same direction, the opposite direction, or not at all.

As a whole, stocks and bonds (not junk bonds, but high-quality bonds) tend to have little to negative correlation. Finding the perfect mix of stocks and bonds, as well as other investments with low correlation, is known among financial pros as looking for the *Efficient Frontier.* The Frontier represents the mix of investments that offers the greatest promise of return for the least amount of risk.

Fortunately, ETFs allow us to tinker easily with our investments so we can find just that sweet spot.

Accusations that MPT is dead are greatly exaggerated

Since the market swoon of 2008, some pundits have claimed that Modern Portfolio Theory is dead. Most experts say that while it's true that markets moved together during the recession, they moved at different paces and the degree to which they recovered has differed significantly. Sectors have performed differently too — sometimes vastly differently — so, the theory is still relevant. You can see these differences in the charts in the upcoming sections "Filling in your style box" and "Buying by industry sector."

The investors who were hurt terribly in 2008 were those who sold their depressed stocks and moved everything into cash or "safe" bonds. The investors who kept the faith in MPT and rebalanced their portfolios, as we discuss fully in Chapter 18, were not so badly wounded. These investors were buying stock in 2008 instead of selling it. And any investors with a fairly well-balanced portfolio of stocks and bonds would have recouped their losses within two years after the market bottomed in March 2009.

The correlation of various ETFs

The following correlations of several iShares ETFs show to what degree different ETFs moved in the same direction during a recent three-year period. The lower the correlation, the better, from a portfolio-building point of view. Low correlations reduce portfolio risk. High correlations do not. Negative correlations are, alas, not that easy to find in the real world, but portfolio managers are forever looking.

ETF 1	ETF 2	Correlation Coefficient	Rating
iShares S&P/TSX 60	iShares DEX Universe Bond	−0.54	Negative correlation
iShares Dow Jones Canada Select Growth Index	iShares Dow Jones Canada Select Value Index	0.73	Modest correlation
iShares China All Cap Index	iShares S&P/TSX Small Cap Index	0.45	Low correlation
iShares S&P/TSX Small Cap Index	iShares MSCI Canada Index (large caps)	0.89	High correlation
iShares Russell 200 Index (U.S. small caps)	iShares S&P/TSX Small Cap Index	0.78	Modest correlation

Mixing and Matching Your Stock ETFs

Reaching for the elusive Efficient Frontier means holding both stocks and bonds — domestic and international — in your portfolio. That part is fairly straightforward and not likely to stir much controversy (although, for sure, experts differ on what they consider optimal percentages). But experts definitely don't agree on how best to diversify the domestic-stock portion of a portfolio. Two competing methods predominate:

✔ One method calls for the division of a stock portfolio into domestic and foreign, and then into different styles: large cap, small cap, mid cap, value, and growth.

✔ The other method calls for allocating percentages of a portfolio to various industry sectors: health care, utilities, energy, financials, and so on.

We suggest the small to mid-sized investor, especially the ETF investor, should go primarily with the styles. But there's nothing wrong with dividing up a portfolio by industry sector. And for those of you with good-sized portfolios, a mixture of both, without going crazy, may be optimal.

Filling in your style box

Most savvy investors make certain to have some equity in each of the nine boxes of the grid in Figure 4-4, which is known as the *style box* or *grid* (sometimes called the *Morningstar grid*).

Large cap value	Large cap blend	Large cap growth
Mid cap value	Mid cap blend	Mid cap growth
Small cap value	Small cap blend	Small cap growth

Figure 4-4:
The style box or grid.

The reason for the style box is simple enough: History shows that companies of differing cap (capitalization) size (in other words, large companies and small companies), and value and growth companies, tend to rise and fall under different economic conditions. We define *cap size, value,* and *growth* in Chapter 5, and we devote the next several chapters to showing the differences among styles, how to choose ETFs to match each one, and how to weight those ETFs for the highest potential return with the lowest possible risk.

Table 4-2 shows how well various investment styles, per Morningstar, have fared in the past several years. Because the U.S. market is larger, we use American figures in this example. Note that a number of ETFs are available to match each style.

Table 4-2	Recent Performance of Various Investment Styles				
	2008	*2009*	*2010*	*2011*	*2012*
Large cap growth	−41.9	44.4	12.9	−2.5	14.0
Large cap value	−36.1	11.4	14.7	−0.8	12.3
Small cap growth	−39.9	33.0	31.3–3.6	−3.6	9.7
Small cap value	−31.7	40.3	26.0–4.4	−4.4	11.0

Buying by industry sector

The advent of ETFs has largely brought forth the use of sector investing as an alternative to the grid (refer to Figure 4-4). Examining the two models toe to toe yields some interesting comparisons — and much food for thought.

One study on industry-sector investing, by Chicago-based Ibbotson Associates, came to the very favourable conclusion that sector investing is a potentially superior diversifier to grid investing because times have changed since the 1960s when style investing first became popular. "Globalization has led to a rise in correlation between domestic and international stocks; large, mid, and small cap stocks have high correlation to each other. A company's performance is tied more to its industry than to the country where it's based, or the size of its market cap," concluded Ibbotson.

The jury is still out, but we give an overview of the controversy in Chapter 10. For now, we invite you to do a little comparison of your own by comparing Tables 4-2 and 4-3. Note that by using either method of diversification, some of your investments should smell like roses in years when others stink. Also, recall what we state earlier about how all stocks crashed in 2008 but recovered at significantly different paces; this is true of various styles and sectors. And it is certainly true for various geographic regions. Modern Portfolio Theory is not dead!

Table 4-3 shows how well various industry sectors (as measured by their respective S&P indexes) fared in recent years. Yes, there are ETFs that track each of these industry sectors — and many more.

Table 4-3	Recent Performance of Various Market Sectors				
	2008	*2009*	*2010*	*2011*	*2012*
Canadian Financials	37.3	38.5	−4.4	−7.5	9.04
Canadian Energy	39.5	37.3	−8.7	−16.8	−7.8
Canadian REITs	−42.3	42.4	−15.1	15.1	6.2
U.S. Health Care	−23.8	−17.1	−0.7	10.2	14.7

Don't slice and dice your portfolio to death

One reason we tend to prefer the traditional style grid to industry-sector investing, at least for the nonwealthy investor, is that there are simply fewer styles to contend with. You can build yourself, at least on the domestic side of your stock holdings, a pretty well-diversified portfolio with just four ETFs: one small value, one small growth, one large value, and one large growth. With industry-sector investing, you would need a dozen or so ETFs to have a well-balanced portfolio, and that may be too many.

We hold a similar philosophy when it comes to global investing. Yes, you can, thanks largely to the iShares lineup of ETFs, invest in about 50 individual countries. (And in many of these countries, you can also choose between large cap and small cap stocks, and in some cases, value and growth.) Too much! We prefer to see most investors go with larger geographic regions: U.S., Europe, Asia, emerging markets. . . .

You don't want to chop up your portfolio into too many holdings, or the transaction costs (especially with ETFs that require trading costs) can start to bite into your returns. Rebalancing gets to be a headache. Tax filing can become a nightmare. And, as many investors learned in 2008, having a very small position in your portfolio, say less than 2 percent of your assets, in any one kind of investment isn't going to have much effect on your overall returns anyway.

As a rough rule, if you have $50,000 to invest, consider something in the ballpark of a 5- to 10-ETF portfolio, and if you have $250,000 or more, perhaps look at a 15- to 25-ETF portfolio. Having many more ETFs than this won't enhance the benefits of diversification but will entail additional trading costs every time you rebalance your holdings. (See our sample ETF portfolios for all sizes of nest eggs in Part IV.)

What creates returns, and what kind of returns will the future bring?

In the world of stock markets, with their by-and-large juicy long-term returns, the juice comes from three sources:

✔ Dividends

✔ Earnings growth

✔ Price/earnings multiples (the measure of market expectations), otherwise known as P/E

Dividends, it may surprise you to hear, account for the lion's share of stock market returns over the past two centuries. The stock market has given us roughly a 7 percent post-inflation rise during that period. Perhaps three-quarters of that 7 percent is attributable to dividends. That story is likely to continue, especially if interest rates stay low for a while. Many companies are increasing their dividends, and businesses that have never paid a yield are starting to give back to investors. People are hungry for income and — because you can't get that from government bonds anymore — look to the equity markets.

The dividend yield on the S&P/TSX Composite Index is about 3 percent, or about 1.2 percentage points higher than a ten-year Government of Canada bond. The price/earnings multiple — the factor by which investors are willing to invest in stocks in hopes of future earnings — soared wildly in the bull market of the 1990s and then fell to extreme lows during the recession, but has since returned to a level that's pretty close to its historical norm. It may grow again, or it may shrink. Who knows? Earnings growth needs to pick up before investors can get those 7 percent after-inflation returns. Will it happen? Who knows?

When we look into our crystal ball (we really try not to do that very often!), we can't see what returns will be, but we do know for sure that the stock market will continue to be volatile, perhaps even more so than it has been in the past. Many investors may end up jumping overboard long before they get to any port where they'll find the Holy Grail. Fortunately, with a well-balanced portfolio of ETFs, you will be in a position to complete the voyage.

But don't presume that you can avoid all risk or that the future will mirror the past, and don't put everything you have into stocks.

Chapter 5

Large Growth: Muscular Money Makers

In This Chapter

▶ Understanding what makes large large and growth growth

▶ Sizing up the size factor in stock investing

▶ Choosing the best options for your portfolio

*P*ick up a typical business magazine and look at the face adorning the cover. He's Mr. CEO. Tough and ambitious and looking for acquisitions under every rock, his pedigree is University of Toronto, his wife is the former Miss Ontario, his salary (not to mention other perks) exceeds the gross national product of Peru, and his house has 14 bathrooms. The title of the cover story emblazoned across Mr. CEO's chest suggests that buying stock in his company will make you rich. Without knowing anything more, you can assume that Mr. CEO heads a large growth company.

In other words, Mr. CEO's company has a *total market capitalization* (the value of all its outstanding stock) of at least $5 billion, earnings have been growing, and growing fast, the company has a secure niche within its industry, and many people envision the Borg-like corporation eventually taking over the universe. Think CN Rail, Scotiabank, Suncor, and Barrick Gold. In the States, think General Electric, IBM, and — even though its CEO may not exactly fit the stereotype — Google.

In this chapter, we explain what role such behemoths should play in your portfolio. But before getting into the meat of the matter, take a quick glance at Figures 5-1 and 5-2. Figure 5-1 shows where large growth stocks fit into a well-diversified stock portfolio. (We introduce this style box or grid, which divides a stock portfolio into large cap and small cap, value and growth, in Chapter 4.) Figure 5-2 shows their historical returns. (We're using American numbers because there's more historical data to look at. The results are similar in Canada.)

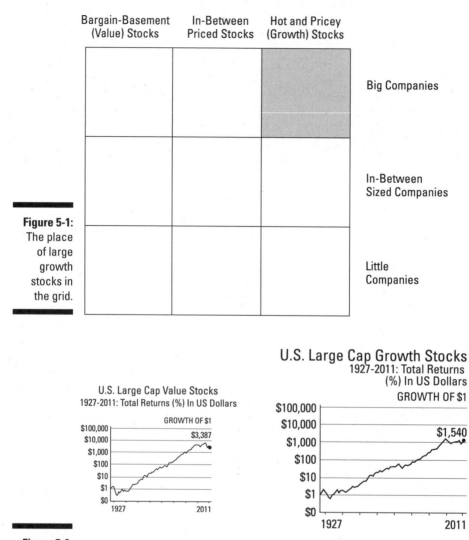

Figure 5-1:
The place of large growth stocks in the grid.

Figure 5-2:
Large growth stocks have given investors ample returns over the decades.

Source: Fama/French data provided by Eugene F. Fama and Kenneth R. French

Style Review

In Chapter 4, we note that one approach to building a portfolio involves investing in different styles of stocks: large cap, mid cap, small cap, value, and growth. How did the whole business of style investing get started? Hard to say. Benjamin Graham, the "Dean of Wall Street," the "Father of Value Investing," who wrote several oft-quoted books in the 1930s and 1940s, didn't give us the popular style grid that you see in Figure 5-1. But Mr. Graham certainly helped provide the tools of fundamental analysis whereby more contemporary brains could figure things out.

In the early 1980s, studies out of the University of Chicago began to quantify the differences between large caps and small caps, and in 1992, two economists named Eugene Fama and Kenneth French delivered the seminal paper on the differences between value and growth stocks.

What makes large cap large?

Capitalization, or *cap,* refers to the combined value of all shares of a company's stock. The lines dividing large cap, mid cap, and small cap are sometimes as blurry as the line between, say, *Rubenesque* and *fat.* The distinction is largely in the eyes of the beholder. If you took a poll, however, you would find that the following divisions are generally accepted:

- **Large caps:** Companies with more than $5 billion in capitalization
- **Mid caps:** Companies with $1 billion to $5 billion in capitalization
- **Small caps:** Companies with $250 million to $1 billion in capitalization

Anything from $50 million to $250 million is usually deemed a *micro cap.* And your local pizza shop, if it was to go public, would be called a *nano cap (con aglio).* Nano cap companies have a market capitalization of less than $50 million. No nano cap ETFs exist. For all the other categories, there are ETFs to your heart's content.

How does growth differ from value?

Many different criteria are used to determine whether a stock or basket of stocks (such as an ETF) qualifies as *growth* or *value.* (In Chapter 6, we list six ways for you to recognize value.) But perhaps the most important measure is the ratio of price to earnings: the *price/earnings (P/E) ratio,* sometimes referred to as the *multiple.*

The P/E ratio is the price of a stock divided by its earnings per share. For example, suppose McDummy Corporation stock is currently selling for $40 a share. And suppose that the company earned $2 last year for every share of stock outstanding. McDummy's P/E ratio would be 20. (The S&P 500 currently has a P/E of about 14, but that ratio changes frequently.)

The higher the P/E, the more investors have been willing to pay for the company's earnings. Or to put it in terms of growth and value:

- ✔ The higher the P/E, the more *growthy* the company. Either the company is growing fast or investors have high hopes (realistic or foolish) for future growth.
- ✔ The lower the P/E, the more *valuey* the company. The business world doesn't see this company as a mover and shaker.

Each ETF carries a P/E reflecting the collective P/E of its holdings and giving you an indication of just how growthy or valuey that ETF is. A growth ETF is filled with companies that look like they are taking over the planet. A value ETF is filled with companies that seem to be meandering along but whose stock can be purchased for what looks like a bargain price.

Putting these terms to use

Today, most investment pros develop their portfolios with at least some consideration given to the cap size and growth or value orientation of their stock holdings. Why? Because study after study shows that, in fact, a portfolio's performance is inexorably linked to where that portfolio falls in the style grid. A mutual fund that holds all large growth stocks, for example, will generally (but certainly not always) rise or fall with the rise or fall of that asset class.

Some research shows that perhaps 90 to 95 percent of a mutual fund's or ETF's performance may be attributable to its asset class alone. In other words, any large cap growth fund will tend to perform similarly to other large cap growth funds. Any small cap value fund will tend to perform similarly to other small cap value funds. And so on. That's why the financial press's weekly wrap-ups of top-performing funds will typically list a bunch of funds that mirror each other very closely. (That being the case, why not enjoy the low cost of the ETF or index mutual fund?)

Big and Brawny

Large growth companies grab nearly all the headlines, for sure. The pundits are forever singing their praises — or trumpeting their faults when the growth trajectory starts to level off. Either way, you'll hear about it; the northeast corner of the style grid shown in Figure 5-1 includes the most recognizable names in the corporate world. If you're seeking employment, we strongly urge you to latch on to one of these companies; your future will likely be bright. But do large growth stocks necessarily make the best investments?

Er, no.

Contrary to all appearances . . .

According to Fama and French (who are still operating as a research duo), over the course of the last 85 years, large growth stocks have seen an annualized return rate (not accounting for inflation) of about 8.8 percent. Not too bad. But that compares to 11.1 percent for large value stocks, with no greater volatility. Theories abound as to why large growth stocks haven't done as well as value stocks. Value stocks pay greater dividends, say some. Value stocks really *are* riskier; they just don't look it, argue others.

The theory that makes the most sense, in our opinion, is that growth stocks are simply hampered by their own immense popularity. Because growth companies grab all the headlines, because investors *think* they must be the best investments, the large growth stocks tend to get overpriced by the time you buy them. In the past few months, for example, everyone has been talking about Facebook, the social network that everyone and their mothers are on. Yes, the company is growing faster than crabgrass. And it probably will continue to grow. But with a price/earnings ratio of 203, your stock investment in Facebook is dependent on continued supersonic growth . . . anything less than supersonic growth, and the stock isn't going to shine. On the other hand, if people had expected the stock to tank (in which case, the P/E would have been much lower), value investors may have jumped in and made a profit even if the company didn't grow at all — but merely didn't tank!

Let history serve as only a rough guide

So given that large value stocks historically have done better than large growth stocks, and given (as we discuss in Chapters 7 and 8) that small caps historically have knocked the socks off large, does sinking some of your investment dollars into large growth still make sense? Oh yes, it does. The past is only an indication of what the future may bring. No one knows whether value stocks will continue to outshine. In the past ten years or so especially, large growth stocks have lagged behind value and have fallen behind smaller stocks by a wide margin. But this trend was itself a reversal of what happened during much of the 1990s when growth trumped value. So perhaps we're going to see yet another reversal.

(Please don't accuse us of market timing! We're not saying that just because large growth stocks have been depressed they are due for a big comeback. We have no idea. But to a small and limited degree, a little timely *tactical* tilting, we feel, is an okay thing. That is, tilting a portfolio *gently* toward whatever industry seem to be sagging and away from sectors that have been blazing may make some sense. If you do that subtly, and regularly, and don't let emotions sway you — and if you watch out carefully for tax ramifications and trading costs — history shows that you may eke out some modest added return. More on tactical tilting in Chapter 18.)

Stocks of large companies — value and growth combined — should make up between 50 and 70 percent of your total domestic stock portfolio. The higher your risk tolerance, the closer you'll want to be to the lower end of that range.

Whatever your allocation to domestic large cap stocks, we recommend that you invest anywhere from 40 to 50 percent of that amount in large growth. Take a tilt toward value, if you wish, but don't tilt so far that you risk tipping over.

ETF Options Galore

The roster of ETFs on the market now includes about 100 broad-based U.S. large cap funds, of which 20 or so are acceptable large growth options. As with every type of ETF, some Canadian options exist, but not as many as you find down south. The remainder of the broad-based (as opposed to industry sector or other specialized) large cap funds are either *blend* (a growth-and-value cocktail) or strictly large value. As we emphasize throughout this book, each and every investment you make should be evaluated in the context of your entire portfolio.

In this chapter, we focus on large growth ETFs. But before you start shopping for a large growth ETF, you need to ask yourself whether one belongs in your portfolio at all. In a nutshell, it does, but only if your portfolio is large enough to be divided into various styles.

Strictly large cap or blend?

All things being equal, we'd like to see you invest in large growth and large value stocks — separately. That approach gives you the opportunity to rebalance once a year and, by so doing, juice out added return while reducing risk. (More on rebalancing in Chapter 18.) But the profit you expect to reap from that tweak must exceed the transaction costs of making two trades (generally, selling shares of the outperforming ETF for the year and adding to the underperformer).

If your portfolio isn't big enough for the profit of the tweaking to outweigh the cost of the trading, you're better off with a blend of value and growth. If your portfolio is so small that any tweaking is unlikely to be profitable, we suggest not having a blend of large value and growth only, but a blend of *everything*. Keep these parameters in mind as you read on.

"Everything" investment options

If you have a portfolio of $10,000 or less, you should either be thinking mutual funds (not ETFs) or be seeking to invest at a brokerage that won't charge you for trading ETFs. Otherwise, the trading costs could eat you alive. If, however, you're unlikely to do any trading in the next several years, an ETF portfolio may make sense. In that case, consider a simple and all-encompassing "everything" (total ball of wax) ETF for your domestic stock holdings.

Canada has one all-in-one fund, the Vanguard MSCI Canada Index ETF (VCE), though it's still heavily weighted toward large caps. Still, it does include some mid cap and small cap names. So if you want to buy a Canadian "everything" fund, consider this one.

Of course, many good U.S. options exist in the "everything" stock category. So think about adding some to your American exposure. Some of the better picks include the iShares Dow Jones U.S. Total Market ETF (IYY), the Vanguard Total Stock Market ETF (VTI), and the Schwab U.S. Broad Market ETF (SCHB). Of the three, we have a slight preference for the Schwab and the Vanguard choices because of their ultra-low costs (0.06 and 0.04 percent, respectively, versus 0.20 percent for the iShares offering).

Note: Several "everything" ETFs exist that allow you to tap into even broader investments than the entire U.S. stock market; we discuss a few of these options in Chapter 11.

Large cap blends

Canadian investors need to go with blended ETFs if they want to have domestic exposure. The average investor should do well with just a large cap blend. Good choices among the large cap blends are the iShares S&P/TSX 60 (XIU), the iShares S&P/TSX Completion Index Fund (XMD), and the Vanguard MSCI Canada Index Fund (VCE).

Large cap growth and value options

If you have a portfolio of more than $20,000, you should split up the large caps into growth and value, though again, you don't have many options to choose from. The one large growth option is the iShares Dow Jones Canada Select Growth Index Fund (XCG). For U.S.-based ETFs, look at the Vanguard Mega Cap 300 Growth ETF (MGK), the iShares Morningstar Large Growth ETF (JKE), and the Schwab U.S. Large Cap Growth ETF (SCHG). See the upcoming section "Large growth options" for details on these ETFs.

Blended options for large cap exposure

Among the *blended* (large cap value and growth) options for smaller portfolios ($10,000 to $20,000), we feel comfortable recommending any of the ETFs discussed in this section.

Please keep in mind that all the expense ratios, average cap sizes, price/earnings ratios, and top five holdings for the ETFs we list here and elsewhere in this book are true as of a certain date and are subject to change. You should verify all key details before making any purchase.

iShares S&P/TSX 60 Index Fund (XIU)

Indexed to: S&P/TSX 60 Index, which is made up of 60 of the largest and most liquid companies on the TSX.

Expense ratio: 0.15 percent

P/E ratio: 13.1

Top five holdings: Royal Bank, TD Bank, Soctiabank, Suncor Energy, Barrick Gold

Bryan's review: This fund is, by far, the most popular Canadian ETF on the market. Though it covers only a small number of TSX-listed companies, it tracks all the big names, which for most Canadian investors is all that really matters. This fund is for anyone who wants broad exposure to the domestic market; its performance is in line with the S&P/TSX Composite Index, and with a 0.15 percent expense ratio, it's also cheap. As well, it's one of the more diversified Canadian ETFs (well, as diversified as a Canadian ETF can get) with a fairly even exposure to financials, energy, and materials. This is a must in most portfolios.

S&P/TSX Capped Composite Index Fund (XIC)

Indexed to: S&P/TSX Capped Composite Index, an index made up of the largest and most liquid stocks on the TSX.

Expense ratio: 0.25 percent

P/E ratio: 13.6

Top five holdings: Royal Bank, TD Bank, Scotiabank, Suncor Energy, Barrick Gold

Bryan's review: Two main differences between this fund and XIU exist: It holds far more companies, and the weighting of each stock can't exceed 10 percent. Look at the weighting for Royal Bank, and you'll see what I mean. In XIU, RBC accounts for 7.42 percent of the fund, while in XIC, it makes up 5.47 percent. That may not seem like much of a difference, but the fact is you're less exposed to one particular company in XIC — each holding has a similar weighting. Though XIC isn't nearly as popular as XIU, many people prefer this fund because it's more diversified and there's less single company risk. However, the higher expense ratio is a turnoff, and it's worth noting that it has underperformed XIU during the last five years. Still, if you want to play the broader Canadian market and with more stocks, then this ETF's for you.

Indexed to: MSCI Canada Index, an index that tracks 100 mostly large cap and mid cap names.

Expense ratio: 0.09 percent

Top five holdings: Royal Bank, TD Bank, Scotiabank, Suncor Energy, Barrick Gold

Bryan's review: Notice something familiar? All three of the Canadian funds listed here share the same top five holdings. That goes to show you just how diversified our market is. Still, this ETF does hold a wider range of stocks than the others (though less actual holdings than XIC) because it includes mid and small cap stocks. Here's the breakdown: 66.3 percent of the portfolio is in large caps, 20.1 percent borders on large and mid caps, 10.5 percent is in mid caps, and 2.8 percent leans toward small caps. The fund was just introduced in late 2011, so it doesn't have any historical returns yet, but it is one of more promising offerings on the market, especially considering its dirt-cheap fee. If you want some extra diversification, then consider buying this fund.

Looking for blended large cap exposure in the States? Consider the following funds.

Vanguard Large Cap ETF (VV)

Indexed to: MSCI U.S. Prime Market 750 Index (750 corporate biggies from both the value and growth sides of the grid)

Expense ratio: 0.10 percent

P/E ratio: 14.6

Top five holdings: Apple, Exxon Mobil, General Electric, Chevron, International Business Machines

Russell's review: The low cost, as with nearly all Vanguard offerings, makes me want to stand up and cheer. The MSCI U.S. Prime Market 750, as the name implies, encompasses a larger universe of stocks than the more popular S&P 500, which translates to holdings with a somewhat smaller average cap size than you'll find with some other large cap options. The MSCI index is also more "indexy" than the S&P 500: The choice of companies is purely quantitative, whereas with the S&P, some human judgment is applied. Personally, I like the hands-off approach. This ETF is an excellent choice for people with smaller portfolios who are trying to limit the number of ETFs they have to manage.

Vanguard Mega Cap 300 ETF (MGC)

Indexed to: MSCI U.S. Large Cap 300 Index (the biggest 300 U.S. companies, regardless of type)

Expense ratio: 0.12 percent

P/E ratio: 14.3

Top five holdings: Apple, Exxon Mobil, General Electric, Chevron, International Business Machines

Russell's review: What the heck? If you're going to go big, why not go all the way? Note that the top five holdings are the very same that you'll find with the other Vanguard blended option, the Vanguard Large Cap ETF (VV). But in the case of this ETF, you won't be getting the lesser sized of the large cap companies. That's less than optimal from a diversification standpoint, and for that reason, I wouldn't recommend MGC over VV as a stand-alone investment. But if you are combining either of these funds with a blended small cap fund, then MGC will give you somewhat lower correlation (in other words, greater simultaneous zig and zag potential), which is a good thing. For most investors' portfolios, either Vanguard option would be an excellent choice.

Schwab U.S. Large Cap ETF (SCHX)

Indexed to: Dow Jones U.S. Large Cap Total Stock Market Index (approximately 750 of America's largest corporations)

Expense ratio: 0.08 percent

P/E ratio: 15.0

Top five holdings: Apple, Exxon Mobil, General Electric, Chevron, Microsoft

Russell's review: For frugality's sake alone, this fund makes a good option. The management fee is one of the lowest in the industry. Most important, the index is a good one. I expect Schwab to do a good job of tracking the index, even though its ETFs were introduced only in late 2009.

Large growth options

Canadians can't buy a domestic fund that's strictly large growth. Of course, Americans can. (They have all the fun!) The one growth and large cap-oriented domestic ETF does have mid caps too, though its top holdings are all fairly large enterprises. We first talk about this ETF and then get into some U.S. options, which are more purely large cap growth funds.

iShares Dow Jones Canada Select Growth Index Fund (XCG)

Indexed to: Dow Jones Canada Select Growth Index. It includes 61 growth-oriented companies.

Expense ratio: 0.50 percent

P/E ratio: 18.1

Top five holdings: Suncor Energy, Canadian National Railway, PotashCorp, Goldcorp, Canadian Natural Resources

Bryan's review: If you have enough money to split between value and growth and believe an economic recovery is on the horizon (growth stocks tend to do better during good times), then this fund can give your portfolio a boost. But watch out for two things: Its management fee is high for an ETF, and it has a 38 percent weighting to the volatile oil and gas sector. That's not surprising — most Canadian growth companies are energy operations — but it's something to be mindful of. Though it's mostly weighted to large and mid caps, it does have some smaller companies too; its largest company has a market cap of $43.9 billion, and its smallest is worth $200 million. The average, though, is $7.1 billion, which is firmly in large cap territory. It's probably not worth buying if you own the broader-based Canadian ETFs; look at it only if you want to get more specific with your securities.

Vanguard Growth ETF (VUG)

Indexed to: MSCI U.S. Prime Market Growth Index (400 or so of the nation's largest growth stocks)

Expense ratio: 0.10 percent

P/E ratio: 17.0

Top five holdings: Apple, International Business Machines, Coca-Cola, Microsoft, Philip Morris International

Russell's review: The price is right. The index makes sense. There's good diversification. The companies represented are certainly large, even though they could be a bit more growthy. This ETF is certainly a very good option.

Vanguard Mega Cap 300 Growth ETF (MGK)

Indexed to: MSCI U.S. Large Cap Growth Index (300 of the largest growth companies in the United States)

Expense ratio: 0.12 percent

P/E ratio: 16.6

Top five holdings: Apple, International Business Machines, Coca-Cola, Microsoft, Philip Morris International

Russell's review: Bigger is better . . . sometimes. If you have small caps in your portfolio, this mega cap fund will give you slightly better diversification than the Vanguard Growth ETF (VUG), but this fund is also a tad less growthy than VUG, so you'll get a bit less divergence from your large value holdings. Nothing to sweat. Either fund, given Vanguard's low expenses and reasonable indexes, would make for a fine holding.

iShares Morningstar Large Growth ETF (JKE)

Indexed to: Morningstar Large Growth Index (90 of the largest and most growthy U.S. companies)

Expense ratio: 0.25 percent

P/E ratio: 19.7

Top five holdings: Apple, Microsoft, Google, Philip Morris International, Coca-Cola

Russell's review: Nothing in life is perfect. This ETF offers the growthiness that the Vanguard ETFs lack, but the flip side is that the diversification leaves something to be desired. Apple and IBM together make up a tad more than 20 percent of the index; that's a little more than I would like to see for two companies that happen to be in a similar industry, especially when the third-largest holding is also in that industry. And perhaps because Morningstar indexes aren't nearly as popular as S&P indexes, this ETF is thinly traded, which can result in a larger spread when you buy or sell. What tips the scales for me, however, and makes this one a contender, is that Morningstar indexes are crisp and distinct: Any company that appears in the growth index isn't going to be popping up in the value index. Even though that crispness may lead to slightly higher turnover, I like it.

Chapter 6

Large Value: Counterintuitive Cash Cows

In This Chapter
▶ Recognizing ETFs that fit the value bill
▶ Choosing the best options for your portfolio

Why do suburbanites gingerly cultivate their daisies yet go nuts swinging spades or spraying poison chemicals at their dandelions? Why is a second cup of coffee in a diner free, but a second cup of tea isn't? Some things in this world just don't make a lot of sense. Why, for example, would slower-growing companies (the dandelions of the corporate world) historically reward investors better than faster-growing (daisy) companies? Welcome to the shoulder-shrugging world of value investing.

We're talking about companies you've probably heard of, yes, but they aren't nearly as glamorous as Google or as exciting as Cisco. We're talking about companies that usually ply their trade in older, slow-growing industries, like finance, energy, and telecom. We're talking about companies such as Bank of Montreal, Sears Canada, Suncor Energy, and BCE.

We see you yawning! But before you fall asleep, consider this: In the past 85 years, large value stocks have enjoyed an annualized growth rate of about 11.1 percent, versus 8.8 percent for large growth stocks — with roughly the same standard deviation (volatility). And thanks to ETFs, investing in value has never been easier.

In this chapter, we explain not only the role that large value stocks play in a portfolio but also why you may want them to be the largest single asset class in your portfolio. Take a gander at Figures 6-1 and 6-2. They show where large value stocks fit into the investment style grid (which we introduce in Chapter 4) and the impressive return of large value stocks over the past eight or so decades. (We're using American figures here, because the data stretches back farther. The results will be similar no matter what country you're looking at.)

Pass the dandelion fertilizer, will ya?

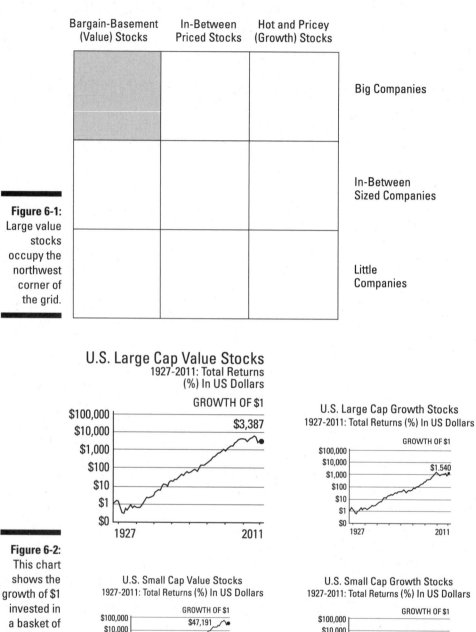

	Bargain-Basement (Value) Stocks	In-Between Priced Stocks	Hot and Pricey (Growth) Stocks	
				Big Companies
				In-Between Sized Companies
				Little Companies

Figure 6-1: Large value stocks occupy the northwest corner of the grid.

U.S. Large Cap Value Stocks
1927-2011: Total Returns (%) In US Dollars

GROWTH OF $1

$3,387

U.S. Large Cap Growth Stocks
1927-2011: Total Returns (%) In US Dollars

GROWTH OF $1

$1.540

Figure 6-2: This chart shows the growth of $1 invested in a basket of large value stocks from 1927 to the present.

U.S. Small Cap Value Stocks
1927-2011: Total Returns (%) In US Dollars

GROWTH OF $1

$47,191

U.S. Small Cap Growth Stocks
1927-2011: Total Returns (%) In US Dollars

GROWTH OF $1

$1,299

Source: Fama/French data provided by Eugene F. Fama and Kenneth R. French

Six Ways to Recognize Value

Warren Buffett knows a value stock when he sees one. Do you? Different investment pros and different indexes (upon which ETFs are fashioned) may define *value* differently, but here are some of the most common criteria:

- **P/E ratio:** As early as 1934, Benjamin Graham and David Dodd (in their book with the blockbuster title *Security Analysis*) suggested that investors should give special consideration to the ratio of a stock's market price (P) to its earnings per share (E). Sometimes called the *multiple,* this venerable ratio sheds light on how much the market is willing to cough up for a company's earning power. The lower the ratio, the more "valuey" the stock. (The P/E ratio as it relates to growth stocks is addressed in Chapter 5.)

- **P/B ratio:** Graham and Dodd also advised that the ratio of market price to book value (B) should be given at least "a fleeting glance." Many of today's investment gurus have awarded the P/B ratio the chief role in defining value versus growth. A ratio well below sea level — generally under 1 times price-to-book — is what floats a value investor's boat. *Book value* refers to the guesstimated value of a corporation's total assets, both tangible (factories, inventory, and so on) and intangible (goodwill, patents, and so on), minus any liabilities.

- **Dividend distributions:** You like dividends? Value stocks are often the ones that pay them.

- **The cover of *Canadian Business:*** Magazine covers are rarely adorned with photos of the CEOs of value companies. While growth companies receive broad exposure, value companies tend to wallow in obscurity.

- **Earnings growth:** Growth companies' earnings tend to impress, but you can expect value companies to have less than awe-inspiring earnings growth.

- **The industry sector:** Growth stocks are typically found in high-flying industries, such as computers, wireless, and biotechnology. Value stocks are more often found in older-than-the-hills sectors, such as energy, banking, transportation, and toiletries.

Looking for the Best Value Buys

Many academic types have looked at the so-called *value premium* and have tried to explain it. No one can agree on why value stocks have historically outperformed growth stocks. (A joke Russell remembers from his college days: Put any three economists in a room, and you'll get at least five opinions.)

Some people say hidden risk exists in value investing that warrants greater returns. They explain that although the standard deviation for the two asset classes is about the same, value stocks tend to plummet at the worst economic times. This argument isn't very persuasive. Although value was hit harder than growth in the market plunge of 2008, the reverse held true in the prior market nosedive of 2000–2002.

Others say that value stocks outperform growth stocks because of the greater dividends paid by value companies. Growth companies tend to plow their cash into acquisitions and new product development rather than issue dividends to those pesky shareholders.

Here's the best explanation for the value premium, if you ask us: Value stocks simply tend to be ignored by the market — or have been in the past — and therefore come relatively cheap. When value stocks do receive attention, it's usually negative. And studies show that investors tend to overreact to bad news. Such overreactions end up being reflected in a discounted price.

Taking the index route

Famous value investors like Warren Buffett make their money finding stocks that come at an especially discounted price. They recognize that companies making lacklustre profits, and even sometimes companies bleeding money, can turn around (especially when Mr. Buffett sends in his team of whip-cracking consultants). When a lacklustre company turns around, the stock that was formerly seen as a financial turd (that's a technical term) can suddenly turn into 14-karat gold. It's a formula that has worked well for the Oracle of Omaha.

Good luck making it work for you.

Unlike Warren Buffett, many or most value stock pickers repeatedly take gambles on failing companies that continue to fail. We say the best way to invest in large value is to buy the index. No better way of doing that than through ETFs exists.

Making an ETF selection

Of the more than 100 or so diversified large cap ETFs on the market (Canadian and American), perhaps 20 or so are worth particular attention for tapping into the value market. The following offer good large value indexes at reasonable prices: iShares Dow Jones Canada Select Value Index Fund ETF (XCV), iShares Canadian Fundamental Index Fund ETF (CRQ), Vanguard Value ETF

(VTV), Vanguard Mega Cap 300 Value Index ETF (MGV), iShares Russell 1000 Value ETF (IWD), and iShares Morningstar Large Value ETF (JKF).

We suggest that you read through the descriptions that follow and make the choice that you think is best for you. Whatever your allocation to domestic large cap stocks (see Chapter 16 if you aren't sure), your allocation to value should be somewhere in the ballpark of 50 to 60 percent of that amount. In other words, we suggest that you tilt toward value, but don't go overboard.

The criteria you use in picking the best large cap value ETF should include expense ratios and appropriateness of the index. If you have a modest portfolio, or if you are making regular contributions, the trading costs need to be factored in as well. Note that the expense ratios, average cap sizes, price/earning ratios, and top five holdings are all subject to change; you should definitely check for updated figures before investing.

As usual, Canada doesn't have nearly as many options that cover the large cap value space as the U.S. does. However, a few domestic ETFs exist. Here are the Canadian ones; some U.S. funds follow.

iShares Dow Jones Canada Select Value Index Fund ETF (XCV)

Indexed to: Dow Jones Canada Select Value Index, which holds 60 mostly large Canadian value companies.

Expense ratio: 0.50 percent

P/E ratio: 12.1

Top five holdings: Royal Bank of Canada, TD Bank, Scotiabank, Barrick Gold, Bank of Montreal

Bryan's review: This basket of value stocks is, as of this writing, undervalued compared to the overall market. This ETF is inexpensive for the same reasons why the stocks it holds are cheap — no one wants to buy it. After six years, it has only $51 million in assets under management, which isn't great for a bunch of big-name buys. Two reasons why it hasn't caught on: It's similar to XIU, the broad-based S&P/TSX-tracking ETF, and 57.5 percent of it is made up of financial stocks. While the average investor may be better served by just buying XIU, the savvier ETF buyer who wants to drill down in his or her picks can own both this and XCG, its growth counterpart.

iShares Canadian Fundamental Index Fund ETF (CRQ) and PowerShares FTSE RAFI Canadian Fundamental Index ETF (PXC)

Indexed to: FTSE RAFI Canadian Index. They look at dividends, cash flow, sales, and book value to determine which companies should make the list.

Expense ratio: 0.65 percent for CRQ; 0.45 percent for PXC

P/E ratio: 14.4

Top five holdings: Royal Bank of Canada, TD Bank, Scotiabank, Encana, Manulife

Bryan's review: Why have I lumped these two ETFs together? Because they both track the same index. The only difference between the two funds is the expense ratio; the PowerShares option is about 0.2 percentage points cheaper. Some investors may prefer these ETFs over XCV because they're more diversified, with only about 43 percent of the fund in the financial sector. However, returns aren't that different; these ETFs slightly outperformed XCV from January to October 2012. When it comes down to choosing among them, look at cost. Because PXC is the cheapest Canadian large cap value stock on the market, it makes a lot of sense to buy this one over the others.

Vanguard Value ETF (VTV)

Indexed to: MSCI U.S. Prime Market Value Index (400 or so of the nation's largest value stocks)

Expense ratio: 0.10 percent

P/E ratio: 13.4

Top five holdings: Exxon Mobil, General Electric, Chevron, AT&T, Procter & Gamble

Russell's review: The price is right. The index makes sense. There's good diversification. The companies represented are certainly large. This ETF is a very good option, although I'd like it even more if it were a tad more valuey. (On the other hand, making it more valuey could increase turnover, which might increase costs.) All told, I like the VTV. I like it a lot. If you already own the Vanguard Value Index mutual fund and you're considering moving to ETFs, this fund would clearly be your choice.

Vanguard Mega Cap 300 Value Index ETF (MGV)

Indexed to: The MSCI U.S. Large Cap Value Index (150 or so of the largest U.S. stocks with value characteristics)

Expense ratio: 0.12 percent

P/E ratio: 13.3

Top five holdings: Exxon Mobil, General Electric, Chevron, AT&T, Procter & Gamble

Russell's review: This fund offers exposure to larger companies than does the more popular VTV featured above. Is bigger better? Could be. If you have small caps in your portfolio (which you should!), this mega cap fund will give you slightly less correlation than you'll get with VTV. As a stand-alone investment, however, I would expect that the very long-term returns on this fund will lag VTV, given that giant caps historically have lagged large caps. Given Vanguard's low expenses and reasonable indexes, either fund makes a fine holding.

iShares Russell 1000 Value ETF (IWD)

Indexed to: The 600 or so more-valuey stocks in the Russell 1000 Index (the largest 1,000 publicly traded companies in the U.S.).

Expense ratio: 0.21 percent

P/E ratio: 14.7

Top five holdings: Exxon Mobil, General Electric, Chevron, AT&T, Pfizer

Russell's review: The cost isn't high, but it is higher than the comparable Vanguard funds. On the other hand, this ETF offers a slightly more valuey lean than the others.

iShares Morningstar Large Value ETF (JKF)

Indexed to: Morningstar Large Value Index (76 of the largest U.S. value stocks, "value" being determined by Morningstar's proprietary formula)

Expense ratio: 0.25 percent

P/E ratio: 13.6

Top five holdings: Exxon Mobil, General Electric, Chevron, AT&T, Pfizer

Russell's review: Exxon Mobil alone makes up about 12 percent of this ETF, and that is less than ideal. Add the 6 percent held in Chevron, and you have nearly one-fifth of the fund in two stocks, both in the same oily industry. (That concentration in the giants means the average cap size of this fund is even greater than Vanguard's Mega Cap ETF.) To boot, Morningstar indexes aren't nearly as popular as S&P indexes, so this ETF is thinly traded, which can result in a larger spread when you buy or sell. On the positive side, however, Morningstar indexes are neat boxes: Any company that appears in the value index isn't going to pop up in the growth index. I think that's worth something, for sure.

Chapter 7

Small Growth: Sweet-Sounding Start-Ups

*O*nce upon a time in the kingdom of Redmond, there was a young company called Microsoft. It was a very small company with very big ideas, and it grew and grew and grew. Its founder and its original investors became very, very rich and lived happily ever after.

Oh, you've heard that story? Then you understand the appeal of small growth companies. These are companies that typically have *market capitalization* (the market value of total outstanding stock) of about $300 million to $1 billion. They frequently boast a hot product or patent, often fall into the high-tech or, in Canada, mining arenas, and always seem to be on their way to stardom. Some of them make it, and along with them, their investors take a joy ride all the way to early retirement.

Unfortunately, for every Microsoft, there are a dozen, or two or three dozen, small companies that go belly up long before their prime. For every investor who gambles on a small company stock and takes early retirement, 100 others still drive their cars to work every Monday morning.

Beep, beep.

In this chapter, we ask you to take a ride with us through the world of small cap growth stocks. We explain what role, if any, they should play in your ETF portfolio. First stop along the ride: Figure 7-1, where you can see how small growth fits into the investment style grid we introduce in Chapter 4. Second stop: Figure 7-2, which shows that small growth stocks, at least over the past eight decades, haven't exactly lit the world on fire.

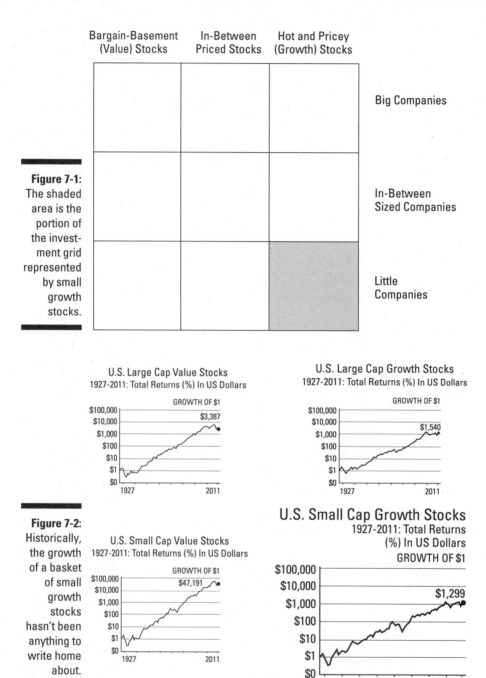

	Bargain-Basement (Value) Stocks	In-Between Priced Stocks	Hot and Pricey (Growth) Stocks
				Big Companies
				In-Between Sized Companies
				Little Companies

Figure 7-1: The shaded area is the portion of the investment grid represented by small growth stocks.

U.S. Large Cap Value Stocks
1927-2011: Total Returns (%) In US Dollars

GROWTH OF $1

$3,387

1927   2011

U.S. Large Cap Growth Stocks
1927-2011: Total Returns (%) In US Dollars

GROWTH OF $1

$1,540

1927   2011

Figure 7-2: Historically, the growth of a basket of small growth stocks hasn't been anything to write home about.

U.S. Small Cap Value Stocks
1927-2011: Total Returns (%) In US Dollars

GROWTH OF $1

$47,191

1927   2011

U.S. Small Cap Growth Stocks
1927-2011: Total Returns (%) In US Dollars

GROWTH OF $1

$1,299

1927   2011

Source: Fama/French data provided by Eugene F. Fama and Kenneth R. French

Getting Real about Small Cap Investments

In the past century, small cap stocks have outperformed large cap stocks just as assuredly as Quebec has produced more Québécois than the rest of Canada. The volatility of small cap stocks has also been greater, just as assuredly as the other Canadian provinces have more Anglophones than Quebec. In terms of return per unit of risk (the risk-adjusted rate of return), however, small caps are clearly winners. And so it would seem that investing in small caps is a pretty smart thing to do. But please know that not all small caps are created equal.

As it happens, the true stars of the small cap world have been small cap *value* stocks rather than small cap *growth* stocks. (Take a look at Chapters 5 and 6 if you aren't sure what we mean by these terms.) How slow-growing, often ailing companies have beat out their hot-to-trot cousins remains one of the great unresolved mysteries of the investing world. But the numbers don't lie.

In fact, if you look at the numbers, such as those in Figure 7-2, you may be inclined to treat small growth stocks as a pariah. Please don't. They belong in a well-diversified portfolio. Some years are clearly small growth years. The best example is in 2010, when markets were on the upswing. The average U.S. small cap growth stock was up about 26 percent, compared to 13 percent for the average U.S. large cap. Back in 2003, small growth was the undisputed King of Returns, clocking in at an astounding 50.37 percent. Generally, small caps do well in good times and market recoveries because people are less afraid to jump into growth stocks. Large caps tend to outperform in periods of uncertainty, when stability and brand name familiarity are key. Small caps underperformed in 2011 and 2012, which isn't surprising given the problems in Europe, China's slowdown, and America's debt issues. People were nervous, so they gravitated to the names they knew. Investors will eventually get more confident with the markets, and when that happens, small caps can soar.

Your Choices for Small Growth

If you have a portfolio of under $20,000 or so, we recommend that you consider a small cap *blend* fund, which combines small value and small growth stocks. Most of the Canadian small cap ETFs are more of a blend anyway. Small cap domestic stocks shouldn't occupy more than 20 percent or so of your portfolio (more on that topic in Chapter 16), and if you divide up 20 percent of less than $20,000, the trading costs (some you'll see, and some that may be hidden) could seriously impact your returns. So keep it simple until your portfolio grows to the point that you can start slicing and dicing a bit more economically.

If you have a portfolio of more than $20,000 and you are a buy-and-hold kind of guy or gal, we suggest that you break up your small cap holdings into a growth ETF and a value ETF using a combination of Canadian and U.S. funds. Given the dramatic outperformance of value in the past, you might tilt in that direction — more so than you do with large caps. A reasonable tilt may call for somewhere between 60 and 75 of your small cap exposure going to value, and 25 to 40 percent going to growth.

Small cap blend funds

A bit of growth, a bit of value, your choice in small cap blend funds should take into consideration such things as expense ratios, average cap size, and P/E ratio (explained in Chapter 5). Keep in mind that these numbers are subject to change, so we recommend checking them before you act.

Two good Canadian-made options for people with limited-size portfolios exist — the iShares S&P/TSX SmallCap Index Fund (XCS) and the iShares S&P/TSX Completion Index Fund (XMD).

iShares S&P/TSX SmallCap Index Fund (XCS)

Indexed to: S&P/TSX SmallCap Index (225 diversified smaller Canadian companies)

Expense ratio: 0.55 percent

P/E ratio: 15.4

Top five holdings: Stantec, Russel Metals, CCL Industries, Dundee Corporation, B2gold

Bryan's review: Most Canadian ETF investors who are interested in small caps likely own this product. It's got an average market cap of 828 million, which should suit smaller-company-seeking investors just fine. Like with most Canadian ETFs, the main drawback is diversification. Yes, the fund has 225 stocks, which is good, but 27.4 percent of the fund is concentrated in materials while 24.5 percent is in energy. That's not surprising — many of our smaller businesses are in the mining and oil and gas sectors — but it's something to be aware of. If oil prices fall, or precious metal prices plummet, this fund will likely be affected. Although the management fee is more expensive than what you'd find with some large caps funds, it's still a lot cheaper than many of the more-specialized small cap mutual funds. It's a good option for people who want to add a little *oomph* to their portfolios.

iShares S&P/TSX Completion Index Fund (XMD)

Indexed to: S&P/TSX Completion Index, an index made up of the mid cap and small cap stocks on the S&P/TSX Composite Index

Expense ratio: 0.55 percent

P/E ratio: 15.7

Top five holdings: Pembina Pipeline, Riocan Real Estate Investment Trust, CGI Group, Alimenation Couche Tard, Intact Financial

Bryan's review: As you know by now, Canadian ETFs are rarely as black and white as their American counterparts. Because our market is so small, getting a pure small cap stock is difficult. Many investors have turned to this product, which is the S&P/TSX Composite Index minus the S&P/TSX 60 stocks, for their small cap needs, though it includes about 80 percent mid cap stocks. The average stock's market cap is 4.2 billion, which is much more in the mid cap range than what some small cap investors may want, but this fund still offers some extra growth potential. It's also a bit more diversified than XCS, with 28.7 percent of its holdings in financials, 26.6 percent in energy, and 15.5 percent in materials. If you want to play the smaller company space but don't want to take on as much risk as you would with XCS, then try this on for size.

American Small Cap Blends

If you've got some extra cash, you may want to consider investing in these small cap blend ETFs. Although these don't hold any Canadian companies, of course, they're more diversified across sector than what you'll find in our neck of the woods.

Vanguard Small Cap ETF (VB)

Indexed to: CRSP U.S. Small Cap Index (About 1,440 broadly diversified smaller U.S. companies)

Expense ratio: 0.10 percent

P/E ratio: 16.2

Top five holdings: Rock Tenn Co., Onyx Pharmaceuticals, B/E Aerospace, Fortune Brands Home & Security, Cheniere Energy

Russell's review: The expense ratio is quite low, especially when compared to most other offerings in the small cap arena. The diversification is lovely too, with only financials exceeding 20 percent of the portfolio (23.8 percent, to be exact). And Vanguard's ETFs — largely because they are pegged to indexes with little turnover — are arguably the most tax efficient of all ETFs. On balance, this is a very good selection, but I'd scrap it for something more refined — a growth and value split — as soon as your portfolio is large enough to allow for such refinement.

iShares Core S&P Small-Cap ETF (IJR)

Indexed to: Roughly 600 companies that make up the S&P Small Cap 600 Index

Expense ratio: 0.16

P/E ratio: 19

Top five holdings: Gulfport Energy, Tanger Factory Outlet Centre, Cymer, Eagle Materials, Hain Celestial Group

Russell's review: This is a perfectly acceptable ETF for small cap exposure at a good price. Although it doesn't hold as many companies as VB, it's slightly more diversified by sector, with financials making up 21.2 percent of the portfolio and four others accounting for between 10 and 18 percent of the pie. It's a little more expensive on a P/E basis than VB. It's not a huge deal, but it may, for some investors, be a deal-breaker.

Strictly small cap growth funds

As we mention earlier, Canadians will have trouble splitting their small cap stocks into growth and value. We've got nothing domestic to present here, but American options are still worth mentioning because Canadians aren't limited in what U.S. funds we can buy. Keep in mind that, typically, any American fund you buy has to be purchased in U.S. dollars, so there will be some currency risk. Because small cap stocks are also more volatile than large caps, it's a good idea to only own these if you have money to spend. Don't put all your retirement savings in U.S.-based small cap stocks — or any American domiciled ETF, for that matter.

Vanguard Small Cap Growth ETF (VBK)

Indexed to: CRSP U.S. Small Cap Growth Index (approximately 950 small cap growth companies in the United States)

Expense ratio: 0.10 percent

P/E ratio: 19.9

Top five holdings: Cheniere Energy, Tenent Healthcare, FleetCor Technologies, Alaska Air, MEDNAX

Russell's review: I really have no complaints. Its price is right, it offers wide diversification and a very definite growth exposure. The Vanguard Small Cap Growth ETF offers an excellent way to tap into this asset class.

iShares Morningstar Small Growth Index ETF (JKK)

Indexed to: Approximately 250 companies from the Morningstar Small Growth Index

Expense ratio: 0.30 percent

P/E ratio: 25.8

Top five holdings: Gulfport Energy, Athenahealth, Cymer, CBOE Holdings, Gentex

Russell's review: My only beef with the Morningstar indexes is that they tend to be a bit too concentrated, at least in the large cap arena. In their small caps, however, concentration isn't a problem. The largest holding here, Gulfport Energy, gets an acceptably small 1 percent allocation. The expense ratio, too, is acceptable, although higher than some others in this category. I like that Morningstar promises no crossover between growth and value. If you own this ETF along with the iShares Morningstar Small Value Index, you should get pleasantly limited correlation.

iShares S&P SmallCap 600 Growth ETF (IJT)

Indexed to: Despite the "600" in its name, this ETF tracks the 335 or so holdings that make up the S&P Small Cap 600.

Expense ratio: 0.25 percent

P/E ratio: 21.8

Top five holdings: Gulfport Energy, Cymer, Eagle Materials, Hain Celestial Group, 3D Systems

Russell's review: S&P indexes are a bit too subjective for me to really love them, but the fund's price is reasonable. It's got decent diversification too, with its top holding only accounting for 1.26 percent of the portfolio. There's no reason to snub this iShares offering.

Smaller than Small: Meet the Micro Caps

If you want to invest your money in companies that are smaller than small, you're going to be investing in micro caps. These companies are larger than the corner delicatessen, but sometimes not by much. In general, micro caps are publicly held companies with less than $300 million in outstanding stock. Micro caps, as you can imagine, are volatile little suckers, but as a group they offer impressive long-term performance. In terms of diversification, micro caps — in conservative quantity — may be a nice addition to your portfolio, although we wouldn't call them a necessity. Take note that micro cap funds, even index ETFs, tend to charge considerably more in management fees than you'll pay for most funds.

Micros move at a modestly different pace from other equity asset classes. The theory is that because micro caps are heavy borrowers, their performance is more tied to interest rates than the performance of larger cap stocks is. (Lower interest rates would be good for these stocks; higher interest rates would not.) Micro caps also tend to be more tied to the vicissitudes of the domestic economy and less to the world economy than, say, the fortunes of Scotiabank or McDonald's.

Given the high risk of owning any individual micro cap stock, it makes sense to work micro caps into your portfolio in fund form, despite the management fees, rather than trying to pick individual companies. To date, one Canadian micro cap fund and a handful of U.S.-based micro cap ETFs have been introduced. They differ from one another to a much greater extent than do the larger cap ETFs.

Despite the differences, all of the funds discussed next have seen rather lacklustre performance since their inception. It may be possible that micro caps are a particular kind of asset class (commodities would be another) where indexed ETFs may be less than the ideal vehicle. The performance may have something to do with the illiquidity of micro caps (it's not always easy to buy and sell shares on the open market). Time will tell. In the meantime, proceed with caution, and if you want to invest in any of these funds, do so with only a modest percent of your portfolio.

S&P/TSX Venture Index Fund (XVX)

Indexed to: S&P/TSX Venture Select Index, an index made up of companies on the S&P/TSX Venture Exchange

Expense ratio: 0.79 percent

P/E ratio: N/A

Top five holdings: Painted Pony Petroleum, Africa Oil, Mart Resources, Raging River Exploration, Americas Petrogas

Bryan's review: If you want to play the Canadian micro cap space, this might be the best way to do it. Taking a bet on one single company is a huge risk, so better to put your money on all of them. As highly concentrated as the S&P/TSX Composite is, the Venture Exchange is even less diversified, so be careful. Just more than 62 percent of this fund is in energy and 28 percent is weighted toward materials. I'll do the math for you: More than 90 percent of XVX is in two sectors. As well, with only $2 million in assets under management, it's a lot smaller and less liquid than most ETFs. You might have trouble selling it if you need to get rid of this in a pinch. Still, if you've got money to burn and can stomach the high fee and low liquidity, then this ETF could end up adding an extra boost to your portfolio. It hasn't started kicking yet — it's down 25 percent since inception (September 2011) — but you never know how it will fare in the future.

iShares Russell Microcap Index ETF (IWC)

Indexed to: About 1,300 of the smallest publicly traded companies, all culled from the Russell 3000 Index

Expense ratio: 0.69 percent

P/E ratio: 14.6

Top five holdings: Radian Group, American Reality Capital, Colony Financial, Infinity Pharmaceuticals, Home Loan Servicing Solution

Russell's review: There aren't a lot of choices in this field, so I'm glad this is one of them. I'm not crazy about paying 0.69 percent, which is high for an ETF, but there seems to be price collusion in the micro cap area, so what are you going to do? (Personal note to ETF firms' attorneys: Hey, I'm only kidding about the price collusion, guys! It just *seems* that way.) Caveat: More than one-quarter of the stocks held in this fund are financial stocks.

Chapter 8

Small Value: Diminutive Dazzlers

ook at the list of some of the top companies represented in the Vanguard Small Cap Value ETF: First Niagara Financial Group, Camden Property Trust, Beazer Homes USA, Corn Products International. . . . These are not household names. Nor are they especially fast-growing companies. Nor are they industry leaders. Nor is there much excitement to be seen in companies such as Corn Products International. ("Our starches, sweeteners and other ingredients are used by our customers to provide everything from sweetness, taste and texture to immune system support, fat replacement and adhesive strength.") As you go farther down the list of holdings, you'll likely find some companies in financial distress. Others may be facing serious lawsuits, expiration of patents, or labour unrest. If you wanted to pick one of these companies to sink a wad of cash into, we would tell you that you're crazy.

But if you wanted to sink that cash into the entire small value index, well, that's another matter altogether. Assuming you could handle some risk, we'd tell you to go for it. By all means. Your odds of making money are pretty darned good — at least if history is our guide.

Don't take our word for it; see Figure 8-2, which shows the enormous growth of value stocks over the past eight decades. On the way there, see Figure 8-1, which shows where small value fits into the investment style grid we introduce in Chapter 4. And then, follow us as we explain the importance of small value stocks in a poised-for-performance ETF portfolio.

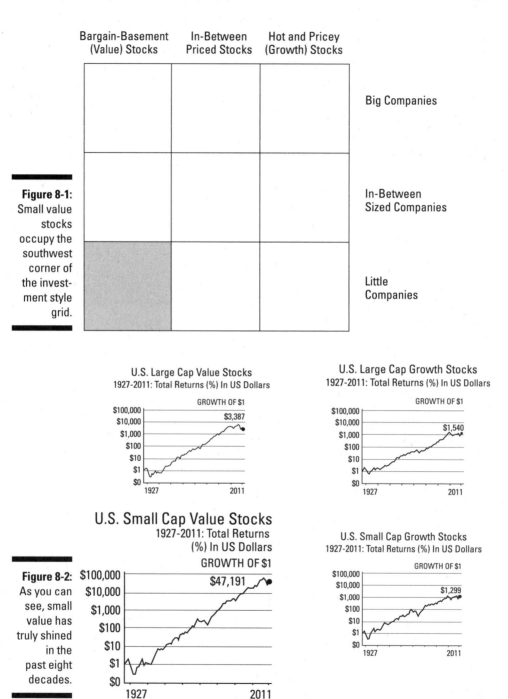

Figure 8-1:
Small value
stocks
occupy the
southwest
corner of
the invest-
ment style
grid.

Figure 8-2:
As you can
see, small
value has
truly shined
in the
past eight
decades.

Source: Fama/French data provided by Eugene F. Fama and Kenneth R. French

It's Been Quite a Ride

Small value stocks collectively have returned more to investors than have large value stocks or any kind of growth stocks. In fact, the difference in returns has been somewhat staggering: We're talking about an annualized return of about 14.2 percent over the past 85 years or so for small value stocks versus 11.1 percent for large value, 8.8 for large growth, and 9.2 for small growth. Compounded over time, the outperformance of small value stocks has been *huge*.

Latching on for fun and profit

To be sure, small value stocks are risky little suckers. Even the entire index (available to you in neat ETF form) is more volatile than any conservative investor may feel comfortable with. But as part — a very handsome part — of a diversified portfolio, a small value ETF can be a beautiful thing indeed.

If we knew the past was going to repeat, such as it did in the movie *Groundhog Day,* you wouldn't have any reason to have anything but small value in your portfolio. But, of course, we don't know that the past will repeat. Bill Murray's radio alarm clock may not go off at sunrise. And the small value premium, like Bill Murray's hairline, may start to seriously recede. Still, the outperformance of small value has historically been so much greater than that of small growth that we favour a good tilt in the direction of value.

But keeping your balance

Whatever your total allocation to small cap stocks (see Chapter 16 for advice), we recommend that anywhere from 60 to 75 percent of that amount be allocated to small value. But no more than that, please. If the value premium disappears or becomes a value discount, we don't want you left holding the bag. And even if small value continues to outperform, having both small value and small growth (along with their bigger cousins, all of which tend to rise and fall in different cycles) will help smooth out some of the inevitable volatility of holding stocks.

Now's a good time to mention that Canadians don't have a lot of choice when it comes to small cap value. As we tell you in Chapter 7, Canadian small cap ETFs that lean toward growth do exist, but none are pure growth or only value. However, the ideas behind adding small cap value still remain, so it's okay to own some American small cap ETFs.

Saying that, we do have one Canadian value-focused ETF that's worth looking at. It actually does hold a lot of small caps, but it owns several mid caps as well. So it's not quite as small as some of the U.S. offerings, but it's not as large as many of the other Canadian ETFs.

iShares S&P/TSX Canadian Dividend Aristocrats Index Fund (CDZ)

Indexed to: S&P/TSX Canadian Dividend Aristocrats Index, an index made up of companies that have increased their dividends every year for the last five years.

Expense ratio: 0.60 percent

P/E ratio: 16.5

Top five holdings: Atlantic Power Corp., AGF Management, Ltd., Ag Growth International, Reitmans Canada, Transcontinental, Inc.

Bryan's review: While this isn't exactly a small cap fund, many of the holdings are of the small and mid cap variety. For instance, its top holding, Atlantic Power, has a market cap of $1.4 billion, while AGF and Ag both have market caps of below $1 billion. What's great about this ETF is that it can reduce volatility in a portfolio. A company that pays dividends every year for five consecutive years is usually more stable than one that doesn't. So a collection of these stocks should reduce some portfolio risk. Smaller companies also tend to grow faster than large ones, so you may get some added capital gains too. One thing to watch out for: Big banks have made their way onto this index in the past, so if you really do want to hold an ETF of smaller cap value stocks, keep an eye out to make sure the index isn't adding large caps, which it could.

Here are some U.S. options to consider:

Vanguard Small Cap Value ETF (VBR)

Indexed to: MSCI U.S. Small Cap Value Index (about 1,000 small value domestic companies).

Expense ratio: 0.21 percent

P/E ratio: 13.8

Top five holdings: BRE Properties, Inc., Westar Energy, Questar Corp., RPM International, East West Bancorp

Russell's review: Low cost, wide diversification, and a very definite value bias — what's not to like? The Vanguard Small Cap Value ETF offers an excellent way to tap into this asset class.

iShares Morningstar Small Value Index (JKL)

Indexed to: Morningstar's Small Value Index (about 230 companies of modest size and modest stock price).

Expense ratio: 0.30 percent

P/E ratio: 12.8

Top five holdings: Ocwen Financial Corp., Dean Foods, Two Harbors Investment Corp., Alaska Air Group, MFA Financial, Inc.

Russell's review: My only complaint with the Morningstar indexes is that they tend to be a bit too concentrated, at least in the large cap arena where a company like Exxon Mobil can hold too much sway. In the Morningstar small cap indexes, that isn't a problem. The largest holding here, Ocwen Financial, gets only a 1.23 percent allocation, which is fine and dandy. The expense ratio, too, is acceptable although higher than some others in this category. I like that Morningstar promises no crossover between growth and value. If you own this ETF along with the iShares Morningstar Small Growth Index, you should get pleasantly modest correlation. (In lay terms, if one fund gets slammed, the other may not.)

iShares S&P Small Cap 600 Value Index (IJS)

Indexed to: It's supposed to mirror the S&P Small Cap 600 Value Index, but it doesn't use a full replication strategy, opting instead to hold only 457 of the 600 names that are on the index.

Expense ratio: 0.25 percent

P/E ratio: 16.7

Top five holdings: Emcor Group, Inc., LaSalle Hotel Properties, Actuant Corp., Susquehanna Bancshares, Inc., Prospect Capital Corp.

Russell's review: S&P indexes are a bit too subjective for me to want to marry them. I'm also a slight bit baffled that the current P/E ratio of this fund, which is supposed to be a value fund, is so similar to the iShares S&P Small Cap 600 Growth Index (IJT). It shouldn't be that way. Of course, P/E ratios can change from week to week, especially with small cap funds, but I've been checking this one out for a while. Nonetheless, this fund's price is reasonable, and there's no reason to entirely snub this iShares offering. (Marry it, but have a pre-nup. You may later decide that you'll do better elsewhere.)

What about the Mid Caps?

In a word, our take on mid cap ETFs is . . . *why?* Yes, for the past several years mid cap stocks — investments in companies with roughly $1 to $10 billion in outstanding stock — have performed especially well. They've done better than large caps and have even given small cap stocks a run for their money. But such outperformance of mid cap stocks is a fluke. So, too, is any underperformance.

If you look at the risk/return profile of mid caps over many years, you find that it generally falls right where you would expect it to fall: smack dab in between large and small cap. Owning both a large cap and small cap ETF, therefore, will give you an average return very similar to mid caps but with considerably less volatility because large and small cap stocks tend to move up and down at different times.

Other investment pros may disagree, but we really don't see the point of shopping for mid cap ETFs. Plus, no domestic options exist anyway (though you have lots of choices in the States). Keep in mind, too, that most large cap and small cap funds are rather fluid: You will get some mid cap exposure from both. Many sector funds — including real estate, materials, and utilities — are also chock-full of mid caps (see Chapter 10).

Chapter 9

Going Global: ETFs without Borders

. . . .

In This Chapter

▶ Understanding how global diversification lowers risk

▶ Calculating how much of your ETF portfolio to allocate overseas

▶ Deciding upon your investment destinations

▶ Choosing your best ETF options

. . . .

*I*f you were standing on a ship in the middle of the ocean (doesn't matter whether it's the Atlantic or Pacific), and you looked up and squinted real hard, you might see investment dollars sailing overhead. For at least a decade now, investors have been steadily adding money to the international side of their stock portfolios.

Just to be clear: The terms *foreign* and *international* are used interchangeably to refer to stocks of companies outside of Canada. Although the terms can be used when talking about American stocks, U.S. equity is typically in a different category than international or foreign securities. The word *global* refers to stocks of companies based anywhere in the whole world, including the United States and Canada, but when Canadians talk about international equity, we're usually referring to Europe, emerging markets, Latin America — anywhere outside of Canada and the U.S.

Many investors have been moving to foreign stocks for the same reason that they move, moth-into-light style, into any other kind of investment: They've been lured by recent high returns, especially the returns of emerging market nation stocks.

As of March 2013, the ten-year annualized return of the MSCI Canada Index stood at about 10 percent. The stocks of the world's emerging market nations — using the MSCI Emerging Market Index — clocked in with a rather astounding 13.6 percent per year for the past decade. Developed nations in the Pacific Rim (Japan, Australia, Singapore) more or less matched Canada for the decade. European stocks (including the United Kingdom), despite some sharp recent losses due largely to a debt mess in Greece and Portugal, showed an average return of about 7 percent.

In the past, most Canadians were woefully under-invested abroad, so we see the recent turn as a decidedly good thing. We're *glad* most investors have finally started to send their dollars abroad — even if some of them are doing it, by and large, for the wrong reasons. In this chapter, we explain our love for global diversification and reveal how you can accomplish it easily with ETFs.

The Ups and Downs of Different Markets around the World

If you expect emerging market stocks to continue to clock such phenomenal returns, you are sure to be disappointed. If you expect European stock markets to do half again as much as the Canadian and U.S. markets, we think you are similarly in for a sad surprise. We do think you can expect that foreign stocks overall may do better than North American stocks in the coming decade or two. (If you want the nitty-gritty of our reasoning, see the section, "Why ETFs are a great tool for international investing.") But we certainly wouldn't bet the farm on international stocks outperforming domestic stocks — or underperforming them either, for that matter. The difference in returns in the future, as it has been in the long-term past, is not likely to be all that extreme.

In all likelihood, international stocks as a whole will have their day. Canadian stocks will then come up from behind. Then international stocks will have their day again. And then Canadian stocks will get the jump. This type of horse race has been going on since, oh, long before *Mr. Ed* was on the air.

The reason to invest abroad isn't primarily to try to outperform the Joneses . . . or the LeBlancs, or the Yamashitas. Rather, the purpose is to diversify your portfolio so as to capture overall stock market gains while tempering risk. You reduce risk whenever you own two or more asset classes that move up and down at different times. Stocks of different geographic regions tend to do exactly that.

Low correlation is the name of the game

Why, you may ask, do you need European and Japanese stocks when you already have all the lovely diversification discussed in past chapters: large, small, value, and growth stocks, and a good mix of industries? (Refer to Chapter 5 if you need a reminder of what these terms mean.) The answer, *mon ami, mi amigo,* is quite simple: You get better diversification when you diversify across borders.

We'll use several iShares ETFs to illustrate our point. Suppose you have a wad of money invested in the iShares S&P/TSX 60 Index Fund (XIU) and you want to diversify:

✔ If you combine XIU with the iShares S&P Completion Index Fund (XMD) — a fund that holds all the stocks in the S&P/TSX Composite Index except the large cap companies in the XIU — you find that your two investments have a three-year correlation of 0.90. In other words, over the past three years, the funds have had a tendency to move in the same direction 90 percent of the time. Only 10 percent of the time have they tended to move in opposite directions.

✔ If you combine XIU with the iShares Dow Jones Canada Select Value Index Fund (XCV), your investments tend to move north or south at the same time 92 percent of time.

✔ If you combine XIU with the iShares S&P/TSX SmallCap Index Fund (XMD), you find that your two investments have tended to move up and down together roughly 87 percent of the time. Not bad. But not great.

Now consider adding some Brazilian stocks to your original portfolio of large growth stocks. The iShares MSCI Brazil Index Fund (XBZ) has tended to move in synch with large cap Canadian stocks only about 76 percent of the time over the last three years. And the ETF that tracks the FTSE China 25 Index (FXI) has moved in the same direction as large cap Canadian stocks only 50 percent of the time. There's clearly more zig and zag when you cross oceans to invest, and that's what makes international investing a must for a well-balanced portfolio.

The increasing interdependence of the world's markets wrought by globalization may cause these correlation numbers to rise over time. Indeed, we saw in 2008 that in a global financial crisis, stock markets around the world will suffer. The trend toward rising correlations has led some pundits to make the claim that diversification is dead. Sorry, those pundits are wrong. In downtimes, yes, stocks of different colours, here and abroad, tend to turn a depressing shade of grey together. When investors are nervous in Toronto, they are often nervous in Berlin. And Sydney. And Cape Town. That's been true for years. The great apple-cart-turnover of 2008 was a particular case in point. But even in 2008, it still paid to be diversified, as Canadian and foreign stocks recovered, and are still recovering, at very different rates.

Diversification lowers, but does not eliminate, stock market risk. Never did. Never will. Your portfolio, in addition to being well-diversified, should also have some components, such as cash and bonds, which are less volatile than stocks.

Remember what happened to Japan

To just "stay home" on the stock side of your portfolio would be to exhibit the very same conceit seen among Japanese investors in 1990. If you recall, that's when the dynamic and seemingly all-powerful rising sun slipped and then sank. Japanese investors, holding domestically stuffed portfolios, bid *sayonara* to two-thirds of their wealth, which, more than two decades later, they have yet to fully recapture. (By March 2013, a basket of large-company Japanese stocks had a ten-year annualized return of 4.66 percent. Based on MSCI Indexes, Canada had a 10.38 percent return. Ouch.) It could happen here. Or worse.

Finding Your Best Mix of Domestic and International

The Canadian market accounts for a measly 4 percent of the entire world stock market. So, should you invest 96 percent of your stock portfolio in international ETFs? No way; that's overdoing it. Many financial experts say 50 percent of your stock holdings should be international, with 25 percent of that in the U.S. We think that percentage works fine, but some experts are now saying that we may want to reduce our domestic exposure, which is often correlated to oil prices, by a bit. Consider putting between 50 to 60 percent in international stocks. This section explains why in more depth.

Why putting 96 percent of your portfolio in foreign stocks is too much

We see five distinct reasons not to overload your portfolio to the tune of 96 percent foreign stocks:

✔ **Currency volatility:** When you invest abroad, including in the U.S., you're usually investing in stocks that are denominated in other currencies. Because your foreign ETFs are denominated in greenbacks, euros, yen, or pounds, they tend to be more volatile than the markets they represent. In other words, if European stock markets fall and the loonie rises (*vis-à-vis* the euro) on the same day, your European ETF will fall doubly hard. If, however, the dollar falls on a day when the sun is shining on European stocks, your European ETF will soar.

Over the long run, individual currencies tend to go up and down. Although it could happen, it is unlikely that the dollar (or euro) would permanently rise or fall to such a degree that it would seriously affect your nest egg. In the short term, however, such currency fluctuations can be a bit nauseating.

✔ **Inflation issues:** Another risk with going whole hog for foreign stock ETFs is that, to a certain extent, your fortunes are tied to those of your home economy. Stocks tend to do best in a heated economy. But in a heated economy, we also tend to see inflation. Because of that correlation between general price inflation and stock inflation, stock investors are generally able to stay ahead of the inflation game. If you were to invest all your money in, say, England, and should the economy here take off while the economy there sits idly on the launch pad, you could potentially be rocketed into a Dickensian kind of poverty.

✔ **Higher fees for foreign ETFs:** In the world of ETFs, the really good buys are to be had on the domestic side of the offerings. For whatever reason, global and international ETFs are about twice the price of broadly diversified Canadian ETFs. For example, while many iShares and BMO domestic ETFs carry management expenses of around 0.20 percent or less, no foreign funds go nearly that low.

✔ **Lower correlation with homegrown options:** Certain kinds of stock funds in Canada offer even lower correlation to the rest of the Canadian market than do many international stock funds, and we suggest leaving room in your portfolio for some of those. We discuss some of these industry-sector funds in Chapter 10. You may also want to make room for *market-neutral* funds, which we discuss in Chapter 15.

✔ **A double tax hit:** Foreign governments almost always hit you up for taxes on any dividends paid by stocks of companies in their countries. If your funds are held in certain accounts, the Canada Revenue Agency may want your money too, and you wind up taking a double tax hit. This is a relatively minor reason not to go overboard when sailing overseas. (Specifics on this tax, and how to avoid getting double-whammied, are at the very end of this chapter.)

Every investor, no matter the location, has some sort of home bias. People like investing in companies or sectors they know rather than in foreign operations they've never heard of. Understanding why someone may want to own Rogers Communications over Britain's Vodafone isn't difficult. You read about Rogers nearly every day, and you may even be a customer. If something goes wrong with this telecom, you'll know. Unless you're a big BBC watcher, you may not even find out that Vodafone got into trouble until a few days after the news gets out. So, investing in domestic companies makes sense from this standpoint, but don't overdo it.

Many investment pros know well — and several have even told us — that they favour a much larger international position than they publicly advocate. Some may be afraid of seeming unpatriotic. Much more prevalent is a certain lemming-over-the-cliff-cover-my-ass mentality. If your financial advisor suggests a portfolio that resembles the S&P/TSX Composite Index and your portfolio tanks, you'll feel a bit peeved but you won't hate the guy. That's because all your friends' and neighbours' portfolios will have sunk as well. If the advisor gives you a portfolio that's 70 percent foreign, and if foreign stocks have a bad year, you'll compare your portfolio to your friends' and neighbours' portfolios, and you may get mad. You may even sue.

No advisor wants that. So most err on the side of caution and give you a portfolio that's more S&P/TSX Composite Index and less foreign — for their own protection, and not in the pursuit of your best interests.

Why ETFs are a great tool for international investing

By mixing and matching your domestic stock funds with around 50 percent international and U.S., you will find your investment sweet spot. In Chapter 16, we pull together sample portfolios that use this methodology. Time and time again, people have run the numbers through the most sophisticated (and perhaps most expensive) professional portfolio analysis software available, and time and time again, 40 to 50 percent foreign is where they find the highest returns per unit of risk. And yes, this range has worked very well in the real world, too.

Although we try not to make forecasts because the markets are so incredibly unpredictable, we will say that if you had to err on the side of either Canadian or foreign stock investment, we would err on the side of too much foreign. The world economic and political climate is telling us that the Canadian stock market may be on relatively shakier ground. We could give you a long list of reasons (high housing prices, record personal debt levels, up and down oil prices), but what's most troubling about Canada — and North America in general — is the extent to which it is becoming a nation of haves and have-nots. If history tells us anything, it is that great inequality leads to great dissension and upheaval.

Personally, we eat our own international cooking: We have fully half of our own stock portfolios in foreign stocks — the vast majority of them held in ETFs.

Not All Foreign Nations — or Stocks — Are Created Equal

At present, you have more than 300 global and international ETFs from which to choose. We're not including U.S.-only ETFs in this figure. Most international ETFs are also American based. You can get some Canadian-listed options and international ETFs that are Canadian currency hedged, which will protect you from currency fluctuations. However, some investors may have to put their money at a bit of additional risk if they want to buy a non-hedged American or foreign-listed fund. (Once again, *global* ETFs hold Canadian as well as international stocks; *international* or *foreign* ETFs hold purely non-North American stocks.) We'd like you to consider the following half dozen factors when deciding which ones to invest in:

✔ **What's the correlation?** Certain economies are more closely linked to the Canadian economy than others, and the behaviour of their stock markets reflects that. The U.S., for example, is more correlated to our market than Western Europe. For the least amount of correlation among developed nations, you want Japan (the world's second-largest stock market) or emerging market nations like Russia, Brazil, India, and China.

✔ **How large is the home market?** Although you can invest in individual countries, we generally wouldn't recommend it. Oh, we suppose you could slice and dice your portfolio to include 50 or so ETFs that represent individual countries (from Belgium to Austria and Singapore to Spain and, more recently, Vietnam to Poland), but that is going to be an awfully hard portfolio to manage. So why do it? Choose large regions in which to invest. (The only exceptions are the United States and perhaps Japan and the United Kingdom, which have such large stock markets that they each qualify, in our minds, as a region.)

✔ **Think style.** If you have a large-enough portfolio, consider dividing your international holdings into value and growth, large and small, just as you do with your domestic holdings. You can also divvy up your portfolio into global industry groupings. We discuss this strategy in Chapter 10. We generally prefer style diversification to sector diversification, but using both together can be truly powerful. You'll note that we take the combined approach in our sample portfolios in Part IV of this book.

✔ **Consider your risk tolerance.** Developed countries (United States, United Kingdom, France, Japan) tend to have less volatile stock markets than do emerging market nations (such as those of Latin America, the Middle East, China, Russia, or India). You want both types of investments in your portfolio, but if you are inclined to invest in one much more than the other, know what you're getting into.

✔ **What's the bounce factor?** As with any other kind of investment, you can pretty safely assume that risk and return will have a close relationship over many years. Emerging market ETFs will likely be more volatile but, over the long run, more rewarding than ETFs that track the stock markets of developed nations. One caveat: Don't assume that countries with fast-growing economies will necessarily be the most profitable investments; see the sidebar "A boom economy doesn't necessarily mean a robust stock market."

✔ **Look to P/E ratios.** How expensive is the stock compared to the earnings you're buying? You may ask yourself this question when buying a company stock, and it's just as valid a question when buying a nation's or a region's stocks. In general, a lower P/E ratio is more indicative of promising returns than is a high P/E ratio. (Refer to Chapter 5 for a reminder of how to calculate a P/E ratio.)

Using ETFs as our proxies for world markets, we find that the Vanguard Total (U.S.) Stock Market ETF (VTI) currently has a P/E of about 15; the Vanguard European ETF (VGK) has a P/E of about 11.5; the Vanguard Pacific ETF (VPL) has a P/E of approximately 15; and the Vanguard Emerging Market ETF (VWO) has a P/E of roughly 10. So it seems as if foreign stocks — led by emerging markets — are currently the "value stocks" of the world.

You want your portfolio to include Canadian, U.S., European, Pacific, and emerging market stocks, but if you are going to overweight any particular area, you may want to consider the relative P/E ratios, among other factors.

Choosing the Best International ETFs for Your Portfolio

Although we're (obviously) huge fans of international investing, and we believe that ETFs are the best way to achieve that end, there are only a dozen or so foreign ETFs that we think really fit the bill for most portfolios. This section introduces our favourites, complete with explanations of why we like them.

A boom economy doesn't necessarily mean a robust stock market

You would think that a fast-growing economy would be the best of places to invest. And yet there is more to stock returns than the growth of a national economy. (Just ask those investors who poured money into China several years ago.) In fact, the mind-blowing conclusion of a handful of recent studies is that the reverse is true: If you look at the stock returns of various national markets over the past 100 years, you actually find an *inverse* relationship. *Slow-growing* economies (such as India's, whose stock market has lately left China's in the dust) generally make for better stock investments!

Several possible explanations for this anomaly exist. Some say that rapid economic growth is attributable more to small, entrepreneurial businesses rather than to larger, publicly held corporations. Others have suggested that the fruits of economic growth often don't go to shareholders. Instead, those fruits may go to labour or consumers or (with the United States being a prime example) top executives and option-holders. Another possible explanation is that the prices of stocks in fast-growing economies (just like domestic growth stocks) often start off overpriced because of higher-than-reasonable expectations. Stocks of slow-growing economies (just like value stocks) may tend to be underpriced.

The moral of the story is to spread your investment dollars around the world. Don't think you can pick countries that will outperform by using projected growth rates as your crystal ball.

Note: This chapter doesn't include American funds. As you know by now, because there aren't a whole lot of Canadian funds to choose from, and because we can easily buy NYSE-listed ETFs, we've included some solid U.S. funds in other parts of this book. Refer to Chapters 5 through 8 for a number of options that can work well for the American part of your portfolio.

We've split our foreign picks up into three major categories: European, Pacific region, and emerging markets. For most portfolios, a reasonable split of foreign stock holdings would be something in the neighbourhood of 40/40/20, with 40 percent going to Europe (England, France, Germany, Switzerland); 40 percent to the developed Pacific region (mostly Japan, with a smattering of Australia, New Zealand, and Singapore); and 20 percent to the emerging market nations (Brazil, Russia, Turkey, South Africa, Mexico, and a host of countries where the entire value of all outstanding stock may be less than that of any S&P 500 company).

A special word on BLDRS

The BLDRS indexes, when these funds first appeared, were restricted to American Depositary Receipts that traded on the NASDAQ. Today the indexes include ADRs traded mostly on the NASDAQ, but also on the New York Stock Exchange. The indexes have attracted some criticism for their apparent randomness. In a way, the critics are right. Building a European ETF out of only ADRs that trade mostly on the NASDAQ is a little like putting together a football team of players whose first names all start with _R_. But all indexes are somewhat random. Some are weighted according to cap size; others are equally weighted; still others are weighted by number of shares outstanding. In point of fact, a team of football players named Robert, Rick, and Raul are not necessarily going to be any better or worse than a team with Clay, Dave, and Sam. And so it is with BLDRS: Their performance has been pretty much on a par with the other ETF options of the same regions.

For more information on any of the international ETFs we discuss next, keep the following contact information handy:

- ✔ **Vanguard:** www.vanguard.com or www.vanguardcanada.ca; 1-877-662-7447

- ✔ **BlackRock iShares:** www.ishares.com or www.ishares.ca; 1-866-486-4874

- ✔ **BLDRS:** www.invescopowershares.com; 1-800-983-0903

- ✔ **BMO:** www.etfs.bmo.com; 1-800-361-1392

- ✔ **Schwab:** www.schwab.com; 1-866-232-9890

Five brands to choose from

The ETFs we discuss here by and large belong to five ETF families: Vanguard, BlackRock (iShares); BMO; Schwab; and BLDRS (pronounced "builders"), a small product line issued by Invesco PowerShares. Yes, there are other global and international ETFs from which to choose. We discuss some of your other options in the next chapter, where we turn to global stocks divvied up by industry sector. As for global stocks that fit into a regional- or style-based portfolio, those mentioned in this section are among your best bets.

Canadian-listed international funds exist, but in many cases buying the U.S.-based ETFs in American dollars makes more sense. The first thing you need to do is ask yourself whether hedging matters to you. If you're holding these funds for a long time, currency fluctuations shouldn't affect your portfolio too much. If you really don't want the volatility, then you can get some Canadian-hedged funds, but you may have to pay a little more for them.

Some iShares ETFs are just TSX-listed versions of U.S.-based funds, which would be great if the fees were the same. But like everything American that comes to Canada (Target, anyone?), the prices are typically higher here. Double-check the fees before investing and decide whether buying Canadian is really that important to you.

Most of the funds listed here are U.S. based, but we do include Canadian options where it makes sense.

BLDRS stands for "Baskets of Listed Depositary Receipts," which is a very fancy way of saying "foreign stocks that trade on American stock exchanges." Vanguard and iShares foreign ETFs also include some Depositary Receipts (often referred to as *ADRs* — the *A* is for "American") but are made up more of true foreign stocks. That is to say that they own mostly foreign stocks only traded on foreign exchanges. For you, the investor, these nuances don't matter much, if at all, if you are holding your stock ETFs for the long haul (which, of course, you are!). In the short run, however, "true" foreign stocks and ADRs may diverge somewhat in performance.

All the world's your apple: ETFs that cover the planet

If you have a portfolio of under $10,000, or if you have a strong desire to keep your investment management simple, you may be best off combining one of the total-market funds we discuss in Chapter 5 with a total international fund, the best of which are the Vanguard Total International Stock ETF (VXUS) and the Schwab International Equity ETF (SCHF). Both of these funds give you instant exposure to everything in the world of stocks, minus U.S. investments. Both ETFs are ultra low-cost (0.09 percent for Schwab, and 0.16 percent for Vanguard) and well-diversified. The iShares MSCI ACWI (All Country World Index) ex-US Index (ACWX) is also a perfectly acceptable option, although it will cost you 0.34 percent a year. Keep in mind that these U.S.-based international funds do hold Canadian stocks. It's a small percentage, but it may be a lot if you're overexposed to domestic companies.

If you want to buy a hedged option, look at the BMO International Equity Hedged to CAD Index ETF (ZDM). The fund tracks stocks in developed markets, excluding Canada and the U.S. With an expense ratio of 0.46 percent, though, it's not cheap.

If you *really* want to keep things simple, you can buy a single ETF that tracks an index of all stocks everywhere — Canadian, U.S., and foreign. That one fund may be the Vanguard Total World Stock ETF (VT), with an expense ratio of 0.19 percent; the iShares MSCI ACWI Index Fund ETF (ACWI), with an expense ratio of 0.34 percent; or the TSX-listed iShares MSCI World Index Fund (XWD), but it comes with a 0.44 percent fee. All are perfectly fine options (though the lower the fee, the better). These indexed ETFs, like practically all others, are self-adjusting. That is, if your goal is to own a single global fund that reflects each country's percentage of the global economy, as that percentage grows or shrinks, so will its representation in these ETFs. Easy!

And if you *really, really* want simplicity — stocks and bonds and the kitchen sink, all in one package — see the end of Chapter 11 for suggestions.

If you have a portfolio larger than $10,000 and you are okay with adjusting its alignment (via rebalancing) once a year or so, we suggest that you keep your stocks and bonds in separate funds and that you furthermore break down your stock holdings into Canada, U.S., and non-U.S. Then, just as we advise for your domestic stocks, assign your foreign holdings to each of at least three categories.

If you've read the preceding Part II chapters, you know our preferred way to split up your domestic stock holdings is by style: large growth, large value, small growth, and small value. On the international side, alas, such a breakdown is difficult to achieve. We're not sure why the ETF purveyors haven't given us international stocks in four neat styles, but they haven't. That's okay. You can slice the pie into regions: European, Pacific, and emerging markets. Or slice it into large value, large growth, and small cap.

We help you weigh the options in the pages that follow. In Part IV, you'll see how both means of diversification can be used to build sample portfolios.

European stock ETFs: From the North Sea to the shores of the Mediterranean

Europe boasts the oldest, most established stock markets in the world: the Netherlands, 1611; Germany, 1685; and the United Kingdom, 1698. Relative to the stocks of most other nations, European stocks, as a whole, are seemingly low priced (going by their P/E ratios, anyway).

Europe's strengths include political stability (well, for the most part . . .), an educated workforce, and a confederation of national economies making for the world's largest single market. Germany, the largest economy in Europe, has been growing its export industry faster than any nation on the planet.

Europe's great weaknesses include a persistently high rate of unemployment (outside of Germany); a rapidly aging population; and a few member nations, most notably Greece and Portugal (and to a lesser extent Spain, Italy, and Ireland), whose governments have racked up some very serious debt. These nations are collectively — and none too flatteringly — known as the "PIGS" (**P**ortugal, **I**reland, **G**reece, **S**pain) or sometimes "PIIGS" (with **I**taly thrown in).

Even with its weaknesses on full display, the European market definitely deserves a piece of your portfolio. The ETFs we present here are good options to consider when you make that investment.

Vanguard FTSE Europe ETF (VGK)

Indexed to: FTSE Developed Europe Index, which tracks approximately 500 companies in 16 European nations

Expense ratio: 0.12 percent

Top five country holdings: United Kingdom, Switzerland, France, Germany, Sweden

Our review: This ETF has everything going for it, including low cost and good diversification. You can't go wrong (unless the European stock market falters, which, of course, could happen). The mix of many nations and currencies (euro, British pound, Swiss franc, Swedish krona) gives this fund an especially good balance and an especially good way to help protect your portfolio from any single-country (or currency) collapse.

BLDRS Europe Select ADR Index Fund (ADRU)

Indexed to: The Bank of New York Mellon Europe 100 ADR Index, a market-weighted basket of 84 ADRs issued by European companies (American Depositary Receipts) representing the United Kingdom (about half the money pot) and major nations of the European continent, in addition to, for some unknown reason, Israel

Expense ratio: 0.30 percent

Top five country holdings: United Kingdom, Switzerland, France, Germany, Netherlands

Our review: Not as diverse as the Vanguard European ETF, but with 84 securities, it's plenty diverse enough. The yearly expense ratio is about midway between the Vanguard European offering and the iShares Europe offering. All told, the BLDRS Europe is a good choice, although it may not be the best. (That, as usual, would be Vanguard.)

Make wheat, not war

In the stock market Olympics of the last century (1900–2000), the overall winner in terms of real stock market return was . . . drum roll . . . the socialist, Volvo-producing, snow-covered nation of Sweden. Sweden's overall rate of return for the century was 7.6 percent. In second place was Australia with 7.5 percent. In third place was South Africa with 6.8 percent. The United States came in fourth with 6.7 percent, and Canada was fifth with 6.4 percent. At the bottom of the world barrel, the Belgian equity market returned only 2.5 percent, with Italy, Germany, Spain, and France dragging closely behind with respective 100-year annualized post-inflation returns of 2.7, 3.6, 3.6, and 3.8 percent.

Here's the conclusion of the authors who pulled these numbers together, a group of distinguished professors from the London Business School: "Generally speaking, the worst performing equity markets were associated with countries which either lost major wars, or were most ravaged by international or civil wars." The best performers, point out professors Elroy Dimson, Paul Marsh, and Mike Staunton, were "resource rich countries."

An updated listing of the long-term stock market winners appears in the Credit Suisse Global Investment Returns Sourcebook 2011, using return data from 1900 through 2010. Australia has now taken the lead with 7.4 percent, South Africa is in second place with 7.3 percent, and Sweden now holds third place (tied with the United States) with a 6.3 percent real stock market return over the past 110 years.

iShares S&P Europe 350 (IEV)

Indexed to: Standard & Poor's Europe 350 Index, a collection of 350 large cap companies in 16 European countries

Expense ratio: 0.60 percent

Top five country holdings: United Kingdom, Switzerland, France, Germany, Sweden

Our review: We really like iShares domestic offerings, and its foreign ETFs aren't bad products — not at all. The diversification is excellent. The indexes make sense. The tax efficiency is top notch. We only wish the darned things didn't cost so much. At roughly 3.3 times the cost of the Vanguard European offering, IEV just isn't anything to write home about.

Pacific region stock ETFs: From Mt. Fuji to that big island with the kangaroos

The nations of the Pacific have evidenced a good comeback in recent years. With the rapid growth of China as the world's apparent soon-to-be largest consumer, surrounding nations may bask in economic glory. Australia, in particular, has benefited greatly from the recent run-up in prices for natural resources caused in part by Chinese demand. And Japan still leads the world in labour productivity, despite some obvious economic challenges (such as a serious real estate collapse and a level of debt greater than that of any other major nation). On the other hand, the threat posed by North Korea, the tensions between China and Taiwan, and the presence of nuclear weapons in unfriendly neighbours India and Pakistan loom like black clouds over the region.

But black clouds and all, the Pacific region merits a chunk of any balanced portfolio. Investing that chunk can be fairly easy; start by considering the ETF options laid out here.

Vanguard FTSE Pacific ETF (VPL)

Indexed to: FTSE Developed Asia Pacific Index, which follows roughly 800 companies in five Pacific region nations

Expense ratio: 0.12 percent

Top five country holdings: Japan, Australia, Korea, Hong Kong, Singapore

Our review: The cost can't be beat. And 800 or so companies certainly allow for good diversification, though Japan — the world's second-largest stock market — makes up 46 percent of this fund. We have a preference for VPL over all other Pacific options.

BLDRS Asia 50 ADR (ADRA)

Indexed to: The Bank of New York Mellon Asia 50 ADR Index, a market-weighted basket of 50 Asian market-based ADRs representing a total of 8 countries (Japan accounts for 48 percent of the pie)

Expense ratio: 0.30 percent

Top five country holdings: Japan, Australia, China, Taiwan, South Korea

Our review: The cost is higher than Vanguard's Pacific ETF, and you're tapping into fewer companies. Still, 50 companies isn't bad diversification. This fund also gives a bit more weight to non-Japan stock markets, which may be a good thing — although note that some of the countries represented are clearly emerging market nations. If you use ADRA, you'll want to factor that fact into your overall portfolio analysis. All in all, ADRA is a good investment, although we'd probably choose the Vanguard ETF.

iShares MSCI Japan (EWJ)

Indexed to: MSCI Japan Index, representing approximately 310 of Japan's largest companies

Expense ratio: 0.51 percent

Top five country holdings: Just Japan here

Our review: We can't understand why iShares doesn't offer a Pacific region ETF. If you want the equivalent of either the BLDRS or Vanguard Pacific ETFs, you need to buy at least two iShares ETFs: the MSCI Japan and the MSCI Pacific ex-Japan (EPP). That's a viable option for larger portfolios, but with a cost ratio several times greater than Vanguard's, we're not sure we see the point.

Emerging market stock ETFs: Well, we hope that they're emerging

When economists feel optimistic, they call them *emerging market* nations. But these same countries are also sometimes referred to as the Third World or, even more to the point, "poor countries." As we write these words, the recent astonishing returns of emerging market stocks are due in good part to sharp increases in the prices of commodities, such as oil, which come largely from these nations. But commodity prices fluctuate greatly. And political unrest, corruption, and overpopulation, as well as serious environmental challenges, plague many of these countries.

On the other hand, emerging market stocks are perhaps still (despite their recent rise) underpriced. Many emerging economies seem especially strong. And — perhaps most important — these countries have young populations. Children tend to grow up to be workers, consumers, and perhaps even investors. Future growth seems almost assured.

Vanguard FTSE Emerging Markets ETF (VWO)

Indexed to: The FTSE Emerging Transition Index, which tracks roughly 1,050 companies in 23 emerging market nations

Expense ratio: 0.18 percent

Top five country holdings: China, Brazil, Taiwan, India, South Africa

Our review: There's no better way that we know to capture the potential growth of emerging market stocks than through VWO. The cost is the lowest in the pack, and the diversity of investments is more than adequate.

BLDRS Emerging Markets 50 ADR (ADRE)

Indexed to: The Bank of New York Mellon Emerging Markets 50 ADR Index, a market-weighted basket of 50 emerging market–based ADRs

Expense ratio: 0.30 percent

Top five country holdings: Brazil, China, Mexico, Taiwan, South Korea

Our review: Yeah, 50 companies fall way short of Vanguard's 1,050, but 50 companies are still enough to give you pretty good diversification. We have no problem whatsoever recommending this ETF as a way to tap into emerging markets, although we do have a preference, once again, for Vanguard. Note that there is some overlap in the countries represented by this fund and the BLDRS Asia fund.

iShares MSCI Emerging Markets (EEM)/iShares MSCI Emerging Markets Index Fund (XEM)

Indexed to: MSCI Emerging Markets Index, a basket of approximately 800 companies in 20 emerging market nations; XEM is the TSX-listed version of EEM — both hold the same stocks

Expense ratio: 0.66 percent for EEM; 0.78 percent for XEM

Top five country holdings: China, South Korea, Brazil, Taiwan, South Africa

Our review: Good funds. Good company. Good index. If they weren't more than twice the price of the other options in this area (the Canadian version costs more), we'd jump to recommend them.

iShares value and growth: Two special ETFs for style investing abroad

Studies show that the same *value premium* — the tendency for value stocks to outperform growth stocks — that seemingly exists here in North America can be found around the world. (See the full value premium discussion in Chapters 6 and 8.) Therefore, we suggest a mild tilt toward value in your international stock portfolio, just as we recommend for your domestic portfolio.

Frontier markets: Nations that may emerge to become emerging markets

Of late, a number of ETFs, including the PowerShares MENA Frontier Countries Portfolio (PMNA), the Guggenheim Frontier Markets ETF (FRN), and the Market Vectors Gulf States Index ETF (MES), have cropped up to allow you to invest in so-called frontier markets. These markets feature economies even smaller, stock markets even newer and potentially less regulated, and governments perhaps even shakier than in emerging market nations.

Do you really want to invest in Bangladesh, Oman, Kuwait, Sri Lanka, and Trinidad and Tobago? Well, maybe . . . the payoff could be big. And the lack of correlation to other markets could be quite sweet.

But before you invest, realize how volatile these holdings are. Please do not invest too much, and diversify. The PMNA and FRN options are probably your best bets for now, but we're sure other frontier market ETFs will appear on the market soon.

If you do want to throw a few dollars into a frontier market ETF (stand advised that they tend to be costly), go for it. We suggest you use money that you otherwise would have allocated to emerging market stocks. But we wouldn't consider frontier markets a necessary part of a diversified portfolio.

You can accomplish this tilt easily by using the iShares MSCI EAFE Value Index (EFV) along with the iShares MSCI EAFE Growth Index (EFG).

Using these two funds together — allotting perhaps 55 to 60 percent to the value fund and 40 to 45 percent to growth — will give you full exposure to large cap, developed nation stocks. You still want to allocate some of your portfolio to emerging markets and to small cap international stocks.

Or, if you've already decided to split your international stocks up by regions — Europe, Pacific, emerging market — then adding a bit of EFV can give you the value lean you seek.

iShares MSCI EAFE Value Index (EFV)

Indexed to: MSCI EAFE Value Index, which is made up of approximately 500 large value companies of developed world nations, with about 40 percent of the fund's net assets in either Japan or the United Kingdom, the second and third largest equity markets on the planet

Expense ratio: 0.40 percent

Top five country holdings: Japan, United Kingdom, France, Australia, Germany

Our review: It's the only fund of its kind, and we're greatly appreciative that it exists. It's a bit costly when compared to the Vanguard funds but still considerably less than most of the other international iShares options.

iShares MSCI EAFE Growth Index (EFG)

Indexed to: MSCI EAFE Growth Index, which is made up of approximately 500 large growth companies of the developed world nations, with about 44 percent of the fund's money invested in the United Kingdom and Japan, the second and third largest stock markets

Expense ratio: 0.40 percent

Top five country holdings: Japan, United Kingdom, Switzerland, Australia, Germany

Our review: Like EFV, this international growth fund is the only one of its kind. We're grateful for its existence, and we're grateful that iShares has kept the expense ratio lower than what it charges for most of its other international funds.

Small cap international: Yes, you want it

Small cap international stocks have even less correlation to North American stock markets than larger foreign stocks. The reason is simple: If North America's economy takes a swan dive, it will seriously hurt conglomerates — Nestle, Toyota, and Suncor, for example — that serve the North American market, regardless of where their corporate headquarters are located. A fall in the U.S. economy and U.S. stock market is less likely to affect smaller foreign corporations that sell mostly within their national borders.

Regardless of the investment vehicle you choose, we suggest that a good chunk of your international stock holdings — perhaps as much as 50 percent, if you can stomach the volatility — go to small cap holdings. The two ETFs we'd like you to consider are from Vanguard and iShares. Note that there are considerable differences between the two.

Vanguard FTSE All-World ex-US Small Cap Index (VSS)

Indexed to: The FTSE Global Small Cap ex-US Index, which tracks more than 3,000 small cap company stocks in both developed nations (about 75 percent of the stocks) and emerging markets (approximately 25 percent)

Expense ratio: 0.25 percent

Top five country holdings: United Kingdom, Canada, Japan, Taiwan, Australia

Our review: For exposure to small cap international, you aren't going to find a less expensive or more diversified avenue. There is some Canadian exposure, which could actually be a good thing if you don't hold any other small cap ETFs. If you do hold a good amount of Canadian small caps already, then owning this may put your portfolio at a bit too much small cap risk.

iShares MSCI EAFE Small Cap Index (SCZ)

Indexed to: The MSCI EAFE Small Cap Index, which tracks more than 1,300 stocks from developed market nations other than the United States

Expense ratio: 0.40 percent

Top five country holdings: Japan, United Kingdom, Australia, Germany, Switzerland

Our review: Although a little more expensive than the Vanguard offering, this fund is still an excellent choice for international small cap exposure. Note, however, that unlike the Vanguard ETF, SCZ does not allocate any portion of its portfolio to emerging markets. If you own SCZ and you want that exposure, you might consider a modest position in one of a handful of small cap emerging market ETFs, such as the SPDR S&P Emerging Markets Small Cap (EWX) or the WisdomTree Emerging Markets SmallCap Dividend ETF (DGS).

Chapter 10

Sector Investing: ETFs According to Industry

· ·

In This Chapter

▶ Getting acquainted with major industry sectors

▶ Weighing the pros and cons of sector and style investing

▶ Listing the ETFs that work best for sector investing

▶ Choosing the best options for your portfolio

· ·

Any *Star Trek* fan (yeah, beam us up) knows that matter and antimatter, should they ever meet, would result in an explosion so violent as to possibly destroy the entire universe or, at the very least, mess up Donald Trump's hair. Despite the firm convictions of zealots on both sides, style investing (large/small/growth/value) and sector investing (technology/utilities/health care/energy) are not matter and antimatter. They can, and sometimes do, exist very peacefully side by side.

In this chapter, we present the nuts and bolts of sector investing: how it can function alone, or in conjunction with style investing, to provide diversity both on the domestic and international sides of your portfolio (or overlapping the two). However you decide to slice the pie (whether by style and/or sector), using ETFs as building blocks makes for an excellent strategy. (Hmm, are we starting to sound like zealots ourselves?)

Selecting Stocks by Sector, Not Style

As of this writing, more than 200 North American industry-sector ETFs exist. The vast majority, surprise, surprise, are U.S. based. The Canadian market has three main sectors — financial, energy, and materials. If you want to buy into health care, consumer goods, technology, or really any sector other than the big Canadian three, then you need to look south. And you do want to buy into other industries in order to diversify. See Figure 10-1 for a bird's-eye view of the U.S. economy and the Canadian economy split into their major industry sectors, each accorded its proper allotment. You'll quickly see why sector investors will want to do some over-the-border shopping.

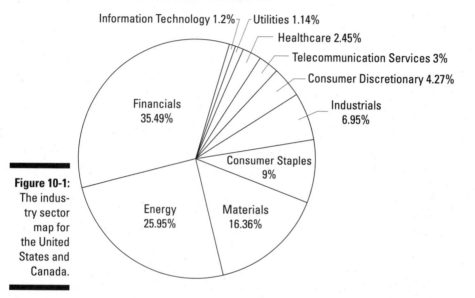

Percentage of Total Canadian Stock Market

- Information Technology 1.2%
- Utilities 1.14%
- Healthcare 2.45%
- Telecommunication Services 3%
- Consumer Discretionary 4.27%
- Industrials 6.95%
- Financials 35.49%
- Consumer Staples 9%
- Energy 25.95%
- Materials 16.36%

Figure 10-1: The industry sector map for the United States and Canada.

Based on the breakdown of the MSCI U.S. Broad Market Index and the MSCI Canada Index, these charts reveal the size of ten industry sectors of the U.S. and Canadian economies. What you're seeing is the total *capitalization* (value of stock) of all public companies within each industry group. ***Note:*** No standard methodology exists for breaking up markets into sectors; MSCI does it one way, and S&P does it a slightly different way.

Some ETFs mirror subsections of the economy, such as semiconductors (a subset of information technology) and biotechnology (a subset of health care). In some cases, subsectors of the economy you may not even know exist — such as nanotech, cloud computing, and water resources — are represented with ETFs!

A good number of newer ETFs allow you to invest in industry sectors in foreign countries (which are not represented in Figure 10-1) or in *global* industries (which is to say U.S., Canada, and foreign countries together; see Figure 10-2). About 150 international and global sector ETFs are available.

(As you look at Figures 10-1 and 10-2, note that one of the biggest differences between the U.S. chart and the global chart is the portion of the pie that goes to health care. Only in the United States does a trip to the dermatologist affect the national economy!)

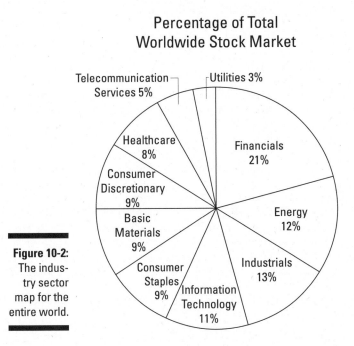

Figure 10-2:
The industry sector map for the entire world.

Certain newer ETFs — such as the BMO Junior Oil Index ETF (ZJO) or the PowerShares S&P SmallCap Health Care Portfolio ETF (PSCH) — allow you to invest in industry sectors *and* styles at the same time.

And finally, the living proof that you can, if you so wish, slice and dice a portfolio to ultimate death: You can even find some ETFs that allow you to buy into a particular industry within a particular country. Examples include the Global X Brazil Financials ETF (BRAF) and Global X China Energy ETF (CHIE). Unless you have a really compelling reason to purchase such a specialized fund (and pay the hefty expenses and subject your portfolio to excess concentration), we suggest you don't.

Speculating on the Next Hot Industry

Is there a God? Does He have a long, white beard, and does He wear sandals? Why do sector investors tend to be speculators, while style investors tend to be buy-and-hold kinds of people? These are questions that sometimes keep us awake at night. We won't attempt to address the first two here. As for the third . . . heck, we have no idea. But there's little question that people who divide their portfolios into large/small/value/growth are much more likely to be long-term investors with long-term strategies than are people who buy into sectors (often through ETFs). That's just the way it is.

Sizzling and sinking

Sector funds are often purchased by investors who think they know which sectors (or sectors within specific countries, such as financials in Brazil) are going to shine, and goshdarnit, they're going to profit by it. Unfortunately, they are often wrong.

Many people can still recall the time when environmental service companies, by dint of the realization that pollution was becoming a serious problem, were going to be a sure bet. But then, lo and behold, environmental service companies seriously lagged the overall market for years. Then it was information technology that couldn't possibly fail to outperform, yet for three brutal years (2000–2002), the technology sector fell like hail. At the time of this writing, real estate is the sector that people are pouring money into. Information technology is also hot (once again) with the entire world, thanks to Facebook's IPO, which didn't do so well but got investors thinking about the sector again. By the time this book comes out, who knows what everyone will be panting after?

Momentum riders and bottom feeders

Interestingly, while most investors are *momentum investors* — they tend to buy what's hot — other investors look for what's not, on the theory that everything reverts to the mean. The two camps are forever trading sector funds back and forth. Right now, the momentum investors are buying materials and energy; the bottom feeders (who prefer to see themselves as value investors) are buying financials and housing construction. Fortunately (or unfortunately), there is no dearth of ETFs to please both crowds.

Note: We're not saying that neither momentum investing nor buying up down-and-out industries has value. Both strategies have been known to make money. But such strategies can't be done helter-skelter. Like any other kind of investing, they require careful thought and study. Many rapid sector traders are not such deep thinkers.

You can tell from our tone, no doubt, that we're not big fans of sector speculation — or speculation of any sort. But what about using sector ETFs as buy-and-hold instruments? Even though few people do it, can a buy-and-hold portfolio be just as easily and effectively divided up by industry sector as it can by investment style? Keep reading.

Doing Sector Investing Right

An in-depth study on industry-sector investing, done several years ago by Chicago-based Ibbotson Associates (now part of Morningstar), came to the very favourable conclusion that sector investing — because times have allegedly changed — is potentially a superior diversifier to grid (style) investing. (We discuss the style grid in Chapters 4 and 5.) Globalization has led to a rise in correlation between domestic and international stocks; large, mid, and small cap stocks have high correlation to each other. A company's performance is tied more to its industry than to the country where it's based or its market capitalization, concluded Ibbotson.

The Ibbotson report didn't end there. It also ballyhooed sector investing as a superior instrument for fine-tuning a portfolio to match an individual investor's risk tolerance. A conservative investor might overweight utilities (a less volatile sector); a more aggressive investor might tilt toward technology (whooeee).

That sounds like a good plan, although the lead author of that study once confided to Russell that he has the bulk of his personal portfolio still broken up into value, growth, large cap, and small cap. However, he does have some industry-sector ETFs (for fine-tuning), as well.

Calculating your optimal sector mix

If you are going to go the sector route and build your entire stock portfolio, or a good part of it, out of industry-sector ETFs, we suggest that before you do anything you take a look at Figures 10-1 and 10-2. Make sure you are able to have allocations to all or most major sectors of the economy.

Some advisors would tell you to keep your allocations roughly proportionate to each sector's share of the broad market. We think that's decent advice, with just a bit of caution: Had you taken that approach in 1999, your portfolio would have been chocked to the top with technology, given the gross overpricing of the sector at that point. (And you would have taken a bath the following year.) We'd suggest that no matter what sectors are hot at the moment, no single sector should ever make up more than 20 percent of your stock portfolio.

(If you've read Chapter 9, you may recall that single-country and especially small single-country ETFs are not something we go out of our way to own. One reason is that a smaller country's economy can be dominated by one or two industries, making its markets especially volatile.)

Start perhaps with roughly allocating your sector-based portfolio according to the market cap of each sector, and then tweak from there — based not on crystal ball predictions of the future but on the unique characteristics of each sector. What do we mean? Read on.

Seeking risk adjustment with high and low volatility sectors

Some industry sectors have historically evidenced greater return and greater risk. (Return and risk tend to go hand-in-hand, as we discuss in Chapter 4.) The same rules that apply to style investing apply to sector investing. Know how much volatility you can stomach, and then, and only then, build your portfolio in tune with your risk tolerance.

As for historical risk and return, Figure 10-3 shows an approximation of how the major sectors rank. Keep in mind that *any* single sector — even utilities, the least volatile of all — will tend to be more volatile than the entire market because there is little diversification. Don't overindulge!

Finally, keep in mind that your allocation between bonds and stocks will almost certainly have much more bearing on your overall level of risk and return than will your mix of stocks. In Part III of this book, we introduce bonds and discuss how an ETF investor should hold them.

The Most Volatile Sector ETFs (with highest return potential)

Technology

Financial (includes REITs)

Healthcare

Consumer Discretionary

Industrial

Materials

Energy

Consumer Staples

Utilities

The Least Volatile Sector ETFs (with lowest return potential)

Figure 10-3: Industry sectors, from most to least volatile.

Knowing where the style grid comes through

There is nothing wrong with dividing up a stock portfolio into industry sectors, but please don't be hasty in scrapping style investing. We really believe that if you're going to pick one strategy over the other, the edge goes to style investing. For one thing, we know that it works. Style investing helps to diffuse (but certainly not eliminate) risk. Scads of data show that.

In addition, style investing allows you to take advantage of years of other data that indicate you can goose returns without raising your risk, or raising it by much, by leaning your portfolio toward value and small cap (see Chapters 6, 7, and 8). When you invest in industry sectors through ETFs, you are most often investing the vast majority of your funds in large caps, and you're usually splitting growth and value evenly. That approach may limit your investment success.

Another reason ETF investors shouldn't scrap style investing: Style ETFs are the cheaper choice. For whatever reason — yes, another one of those eternal mysteries that keeps us awake at night — style ETFs tend to cost much less than industry-sector ETFs. On average, they're about half the cost. Go figure.

And one final reason to prefer style to sector for the core of your portfolio: You will require fewer funds. With large growth, large value, small growth, and small value, you pretty much can capture the entire stock market. With sector funds, you need nearly a dozen funds to achieve the same effect. Each sector fund offers minimal diversification because the price movements of companies in the same industry sector tend to be closely correlated.

Combining strategies to optimize your portfolio

There's no point in having dozens of ETFs in your portfolio if they are only going to duplicate each other's holdings. So if you already own the entire market through diversified ETFs in all corner quadrants of the style grid — large, small, value, and growth — why add any industry sectors that are obviously already represented?

Adding a peppering of semiconductor stocks or utility stocks would make sense if you knew that semiconductors or utilities were going to blast off. (Of course, a rational investor would never say she knew anything about the future, other than that the sun will probably rise tomorrow.) And yet, taking on an added dose of semiconductors or utilities may still make sense if that added dose of either industry sector somehow were to raise your performance potential without raising risk. That could happen only if you chose an industry sector that is not closely correlated to the broader market.

Seeking low correlations for added diversification

Some sectors, or industry subsectors, even though they are part of the stock market, tend to move out of lockstep with the rest of the market. By way of example, consider REITs: real estate investment trusts. We devote Chapter 13 almost entirely to REITs, and especially REIT ETFs. For example, consider that in 2011, when the Canadian stock market tanked by almost 11 percent, Canadian REITs were up 14 percent.

Of late, the Canadian mining sector has shown an unfortunate lack of correlation (unfortunate for mining investors) with the rest of the market. As we write these words, this sector — comprised of companies involved in the mining and refining of precious and industrial metals, and the manufacture of chemical and fertilizer products — has thus far in 2013 been one of the worst performing sectors, while the overall market is in positive territory.

So it can go both ways. That's why, if you want to invest by sector, you need to make sure you're still diversified. If one goes down, you'd better hope another goes up. In Chapter 16, where we draw up some sample portfolios, you can see some examples of what we're talking about.

Newness is a red flag

At about 350 and counting (roughly one-third of all ETFs), you can find an ETF to mirror just about any sector or subsector of the global economy. The latest arrivals include a host of commodity funds . . . dozens and dozens of them. And new ones are sure to arrive shortly. Proceed with caution. New sector offerings occur most often after recent run-ups in price. The sector is hot. The public is buying. The financial industry is accommodating. Everyone is happy, for the moment. But maybe a bubble is about to burst.

If you decide to build your portfolio around industry sector funds, we urge you at the very least to dip into the style funds to give yourself the value/small cap tilt that we discuss in Chapters 6, 7, and 8. Again, in Chapter 16, we offer a few sample portfolios to illustrate workable allocations.

Sector Choices by the Dozen

After you decide which industry sectors you wish to invest in, you need to pick and choose among ETFs. BlackRock's iShares offers about 16 Canadian selections, about 40 U.S. ETFs, and 40 global or international selections. BMO has five domestic, three U.S., and three global. PowerShares has about 50 U.S. and a dozen international sector funds. State Street Global Advisors offers about two dozen SPDRs that cover U.S. industry sectors and nearly as many that cover international and global markets. Vanguard has 11 U.S. sector funds, one Canadian, and one international. And there are other players, too.

Begin your sector selection here:

- ✔ **Do you want representation in large industry sectors (health care, technology, utilities)?** Your options include Vanguard ETFs, BlackRock's iShares, and State Street Global Advisors Select Sector SPDRs, as well as funds from FocusShares, Guggenheim, Jefferies, and WisdomTree.

- ✔ **Do you want to zero in on narrow industry niches (insurance, oil service, nanotech)?** Consider PowerShares, First Trust, or Market Vectors ETFs. You can also choose State Street Global Advisors (non-Select Sector) SPDRs.

- ✔ **Are you looking for sometimes ridiculously narrow industry niches (aluminum) or sectors within sectors within small countries?** You should look at EG Shares, Global X, and Guggenheim ETFs.

    ✔ **Do you want to keep your expense ratios to a minimum?** Vanguard's
    ETFs, the State Street Global Advisors Select Sector SPDRs, and
    FocusShares from Scottrade tend to cost the least.

    ✔ **Do you want to invest in non-Canadian sectors but don't like currency
    risk?** iShares and BMO offer some Canadian dollar hedged sector ETFs.
    This option isn't available for most sectors, but there are a few.

In the following sections, we give you a more in-depth view of the sector
offerings available to you.

iShares Canada

The iShares Canada industry sector offerings include the following:

International Sector Fund Name	Ticker
iShares Oil Sands Index Fund	CLO
iShares Equal Weight Banc & Lifeco Fund	CEW
iShares S&P/TSX Capped Consumer Staples Index Fund	XST
iShares S&P/TSX Capped Energy Index Fund	XEG
iShares S&P/TSX Capped Financials Index Fund	XFN
iShares S&P/TSX Capped Information Technology Index Fund	XIT
iShares S&P/TSX Capped Materials Fund	XMA
iShares S&P/TSX Capped REIT Index Fund	XRE
iShares S&P/TSX Capped Utilities Index Fund	XUT

Global Sector Fund Name	Ticker
iShares Global Real Estate Index Fund	CGR
iShares Global Infrastructure Index Fund	CIF
iShares S&P/TSX Global Mining Index Fund	CMW
iShares Global Agriculture Index Fund	COW
iShares S&P Global Water Index Fund	CWW
iShares S&P/TSX Global Base Metals Index Fund	XBM
iShares S&P/TSX Global Gold Index Fund	XGD
iShares S&P/TSX Global Healthcare Index Fund (CAD-Hedged)	XHC

It doesn't take an expert investor to see that sector investing isn't easy for
Canadians. Although iShares has a number of sector funds to choose from,
the diversity in its offerings leaves much to be desired. It's mostly energy,
financials, and materials, which shouldn't come as a surprise because that's
what makes up most of our market. The majority of investors won't need to

buy any of the Canadian funds — you can get plenty of exposure to these sectors by owning some of the more broad-based iShares funds. They're also quite a bit more expensive than XIU or XIC.

What is interesting are the global sector ETFs. Investors can get access to international agriculture, health care, and infrastructure investments, while the global metals and gold indexes give you a chance to diversify your exposure beyond Canadian companies.

Before buying any of these, check the sector exposure in your other funds. For instance, XIC has a 33 percent weighting in financials. Do you really need more? On the other hand, it has a 2 percent weighting in health care, which many people believe is a major growth industry. If you believe that to be true, then maybe buy a health care ETF to bump up your exposure.

iShares U.S.

Following are the myriad sector funds from iShares U.S. As we've said before, Canadians can buy American ETFs, and, particularly when it comes to sector investing, they probably should. The U.S. market is much more diversified, so you'll find a number of funds you won't see on the domestic list. (iShares also has several U.S.-focused energy and financial funds too. You may or may not want to stay away from these. It depends on your view of the market. The names in these funds will be different from the TSX-listed ETFs, so although you'll get exposure to some interesting companies, be mindful of holding too many energy or financial operations.)

U.S. Sector Fund Name	*Ticker*
iShares Dow Jones U.S. Basic Materials Sector Index Fund	IYM
iShares Dow Jones U.S. Consumer Goods Sector Index Fund	IYK
iShares Dow Jones U.S. Consumer Services Sector Index Fund	IYC
iShares Dow Jones U.S. Energy Sector Index Fund	IYE
iShares Dow Jones U.S. Financial Sector Index Fund	IYF
iShares Dow Jones U.S. Financial Services Index Fund	IYG
iShares Dow Jones U.S. Healthcare Sector Index Fund	IYH
iShares Dow Jones U.S. Industrial Sector Index Fund	IYJ
iShares Dow Jones U.S. Real Estate Index Fund	IYR
iShares Dow Jones U.S. Technology Sector Index Fund	IYW
iShares Dow Jones U.S. Telecommunications Sector Index Fund	IYZ
iShares Dow Jones Transportation Average Index Fund	IYT
iShares Dow Jones U.S. Utilities Sector Index Fund	IDU
iShares Cohen & Steers Realty Majors Index Fund	ICF

International Sector Fund Name	Ticker
iShares MSCI ACWI ex-US Energy Sector Index Fund	AXEN
iShares MSCI ACWI ex-US Consumer Staples Sector Index Fund	AXSL
iShares MSCI ACWI ex-US Materials Sector Index Fund	AXMT
iShares MSCI ACWI ex-US Industrials Sector Index Fund	AXID
iShares MSCI ACWI ex-US Telecommunication Services Sector Index Fund	AXTE

Global Sector Fund Name	Ticker
iShares S&P Global Energy Sector Index Fund	IXC
iShares S&P Global Materials Sector Index Fund	MXI
iShares S&P Global Technology Sector Index Fund	IXN
iShares S&P Global Timber & Forestry Sector Index Fund	WOOD
iShares S&P Global Utilities Sector Index Fund	JXI

BMO ETFs

The BMO industry sector offerings include the following:

Domestic Sector Fund Name	Ticker
BMO S&P/TSX Equal Weight Banks Index ETF	ZEB
BMO S&P/TSX Equal Weight Oil and Gas Index ETF	ZEO
BMO Equal Weight Utilities Index ETF	ZUT
BMO Equal Weight REITs Index ETF	ZRE
BMO S&P/TSX Equal Weight Industrials Index ETF	ZIN

U.S. Sector Fund Name	Ticker
BMO Equal Weight U.S. Health Care Hedged to CAD Index ETF	ZUH
BMO Equal Weight U.S. Banks Hedged to CAD Index ETF	ZUB

Global Sector Fund Name	Ticker
BMO Global Infrastructure Index ETF	ZGI
BMO S&P/TSX Global Base Metals Hedged to CAD Index ETF	ZMT
BMO Equal Weight Global Gold Index ETF	ZGD

Small Cap Sector Fund Name	*Ticker*
BMO Junior Gold Index ETF	ZJG
BMO Junior Oil Index ETF	ZJO
BMO Junior Gas Index ETF	ZJN

Like iShares, BMO offers a number of sector ETFs that you probably don't need to hold. They're also much more expensive than the company's own broad-based domestic fund. These funds are *equal weighted,* meaning the allocation to each company in a fund is almost the same. ZEB, for instance, holds six banks and each has about a 16 percent allocation. For people who want to buy something even more focused, BMO does have some interesting options, such as its junior gold, oil, and gas funds, which give investors exposure to potentially high-flying small cap energy companies. So there are options here for the savvier investor. Just watch out for the fees and your overall exposure to one sector.

Vanguard ETFs

Vanguard Canada offers only one domestic sector ETF. The rest of the funds on this list are U.S.-listed securities.

Canadian Sector Fund Name	*Ticker*
Vanguard FTSE Canadian Capped REIT Index ETF	VRE

U.S. Sector Fund Name	*Ticker*
Vanguard Consumer Discretionary ETF	VCR
Vanguard Consumer Staples ETF	VDC
Vanguard Energy ETF	VDE
Vanguard Financials ETF	VFH
Vanguard Health Care ETF	VHT
Vanguard Industrials ETF	VIS
Vanguard Information Technology ETF	VGT
Vanguard Materials ETF	VAW
Vanguard REIT Index ETF	VNQ
Vanguard Telecommunications Services ETF	VOX
Vanguard Utilities ETF	VPU

Yes, only one measly Canadian sector offering from Vanguard. But don't be upset! It's 20 basis points cheaper than the iShares capped REIT fund. So if you want exposure to Canadian real estate, this isn't a bad choice.

The real value of Vanguard, though, is that it's created an ETF for every U.S. sector. That makes filling gaps easy for Canadian investors. Need some telecom? Buy VOX. Looking to add consumer discretionary stocks? Load up on VCR. Most of the holdings are of the large cap variety, which should be fine for most investors — you don't typically want to take on currency risk and hold volatile small caps.

These funds are also ridiculously cheap, at least compared to Canadian sector funds. Most have an expense ratio of around 0.14 percent, though the range is between 0.10 and 0.19 percent.

Seeking sector funds down south

Besides iShares, BMO, and that one Vanguard ETF, no other Canadian company sells sector funds. So, you'll have to look to the U.S. if you want to invest by industry. We've listed some of the U.S. iShares and Vanguard funds earlier in this section. Here's what some other American companies offer.

Select Sector SPDRs: State Street Global Advisors (Part 1)

In this section, we focus on *Select* Sector SPDRs. In the next, we introduce just plain old SPDRs representing industry sectors. What's the difference? Keep reading because we explain in the next section. First, let us acquaint you with some fund names.

Select Sector SPDR offerings include the following:

U.S. Sector Fund Name	Ticker
Biotech Select Sector SPDR	XBI
Consumer Discretionary Select Sector SPDR	XLY
Consumer Staples Select Sector SPDR	XLP
Energy Select Sector SPDR	XLE
Financial Select Sector SPDR	XLF
Health Care Select Sector SPDR	XLV
Industrial Select Sector SPDR	XLI
Materials Select Sector SPDR	XLB
Technology Select Sector SPDR	XLK
Utilities Select Sector SPDR	XLU

Overall, we put the Select Sector SPDRs on a par with the Vanguard sector ETFs. Like the Vanguard funds, they represent large U.S. industry groupings.

They follow reasonable indexes, and they will cost you about the same as the Vanguard ETFs in management fees.

SPDRs: State Street Global Advisors (Part II)

SPDRs industry sector offerings are as follows:

U.S. Sector Fund Name	Ticker
SPDR S&P Biotech ETF	XBI
SPDR KBW Bank ETF	KBE
SPDR KBW Capital Markets ETF	KCE
SPDR KBW Insurance ETF	KIE
SPDR S&P Oil & Gas Exploration & Production ETF	XOP
SPDR S&P Oil & Gas Equipment & Services ETF	XES
SPDR S&P Health Care Equipment ETF	XHE

International Sector Fund Name	Ticker
SPDR S&P International Consumer Staples Sector ETF	IPS
SPDR S&P International Materials Sector ETF	IRV
SPDR S&P International Energy Sector ETF	IPW
SPDR S&P International Technology Sector ETF	IPK
SPDR S&P International Utilities Sector ETF	IPU
SPDR Dow Jones International Real Estate ETF	RWX

Global Sector Fund Name	Ticker
SPDR Dow Jones Global Real Estate ETF	RWO
SPDR S&P Global Natural Resources ETF	GNR

Ready to find out what distinguishes a Select Sector SPDR from a plain old industry sector SPDR? Both are industry sector funds. Both are owned and run by megabank State Street Global Advisors. But the two ETF lineups are somewhat different. Retailers and car manufacturers call the differentiation *product-line extension.* So just as Honda has its Acura line of cars as well as plain old Hondas, and Toyota has its Lexus line in addition to the plain old Toyotas, State Street has both SPDRs and Select Sector SPDRs.

A big difference between the two lineups (just as with Hondas and Acuras, and Toyotas and Lexuses) is price, but if you assume that the "Select" names will cost you more, surprise! Whereas the Select Sector SPDRs charge 0.18 percent in management fees, the non-Select Sector SPDRs charge 0.35 percent for the domestic options and 0.50 percent for the international.

Another difference is the exposure. Select Sector SPDRs track large sectors of the economy, such as health care and energy. The plain old SPDRs, which happen to be darlings among day traders, track more narrow segments of the market. Instead of energy, you're looking at Oil & Gas Exploration & Production or Oil & Gas Equipment & Services, for example. Instead of health care, you're looking at just health care equipment. Because we prefer larger segments of the market, and we certainly prefer lower prices, we tend to prefer the Select Sector SPDRs over the SPDRs for any kind of U.S. stock exposure.

The SPDRs website — www.sectorspdr.com — is full of fabulous tools. Check out especially the Correlation Tracker, SPDR Map of the Market, and the Sector Tracker. (You don't have to be a SPDRs investor to use the tools.)

PowerShares

PowerShares industry sector offerings include the following:

U.S. Sector Fund Name	Ticker
PowerShares Dynamic Biotechnology & Genome Portfolio Fund	PBE
PowerShares Dynamic Building & Construction Portfolio Fund	PKB
PowerShares Dynamic Energy Exploration & Production Portfolio Fund	PXE
PowerShares Dynamic Food & Beverage Portfolio Fund	PBJ
PowerShares Dynamic Leisure & Entertainment Portfolio Fund	PEJ
PowerShares Dynamic Media Portfolio Fund	PBS
PowerShares Dynamic Networking Portfolio Fund	PXQ
PowerShares Dynamic Oil & Gas Services Portfolio Fund	PXJ
PowerShares Dynamic Pharmaceuticals Portfolio Fund	PJP
PowerShares Dynamic Retail Portfolio Fund	PMR
PowerShares Dynamic Semiconductors Portfolio Fund	PSI
PowerShares Dynamic Software Portfolio Fund	PSJ
PowerShares Dynamic Utilities Portfolio Fund	PUI
PowerShares Lux Nanotech Portfolio Fund	PXN
PowerShares Aerospace & Defense Portfolio Fund	PPA
PowerShares WilderHill Clean Energy Portfolio Fund	PBW
PowerShares Water Resources Portfolio Fund	PHO

Global Sector Fund Name	Ticker
PowerShares Global Water Portfolio	PIO
PowerShares Global Agriculture Portfolio	PAGG
PowerShares Global Clean Energy Portfolio	PBD
PowerShares Global Gold and Precious Metals Portfolio	PSAU

On the downside, PowerShares charges 0.50 percent for its domestic offerings and 0.75 percent for its global funds: That's a whole lot more than most of the competition is charging or would dare charge. The funds are also "dynamic," which means that the indexes it tracks are actively managed (someone somewhere is picking stocks). Many investors would see that as a plus; we don't. It means added expense, both up front and behind the scenes. On the upside, however, the PowerShares selection of industry groupings, in both its U.S. and global offerings, has been innovative, to say the least.

Unhealthy investments

A few years ago, a number of truly loony ETFs began hitting the market. There used to be about a dozen ETFs that invested in companies involved in treating specific diseases. You could have invested in the Ferghana-Wellspring (FW) Derma and Wound Care Index Fund, or the FW Metabolic-Endocrine Disorders Index Fund, or the FW Respiratory/Pulmonary Index Fund. Is there any good reason to invest in these funds? We can't think of any, unless you like to gamble and want to roll the dice on such small market niches. Should a cure to cancer be found, the company that nails it will see its stock skyrocket, for sure. The other however-many companies? Their stocks may well plummet. If you're holding the entire basket, it's a flip of the coin to say which way your investment may head. If you like flipping coins, fine, but please don't bet your retirement money on such foolishness. Many of these funds folded soon after they were created. You'd think people would learn that these über-specific ETFs are no different than betting on black at the casino, but we're sorry to say that many more crazy ETFs continue to pop up all the time. Many of them, if not most, track industry sectors.

Because commodities have been hot (and investors just love what's hot), we've seen lately the arrival of funds that allow you to invest in every conceivable individual commodity, from aluminum and potash to uranium and jelly beans. (We're kidding about the jelly beans; alas, serious about the rest.) Many sector funds are leveraged, promising to generate — for better or for worse — some multiple of their underlying index's returns; they bear names like the Direxion Daily Natural Gas Related Bull 3x Shares (GASL). Or they are inverse funds, moving opposite to their index, such as the PowerShares DB Crude Oil Short ETN (SZO). Or they are inverse *and* leveraged, such as the Direxion Daily Gold Miners Bear 3x Shares ETF (DUST — a ticker symbol that could end up being an apt description of the fate of invested capital). Other exotic sector funds represent narrow sectors within small stock markets, such as the Global X Brazil Financials ETF (BRAF).

Most of these inverse/leveraged/tiny-sliver-of-some-market funds are not only crazy to begin with (unless perhaps you are a very seasoned trader with vastly superior information . . . and if you're reading this book, chances are you're not one), but they also charge ongoing fees that are three, four, or five times what most ETFs charge. Keep your portfolio healthy, and avoid these gimmicky funds. Please.

Chapter 11

Specialized Stock ETFs

- -

In This Chapter

▶ Unearthing some facts about socially responsible investing

▶ Determining the potential payoff of dividend funds

▶ Introducing an opportunity to invest in initial public offerings

▶ Assessing funds that thrive (allegedly) when the market falters

▶ Considering a leveraged fund (woooeeee!)

▶ Examining lifecycle and asset-allocation options

- -

*I*n this chapter, we introduce a few stock ETFs that don't fit into any of the categories we discuss in previous chapters. They are neither growth nor value, large nor small. They are not industry sector funds, nor are they international. If ETFs were ice cream, the funds presented here would not represent chocolate and vanilla, but rather, the outliers on the Baskin Robbins menu: Turtle Cheesecake, Tiramisu, No Sugar Added Chocolate Chip, Pink Bubblegum, and Wild 'N Reckless (a swirl of green apple, blue raspberry, and fruit punch sherbet).

Wild 'N Reckless? We wouldn't say that these funds are necessarily wild or reckless, but nonetheless, they are stock funds, by and large, and anything related to stocks — trust us on this — carries risk. That being said, we present you with a few ETFs that bill themselves as socially responsible, a slew of funds that focus on companies paying high dividends (they're especially hot at the moment we're writing this chapter), one that invests only in corporations that have fairly recently begun selling shares to the public, and a few funds that go up when everything else is going down (don't get too excited; it isn't as good as it sounds). We also describe a few all-in-one funds for the ultimate couch-potato approach to investing. And we describe one hypothetical specialized stock ETF (see the sidebar "The authors' pipedream") that we wish someone would introduce.

Investing for a Better World

An increasing number of people — both individuals and institutions — are investing using some kind of moral compass. The investments chosen are screened not only for potential profitability but also for social, environmental, and even biblical factors. Some screens, for example, attempt to eliminate all companies that profit from tobacco or weapons of mass destruction. Others try to block out the worst-polluting companies, or companies that use child labour in countries that have no effective child labour laws.

The total amount of money across North America invested in socially screened portfolios has grown from about $1 trillion in 1997 to an estimated $3 trillion or so today. Most of that money is, of course, in U.S.-based mutual funds, pensions, university endowments, ETFs, and more. As for Canada, according to the Social Investment Organization, socially responsible funds account for one-fifth of total assets under management here.

Many of the funds that call themselves socially responsible (otherwise known as *SRI funds* – the *I* stands for "investment") not only invest with a purpose but also use their financial muscle to lobby companies to become better world citizens. The movement's greatest victory to date may have been the role it played in ending apartheid in South Africa. SRI seems to have had some impact on corporate North America as well, most notably by pushing certain auto, oil, and utility companies to research ways to reduce emissions of greenhouse gasses. Other victories include a ban on mercury thermometers and commitments from various corporations to start recycling programs, reduce toxic waste emissions, and end discrimination against employees based on their sexual orientation.

In this section, we discuss how SRI funds have performed in their relatively short history, the social aims of various types of funds, and some specific options available for your portfolio.

Tracking the history of SRI performance

Whereas investing in a socially responsible mutual fund or ETF may do the world some good, the question remains whether it will do your portfolio any good. Proponents believe that nice companies, like nice salespeople, will naturally be more successful over time. Skeptics of investing with a social screen not only scoff at the notion of good karma but also say that limiting a fund manager's investment choices can lead to *lower* performance.

So far, no solid evidence exists that either side is right — or wrong. During the past decade or so, the collective performance of socially responsible mutual funds has been very similar to that of all other mutual funds. One could argue that a tie should be resolved in favour of socially responsible investing. If one can achieve market returns while at the same time prodding companies to improve their behaviour, why not do that?

What about the specific performance of the socially responsible ETFs? Well, in Canada there's only one — the iShares Jantzi Social Index Fund (XEN) — and it hasn't done that well. But it was introduced in 2007, about a year before the market tanked, so we should cut it some slack. Generally, SRI ETFs haven't been around long enough for their collective performance record to count for much. And, of course, performance is only one factor to look at when deciding whether to recommend an ETF. But if it matters to you, consider the performance of the oldest socially responsible ETF, the iShares MSCI USA ESG Select Index (KLD), founded in January 2005. KLD has a five-year annualized return of about 5.51 percent, which is better than XEN's 1.77 percent. If you compare them to the broader-based ETFs though, such as XIU or SPY, the returns are similar. So, while these funds aren't necessarily beating other, more inclusive ETFs, it appears that you can invest responsibly without sacrificing much return. In a few years, when these funds have longer track records, we'll be able to know for sure.

Your growing number of choices for social investing

If you decide that you want to be a socially responsible investor, you have many choices: More than 65 Canadian mutual funds now invest with some social screen. About two dozen U.S. ETFs exist that are designed to appeal to your conscience too, though there's only one Canadian one. Because of the lack of choice in the Canadian ETF space, we're going to focus on the American funds, which Canadians can buy through most domestic brokerages.

ETFs exist that emphasize environmental awareness, social responsibility, clean energy, religious values, and more. For example, two U.S. ETFs that aim to show commitment to broad social issues are the iShares KLD 400 Social Index ETF (DSI) and Pax MSCI North America ESG Index ETF (NASI). For the same kind of stock exposure on the international side, you find the Pax MSCI EAFE ESG Index ETF (EAPS). Funds that invest in global stocks focused on clean energy include the Market Vectors Global Alternative Energy ETF (GEX) and Guggenheim Solar ETF (TAN).

Reasonable people can sometimes disagree on the specifics of what is and is not socially responsible corporate behaviour. If you decide to invest in an SRI fund, we urge you to review a fund's statement of values before investing. Otherwise, you could end up investing at cross purposes with your own values.

A close-up look at your SRI options

The two oldest and most popular ETFs that use social screens are as different as night and day. The iShares MSCI USA ESG Select Index ETF (KLD) is a broad-based large cap *blend* (both value and growth) fund. The PowerShares WilderHill Clean Energy Fund (PBW) is a narrow industry sector fund *and* a style fund (overwhelmingly small growth) *and* — whew — something of a global fund as well. (Approximately 25 percent of the holdings are non-U.S.)

Unlike our reviews of other kinds of ETFs (found in Chapters 5 through 10), we review these two funds together. That way, we avoid repeating ourselves because our feelings about both — and, in fact, about most of the socially conscious ETFs — are the same: We're absolutely, positively, conclusively ambivalent. Our double-shot-plus review follows a brief synopsis of the two most popular SRI funds. Our review of the one Canadian SRI follows after.

iShares MSCI USA ESG Select Index ETF (KLD)

Indexed to: The MSCI USA ESG Select Social Index (*ESG* stands for environment, social, and governance). The index starts with 250 or so fairly large U.S. corporations. Based on each company's record for social justice and environmental performance, it overweights purportedly ethical companies and underweights supposedly unethical ones while making sure that all industries other than tobacco are represented. (Tobacco is totally snuffed.)

Expense ratio: 0.50 percent

Top five companies: Apple, IBM, Starbucks, Spectra Energy, Procter & Gamble

Top five industries: Information technology, financials, consumer discretionary, health care, consumer staples

PowerShares WilderHill Clean Energy Fund (PBW)

Indexed to: The WilderHill Clean Energy Index, which tracks three dozen companies that invest in solar energy, windmills, hydrogen fuel cells, rechargeable batteries, and other forms of environmentally friendly power.

Expense ratio: 0.76 percent

Top five companies (most of which you've probably never heard of): First Solar, Cosan Ltd., Air Products & Chemicals, Polypore International, Inc., OM Group, Inc.

Top five countries: United States, China, Brazil, Canada, Chile

Russell's double-shot-plus review: These two funds are very different from each other. KLD covers a large swath of the market, while PBW is more narrowly focused. Both funds cost less than half of what the average socially conscious mutual fund would cost, which is certainly a good thing. On the other hand, SRI ETFs charge considerably more than many other ETFs. (The average expense ratio for the entire SRI category is about 0.70 percent, whereas many ETFs carry expense ratios of 0.20 percent or less.)

iShares Jantzi Social Index Fund (XEN)

Indexed to: The Jantzi Social Index, an index made of up Canadian companies — as chosen by Jantzi Research (now Sustainalytics) — that have a higher standard of environmental and social performance.

Expense ratio: 0.50 percent

Top five companies: Royal Bank, TD Bank, Scotiabank, Suncor Energy, Bank of Montreal

Top five sectors: Financials, oil and gas, basic materials, industrials, telecommunications

Bryan's review: If SRI investing helps you sleep better at night, then there's nothing wrong with owning this fund. However, it does hold some oil and gas companies, which some ethical investors may not want to own. If you must buy this, then we suggest selling off your shares in the iShares S&P/TSX 60 Index Fund (XIU) because it's almost the same, other than holding some more energy and gold companies. Actually, if you can stomach holding a few less ethical operations, then own XIU instead. It's cheaper, more diversified, and far more liquid than the SRI alternative.

Keep in mind that SRI ETF providers don't offer or promise the same kind of shareholder activism that you get with some of the more aggressive mutual fund companies. That's because most mutual funds are more actively managed than ETFs. As we explain in Chapter 2, passive management is part of what makes ETFs so appealing, because it leads to lower management fees and greater transparency. However, active management — such as that found with many mutual funds — may help keep an SRI fund more closely aligned with its stated values. Depending on the level of activism you'd like to see in your SRI fund company, this fact may lessen the appeal of pursuing socially responsible investing via ETFs.

For some, XEN may have too liberal a definition of "socially responsible." (We mean *liberal* not in the political sense but in the ease with which a stock can survive its screen — although some people may deem social responsibility itself to be a political statement.) The fund owns oil and gas companies, mining operations, and gold-producing businesses, which a lot of SRI investors try to avoid.

In terms of diversification, we like to see large cap stocks split distinctly into value and growth. With the SRI ETFs, however, you get a mushier exposure to these large cap categories. Looking through the lens of diversification, PBW offers up a small sliver of the economy and, as such, can involve considerable risk. As for XEN, 40 percent of the fund is in financials. That likely wouldn't fit many people's definition of a well-diversified portfolio.

If you want to invest for a better world and a better portfolio, we suggest you do additional research. One person's idea of socially responsible may be very different than another's. What works for one portfolio may not work for another. You can find a ton of information on the website of Canada's Social Investment Organization: www.socialinvestment.ca.

Dividend Funds: The Search for Steady Money

The check is in the mail. When you know it's true (it isn't always), perhaps no sweeter words exist in the English language. To many investors, the thought of regular cash payments is a definite turn-on, especially today when you can barely squeeze a few bucks out of bonds. Always willing to oblige, the financial industry of late has been churning out dividend funds — both mutual funds and ETFs — like there's no tomorrow.

The idea behind *dividend funds* is simple enough: They attempt to cobble together the stocks of companies that are issuing dividends, have attractive dividend growth rates, or promise future dividends. In this section, we spell out some of the dividend ETF options and then debate the value of investing in them.

Your dividend ETF options

The oldest and largest of the ETF dividend funds is the U.S-based iShares Dow Jones Select Dividend Index Fund (DVY). For Canadian domestic investments, here are some other options:

- ✔ iShares Dow Jones Canada Select (XDV)
- ✔ iShares S&P/TSX Canadian Dividend Aristocrats (CDZ)
- ✔ BMO Canadian Dividend (ZDV)

Canadian investors may also want to consider buying a U.S. dividend-paying ETF too. Here are a few of your options:

- ✔ SPDR S&P Dividend ETF (SDY)
- ✔ Vanguard Dividend Appreciation ETF (VIG)
- ✔ First Trust Morningstar Dividend Leaders Index Fund (FDL)
- ✔ PowerShares Dividend Achievers Portfolio (PFM)
- ✔ PowerShares High Yield Equity Dividend Achievers Portfolio (PEY)

Why *two* domestic iShares dividend ETFs? CDZ used to belong to Claymore Investments, which was purchased by BlackRock, the parent of iShares, in January 2012. The company continues to sell both funds, which is fantastic for investors who want more dividend investments to choose from.

The two funds are quite different, too. CDZ is far more diversified than XDV — it has a 19.74 percent weighting to financials versus 51.77 percent, for example. It also holds more smaller cap companies, which are spread across more of the Canadian economy. Because they don't resemble each other, their returns and distributions are different. XDV pays a 4.16 percent yield (because of the higher bank exposure), while CDZ pays 3.3 percent. The latter's return for 2012 was 5.3 percent, while the former's was 4 percent. So there are pros and cons to both. To decide which one to buy, ask yourself how comfortable you are with all that financial sector exposure.

You probably noticed that there are also two PowerShares dividend ETFs on the U.S. list. The first one (PFM) "seeks to identify a diversified group of dividend paying companies." The second one (PEY) "seeks to deliver high current dividend income and capital appreciation." If you're having a hard time telling these dividend funds apart based on their descriptions, you aren't alone. We're confused as heck!

And if all those choices aren't enough — or aren't confusing enough — you could also go with the PowerShares International Dividend Achievers Portfolio (PID), which "seeks international companies that have increased their annual dividend for five or more consecutive fiscal years."

And if *that* isn't enough choice (or confusion), the newest kids on the ETF block, WisdomTree and Guggenheim, offer about 20 *other* high dividend funds . . . with every wrinkle or subwrinkle imaginable.

In a way, seeking dividends makes sense. In another, larger way, the logic is a bit loopy, just as the marketing (sort of like toilet paper and breakfast cereal marketing) is a bit intense and sometimes silly. Let us explain.

Promise of riches or smoke and mirrors?

Dividends! Dividends! On the face of it, they look like free money. But nothing in life is quite so simple. Here are the typical arguments for buying a high dividend fund, along with our retort to each:

- **Argument for dividends #1: Steady money is just like honey.** Huh? Are you crazy, guys? Who in their right mind wouldn't want dividends? A stock that pays dividends is *obviously* more valuable than a stock that doesn't pay dividends. If I buy a high dividend ETF, my account balance will grow every month.

  Retort. Suppose you own an individual share of stock in the McDummy Corporation (ticker MCDM), and MCDM issues a dividend of $1. The market price of your one share of MCDM, as a rule, will fall by $1 as soon as the McDummy Corporation sends out the dividend. That's because the dividend comes from the company's cash reserves, and as those cash reserves diminish, the value of the McDummy Corporation diminishes (just as it would if it gave away, say, 100 plastic pink flamingoes from the front lawn of its corporate headquarters, or any other asset for that matter). As the value of the company diminishes, so too does the value of its shares. And the very same holds true for every stock held in an ETF.

- **Argument for dividends #2: They lower my tax hit.** But . . . but . . . suppose I need a steady stream of income? Isn't it better that I rely on dividends, which, if you're in the highest tax bracket, are taxed at 19 percent (in a non-registered account), instead of interest from bonds, which is taxed at my higher income tax rate?

  First retort. First, if you need a steady stream of income, nothing is stopping you from creating *artificial dividends* by selling off any security you like. In the end, whether you pull $1,000 from your account in the form of recently issued dividends or $1,000 from the sale of a security, you are withdrawing the same amount. And what if one month you find you don't need the income? You can sell nothing and pay no tax, whereas with a dividend ETF, you'll pay the tax regardless. (However, capital gains are taxed at a lower rate, so you won't end up with exactly the same amount if you sell a fund versus buying dividends.)

  Second retort. If you're really concerned about taxes, maybe you should be investing in a tax-free savings account or your RRSP.

✔ **Argument for dividends #3: It's a new world!** You guys sound like sticks in the mud. This is an exciting new development in the world of investments.

Retort. New development? Really? Equity income funds have been around for years and years, and they haven't exactly set the world on fire. And consider the age-old *Dogs of the Dow* strategy. Many people believe that if every year you purchase the ten highest paying dividend stocks in the Dow (the so-called *Dogs*), you can rack up serious returns. The strategy has been well studied, and it clearly isn't as powerful as the hype. The Dogs do seem to have some bark, but no more so than any other similarly sized and similarly volatile stocks. In other words, if you put a value lean on your portfolio, as we suggest in numerous places throughout this book (see especially Chapters 6 and 8), you'll be getting plenty of dividends and much of the edge that high dividend investors seek.

✔ **Argument for dividends #4: Don't you read history?** Over the course of history, much of the stock market's returns have come from dividends. You should know that.

First retort. Yeah, so? During the longest bull market in history — the 1990s — stock market returns were running double digits a year, and very little was being shelled out in dividends. A company that isn't paying dividends is either investing its cash in operations or buying back its own stock. Either way, shareholders stand to gain. Just because much of the stock market's past returns have come from dividends doesn't mean that future returns must or will come from the same source.

Second retort. If you look at high-dividend-paying sectors of the economy, you don't necessarily find that those sectors beat the broader market over long periods of time. The utilities sector is a perfect example. If the power of dividends was as great as the dividend hawks say it is, wouldn't the historical return of the utilities industry and financial stocks clobber the S&P 500? That isn't the case.

✔ **Argument for dividends #5: Dividends offer protection.** Stocks that pay high dividends are going to be less risky than stocks that don't. Those dividends create a floor, even if only psychologically. High-dividend-paying stocks cannot become worthless.

Retort. You would think that high-dividend-paying stock ETFs would be less likely to fall precipitously if there is a major downturn in the stock market. On the face of it, the argument seems logical. In the real world, however, studies of high-dividend-paying stocks reveal that they actually tend to be somewhat *more* volatile than the broad market. Go figure. Besides, if your main goal is to temper risk, you have other, more effective, ways of doing that. (See Chapter 12 on bonds.)

✔ **Argument for dividends #6: But still, it can't hurt.** All right, I concede, maybe these funds aren't the greatest thing since sliced bread. Still, can it hurt to buy one?

Retort. Look, we don't *despise* these funds. Far from it. If you want to buy one, buy one. Put it into your retirement account, if there's room in there, and you won't even have to worry about any tax on the dividends. But don't assume that you're going to beat the broad market over the long haul. And know that you are buying a fund that is mostly large value stocks, typically within just a handful of industries (notably financials, energy, utilities, and telecom). Your risk may be greater than you think. And if dividend-paying stocks are incredibly hot at the moment (as they are while we write these words), be aware that their prices may be inflated.

✔ **Final argument: I want my dividends!** I don't care what you say. I'm going to buy a high dividend ETF.

Final retort. Fine. Consider the Vanguard option (VIG) or the SPDR (SDY). With expense ratios of 0.18 percent and 0.35 percent, respectively, they are considerably less costly than the competition — and a lot less than the Canadian dividend ETFs, which have management fees of between 0.35 percent and 0.60 percent.

Last but not least, if you're not going to be using that dividend money right away, make sure your ETF is held in an account at a brokerage house that will reinvest your dividends without charging you a commission. Not all companies offer dividend reinvestment programs — called DRIPs — so double check before buying.

Initial Public Offerings

Want to take a real joyride? In April 2006, First Trust Advisors introduced the First Trust IPOX-100 Index Fund (FPX). You can invest in an ETF that, according to the prospectus, tracks the 100 "largest, typically best performing, and most liquid initial public offerings" in the United States. No Canadian equivalent exists.

Just before the introduction of the fund, the index on which it is based clocked a three-year annualized return of 33.74 percent. Needless to say, with that kind of return, this new ETF got the attention of a good number of investors. Those who jumped on board didn't exactly have a smooth ride. When the market tanked in 2008, FPX lost 43.79 percent — almost 7 percentage points more than the S&P 500 lost. Oooo, the pain. But in 2009, this fund gained 44.56 percent, and as of this writing, it has continued to outperform the broad market.

Thinking about plunking some cash into FPX? We may not have a crystal ball, but we do have an inkling of what the future will bring for this fund: more volatility. Keep reading to find out why.

The rollercoaster of recent IPO performance

When times are good for small and mid cap stocks, as they were in the three years prior to the launch of FPX, times are typically very good for IPOs. But when times are bad, you can guess what happens. The index on which this ETF is based suffered terribly during the bear market of 2000, 2001, and 2002, with respective annual dips of –24.55 percent, –22.77 percent, and –21.64 percent. (If you started with $10,000 in 2000, you would have been left at the end of 2002 with a rather pathetic $4,566.04.) And we've already addressed the more recent recession of 2008.

Taking a broader look at IPOs

But what about the very long-term performance of IPOs? Jay Ritter, a professor of finance at the University of Florida, keeps copious records on the returns of IPOs. Dr. Ritter asserts that, collectively, they haven't done all that well vis-à-vis the broad market. But he hastens to add that long-term performance is dragged down by the smaller IPOs, and that larger IPOs — the ones included in the IPOX ETF — as a group have modestly outperformed the market, albeit with greater volatility.

Indeed. As the IPOX Index now stands, tech stocks, volatile as heck in their own right, make up slightly more than 28 percent of the roster. The top three companies together represent nearly one-third of the index's value. Do you really want that kind of swing in your portfolio, on top of an expense ratio of 0.60 percent?

Maybe you do. But if you are inclined to take such a gamble, please don't do it with any more money than you can afford to lose. Of course, that's true of all stocks, but especially of these youngsters.

Funds That (Supposedly) Thrive When the Market Takes a Dive

In June 2006, an outfit called ProShares introduced the first ETFs designed to *short* the market. That means these *inverse* ETFs are designed to go up as their market benchmark goes down, and vice versa. The four original ProShares ETFs are the Short QQQ fund (PSQ), which is betting against the NASDAQ-100; the Short S&P500 (SH); the Short MidCap400 (MYY); and the Short Dow30 (DOG).

In Canada, Horizons Exchange Traded Funds has a number of inverse products, including the BetaPro S&P/TSX Capped Energy Inverse ETF (HIE) and the BetaPro S&P/TSX 60 Inverse ETF (HIX).

If we were to devise a ticker for the entire lot, it would be "HUH?"

As it happens, this HUH? category of ETFs and exchanged-traded notes (ETNs) has proliferated like no other — though mostly in the States. You can now find well more than over 100 exchange-traded products, from ProShares, PowerShares, Direxion, Guggenheim, and iPath, allowing you to short anything and everything, including the kitchen sink (see the ProShares UltraShort Consumer Goods ETF (SZK)). From the Canadian and U.S. stock markets, to various industry sectors, stock markets of other countries, Treasury bonds and gold and oil, it is now easy to bet that prices are heading south.

For the truly pessimistic investor, many of these short ETFs now allow you to bet in *multiples*. In other words, if the market falls, these funds promise to rise on a leveraged basis. For example, the Direxion Daily Semiconductor Bear 3x Shares (SOXS) is designed to rise 30 percent if the market for semiconductor stocks falls 10 percent.

From where we sit, these funds look an awful lot like legalized gambling. If you're considering putting your bag of nickels in any of these slots, keep reading for our two cents.

Entering an upside-down world

In other parts of this book, we talk about correlation and how wonderful it is when you can find two asset classes that go up and down at different times. Heck, it would seem that funds that short the stock and bond markets would be ideal additions to a portfolio. Talk about diversification! Ah, but there are hitches. For example, when you diversify, you want to find various asset classes that move out of synch but that are all expected to move upward over time, making money for you. Funds that short the stock and bond markets fail to meet the long-term test.

Sure, sometimes stocks decline. But over the long run (granted, the very long run), they rise. If they didn't, we wouldn't have a stock market. Who would invest? So over the long run, you would expect the short funds to lose money. Just about the only way to make money with these funds is to time the market just right: to jump in just as the market is about to dive and then pull out before the market goes up. Good luck! Market timing, we're not the first to say, is a fool's game.

Here's another hitch: These short ETFs are designed to move against the market on a *daily* basis. That means if the market goes down 5 percent on Wednesday, your fund should go up 5 percent (or, if your fund is leveraged, 10 percent or 15 percent) on Wednesday. But the mathematics of this, as we show you in the upcoming section "Funds That Double the Thrill of Investing (for Better or for Worse)," is very tricky. This tricky math means that if you invest in these funds for more than a very brief spell, you are very likely to lose money, regardless of which way the market moves!

Boasting a track record like none other

Don't take our word for anything we state in the preceding section. Just check the long-term performance records of these beasts. All of the original ProShares ETFs introduced in 2006 have lost a bundle. The ProShares Short QQQ (PSQ), for example, has lost 12.51 percent annually since inception. But to truly appreciate the losing power of these funds, you need to look at ProFunds, the mutual funds produced by the very same people who produce ProShares ETFs. The company's so-called *inverse* mutual funds and the company's short ETFs are very similar. Ready for some depressing numbers? See http://www.profunds.com/funds/performance.html.

Here, for example, are the annualized returns for the UltraShort NASDAQ-100 ProFund mutual fund, which has been proudly torturing investors since June 2, 1998:

- One year: –49.70 percent
- Five years: –30.06 percent
- Ten years: –32.46 percent
- Since inception: –33.53 percent

Sure, the stock market could tumble at any time, and you could profit by buying inverse or short funds. But you'll need to time that stock market tumble just right, and the odds of doing so are very slim. Moreover, playing this stacked game will cost you dearly: None of the short ETFs charge less than 0.75 percent, and most carry an expense ratio of 0.95 percent, making them just about the most expensive ETFs on the market.

Funds That Double the Thrill of Investing (for Better or for Worse)

ProShares introduced four other ETFs in 2006, targeting investors at the other end of the sentiment spectrum: extreme optimists. These are leveraged funds that include the Ultra QQQ (QLD), which "seeks daily investment results, before fees and expenses, that correspond to twice (200%) the daily performance of the NASDAQ-100 Index," and the similarly designed Ultra S&P500 (SSO), Ultra MidCap400 (MVV), and Ultra Dow30 (DDM). Horizons has a number of leveraged ETFs, such as the BetaPro S&P/TSX 60 Bull+ ETF (HXU) and the BetaPro S&P 500 Index Bull+ ETF (HSU).

You think the market is going to rock? These funds, which use futures and other derivatives to magnify market returns, promise to make you twice the money you would make by simply investing in the S&P/TSX Composite Index, the NASDAQ-100, the S&P 500, the S&P Mid Cap 400, or the Dow. Of course, you'll have to accept twice the volatility. It seems like it may be a fair bet. But it really isn't.

Suppose you invest in the BetaPro S&P/TSX 60 Bull+ ETF (HXU), as opposed to, say, the iShares S&P/TSX 60 Fund (XIU). On a daily basis, if the underlying index goes up, your investment will go up twice as much. If the underlying index goes down, your investment will go down twice as much. Clearly, the volatility is double. But you have to look at the potential returns, as well.

The XIU is going to cost you 0.17 percent in operating expenses. The HXU is going to cost you 1.15 percent. That's a difference of 0.98 percent a year, or $490 on a $50,000 investment. You can expect about 2.7 percent in annualized dividends on XIU. Because HXU invests largely in futures, you aren't going to get any dividends. On a $50,000 investment, that's a difference of an additional $1,350 or more. Already you've lost $1,790 ($1,300 + $490), regardless of which way the market goes.

But the loss of dividends or the high operating expenses isn't actually what will hurt you the most with leveraged funds. It's more the added volatility — daily volatility — that will eat up and spit out your principal regardless of which way the market goes.

Follow closely:

Suppose you invest $1,000 in HXU, which seeks a return of 200 percent of the return of the S&P/TSX 60 Index. Now suppose that the index goes up 10 percent tomorrow but then drops 10 percent the day after tomorrow. You think you're back to $1,000? Guess again. The math of compounding is such that, even if you had invested in the index itself — unleveraged — you'd be in the hole after Day Two. Run the numbers: Your 10 percent gain on Day One would take you up to $1,100, but your loss of 10 percent of $1,100 the next day equals $110. Subtract that amount from $1,100, and you're left with $990 on Day Two, or an overall loss of 1 percent.

With HXU, you're going to get double socked. On Day One, you'll happily be up 20 percent to $1,200. But on Day Two, you'll lose 20 percent of that amount and find yourself with $960. You didn't lose the promised *double* (2 percent); you just lost *quadruple* (4 percent). Pull out your calculator if you don't believe us.

In a classic illustration of the principle that life is not fair, you are not helped if the market goes down and then up, instead of the other way around. Lose 10 percent of $1,000, and you've got $900. Gain 10 percent the next day, and what do you have? $990 ($900 + $90). The situation is magnified with HXU: You would lose 20 percent on Day One for a balance of $800, and gain 20 percent on Day Two to bring you right back to the same $960 you were left with in the first example.

And *that,* dear reader, is how these funds eat up your hard-earned savings, and why we strongly suggest that you do not use them.

The authors' pipe dream

We would love to see someone create a "Reasonably-Paid-Top-Executives ETF." We might buy into it if it did exist. It stands to reason that when corporations pay astronomical salaries to their CEOs, shareholders may stand to lose. After all, those millions and millions (indeed, sometimes billions) have to come from *somewhere.*

According to compensation researchers Lucian Bebchuk of Harvard University and Jesse Fried of the University of California at Berkeley, the pay of top executives at America's largest corporations eats seriously into U.S. corporate profits. Not too surprisingly (at least in our minds), one study by the Institute for Policy Studies and United for a Fair Economy found that those reduced profits are indeed hurting shareholders. The study looked at stock market returns for major U.S. corporations between 1991 and the end of 2004. Sure enough, the "Greedy CEO Portfolio" — a portfolio of those corporations that pay their CEOs the most — severely underperformed the S&P 500. Hence, an ETF composed of stocks in companies that curb executive pay just may be expected to outperform the market.

All-in-One ETFs: For the Ultimate Lazy Portfolio

The rest of this chapter introduces you to ETFs that tend to focus fairly narrowly in order to meet your investing needs (or, in the case of short and leveraged funds, your gambling needs). In this section, we introduce you to funds that cast a much wider net, allowing you to invest in enormous pools of stocks and bonds without having to focus at all. First we present a handful of ETF options that fit the bill, and then we explain why you probably don't want them.

Getting worldwide exposure to stocks and bonds

Even the laziest investor has to make choices: Do you want worldwide exposure to stocks only? Or to stocks and bonds? Do you want the allocation between stocks and bonds to remain the same for the life of your investment? Or do you want that allocation to adjust as you get closer to retirement? In this section, we lay out your options.

Buying into the world's stock markets

If you want instant exposure to the broadest possible index of stocks, including Canadian and all sorts of foreign stocks (from both developed and emerging market countries), here are your options as of this writing:

- iShares MSCI ACWI Index Fund (ACWI), with 1,348 stock holdings and management fees of 0.34 percent
- Vanguard Total World Stock ETF (VT), with 3,867 holdings and management fees that are slightly lower at 0.22 percent

Adding bonds to the mix

Not enough diversity for you? Never fear: You can go even broader than the worldwide stock funds, buying one ETF that will give you exposure not only to the entire world of stocks but to bonds as well. (We discuss bond ETFs in Chapter 12.)

These all-in-one ETFs are referred to as *asset allocation funds* when they are *static,* meaning the division between stocks and bonds stays more or less the same for the life of the fund (for example, 50 percent stock and 50 percent bonds). The folks from iShares offer a dozen of these babies, including these (the first two are Canadian products):

- ✔ iShares Balanced Income CorePortfolio (CBD)
- ✔ iShares Balanced Growth CorePortfolio (CBN)
- ✔ iShares S&P Aggressive Allocation Fund (AOA)
- ✔ iShares S&P Conservative Allocation Fund (AOK)
- ✔ iShares S&P Moderate Allocation Fund (AOM)

The last three funds listed carry total management expenses of about 0.30 percent and offer varying exposure to stocks and bonds depending on how aggressive a portfolio you want.

Picking a retirement date and investing accordingly

If a fund seeks to change its asset allocation over time, growing more conservative as you get older and less able or willing to handle market risk, it may be called a *lifecycle* or *target-date* fund (rather than an asset allocation fund). iShares offers a bevy of these funds, including these three:

- ✔ iShares S&P Target Date 2020 Index Fund (TZG)
- ✔ iShares S&P Target Date 2025 Index Fund (TZI)
- ✔ iShares S&P Target Date 2030 Index Fund (TZL)

The dates refer to anticipated retirement dates. These funds start off more aggressive (stressing stocks over bonds) and wind up, by your expected retirement date, holding a more conservative portfolio. The expense ratio for each is 0.30 percent.

Both the iShares asset allocation funds and the target-date funds are actually funds of funds (mostly other iShares ETFs). The expenses you see include the fees for both the component funds and the all-in-one fund wrapper.

Deutsche Bank DBX Strategic Advisors offers five funds of similar nature to the iShares. These funds, which include the db-X 2030 Target Date Fund (TDN) and the db-X 2040 Target Date Fund (TDV), carry expense ratios of 0.65 percent.

Bryan and Russell's average review for the average reader on an average day

"For every complex problem," said H. L. Mencken, "there is an answer that is clear, simple — and wrong." Certainly, finding the optimal portfolio is a complex problem. The all-in-one ETFs we introduce in this section provide an answer that is clear, simple — and usually wrong. Never mind the high expense ratios; what's wrong is that no one-size-fits-all portfolio that makes sense for most people exists. Oh, we suppose if you were the average 50-year-old, with the average amount of money, looking to work an average number of years, expecting to die at the average age, and you were willing to take on an average amount of risk. . . . Well, if you were all those things and planned on remaining forever average, these funds might make sense for you.

But if you are anything other than perfectly average, we urge you to move on to Part IV of this book whenever you feel ready. Take a look at our model portfolios, and craft an ETF portfolio that makes sense for *you*.

Part III
Adding Bonds, REITs, and Other ETFs to Your Portfolio

The 5th Wave   By Rich Tennant

"I've brought in Tom, Denise, and Kyle, to talk about our REIT, Bond, and metal ETFs respectively."

In this part . . .

The majority of ETFs — all those we discuss in Part II — represent common stock holdings. In this part, we introduce you to the minority: those ETFs that represent bonds, real estate investment trusts (REITs), and commodities such as gold, silver, and oil. Such holdings (especially bonds) have enormous diversification power: the power to protect you when the stock market takes a big roll, as it inevitably does from time to time. (We probably don't need to tell you that!)

For sure, you have various means of owning such holdings. You can buy individual bonds, investment properties from foreclosure sales in Florida, gold coins, and silver bullion. Heck, you can fill your garage with barrels of oil. But no method is as easy, efficient, and frugal as holding them as ETFs.

Chapter 12

For Your Interest: The World of Bond ETFs

*A*s we write this book, many investment experts are saying that fixed income is for fools. Interest rates are so low that it's nearly impossible to make a buck in bonds, especially Government of Canada bonds. To make matters worse, when interest rates rise — and they will — bond prices will fall. So, in some ways, these pros are right; it's hard to make any moolah in fixed income.

Yet, people have been flocking to bonds. According to EPFR Global, a company that tracks mutual fund inflows and outflows, a whopping $470 billion went into fixed income funds in 2012, while $70 billion left equity funds. So, should you be in bonds or not?

The short answer: Most definitely. If equities are a wild Canada's Wonderland roller coaster, fixed income is the seat belt that keeps you strapped in and safe. Although it's true that, these days, bonds yield next to nothing and that you won't make much money owning them, it's fixed income that keeps your portfolio from plummeting. In other words, when the going gets rough and you hit a big bump (remember 2008?), you'll be very, very glad you bought some bonds.

Plain and simple, no time-honoured diversification tool for your portfolio even comes close to bonds. They are as good as gold . . . or even better than gold when you look at the long-term returns. Bonds are what may have saved your grandparents from selling apples on the street following the stock market crash of 1929.

The one thing that grandpa and grandma never had — but you do — is the ability to invest in bond ETFs. Like stock ETFs, most bond ETFs (at least the ones we're going to suggest) are inexpensive, transparent (you know exactly what you're investing in), and highly liquid (you can sell them in a flash). Like individual bonds or bond mutual funds, bond ETFs can also be used to bring stability to a portfolio. They can also provide regular interest payments — though those distributions can fluctuate depending on the ETF's holdings — which makes them especially popular among grandparent types of any generation.

Throughout this chapter, we discuss a few things about bond investing in general. Then, without knowing the intimate particulars of your individual economics, we try our best to help you decide if bond ETFs belong in your portfolio, and if so, which ones. We also address that all-important and highly controversial question of how to achieve an optimal mix of stocks and bonds.

The single, most important investment decision you ever make may occur when you determine the split between stocks and bonds in your portfolio. No pressure.

Tracing the Track Record of Bonds

Bonds, more or less in their present form, have been used as financial instruments since the Middle Ages. Then, as now, bonds of varying risk existed. (See the sidebar "The three risks of bond investing.") Then, as now, risks and returns were highly correlated.

For the most part, bonds are less volatile than stocks, and their returns over time tend to be less. Over the past 80 years, the average annualized total return of the Dow Jones Industrial Average has been around 10 percent, while the return of long-term U.S. government bonds has been approximately 5.5 percent.

Comparing the *real* returns of stocks versus bonds (the return *after* inflation, which happens to be the return that really counts), stocks over the past 80 years clock in at about 6.7 percent and bonds at 2.4 percent — a huge difference. A dollar invested in the stock market in 1926 (ignoring all taxes, investment fees, and so on) would today be worth about $243.00. That same dollar invested in bonds would be worth around $7.65.

These numbers may lead you to look at bonds and say to yourself, "Why bother?" Well, in fact, there's good reason to bother. Please read on before you decide to forsake this all-important asset class.

The three risks of bond investing

When you buy a stock, your risks are plenty: The company you're investing in may go belly up; the public may simply lose interest in the stock, sending its price tumbling; or the entire economy may falter, in which case, your stock, like most others, may start to freefall. In the world of bonds, the risks aren't quite so high, and they tend to differ. Here are the three major risks of investing in bonds or a bond ETF:

✔ **Risk of default:** A bond is a promissory note. The note is only as good as the government, agency, or company that makes the promise to repay. If you buy a bond from ABC Corporation and ABC Corporation can't pay, you lose. This risk of default is mostly an issue with high-yield ("junk") bonds. Don't invest in high-yield corporate bonds unless you're willing to shoulder some serious risk. Keep in mind when buying a high-yield bond ETF that if the economy tanks and shaky companies start to sink, you'll possibly lose both the income from the bonds and the principal. And that could hurt. High-yield bonds, for example, were little comfort to those who lost money in the stock market in 2008. The SPDR Barclays Capital High Yield Bond ETF (JNK), for example, saw returns in 2008 of –24.68 percent.

✔ **Interest-rate risk:** Suppose you are holding a bond with a 5 percent coupon rate, bought at a time when interest rates in general were 5 percent. Now suppose that the prevailing interest rate jumps to 10 percent. Are you going to be happy that you're holding a bond that is paying 5 percent? Of course not. If you hold the bond to maturity, there's a great opportunity cost. If you try to sell the bond before maturity, no one will give you full price; you'll need to sell it at a deep discount and take a loss. The longer the maturity of the bond, the greater the interest-rate risk. For that reason, the BMO Long Federal Bond Index ETF (ZFL), for example, carries substantial interest-rate risk, while the iShares DEX Short Term Bond Index Fund (XSB) carries very little. Most of the other funds are somewhere in between. (There's a flip side to interest-rate risk: If you are holding a bond with a 5 percent coupon rate and the prevailing interest rate drops to 3 percent, your bond will suddenly become a very hot ticket, selling at a juicy premium.)

✔ **Inflation risk:** Plain and simple, if you are holding a bond that pays 5 percent and the inflation rate is 8 percent, you are in trouble. This is perhaps the biggest risk with bonds, especially low-yielding bonds, such as short-term and, these days, Government of Canada bonds. The only bonds immune to this risk are inflation-protected bonds, which is why part of your bond portfolio should be invested in a fund such as the iShares DEX Real Return Bond Index Fund (XRB). Such bonds do, however, carry interest-rate risk, and another risk that's unique to them: *deflation* risk. If consumer prices start to drop, your inflation adjustment will be worth zero, and you'll be left holding the lowest yielding bond in the land.

Portfolio protection when you need it most

When determining the attractiveness of bonds, you need to look not only at historical return but also at volatility. We look at U.S. government bonds in this section because there's more history to consider. Long-term U.S. government bonds (which tend, like all long-term bonds, to be rather volatile) in their worst year *ever* (2009) returned –17.2 percent. In their second worst year ever (1980) they returned –14.6 percent. Those are big moves but still a walk in the park compared to the worst stock market years of 1931 (–43.3 percent), 1937 (–35 percent), 1974 (–26.5 percent), and 2008 (–36.7 percent).

As we note in the introduction to this chapter, during the Great Depression years, bonds may have saved your grandma and grandpa from destitution. The annualized real return of the S&P 500 from 1930–1932 was –20 percent. The annualized real return of long-term U.S. government bonds during the same three years was 14.9 percent.

There are two reasons that U.S. — and Canadian — government bonds (and other high-quality bonds) often do well in the roughest economic times:

- ✔ People flock to them for safety, raising demand.

- ✔ Central banks often cut interest rates often (not always, but often) during tough economic times to spur growth. Interest rates and bond prices have an inverse relationship. When interest rates fall, already-issued bonds (carrying older, relatively high coupon rates) shoot up in price.

As in the past, bonds may similarly spare your hide if the upcoming years prove disastrous for Wall Street and Bay Street. (You never know.) Whereas international stocks and certain industry sectors, like energy and real estate, have limited correlation to the broad stock market, bonds (not junk bonds, but most others) actually have a slight *negative* correlation to stocks. In other words, when the bear market is at its growliest, the complicated labyrinth of economic factors that typically coincide with that situation — lower inflation (possible deflation), lower interest rates — can bode quite well for fixed income. They certainly have done so in the past.

The way in which bonds tend to zig when stocks zag (and vice versa) is beautifully illustrated in Figure 12-1, provided by Vanguard Investments.

And also consider Figure 12-2, which shows how stocks and bonds have fared in some of the most exciting (read: volatile) investment years in the past eight decades.

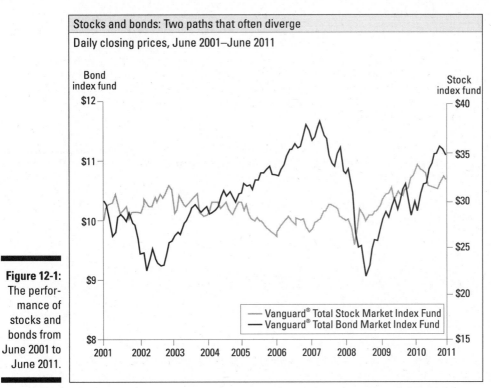

Stocks and bonds: Two paths that often diverge

Daily closing prices, June 2001–June 2011

Figure 12-1: The performance of stocks and bonds from June 2001 to June 2011.

Source: Vanguard, with permission.

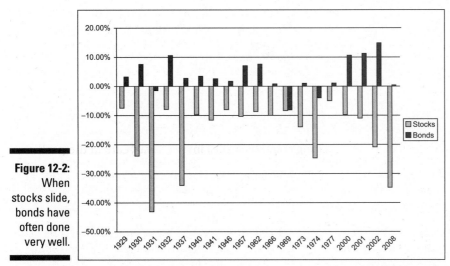

Figure 12-2: When stocks slide, bonds have often done very well.

Source: Vanguard, with permission.

History may or may not repeat

Of course, as investment experts say again and again (although few people listen), historical returns are only mildly indicative of what will happen in the future; they are merely reference points. Despite all the crystal balls, tea leaves, and BNN commentators in the world, we simply don't know what the future will bring.

Although the vast majority of financial professionals use the past century as pretty much their sole reference point, some point out that in the 19th century stocks and bonds actually had more similar — nearly equal, in fact — rates of return. And perhaps that may be true for the 21st century as well. Time will tell. In the meantime, given all this uncertainty, having both stocks and bonds represented in your portfolio would be most prudent.

Tapping into Bonds in Various Ways

Like stocks, bonds can be bought individually, or you can invest in any of the hundreds of bond mutual funds or the many Canadian and U.S. bond ETFs. The primary reason for picking a bond fund over individual bonds is the same reason you might pick a stock fund over individual stocks: diversification.

Sure, you have to pay to get your bonds in fund form, but the management fees on bond ETFs tend to be very low, as you'll see later in this chapter. Conversely, the cost to trade individual bonds can be quite high. Like ketchup at Costco, you can get a better price on a bond if it's bought in bulk. Unfortunately, most retail investors don't have enough money to make a dent in the purchase price. Funds, though, buy lots of bonds at once and, therefore, get a better rate. So, in many cases, buying a bond fund is actually a cheaper way to get into the fixed income market, even with management fees.

We're not saying that you shouldn't consider ever buying individual bonds. Doing so may make sense, provided that you know how to get a good price on an individual bond (if not, please read Russell's book on that topic, *Bond Investing For Dummies,* published by Wiley) and provided that you're buying a bond with little default risk (such as a Government of Canada bond). That's especially true when you know that you will be needing x amount of money on y date. But for the most part, investors do better with low-cost, indexed bond funds.

Like stocks, bonds can (and should, if your portfolio is large enough) be broken up into different categories. Instead of Canadian and international, large, small, value, and growth (the way stocks are often broken up), bond categories may include Canadian Government (both conventional and inflation-adjusted), corporate, and international — all of varying maturity dates and credit ratings. Unless you're a billionaire, you simply can't effectively own enough individual bonds to tap into each and every fixed-income class.

Finding strength in numbers

To be honest, diversification in bonds, while important, isn't quite as crucial as diversification in stocks. If you own high-quality Canadian government bonds (as long as they aren't terribly long-term) and you own a bevy of bonds from the most financially secure corporations, you are very unlikely to lose a whole lot of your principal, as you can with any stock. But the benefits of diversification are more than protecting principal. There's also much to be said for smoothing out returns and moderating risk.

Bond returns from one category of bonds to another can vary greatly, especially in the short run. In 2008, for example, U.S. high-yield corporate bonds, as represented by the SPDR Barclays Capital High Yield Bond ETF (JNK), saw a return of –24.68 percent. That same year, U.S. Treasury bonds (another name for government bonds), as represented by the iShares Barclays 7–10 Year Treasury Bond ETF (IEF), returned 17.9 percent. But the very next year, 2009, was a terrible year for Treasury bonds; IEF sagged –6.56 percent and JNK shot up 37.65 percent. (The junk bond ETF category in Canada is limited, which is why we're using U.S. examples. But the point is the same wherever you reside.)

By owning a handful of bond funds, you can effectively diversify across the map. You can have government bonds of varying maturities, corporate bonds of varying creditworthiness, and international bonds of varying continents and currencies. As you'll see throughout the rest of this chapter, we urge investors primarily to seek safety in bonds. If you're looking for high returns, go to stocks. The purpose of bonds, as far as we're concerned, is to provide ballast to a portfolio.

The purposes served by bond funds are to make your bond investing easy, help you to diversify, and keep your costs low. Just as in the world of stock funds, all bond funds are not created equal. Some government funds are better than others. Some corporate bond funds are better than others. Ditto for funds holding foreign bonds.

Considering bond fund costs

Low costs are even more essential in picking a bond fund than they are in picking a stock fund. When you're looking at maybe earning a percent or two above inflation today — it's also highly possible you'll earn less than inflation — paying a manager even 1.2 percent a year is going to cut your profits in half . . . more than half if you are paying taxes on the bond dividends. Do you really care to do that?

The most economical bond funds are index funds, and you have a number of excellent index bond mutual funds to choose from. The index bond ETFs we highlight in this chapter include some of the cheapest funds on the planet, which is a reason to like them.

Although we're big proponents of ETFs, we must tell you that the ETF edge in the fixed income arena isn't nearly as sharp as it is in stocks. Bonds pay interest — that's how you make money with bonds — and they rarely see any substantial capital gains. To the extent that they do have capital gains, however, ETFs may have an edge over mutual funds. But that's generally not going to be any big deal.

In the next section, we provide a menu of bond ETFs. These are, by and large, very good options for the fixed-income side of your portfolio.

Sampling Your Basic Bond-ETF Menu

When it comes to bond ETFs, there's actually a lot of choice in Canada. Most investors will want to hold some Canadian government bonds, and most of the firms that sell ETFs have some good options. What you decide to buy will depend on what kind of bonds you want to hold — you can buy short-term, long-term, government, higher yielding, or currency hedged ETFs, and more.

That said, many investors will also want to look at U.S. options, especially corporate and high-yield bonds. Our corporate market isn't nearly as developed as it is down south. There are simply way more companies in America than there are here. It's similar to stocks — there are some things you can only buy in the States, and if you want a truly diversified portfolio, you need to look outside of Canada. However, start with what we have here and then build out from there.

Please note that with the discussion of each bond ETF, we include the *current yield:* how much each share is paying as a percentage of your investment on the day we're writing this chapter. We do so only to give you a flavour of how the yields differ among the funds. Current yields on a bond or bond fund, especially a long-term bond or bond fund, can change dramatically from week to week. So, too, can the difference in yields between short- and long-term bonds (known as the yield *curve*). You can check the current yield of any bond fund, as well as the yield curve, on the sites of the ETF providers themselves (see Appendix A) or on general investing sites such as www.morningstar.ca.

Note that several different kinds of bond yield exist. (For detailed information, once again we refer you to Russell's book *Bond Investing For Dummies.*) For the sake of consistency, the bond yield we refer to when talking about Canadian ETFs is *Distribution Yield.* What does that mean? Basically, it's the annual yield an investor would get if a fund's distribution always stayed the same. This isn't the total return of the fund; it represents a single distribution. It's not an exact science either, especially considering that the makeup of a fund can change and then that would affect the yield. Still, it's a good indication of the type of income an investor can receive from a particular bond ETF.

Buying broad-based funds

For decades, the most popular type of fixed income investment has been the government bond. Why? Because it's always been highly unlikely that Canada, the U.S., and other developed nations would default on their debt obligations. A government bond has been about as risk free of an asset as you can get.

Since the recession, however, some government bonds have lost that risk-free status and may actually be dangerous to hold — think Greek or Spanish bonds. Other government bonds, especially Canadian fixed income bonds, are perceived as safe-haven investments because the chance of our country going bust is next to nothing. Although it's great that people have so much confidence in our financial health, the popularity of our bonds — and the little risk associated with them — means that interest rates are incredibly low. At the time of writing, a ten-year government bond yields around 1.8 percent.

Still, many investors will want to hold some government bonds as a way to protect their portfolios from another downfall. Because these investments are so safe, it's almost certain that they won't fall in value if we experience another crash, or at least they won't drop that much. Fortunately, owning bonds is easy for ETF investors. A number of Canadian government ETFs exist, and they come in all shapes and sizes. You can buy short-term or long-term Government of Canada ETFs, and you can get access to provincial bonds — which are still pretty safe, but they do have a higher yield than federally issued bonds — too.

We start off with some of the broader Canadian bond ETFs. The following picks should serve most investors well. They're diversified and hold a variety of debt instruments. For savvier shoppers, you can diversify with shorter-duration and higher-yielding options. We'll get to those later.

iShares DEX Universe Bond Index Fund (XBB)

Indexed to: The DEX Universe Bond Index, the main bond benchmark in the country; this index includes government and corporate fixed income

Expense ratio: 0.30 percent

Distribution yield: None

Average weighted maturity: 9.71 years

Bryan's review: With nearly $2 billion in assets under management, this is one of the most popular Canadian bond ETFs. That shouldn't come as a surprise. With 730 holdings in federal, provincial, and corporate bonds, it offers an incredibly well-diversified basket of securities. In January 2013, it held nearly 40 percent of its assets in Government of Canada bonds, almost 29 percent in provincial issues, and the rest in company fixed income. (About 13 percent is in the financial sector.) Perhaps the one downside is that it has a longer average maturity than some other bond funds, so if interest rates rise, the ETF's price may fall. Although it does have 13 percent of its holdings in bonds with a 25-year-plus maturity date — long-term bonds are more interest rate sensitive than short-term ones — 41 percent of this ETF's assets mature in one to five years. So don't worry too much about the term.

BMO Aggregate Bond Index ETF (ZAG)

Indexed to: The DEX UniverseXM Bond Index, which is basically the DEX Universe Bond Index minus municipal bonds

Expense ratio: 0.20 percent

Distribution yield: 3.47 percent

Average weighted maturity: 9.61 years

Bryan's review: One significant difference exists between this broad-based bond ETF and XBB: price. For some, the fact that this is cheaper, and significantly so, will make the decision as to which fund to buy easy. But you should be aware of a few things. Most of this fund is invested in other BMO ETFs, such as the BMO Short Federal Bond ETF and the BMO Short Corporate Bond ETF. That's not necessarily a bad thing, but this ETF isn't actually holding the bonds themselves, at least in this particular fund. (The bonds are being held in the other ETFs.) Still, it offers the same broad diversification — minus access to municipal bonds, which won't matter much — as XBB. If price is all that matters, then take a closer look.

Vanguard Canadian Aggregate Bond Index ETF (VAB)

Indexed to: Barclays Capital Global Aggregate Canadian Float Adjusted Bond Index

Expense ratio: 0.20 percent

Distribution yield: 3 percent

Average weighted maturity: 10.40 years

Bryan's review: No big difference exists between VAB and XBB, other than price. It's broadly diversified, with holdings in federal, provincial, municipal, and corporate bonds, and it's also got a healthy portion of assets in short-term issues. The main downside is that it's fairly new — it launched at the end of 2011 — so it doesn't have as long a track record as the others. However, between December 2011 and January 2013, it slightly outperformed XBB.

Keep it short

Although a broad-based fund like XBB should cover all of an investor's bases, if you're a little more risk-averse then you may want to own a short-term bond fund instead. In today's low interest rate environment, short duration bonds are a better buy because their prices will fall less than long bonds when rates rise. In other words, short-term bonds are a less volatile form of fixed income. Of course, because you're taking on less risk, yields will be lower. Still, if you're really worried about rising interest rates, then consider these short-term fixed income ETFs.

iShares DEX Short Term Bond Index Fund (XSB)

Indexed to: The DEX Short Term Bond Index, a broadly diversified index of bonds with maturity dates of between one and five years

Expense ratio: 0.25 percent

Distribution yield: 2.77 percent

Average weighted maturity: 2.83 years

Bryan's review: This fund — the largest bond ETF in the country, with more than $2.2 billion in assets under management — is ideal for investors who don't want to put their fixed income portfolios at risk. With 52 percent of its holdings in federal bonds, 13 percent in provincial, and most of the rest in corporates (it has 22 percent in financials), it's almost as well-diversified as the broad-based funds. The only difference is duration. Nearly 93 percent of this fund is in bonds that mature between one and five years. Although this fund's price will still fall if rates rise, it will fall much less than funds with longer durations.

Vanguard Canadian Short-Term Bond Index ETF (VSB)

Indexed to: The Barclays Capital Global Aggregate Canadian Government/ Credit 1–5 Year Float Adjusted Bond Index

Expense ratio: 0.19 percent

Distribution yield: 2.50 percent

Average weighted maturity: 3 years

Bryan's review: Vanguard is clearly trying to compete in Canada on price. This fund isn't much different than XSB, but it's a lot cheaper, which, in this case, is all that matters. The fund hasn't been around as long as XSB, so it's lacking a track record, but with the Vanguard name behind it and the lower management fee, this fund will likely be siphoning off assets from its iShares counterpart soon.

BMO Short Federal Bond Index ETF (ZFS)

Indexed to: The DEX Short Term Federal Bond Index

Expense ratio: 0.20 percent

Distribution yield: 2.53 percent

Average weighted maturity: 2.70 years

Bryan's review: For the truly risk-averse, there's this short-term government bond ETF. It holds only AAA-rated Canadian federal fixed income bonds with maturity dates of between one and five years. Because it holds no corporates, its yield is lower, but that won't matter much to people who want this ETF. Buy ZFS only if you want to take on essentially no risk. Otherwise, stick to XBB or VSB.

Bonds, bonds, and more bonds

Too many Canadian fixed income ETFs exist for us to go through each one, but needless to say there's something for everyone. For instance, in January 2013 First Asset launched a provincial bond ETF (PXF) that tracks, you guessed it, provincial bonds. BMO also has a provincial bond ETF (ZPS) in addition to a real-return bond ETF (ZRR) — *real return* is another way to say *inflation-protected* — a mid-term federal bond ETF (ZFM), and much more. RBC has a slate of target-date corporate bond ETFs. You can also buy long-term bond ETFs, which would pay more right now, but they'll certainly fall in price when rates rise. If you want to get more creative, talk to an advisor to see which fund best suits your portfolio. Otherwise, stick to the basics, such as XBB.

Banking on business: Corporate bond ETFs

We think you should consider one other type of bond: debt issues by corporations. Corporate bonds come in a dizzying array of maturities, yields, and ratings, which is why buying these things through an ETF is usually better. Corporate bonds typically pay higher rates than government bonds do (historically about 1 percent a year higher), so you can expect the long-term payout from this type of ETF to be higher than any government bond ETF, except perhaps for the longest of the long-term government bond ETFs.

Understanding bond ratings

The highest bond rating — AAA — is usually reserved for governments. Why? Because things have to get pretty bad for a government to default on its debt obligations. Governments have a host of tools to raise money, like increasing taxes, so even if the wallet gets tight, they can raise more money to pay back the dollars you loaned them.

However, a government's AAA rating isn't guaranteed anymore. In August 2011, the credit rating agency Standard & Poor's (S&P) downgraded U.S. Treasury bonds from the highest rating (AAA) to a smidgeon below (AA+). Other bond raters didn't follow suit. Despite S&P's dramatic announcement, U.S. Treasury bonds are still considered by nearly all to be the safest bonds in the land (though Government of Canada bonds are technically safer because they still have an AAA rating) because they're backed by the full faith and credit of the U.S. government.

Bonds issued by corporations can vary in safety from quite high to very low, depending on the financial strength of the issuer. The financial strength of the issuer is judged by credit rating agencies such as S&P and Moody's. Following are the most common ratings.

S&P Rating	Moody's Rating	Quality	What It Means
AAA	Aaa	Highest grade	Your money is safe; there's no risk of default.
AA	Aa	High grade	Your money is safe; there's almost no risk of default.
A	A	Medium grade	Your money is likely safe.
BBB	Baa	A little shaky	Your money is probably safe.
BB	Ba	Somewhat speculative	With a little luck, you'll get your money back.
B	B	Very speculative	With a lotta luck, you'll get your money back.
CCC	Caa	Possibly in default	Pray!
CC	Ca	Toilet paper	Pray harder!

Keep in mind that Canada doesn't have a deep corporate bond market, so although there are domestic corporate bond ETFs that should be considered in a portfolio, you may want to look at some U.S. options — which we list after the Canadian ones — to create a more diverse corporate bond portfolio.

In the area of corporate bonds, credit ratings are essential. Know that the average bond rating of the iShares DEX All Corporate Bond Index Fund is A, which means, more or less, that the bonds are issued by companies that are fairly solvent (although certainly not on a par with the Canadian government — yet, anyway). See the sidebar "Understanding bond ratings" if you wish to know more.

In addition to the corporate bonds we list here, consider the following: BMO has mid-term, long-term, and high-yield U.S. corporate bond ETFs (ZCM, ZLC, and ZHY, respectively). iShares has a one- to ten-year laddered corporate bond fund (CBH) and a popular corporate bond that tracks the DEX All Corporate Bond Index Fund (XCB). And other companies offer even more options.

iShares 1–5 Year Laddered Corporate Bond Index Fund (CBO)

Indexed to: DEX 1–5 Year Corporate Bond Index; it's a laddered bond index that's not allowed to hold more than 60 percent in financial corporates or more than 40 percent in bank names

Expense ratio: 0.25 percent

Distribution yield: 4.41 percent

Average credit quality: A

Average weighted maturity: 2.80 years

Bryan's review: This fund was one of the most popular Claymore Investments ETFs, and it continues to do well under the iShares banner. The fund holds 38 Canadian corporate bonds — its highest weightings are in TD Bank, the Bank of Montreal, and Thomson Reuters. This fund has two benefits: The first is that all the holdings mature between one and five years. The second is that it's _laddered_ — meaning that some bonds will mature this year, some next year, and so on. The money received from the bonds that mature in 2013 will be reinvested in bonds that mature five years from now. A lot of people like this strategy because it can reduce interest rate risk. The bonds that mature in a few months will be affected less by rising rates than the ones that mature in five years will be. In other words, it's an added layer of diversification.

BMO Short Corporate Bond Index ETF (ZCS)

Indexed to: The DEX Short Term Corporate Bond Index, an index of Canadian corporate fixed income bonds with maturity dates of between one and five years

Expense ratio: 0.30 percent

Average yield to maturity: 3.52 percent

Average credit quality: A

Average weighted maturity: 2.90 years

Bryan's review: This is another short-term bond, but it's not laddered like CBO. Still, it is diversified among maturity dates, with 34 percent of its holdings coming due in two years and 33 percent in three years. One of the pluses to this ETF is that, with 188 holdings, it's far more diversified than CBO. However, nearly 70 percent of its assets are in financials, which some people, especially equity investors who already own a lot of financial stocks, may not like.

Investing in the U.S.

Although Canadian investors are probably fine with a domestic bond fund, more adventurous folks can look stateside for their fixed income. It's just another way to diversify and get exposure to different markets, which is never a bad thing. Be aware of currency risk, because you're buying these funds in U.S. dollars. Here are some potentially useful U.S.-based bond funds.

Note: U.S. funds use what's called an SEC yield. Here's how it works: If you (or the fund manager) were to hold to maturity each and every one of the bonds in a fund's portfolio, as they stood over the past 30 days, and reinvest all interest payments (that is, you plow those interest payments right back into your bond portfolio), your SEC yield is what you'd get over the course of a year. It takes into account all fund fees and expenses. The formula was created, and the methodology is enforced, by the U.S. Securities and Exchange Commission, which is where the "SEC" in the formula's name comes from.

iShares iBoxx $ Investment Grade Corporate Bond Fund (LQD)

Indexed to: The iBoxx $ Liquid Investment Grade Index — an index of bond issues sponsored by a chorus line of companies rated *investment grade* (which means highly unlikely to go bankrupt any time soon) or above. Technically, we're speaking of bonds rated BBB or better by S&P. About 600 bonds are typically used to create a representative sampling of this universe.

Expense ratio: 0.15 percent

Current SEC yield: 2.93 percent

Average credit quality: A

Average weighted maturity: 12 years

Russell's review: Investment-grade corporate bonds have done a pretty good job of holding their own in bad times. You get a bit more return than you do with government bonds of equal maturity. This fund is nicely diversified with investments in all the major sectors.

Vanguard Short-Term Corporate Bond ETF (VCSH)

Indexed to: The Barclays U.S. 1–5 Year Corporate Index, a pot of about 1,400 bonds from corporations that the raters think have little chance of going belly up

Expense ratio: 0.12 percent

Current SEC yield: 1.22 percent

Average credit quality: A

Average weighted maturity: 3 years

Russell's review: For more conservative investors especially, VCSH, during times of very low interest rates, may warrant half your U.S. bond allocation to corporate bonds. When interest rates start to climb back up to more normal historical levels, you may then want to move some or all of the money in VCSH to LQD.

Vanguard Total Bond Market (BND)

Indexed to: The Barclays Capital U.S. Aggregate Float Adjusted Index, which is made up of about 8,000 bonds, two-thirds of which are U.S. government bonds and one-third of which are higher quality corporate bonds

Expense ratio: 0.10 percent

Current SEC yield: 1.59 percent

Average credit quality: AA

Average weighted maturity: 7.10 years

Russell's review: How can you go wrong with the world's largest provider of index funds tracking the entire U.S. bond market for you and charging you only 0.10 percent (that's 10 percent of 1 percent)? It's a great way for a Canadian to get total exposure to the U.S. bond market.

Vanguard Short-Term Bond (BSV)

Indexed to: The Barclays Capital U.S. 1–5 Year Government/Credit Float Adjusted Index, which is about 2,300 bonds, two-thirds of which are short-term U.S. government and one-third of which are higher quality corporate bonds, also of short-term maturity

Expense ratio: 0.11 percent

Current SEC yield: 0.53 percent

Average credit quality: AA

Average weighted maturity: 2.80 years

Russell's review: If you're worried about rising interest rates, consider this fund over BND. When interest rates start to climb back up to historical norms, you may then want to move some or all of your U.S. fixed income assets out of BSV and into BND.

Moving Beyond Basics: Foreign Bonds

Every investor needs bonds. Not every investor needs foreign bonds. But for those with larger bond portfolios, the added diversification of foreign bonds is something to consider very seriously.

Foreign bonds for fixed income diversification

Over the long haul, bonds of similar default risk and maturity will likely yield about the same percentage. But in the short run, substantial differences can exist in the yields and total returns of Canadian versus foreign bonds. The big difference is often due to currency exchange rates. If you are holding foreign bonds and the dollar drops *vis-à-vis* your foreign currencies, your foreign bond funds tend to do better. If the dollar rises, you'll likely be disappointed in your foreign bond fund returns.

If you follow our advice on the stock side of the portfolio and allocate roughly half your equities to overseas positions, you'll have plenty of exposure to foreign currencies. But still, if you have a fairly large portfolio and half or more of it is in bonds, allocating perhaps 10 to 25 percent of your bonds to overseas ETFs such as the ones we discuss next would enhance the benefits you can achieve from diversification. At the same time, you should understand that because of their exposure to foreign currencies, these bond funds tend to be more volatile than Canadian and U.S. bond funds.

Note that as is the case with Canadian bonds, international bonds can be of the conventional type or inflation adjusted. Whereas we believe strongly that inflation-protected bonds deserve an allotment in most portfolios, foreign inflation-protected bonds just don't make as much sense (unless you plan to retire abroad or take a lot of senior world cruises). Nevertheless, for the sake of added diversification, if you want to add a small dose of inflation-adjusted foreign bonds to your portfolio, we won't object.

As you can see in our recommendations, we have a preference for the iShares offerings in the foreign bond arena.

iShares S&P/Citigroup International Treasury Bond Fund (IGOV)

Indexed to: The S&P/Citigroup International Treasury Bond Index Ex-US, which holds about 100 bonds that, collectively, track the sovereign debt of developed foreign nations, mostly in Western Europe and Japan

Expense ratio: 0.35

Current SEC yield: 1.79 percent

Average credit quality: AA

Average weighted maturity: 8.40 years

Top five countries: Japan, Italy, France, Germany, United Kingdom

Russell's review: This may be your best option for one-shot foreign bond exposure. Be aware that while you can buy this fund in U.S. dollars, its holdings are denominated in other currencies. Your returns will therefore be very dependent on the euro-USD or Japanese yen-USD exchange rate. (And then the USD-CDN rate if you want to convert your investment back into loonies.) It also holds about 4 percent of its assets in Canadian bonds, so you should decrease your domestic exposure by that amount if you want to hold this.

iShares International Inflation-Linked Bond Fund (ITIP)

Indexed to: The BofA Merrill Lynch Global ex-US Diversified Inflation-Linked Index, which compiles about 40 inflation-linked bonds of both developed and emerging-market nations

Expense ratio: 0.40 percent

Current SEC yield: 3.92 percent + inflation bump

Average credit quality: AA

Average weighted maturity: 12.40 years

Top five countries: Brazil, United Kingdom, France, Italy, Mexico

Russell's review: This fund will mitigate any rise in inflation, which is a good thing. It, too, has about 4 percent of its assets in Canada, so, again, reduce your domestic bond exposure if you buy this security.

Emerging-market bonds: High risk, high return

We don't like U.S. high-yield ("junk") bonds and there aren't enough Canadian junk bonds to choose from. American high-yield bonds tend to be highly volatile, and they tend to move up and down with the stock market. In other words, they don't provide much of the diversification power or soft cushion that bonds are famous for. Foreign junk bonds are different. These bonds, issued by the governments of countries that may not be entirely stable, are just as volatile as bonds issued by unstable U.S. corporations, but they don't tend to go up and down with the U.S. stock market (although they certainly may at times . . . and did so in 2008).

For reasons of diversification, investors with fairly good sized portfolios may want to consider allocating a modest part of their portfolios to emerging-market debt. In Russell's personal portfolio, he has allocated 5 percent of the total to this asset class. Note that we're not referring to Russell's "bond portfolio" but to his "portfolio." He actually thinks of his holdings in emerging-market debt as more of a stock-like investment than a true bond investment. After all, you're likely to see stock-like volatility and long-term stock-like returns with these investments.

Although these ETFs have been around for only a few years, emerging-market bond mutual funds have been in existence for much longer. The T. Rowe Price Emerging Markets Bond Fund (PREMX), for example, has a 15-year average annual return of 11.45 percent. But there has been volatility, for sure: In 2008, the fund lost nearly 18 percent of its value.

iShares J.P. Morgan USD Emerging Markets Bond Fund (EMB)

Indexed to: The JPMorgan EMBI Global Core Index, which is made up of about 80 bond issues, all U.S. dollar denominated, from various emerging-market nations

Expense ratio: 0.60

Current SEC yield: 3.29 percent

Average credit quality: BBB

Average weighted maturity: 11.84 years

Top five countries: Brazil, Russia, Turkey, Mexico, Philippines

Russell's review: The expense ratio is a bit high, but there isn't a lot of choice in this arena. The iShares fund is a perfectly good way to tap into this asset class. You can also buy a Canadian-dollar hedged version from iShares Canada.

PowerShares Emerging Markets Sovereign Debt Portfolio (PCY)

Indexed to: The DB Emerging Market USD Liquid Balanced Index, which tracks the returns of approximately 22 emerging-market sovereign bonds

Expense ratio: 0.50

Current SEC yield: 3.94 percent

Average credit quality: BB–BBB

Average weighted maturity: 15.40 years

Top five countries: Turkey, Hungary, Romania, Croatia, Lithuania

Russell's review: This fund is slightly cheaper than the iShares emerging-market fund, and I like that. And I like the higher yield, too. But the dicey mix of nations and lengthy average maturity also make this fund considerably more volatile. (Ah, that old risk and return thing again!) In 2008, this fund lost 18.79 percent; EMB, in contrast, lost 2.09 percent in that sorry year.

Determining the Optimal Fixed Income Allocation

Okay, now that we've discussed which bonds to buy, it's time to tackle the really tough question: How much of your portfolio should you allocate to (non-emerging-market) bonds? The common thinking on the subject — and we're not above common thinking, especially when it is right on the mark — is that a portfolio becomes more conservative as its percentage allocation to bonds increases.

Of course, that doesn't answer the $64,000 question (or however much that question would now be worth with inflation factored in): Just how conservative do you want your portfolio to be? Different financial planners use different approaches to arrive at an answer to this question. We feel confident that our approach is best (otherwise, we wouldn't use it); in the interest of brevity, let us present it in the simplest terms.

Here's our take: We reckon that stocks are very likely — but by no means certain — to outperform bonds over the next decade or two. But as in the past, we will see up years and down years in both markets. The down years in the stock market are the far more dangerous. Bear stock markets, historically, don't last for more than a few years, although some have been particularly brutal and have lasted a decade or more. (Think about the 1930s, the late 1960s to mid 1970s, and 2000 to 2009.)

Yet for most investors over the past 100 years, stocks have paid off handsomely. So it's a balancing act. Too much in the way of stocks and, should the markets go sour, you risk quick poverty. Too much in the way of bonds and, should consumer prices rise too much, you risk slow poverty as the interest you collect just barely stays ahead of inflation, or not even that, and you are forced to eat into your capital to pay the bills. In this section, we show you how to begin thinking about your own balancing act.

60/40? 50/50? Finding a split that makes sense

The balance between stocks and bonds is usually expressed as "[% stocks]/[% bonds]," so a 60/40 portfolio means 60 percent stocks and 40 percent bonds. The optimal balance for any given person depends on many factors: age, size of portfolio, income stream, financial responsibilities, economic safety net, and emotional tolerance for risk.

In general, we like to see working investors hold three to six months of living expenses in cash (money markets or high-interest savings accounts) or near-cash (very short-term bond funds or short-term GICs). Non-working investors living largely off their portfolios should set aside much more, perhaps one to two years of living expenses. Beyond that, most people's portfolios, whether they're working or not, should be allocated to stocks (including REITs, which we discuss in Chapter 13), intermediate-term bonds, and perhaps a few alternative investments, such as market-neutral funds and commodities (including precious metals).

 In determining an optimal split, we would first ask you to pick a date when you think you may need to start withdrawing money from your nest egg. How much do you anticipate needing to withdraw? Maybe $30,000 a year? Or $40,000? If you haven't given this question much thought, please do! Start with your current job income. Subtract what you believe you'll be getting in CPP and OAS payments or other pension income. The difference is what you would need to pull from your portfolio to replicate your current income. But most retirees find they need perhaps 80 to 90 percent of their working-days income to live comfortably. (You likely put less in the gas tank, buy fewer lunches out, have lower wardrobe expenses, and pay lower taxes.)

Take a minute, please. Come up with a rough number of how much you're going to need to take from your nest egg each year.

Got it?

Whatever the number, multiply it by 10. That amount, ideally, is what we'd like to see you have in your bond portfolio, at a minimum, on the day you retire. In other words, if you think you'll need to pull $30,000 a year from your portfolio, we'd like to see you have at least $30,000 in cash and about $300,000 ($30,000 × 10) in bonds. That's regardless of how much you have in stocks — and, with the assumptions outlined above, you should have at least an equal amount in stocks. (See more on building an adequate nest egg in Chapter 19.)

So here's the rough rule we're suggesting (keeping in mind, please, that all rough rules can get you into trouble sometimes): If you are still in your 20s or 30s and want to keep the vast lion's share of your portfolio in stocks, fine. But as you get older and start to think about quitting your day job, begin to increase your bond allocation with the aim of getting to your retirement date with at least ten times your anticipated post-retirement withdrawals in bonds. Most people (who aren't rich) should have roughly one year's income in cash and the rest in a 50/50 (stock/bond) portfolio on retirement day.

With at least one year's living expenses in cash and ten years of living expenses in bonds, you can live off the non-stock side of your portfolio for a good amount of time if the stock market goes into a swoon. (You then hope that the stock market recovers.)

If this rule seems too complex, you can always go with an even rougher rule that has appeared in countless magazines. It says you should subtract your age from 110, and that's what you should have, more or less, in stocks, with the rest in bonds. So a 50-year-old should have (110 – 50) 60 percent in stocks and 40 percent in bonds. A 60-year-old would want a portfolio of about (110 – 60) 50 percent stocks and 50 percent bonds. And so on and so on. This rough rule — even rougher than ours! — may not be bad, assuming that you are of average wealth, are going to retire at the average age, will live the average life expectancy, and expect that the markets will see roughly average performance!

Meet Joe, age 67, with a little more than $600,000 in the bank

Consider Joe. He's a single guy with no kids who figures he's going to retire in one year. His salary is $45,000 a year ($35,000 after taxes). He has $600,000 in investments. He also has about $35,000 in cash and short-term GICs. He estimates that after CPP and his very decent government pension, he needs to pull another $24,000 a year out of savings to pay all the bills. It seems to us that Joe can do that and have a very good chance that his money will last as long as he lives. (Chapter 19 explains why.) How much should Joe invest in bonds and how much in stocks?

As a ballpark figure, without knowing much more about Joe (and ignoring for the moment such sticky things as present value and future taxes and Joe's expected longevity), we'd start by urging Joe to keep the amount he has in cash and short-term GICs ("near cash") exactly where it is. Then we'd take about $240,000 ($24,000 × 10) of the $600,000 and plunk it into a handful of fixed income funds that would almost certainly include a conventional bond (such as XBB), a real-return bond fund (perhaps the iShares Real Return Bond Index Fund (XRB)), and a high-quality corporate bond fund (such as the iShares 1–5 Year Laddered Government Bond Index Fund (CLF)).

We'd invest the rest of Joe's money in a widely diversified portfolio made up mostly of stock ETFs.

Thus, Joe might be looking at an allocation of $360,000 stocks/$240,000 bonds, or a 60/40 allocation. Joe also might be a good candidate for an immediate fixed annuity that would guarantee him the $24,000 a year he needs, or a good portion of it. (***Important note:*** Many annuities are financial dogs, and even the best annuities aren't for everyone. Please see our discussion in Chapter 15.)

A 60/40 allocation may be considered too risky for a 67-year-old. Many retirement models would allocate more to the tune of 50/50, or even be less aggressive than that. We would opt for a more conservative route, too, if Joe didn't have his secure pension. Note, too, that we would use 60/40 only as our starting point. After taking all aspects of Joe's personal circumstances into consideration, including his guaranteed income stream, expected longevity, risk tolerance, and legacy desires (would he be okay with the idea of dying broke?), we might end up suggesting a 50/50 portfolio, or perhaps even 40/60.

Meet Betsy and Mike, age 36, with $30,000 in the bank

Betsy and Mike are happily married. (Yes, happy is important, from both a financial and a non-financial point of view!) They both work and make decent incomes — enough so that if they needed to, they could live on one income. Betsy works in academia. Mike is a self-employed landscaper and a piano teacher. They have no children. They have no debt. They would like to retire by age 62 and do a lot of travelling.

Betsy and Mike obviously need to accumulate a lot more than $30,000 if they want to retire by their early 60s and travel to anyplace other than nearby Montreal. Their situation, we feel, warrants taking about as much risk as any investor should take. We might suggest a 75/25 portfolio, or even (if Betsy and Mike were the type of people who could emotionally handle the volatility) an

80/20 portfolio. The 25 or 20 percent in bonds — $7,500 or $6,000 — we might allocate to XBB or VAB.

We can hardly imagine any investor for whom we would want to see any portfolio more aggressive than 80/20 (80 percent stock, 20 percent bonds) or more sedate than 20/80. Here's why:

- ✔ Studies show that 20 percent in bonds doesn't really lessen a portfolio's long-term performance all that much. Reason: When the market crashes, as it does every once in a while, you want some "dry powder" (such as bonds) that you can use to take advantage of the opportunity to purchase stock at fire-sale prices.

- ✔ Conversely, 20 percent in stocks doesn't really raise a portfolio's volatility all that much (and it may even lessen the volatility). Reason: Bond prices tend to drop the most when interest rates rise sharply. Interest rates tend to rise sharply when the economy is humming and stocks are doing well. Zig and zag. When you have no zig, you are more susceptible to heavy zag. And you can quote us on that!

Chapter 13

Real Estate Investment Trusts (REITs): Becoming a Virtual Landlord

*E*ver wish you could be a real estate mogul à la Donald Trump? Sure you do. There isn't a single person who wouldn't love to own a few shopping malls, or some big office buildings, and collect thousands of dollars in rent month after month. Of course, most of us don't have the millions of dollars it would take to buy prime Bay Street real estate. However, that doesn't mean you can't own your own office building.

Investors can get access to real estate assets through *real estate investment trusts*, or *REITs,* which are, in a nutshell, companies that hold portfolios of properties, such as shopping malls, office buildings, hotels, amusement parks, or timberland. Or they may hold certain real estate-related assets, such as commercial mortgages. Many Canadian REITS are publicly held, and their stocks trade on the open market just like any other stock.

Via dozens of mutual funds, you can buy into a collection of REITs at one time. You can similarly buy a bevy of REITs via ETFs. And that may not be a bad idea. Between October 2002 and October 2012, the S&P/TSX Capped REIT Index had an annualized return of about 12 percent. That outshines by about four full percentage points per year the S&P/TSX Composite Index's 8 percent return during the same period. In the last two years — 2009 to 2012 — REITs really shined, with the index returning a 29 percent or so annualized return.

Some holders of REITs and REIT funds believe (and fervently hope) that such performance will continue. Others argue that the glory of REITs may be over. In this chapter, we provide you with several reasons why REITs deserve a permanent allocation in most portfolios.

Considering Five Distinguishing Characteristics of REITs

You may wonder why an entire chapter of this book is devoted to REIT ETFs. Why, you may ask, didn't we merely include them in Chapter 11 with the other specialized stock ETFs, like dividend and socially responsible funds? Or in Chapter 10 where we talk about industry sector ETFs? Good question!

There are *five* reasons. Any one alone probably wouldn't justify giving REITs a chapter of their very own. All five together do, however. The first three reasons explain why REITs deserve some special status in the world of investments. The last two reasons are less compelling than the first three, but we include them in the interest of completeness.

Less correlation to the broad markets

An index of Canadian REITs has evidenced a correlation of about 0.6 with the S&P/TSX Composite Index over the past ten years. That means the price of an S&P/TSX Composite index fund and the share price of a REIT index fund have tended to move in the same direction about half the time. The REIT index has practically no correlation to bonds.

Holding 20 percent REITs in your portfolio over the past ten years — regardless of whether your portfolio was made up of mostly stocks or bonds — would have both raised your returns and lowered your volatility. It's the Efficient Frontier (as we discuss in Chapter 4) in action.

Will REITs continue to work their magic? Some experts caution investors to be careful. REITs are becoming somewhat the victims of their own success. As they have become more mainstream investments, they have come to act more like other equities. Years ago, practically no one held REITS in their portfolios. Nowadays, according to one recent poll, fully two-thirds of professional money managers are using them.

Investors have also piled into REITs because they pay a hefty dividend (which we talk about next) in a low-return market. That's pushed up prices and valuations, which are higher than they've been in years. That has some people worried about REITs. If investors leave the asset class, the price could drop quickly. A falling commercial real estate market in Canada (at the time of writing, the residential market is experiencing some volatility) will affect prices too. However, the high dividends should keep people in the market until other traditional income investments, such as bonds, become attractive again.

Unusually high dividends

REITs typically deliver annual dividend yields significantly higher than even the highest dividend-paying non-REIT stocks, and twice that of the average stock. (Many stocks, of course, pay no dividends.) At the time of this writing, the iShares S&P/TSX 60 Index Fund (XIU) is producing a yield of 2.73 percent, versus 4.32 percent for the iShares S&P/TSX Capped REIT Index Fund (XRE).

So the cash usually keeps flowing regardless of whether a particular REIT's share price rises or falls, just as long as the REIT is pulling in some money. That's because REITs, which get special tax status, have a *payout ratio* — the amount of cash flow paid to shareholders in dividends — of about 80 percent. In the U.S., REITs are required, by law, to pay out 90 percent of their income as dividends. Cool, huh?

Still, REITs, like other stocks, can be expected also to see growth in share prices. Over the last decade, the Canadian REIT Index is up about 70 percent.

Different taxation of dividends

Because REITs are blessed in that they don't have to pay income taxes, their dividends are usually fully taxable to shareholders as ordinary income. In other words, whatever dividends you get will be taxed at year-end according to your income tax bracket. Few, if any, REIT dividends you receive will qualify for the special 19 percent dividend tax rate. For that reason, your accountant will undoubtedly urge you to handle your REITs a bit carefully. We urge you to do so, as well.

Special status among financial pros

The vast majority of wealth advisors — whether they primarily use style investing, sector investing, or astrology charts and tea leaves — recognize REITs as a separate asset class and tend to include it in most people's portfolios. Is that distinction logical and just? Yes, but . . . ask yourself this question: If REITs deserve that distinction of honour, what about some other industry sectors, such as utilities? After all, the utilities sector has lately shown less correlation to the S&P/TSX Composite than have REITs. Doesn't it deserve its own slice of the portfolio pie?

We don't mean to slam REITs; we like REITs. But one possible reason they are seen as a separate asset class (in addition to the three reasons we explain in the preceding sections) may be that the REIT marketers are savvier than the marketers of utility stocks (which, in addition to having low correlation to the broad market, *also* pay exceptionally high dividends).

Connection to tangible property

Some people argue that REITs are different than other stocks because they represent tangible property. Well yeah, REITs do represent stores filled with useless junk and condos filled with single people desperately look-ing for dates, and we suppose that makes them different from, say, stock in Microsoft or BCE. (Aren't Maple Leaf tickets tangible?) But the reality is that REITs are stocks. And to a great degree, they behave like stocks. If REITs are different from other stocks, dividends and reduced market correlation are the likely distinctions — not their tangibility.

Calculating a Proper REIT Allocation

These days, the main reason to buy REITs is for the income they provide. Fortunately, they also offer diversification and, if the real estate market stays strong, access to a historically well-performing asset class. In other words, your primary motivations for buying REITs should be income, diversification, and potential growth. In this section, we help you consider how much of your portfolio you may want to allot to REITs.

Judging from the past

If we could go back in time 20 years, we'd have you put, heck, *everything* in Apple. But REITs would not have been a bad option either. After all, they've done fabulously well, beating the S&P 500 and many other investments. Looking forward, of course, the picture's a bit less clear. However, we think we can presume fairly safely that REITs will continue to move in somewhat different cycles than other stocks.

We think we can also presume fairly safely that REITs will continue to produce healthy gains, although people who poured money into them more recently, after prices were run up thanks to income-seeking investors, will probably be disappointed. You will *not* see annual gains of 28+ percent a year for years to come — we're sure of that. And you *will* see some bad years, such as in late 2008 and early 2009, when the collective Canadian REIT market fell by 28 percent.

Putting all the factors together, we suggest that most investors devote 10 to 15 percent of the equity side of their portfolios to REITs. If your portfolio is 50 percent stock and 50 percent bonds, we suggest that 5 to 7.5 percent of your entire portfolio be devoted to REITs.

What if, like many people, you're a homeowner whose home represents most of your net worth? You may want to play it a little light on the REITs, but don't let the value of your home affect your portfolio decisions to any great degree. (See the sidebar "Your residence, your portfolio.")

Splitting the baby: Domestic and international REIT funds

International REITs, including American ones, are worth breaking out of your international stock holdings for all the same reasons that Canadian REITs are worth having tucked into a larger portfolio of Canadian stocks. The REIT allotment you give to your portfolio may be evenly split between Canadian and international REITs, in keeping with the 50/50 split between Canadian and non-U.S. stocks that we suggest for your overall portfolio.

As we discuss in Chapter 9, the vast majority of the world's stocks are non-Canadian; so, it stands to reason that an optimally diversified portfolio will have good exposure to foreign stocks. If you follow this advice, you may have two REIT funds, and each may be given a 4 to 5 percent allocation in your portfolio. If you have a very handsome portfolio ($500,000+), and *only* if you have such a portfolio, you may also want to consider one or two individual timber REITs, which can sometimes zig when other REITs zag.

Lumber over to Chapter 15, where we discuss how to work non-ETFs into your portfolio, and you'll get all the specifics.

Your residence, your portfolio

If you bought your home for, say, $130,000 some 26 years ago, and that home is now worth $1.3 million, we say, "Congratulations!" (Yeah, even though it may have been worth $1.6 million in 2012.) But don't let that bounty affect your portfolio decisions very much. After all, you'll always need a place to live. Sell the house today, and you'll presumably need to buy another (made of a similarly overpriced bundle of tiles and plywood).

Of course, someday you may downsize, and at that time you will be able to allot part of the value of your home to your portfolio. For that reason, and that reason alone, you may want to consider that the value of domestic real estate and the value of commercial real estate, while two different animals, are related. If your home represents a big chunk of your net worth, and especially if you are approaching a stage in life when you may consider downsizing, you may want to invest less in REITs than would, say, a renter of similar means. Or you may forget about Canadian REITs altogether and invest only in foreign REITs.

Picking REIT ETFs for Your Portfolio

If you want REITs in your portfolio, you won't get a whole lot of them unless you purchase a REIT fund. For all the room they take up, REITs simply don't make up that large a segment of the economy.

If, for example, you were to buy an S&P/TSX Composite Index fund, less than 1 percent of that fund would be made up of stock from REITs. A Canadian mid cap index fund (most REITs would probably qualify as mid caps) would have more exposure to this asset class, but it's still not enough to get the diversification we've been talking about.

So if you want to own REITs, you need to go out of your way to get them. But thanks to ETFs, doing so shouldn't be much of a hassle, and you get many of ETFs' other benefits in the bargain, including rock-bottom expenses.

Distributions on REITs are taxable as income. For that reason, all REIT funds — ETFs or otherwise — are best kept in tax-advantaged retirement accounts, such as a TFSA or RRSP.

More than 30 U.S. REIT ETFs are available — which Canadians can buy for international REIT exposure — but only two pure Canadian REIT ETFs exist. Fortunately they offer good exposure to the REIT market, and best of all, they're cheap.

If you're curious to see the whole buffet of U.S. REIT ETFs available, visit www. reit.com. In the "Investing" tab menu, click on "Investor Categories," then "Individual Investors." Under the "List of REIT Funds," click on "Exchange-Traded Funds." You'll notice that some are leveraged (such as ProShares Ultra Real Estate (URE)), but stay away from these ones for reasons we discuss in Chapter 11. Others are focused on slivers of the REIT market (such as the iShares FTSE NAREIT Industrial/Office Capped Index Fund (FNIO)), and we'd rather you steer clear of those, too. (You can slice and dice a portfolio to death, but why do so?) Of what's left, several are quite good.

Canadian domestic REIT ETFs

Two REIT ETFs exist in Canada — one is offered by the Bank of Montreal and the other is by (who else?) iShares. Here, we go through each one.

iShares S&P/TSX Capped REIT Index Fund (XRE)

Indexed to: The S&P/TSX Capped REIT Index, which tracks roughly half of the Canadian REIT market and only companies that are on the S&P/TSX Composite Index

Expense ratio: 0.55 percent

Number of holdings: 14

Top five holdings: RioCan, H&R REIT, Dundee REIT, Calloway REIT, Cominar REIT

Bryan's review: For about eight years, until 2010, this ETF was the only option for index-hungry REIT investors. So it's no surprise that it's, by far, the biggest REIT ETF in the country, with a net asset value of $1.4 billion. This fund holds most of the big-name REITs, so you're getting access to quality companies that own a lot of property. Unlike its competition, it's not equal weighted, so portfolio allocation percentages change depending on the market cap of each company. As of this writing, RioCan accounts for 20.55 percent of the fund, much more than the second-largest holding, H&R, which makes up 11.76 percent. If RioCan makes a spectacular mistake and its share price is affected, the ETF's price will certainly be affected. Some people don't like these types of funds because too much of the portfolio is weighted to one company. That doesn't necessarily make it better or worse than the alternative — it really comes down to preference.

BMO Equal Weight REITs Index ETF (ZRE)

Indexed to: Dow Jones Canada Select Equal Weight REIT Index, which tracks a number of TSX-listed REITs. These companies do not have to be part of the S&P/TSX Composite Index

Expense ratio: 0.55

Number of holdings: 19

Top five holdings: Chartwell Seniors Housing, Dundee International REIT, Allied Properties REIT, Boardwalk REIT, Brookfield Office Properties Canada

Bryan's review: This is the latest (and second) entrant to the REIT ETF game. This BMO fund was launched in 2010 and offers a solid alternative to the XRE. With only $322 million in assets, it's small right now, but you can bet it'll grow. Two main differences between this fund and the iShares offering exist. Because ZRE isn't tied to the S&P/TSX Composite, it can own REITs that XRE can't, so it's more diversified (it also holds some smaller operations) than its competitor. The bigger difference, though, is that it's equal weighted, which means every company gets roughly the same weighting in the ETF — about 5 percent. In this fund, RioCan makes up just 5.47 percent of the portfolio — far less than it does in XRE. Its largest holding, Chartwell, accounts for only 5.88 percent of the portfolio. ZRE's returns were about 2 percent higher between January and October 2012 (when we wrote this chapter), so there's not a clear winner between ZRE and XRE. The decision really depends on how much of each company you want your ETF to own.

U.S. and global REIT ETFs

If you want to get adventurous, you can buy U.S. and international REIT ETFs. Here are some non-Canadian investments that can help diversify your portfolio.

Vanguard REIT Index ETF (VNQ)

Indexed to: The MSCI U.S. REIT Index, which tracks roughly two-thirds of the U.S. REIT market

Expense ratio: 0.10 percent

Number of holdings: 111

Top five holdings: Simon Property Group, Inc., Public Storage, HCP, Ventas REIT, Equity Residential

Russell's review: Once again, Vanguard brings to market the most economical investment vehicle. You can't find a better way to invest in the U.S. REIT market than through VNQ. This is a broadly based ETF with an ultra-low expense ratio. Be aware, however, that even with all the advantages of an ETF, this ETF, because of its distributions, will represent something of a tax burden. For that reason, consider purchasing an ETF as a long-term investment and keeping it in a tax-advantaged retirement account.

Vanguard Global ex-U.S. Real Estate ETF (VNQI)

Indexed to: The S&P Global ex-U.S. Property Index, which tracks the performance of REITs in both developed and emerging markets outside of the United States

Expense ratio: 0.35 percent

Number of holdings: 463

Top five holdings: Mitsubishi Estate Company, Sun Hung Kai Properties, Westfield Group, Cheung Kong Holdings, Unibail-Rodamco

Top five countries: Japan, Hong Kong, Australia, Singapore, United Kingdom

Russell's review: Go for it. No less expensive way exists to tap into this asset class. However, be aware that the fund does hold 4.7 percent of its assets in Canadian REITs. That's not a ton, so you won't be too exposed to Canada if you own a domestic REIT too, but just keep this in mind as you're allocating funds to real estate investments. Also be aware that foreign REITs, like all foreign stocks, are going to be subject to currency flux as well as market volatility. (As well, you'll have to buy the ETF in U.S. dollars, so there's currency risk there too.) In other words, expect a bit more of a rollercoaster ride with this and all non-currency hedged foreign ETFs than you would expect of domestic ETFs.

SPDR Dow Jones Global Real Estate (RWO)

Indexed to: The Dow Jones Global Real Estate Securities Index, an index based on the publicly traded real estate market in both developed and emerging-market nations

Expense ratio: 0.50 percent

Number of holdings: 213

Top five holdings: Simon Property Group, Inc., Westfield Group, Unibail-Rodamco, Public Storage, HCP

Top five countries: United States (54 percent of the fund), Australia, Japan, United Kingdom, Hong Kong

Russell's review: This may be a good ETF for someone who wants exposure to the U.S. and the rest of the world. It holds REITs from 17 countries — but it, too, has around 4.7 percent of its holdings in Canadian companies — and has a healthy weighting to American operations. The one downside is its fees. Purchase VNQ and VNQI, and you'll wind up with a similar mix of REITs for less money.

Chapter 14

All That Glitters: Gold, Silver, and Other Commodities

*O*ne of Russell's childhood passions was collecting coins from around the world. Sometime during the Johnson administration, on his meagre allowance of $1 a week, he saved up for three months or so to buy himself a gold coin: an uncirculated 1923 50-kurush piece from Turkey. Maybe you can remember getting a shiny new bicycle for Christmas when you were 5 or 6. Maybe, like Citizen Kane, you remember getting your first sled. His most prized possession from childhood was that gold coin, smaller than a dime but absolutely gorgeous.

He still has it.

Most coin-collecting kids don't think of their pieces of gold as investments. But for many people, gold is just that. Historically, the soft and shiny metal has been seen as the ultimate hedge against both inflation and market turmoil. Most people through the ages have bought gold: as coins, or sometimes in bricks. Alternatively, in more recent decades, they may have invested in shares of gold-mining companies.

Whether people invested in the physical metal or the stock of companies that mined it, the traditional ways of investing in gold have always been a pain in the neck. With shares of gold-mining companies, factors other than the price of gold come into play. For example, political turbulence in South Africa, or a fall in the value of the rand, might send your stock down the mines. Buying gold coins entails hefty commissions. Likewise for gold bricks, with possible added expenses for assaying. And both bricks and coins have to be stored and should be insured.

All these hassles became optional for gold investors with the introduction of the first gold ETF in November 2004. Suddenly it became possible to buy gold at its spot price — in an instant — with very little commission and no need to fret about storage or insurance. Thanks to ETFs, you can now also buy silver in the same way. Or platinum.

In fact, you can invest in just about any commodity you please. You can invest in just about any precious or industrial metal: tin, nickel, you name it. Even natural gas, or crude oil, if that's your cup of Texas tea, can be purchased (sort of) with an ETF, as can coffee futures and contracts on wheat, sugar, or corn. Indeed, it seems the only commodity that's not available for purchase by the retail investor is weapons-grade plutonium.

In this chapter, we discuss the whys and wherefores of investing in commodity ETFs, as well as certain commodity pools and exchange-traded notes (products that differ from ETFs). We also explain why investing in ETFs that feature stocks of commodity-producing companies and countries may be a somewhat better long-term play than investing in the commodities themselves.

Oh, by the way, Russell recently saw that a 50-kurush gold coin just like his sold online for $219. But he makes it clear that he's not selling!

Canada and Commodities

Before we get into the nitty gritty, we must point out that it's nearly impossible for Canadian investors not to hold some commodities. The energy and materials sectors make up a big chunk of our market, so you don't actually need to buy a commodity fund to get exposure to things like oil, gas, and gold. If you own just XIU, you'll have a 23.8 percent weighting to energy sector stocks and 15 percent to materials companies. Buy a dividend fund on top of that, and you'll have even more.

For most Canadians, that's enough, but savvier investors who have a particular investment idea can still add specific exposures by using ETFs. For instance, if you think natural gas prices are going to rise, then maybe you want to buy a fund that holds more natural gas companies. Holding gold, as we explain next, does help with diversification, so you still may want to hold a bit. If however, you want only a 5 percent exposure to gold and the domestic fund you hold has a 4 percent weighting, then invest just 1 percent of your assets in a gold-related fund.

Knowing about energy and commodity funds specifically is still important, but keep in mind that you've likely already got a good weighting to these sectors.

Gold, Gold, Gold!

Stocks and bonds rise and fall. Currencies ebb and flow. Economies go boom and then bust. Inflation tears nest eggs apart. And through it all, gold retains its value. Or so we're told.

The primary reason for buying gold, according to the World Gold Council (www.gold.org), is that

> *Market cycles come and go, but gold has maintained its long term value. Jastram [1977] demonstrated that in inflationary and deflationary times, in the very long term, gold kept its purchasing power. The value of gold, in terms of real goods and services that it can buy, has remained remarkably stable.*

Hmm. We're not sure who Jastram was, and we don't know exactly what is meant by "very long term," but we've done a bit of research on this subject. Although we don't claim that our research is exhaustive or in any way conclusive regarding the investment merits of gold, it does cast *some* doubt on the veracity of the World Gold Council's claim.

Table 14-1 shows the price of gold in a sampling of years between 1980 and 2010; the average price of a basic Hershey chocolate bar in those years (which we found on a website called www.foodtimeline.org); and how many Hershey bars you could buy with an ounce of gold. Note that one ounce of gold in 1980 bought 2,460 Hershey bars, but 20 years later, in 2000, it bought a mere 558 bars. At 2010 prices — about $1,500 for an ounce of gold and about 80 cents for a Hershey bar — you'd get 1,875 chocolate bars for the same nugget.

Table 14-1	Trading Gold for Hershey Bars		
Year	*Average price of a Hershey bar*	*Average price of an ounce of gold*	*Hershey bars per ounce of gold*
1980	$0.25	$615	2,460
2000	$0.50	$279	558
2010	$0.80	$1,500	1,875

Midas touch or fool's gold?

Okay, we'll give the World Gold Council the benefit of the doubt and assume that gold, in the very long term, does maintain its purchasing power. Maybe Hershey bars are an anomaly. Maybe the years 2000 and 2010 were anomalies. Still, you would hope that your investments would do better than merely keep their purchasing power. If that is all gold can do, why hold it as an investment? (After all, it is an unproductive lump of metal, so what should you really expect?)

GREED ALERT

Well, if you type "gold" into your favourite search engine, you'll find 10,000 vendors selling it and 10,000 reasons, according to those vendors, why *now* is the time to buy. (Um, excuse us, ladies and gentlemen, but if the price of gold "can only go up," why are you trying so hard to sell it?) Every day we hear one explanation or another as to why gold "must" go up from here on (India's demand for gold . . . dentists' demand for gold . . . the mines are drying up . . . gold demand in the tech industry . . . and so on and so on). These are the very same arguments we've been hearing for years. Only now there's one more: All these ETF investors are demanding gold!

We believe that the best you can expect from gold over the very long term, as the World Gold Council puts it, is that it will maintain its purchasing power. But, hey, that's not a bad thing when every other investment is tanking. Gold, as it happens, does show little long-term correlation to other assets. And when the going gets really tough — or even seems that way — when people run from most investments, they often turn to gold. Then, as a self-fulfilling prophecy, the price rises. Indeed, that seems like a plausible explanation for gold's run-up in the years following 9/11, when we've seen wars in Iraq and Afghanistan, mounting federal deficits and debt, a financial crisis, and growing doubts about the true value of paper currencies.

In the final analysis, it probably wouldn't hurt you to hold gold in your portfolio. But please don't buy the nonsense that gold "must go up." It will go up. It will go down. It will go up again. Have a ball. Just don't bank your retirement on it, okay?

If you allot a small percentage of your portfolio to gold — no more than, say, 5 percent please (actually make that 5 percent *total* precious metals) — and keep that percentage constant, you'll likely eke out a few dollars over time. Every year, if the price of gold falls, you might buy a bit; if the price rises, perhaps you sell. That strategy is called *rebalancing,* and we recommend it for all your portfolio allocations. (See our discussion of yearly portfolio rebalancing in Chapter 18.)

And if all goes to hell in a handbasket, your gold may offer you some protection.

A vastly improved way to buy the precious metal

When, in November 2004, State Street Global Advisors introduced the first gold ETF, it was a truly revolutionary moment. You buy a share just as you would buy a share of any other security, and each share gives you an ownership interest in one-tenth of an ounce of gold held by the fund. Yes, the gold is actually held in various bank vaults. You can even see pictures of one such vault filled to near capacity (very cool!) on www.spdrgoldshares.com.

If you are going to buy gold, this is far and away the easiest and most sensible way to do it.

You currently have several ETF options for buying gold. Two that would work just fine include the original from State Street — the SPDR Gold Shares (GLD) — and a second from iShares introduced months later — the iShares Gold Trust (IAU). Both funds are essentially the same. Flip a coin (gold or other), but then go with the iShares fund, simply because it costs less: 0.25 percent versus 0.40 percent.

Silver: The Second Metal

Talk about a silver bullet. In early 2006, after years of lacklustre performance, the price of silver suddenly, within three short months, shot up 67 percent. Why? Largely, the move served as testimony to the growing power of ETFs!

The price jump anticipated the introduction of the iShares Silver Trust (SLV) ETF in April 2006. SLV operates much the same as the iShares Gold Trust (IAU). When you buy a share of SLV, you obtain virtual ownership of 10 ounces of silver.

To be able to convey that ownership interest, iShares had to buy many ounces of silver (initially 1.5 million), and that pending demand caused the silver market to bubble and fizz. Within several weeks after the introduction of the ETF, the price of silver continued to rise, reaching a 23-year high in May 2006 ($14.69 an ounce) before tumbling in the following weeks. The volatility has continued to this day as the price has darted above and below $40 an ounce.

Quick silver on the move

To say that silver is volatile is a gross understatement. In 1979, the price of an ounce of silver was about $5. It then rose tenfold in less than a year — to as high as $54 an ounce in 1980 — after the infamous Hunt brothers had cornered the silver market (until they were caught, because, y'know, it's illegal to corner the market in just about anything). The price then fell again. Hard.

Fast forward to April 2011. The price of silver, having risen steadily and sharply since the introduction of the first silver ETF, had topped $48 an ounce and seemed headed back to the highs of 1980. And then . . . pop! Within a mere several days, the price fell about 30 percent to slightly under $34. Then it rose back up in the following months to $42, and then, in September 2011 . . . pop! In a mere two days, it fell back down to $30. In January 2013, the price of silver was about $28.

If there is any reason to stomach such volatility, it stems from the fact that silver has a very low correlation to other investments. For the three years prior to our writing these words, the price of silver has had very, very little correlation to stocks (except for some modest correlation to the stocks of silver-producing countries, such as Chile), almost no correlation to bonds, and even a decidedly limited correlation (0.75) to the price of gold.

If you must . . .

If you're going to take a position in silver, the iShares ETF is the way to go. The expense ratio of 0.50 percent will eat into your profits or magnify your losses, but it will still likely be cheaper than paying a commission to buy silver bars or coins and then paying for a good-sized lockbox.

In the very long run, we don't think you're likely to do as well with silver as you would with either stocks or bonds. Note, however, that unlike gold, silver has many industrial uses. Demand for silver can come from diverse sources — not just jewellers and collectors — which can cause the metal's price to fluctuate with changing expectations for industrial production. Because the uses for silver effectively "consume" the metal, the laws of supply and demand may influence the future prospects of silver prices in a way that doesn't apply to gold. In the end, silver may prove useful as a hedge, maybe even better than gold. But we would urge you to invest very modestly; no more than 5 percent of your portfolio should be allocated to precious metals.

Oil and Gas: Truly Volatile Commodities

The United States Oil Fund (USO) opened on the American Stock Exchange on April 10, 2006. Even though the fund is technically not an ETF but a very close cousin called a *commodity pool*, in our minds that date marks a sort of end to the Age of Innocence for ETFs. The United States Oil Fund, as official as that sounds, is run by a group called United States Commodity Funds LLC, which we will turn to in just a moment.

Don't mistake this fund for something like the U.S.-listed Vanguard Energy ETF (VDE) or Canada's iShares S&P/TSX Capped Energy Index Fund (XEG) (refer to Chapter 10), which invest in oil companies like Exxon Mobil Corp. and Suncor Energy, respectively. Don't mistake this fund for something like the precious metal commodity funds discussed in the preceding sections. U.S. Commodity Funds is not filled with oil. Whereas Barclays and State Street maintain vaults filled with gold and silver, this company deals in paper: futures contracts, to be exact.

In other words, this company uses your money to speculate on tomorrow's price of oil. If the price of oil rises in the next several weeks, you should, theoretically, earn a profit commensurate with that rise, minus the fund's costs of trading and its expense ratio of 0.75 percent. When the price of oil and gas go on a tear, this fund promises to give you a piece of that action, perhaps offering warm comfort every time you pull up to the pump and have to yank out your credit card. So should you pump your money into USO and others like it? (Horizons offers Canadians a few futures-using commodity funds, such as its NYMEX Crude Oil ETF (HUC).) Keep reading for our opinion about these slick investments.

Oily business

If you buy into USO or HUC and the price of oil escalates, you stand to make money. But is there reason to believe that the price of oil will always (or even usually) escalate? It has certainly gone up and down over the years, as have oil futures.

All-in-one ETF for precious metals

One simple approach to precious-metals investing is worth considering: the ETFS Physical Precious Metals Basket Shares (GLTR), an ETF that was introduced in October 2010. In one fund, you get a basket of four precious metals — gold, silver, platinum, and palladium — each in proportion to its economic footprint. Shares are backed up by the physical metals held in vaults. The fund's cost is 0.60 percent a year.

The famed economist John Maynard Keynes in 1930 theorized that commodity futures, over time, will offer compensation above and beyond any rise in the price of a commodity. He speculated that speculators will somehow be rewarded for taking the risk of future price uncertainty. Keynes's theory was very controversial for very many years, and in the past few years it has come to look as if Keynes was wrong. Of course, he didn't know that so many investors, largely thanks to ETFs such as USO, were going to pile into the commodity-futures arena. Such piling on has resulted in some ugly discrepancies between commodity future prices and the price of the actual commodity.

But even if Keynes were right, and even if the futures market more accurately tracked the price of the actual commodity (a.k.a. the *spot price*), why pick a single commodity to invest in? Why not diversify your risks with a variety of commodities? A good number of ETFs attempt to do that, and more are on the way. (We discuss these options next in this chapter.) We equate the arrival of USO with the end of ETFs' Age of Innocence because as we see things, USO is clearly pandering to people's disgust over high oil and gas prices.

The sad saga of contango

As fate would have it, the promise of the United States Oil Fund has turned out to be nothing like the reality. Consider this: The price of an actual barrel of oil rose from about $40 in January 2009 to nearly $100 in June 2011. In the same time period, USO's share price went from about $35 to $38 — not much of an increase.

That meagre return, however, might be considered pure gravy compared to the return suffered by investors in the company's United States Natural Gas Fund (UNG), introduced on April 18, 2007. Through early 2013, this fund's share price, which started at about $90 a share, fell to — are you ready? — roughly $19 a share. Investors in UNG have had anything but a gas.

The explanation for USO's stagnant share price and UNG's sink-like-a-rock share price can be found in something called *contango.* That's a word that nearly all investors in commodity ETFs, at least those that rely on futures contracts, wish to heck they had never heard.

Contango refers to a situation where distant futures prices for a particular commodity start to run well ahead of near futures prices. In other words, if you want to maintain a futures position that looks one month out, you buy futures contracts for the next month that expire in 30 days. Then one month later you replace them with contracts that contango has made more expensive. The effect is sort of like holding a fistful of sand and watching the sand sift through your fingers until you are left with nothing but an empty hand.

It's actually not as mysterious a situation as it might sound like. The reason the price is higher in the future is because it costs money to store and finance the commodity. For instance, you can go to the gas station and buy 100 litres of oil right now for $1.30. If, for some reason, you wanted to take that gas home next month, the gas station owner would charge you a fee to store the gas, plus some interest charges. There might also be some expectation in supply and demand shifts built into the price, but that's mostly for near-term futures that expire within a few months.

Many people think that futures prices represent a commodity's price in the future (the word "futures", understandably, is why people think this), but it actually represents today's price adjusted for storage and financing.

Because of these extra costs, many commodity investors have lost money, and some have lost lots of money, in recent years. If the price of gas falls, you'll still be on the hook to buy it for that $1.30, plus the storage and interest costs. You can even lose money on the transaction if prices rise too.

For you, the ETF investor, we would advise much caution before investing in commodities, especially in funds that use futures and other derivatives.

(Somewhat) Safer Commodity Plays

Just as diversification works to dampen the risks of stock investing, it can similarly smooth out — to a degree — the ups and downs of investing in commodities. If you're willing to accept contango and the natural volatility of most commodities (other than perhaps clay or granite), we urge you at least to diversify. In this section, we show you how to do so.

If you can handle the volatility but are put off by contango, consider one of the alternative commodity plays we discuss in the final section of this chapter.

General commodity index funds

In this section, we tell you about three funds that allow you to tap into a broad spectrum of commodities. We begin with a commodity pool offered by iShares and then discuss two exchange-traded notes issued by Barclays.

iShares Broad Commodity Index Fund (CAD-Hedged) (CBR)

Make no mistake, the CBR fund, issued in February 2010, is a volatile investment. (In 2012 alone it went down 7 percent then up 1 percent then back down and up again.) Not a true ETF, this fund (like USO) is a *commodity pool* that deals in commodities futures.

Unlike USO, or the gold and silver ETFs, the iShares offering has a bit of diversity to protect you if one commodity suddenly heads south. That diversity, alas, is somewhat limited. The fund entails 11 commodity classes, but 3 of the top 6 are energy-related: Brent crude oil (10.8 percent); gasoil (also known as diesel) (8.88 percent); heating oil (6.4 percent); gasoline (12.4 percent); and natural gas (5.5 percent). That adds up to about 31.9 percent. The remaining 68 percent is allocated to various metals and agricultural products.

CBR's expense ratio — 0.87 percent — is close to outrageous by ETF standards, but cheap is hard to find in this category. We like the idea of a general commodity fund, but we're not wild about CBR.

iPath commodity ETNs

In June 2006, Barclays issued two funds that may offer better options for investing directly in commodities . . . or, more specifically, investing in a diversified mix of commodities using futures. They are the iPath S&P GSCI Total Return Index ETN (GSP) and the iPath Dow Jones-USB Commodity Index Total Return ETN (DJP). (In 2012, iPath launched three Canadian-listed ETNs — the first TSX-listed notes — but these two aren't part of its offering. You can still buy GSP and DJP via an online brokerage firm; just be aware that you're purchasing them in U.S. dollars.)

These securities are *exchange-traded notes* (ETNs) and are very different from iShares ETFs. (Note that the iShares ETFs were originally a product of Barclays and were then purchased by BlackRock, Inc. Barclays held onto its lineup of ETNs.) ETNs are actually debt instruments, more like bonds than anything else. By buying them, you are lending Barclays your money, and you are counting on Barclays to give it back. (If Barclays were to go under, you lose.) That's not the case with iShares or any other ETF, where the ETF provider is acting more as a custodian of your funds than anything else. ETNs are becoming more popular, and we talk more about them in Chapter 15.

Barclays is rated a stable company (A by S&P; A3 by Moody's), so we wouldn't worry too much about its going under (although anything is possible, of course). Your bigger worry is the future direction of commodity prices. Barclays promises to use "any tool necessary" to use your money to track commodity prices. Presumably, it works something like the iShares fund in that it uses primarily futures contracts. But Barclays won't say. ETNs are not transparent like ETFs, so you don't know exactly what you're holding.

Why do we like these funds more than the iShares fund? It's not because of the expense ratio. At 0.75 percent, the Barclays funds are only a tad less expensive. The reason we prefer the Barclays funds is that they offer somewhat better diversification. Both ETNs invest in a number of commodities, from oil and natural gas to gold and silver to cocoa and coffee.

Of the two Barclays funds, we prefer DJP for its well-established index and the balanced weightings of its holdings: energy (34 percent), livestock (6 percent), precious metals (15 percent), industrial metals (17 percent), and agriculture (28 percent). Still, even when diversified, commodities are volatile, and their long-term returns are not as well-established as the long-term returns on stocks and bonds.

If you buy into a Barclays ETN, you should do so for the right reason: lack of correlation to your other investments. Both of the iPath funds have shown almost no correlation to either stocks or bonds. For more information on these funds, Barclays has a special website: www.ipathetn.com.

As with precious metals funds, devoting 5 percent of your portfolio to either of the iPath funds would be plenty. No more than that, please.

Actively managed, or quasi-actively managed, commodity funds

In Chapter 15, we discuss actively managed funds and whether and how to work non-ETFs into your portfolio. Given all the challenges with investing in commodities by using exchange-traded vehicles, as discussed so far in this chapter, we're inclined to believe that active management may be just the place to go if you want to invest in commodities. (And, by the way, you don't need to do so; you can invest indirectly in commodities in ways that may make more sense. More on that topic in just a moment.)

If you want direct commodity exposure, consider that a number of the newest ETFs and ETNs are promising to deal with some of the problems of the first-generation commodity funds. The leader in this brigade is iPath, which in April 2011 introduced a new lineup of ETNs called *Pure Beta* indexes. We wouldn't quite call these funds actively managed, but they aren't quite passively run, either. The Pure Beta ETNs promise to "mitigate the effects of certain distortions in the commodity markets" (this language refers to contango) by rolling over futures contracts in an allegedly more intelligent manner (less mechanically) than the older commodity funds that used futures.

It's too soon to say whether Barclays' strategy will prove successful, but keep your eye on the iPath Pure Beta Broad Commodity ETN (BCM), which uses this newfangled strategy to track a basket of commodities consisting of energy (37 percent), agricultural products (24 percent), precious metals (20 percent), industrial metals (16 percent), and livestock (2.5 percent). The management fee is 0.75 percent. We're ignoring the rest of the Barclays' Beta lineup that allows you to speculate on individual commodities, such as lead, nickel, and aluminum. (The ticker for that last fund is FOIL — cute, eh?)

Another ETN worth considering for commodity exposure is the ELEMENTS S&P CTI ETN (LSC). This fund tracks the S&P Commodity Trends Indicator–Total Return index. The fund tracks 16 different commodities, using futures contracts. Unlike Barclays' funds, LSC uses a momentum strategy, buying "long" those commodities rising in price and selling "short" those commodities falling in price.

Backtesting of the index showed that this strategy, known as a managed futures strategy, has been successful for investing in commodities. (Of course, backtested strategies are notorious for performing less well in real time than their hypothetical numbers suggest.) The fund was born in October 2008, and although the strategy shows promise, it is far from proven. And just like any other kind of futures investing, but even more so, a managed futures strategy will not necessarily reflect ups and downs in the spot prices of commodities.

Because LSC is an ETN and not an ETF, remember that you get your money back only if the issuer remains solvent. This fund is issued and backed by HSBC Bank USA, which has high credit ratings like Barclays.

Awaiting new developments

Given all the confusion about how best to invest in commodities, we're certain that other ETF and ETN providers will soon introduce all sorts of new strategies to tap into this asset class. Some will likely be crazy; others may turn out to be golden.

Keep in mind also that many commodity mutual funds exist. If you want to try an actively managed approach and don't want the credit risk that comes with ETNs, some of the available funds may be reasonable options. Because this book is not about mutual funds, we won't go into much depth here, but one mutual fund worth considering is the PIMCO Commodity Real Return Strategy Fund (PCRDX). It's been around since 2002 and has a rather positive history thus far — better than many of the commodity ETFs. See www.pimco funds.com.

Playing the Commodity Market Indirectly

In a recent interview with the *Journal of Indexes,* famed investment guru Burton G. Malkiel, professor of economics at Princeton and author of *A Random Walk Down Wall Street,* had this to say about commodity investing: "I think [commodities] should be in every portfolio, but for individuals, my sense is that the way they should get them is through ensuring that they have in their portfolios companies that mine or manufacture the commodities."

He is not alone. Frustrated with the problems of commodity investing we've outlined in this chapter, and doubtful that commodity investing in the very long run will provide returns commensurate with the risk, many investment advisors of late have turned to Malkiel's solution. The drawback is that stocks in commodity-producing companies are not going to show the same lack of correlation, or offer the same diversification power, as pure commodities do. Investing in commodities this way is a trade-off.

Consider splitting the difference: Put perhaps 3 to 4 percent of a portfolio in pure commodities and perhaps another 3 to 4 percent in one of the funds we outline next.

Tapping into commodity companies

In this section, we introduce you to ETFs that let you invest in the stocks of companies in the oil and gas sector, in mining, and in the broader category of "natural resources" or "materials."

Oil and gas ETFs

More than a dozen ETFs allow you to invest in the stocks of oil and gas companies. Among them are these options — the first five are Canadian focused, the rest American:

- iShares S&P/TSX Capped Energy Index Fund (XEG)
- iShares Oil Sands Index Fund (CLO)
- BMO S&P/TSX Equal Weight Oil & Gas Index ETF (ZEO)
- BMO Junior Oil Index ETF (ZJO)
- BMO Junior Gas Index ETF (ZJN)
- Vanguard Energy ETF (VDE)

- ✔ Energy Select Sector SPDR (XLE)
- ✔ iShares Dow Jones U.S. Energy Index (IYE)
- ✔ PowerShares Dynamic Energy Exploration & Production (PXE)
- ✔ iShares Dow Jones U.S. Oil Equipment & Services Index Fund (IEZ)
- ✔ iShares S&P Global Energy Index Fund (IXC)
- ✔ Global X Oil Equities ETF (XOIL)

The funds all sound different from each other, but when you look at each of their rosters, they are actually quite similar. (Canadians compared to Canadians, and Americans to Americans, of course.) The BMO junior ones are interesting, though, as they hold a number of smaller Canadian energy companies that the larger cap ETFs don't own.

Keep in mind that the energy sector represents a large segment of the Canadian economy. Energy companies make up about 25 percent of the capitalization of the Canadian stock market. So just being invested in the market gives you decent exposure to energy.

Mining ETFs

Several ETFs allow you to invest in mining companies. These include

- ✔ iShares S&P/TSX Global Mining Index Fund (CMW)
- ✔ iShares S&P/TSX Global Base Metals Index Fund (XBM)
- ✔ BMO S&P/TSX Equal Weight Global Base Metals Hedged to CAD Index ETF (ZMT)
- ✔ Global X Pure Gold Miners ETF (GGGG)
- ✔ Market Vectors Gold Miners ETF (GDX)
- ✔ SPDR S&P Metals and Mining ETF (XME)
- ✔ Global X Silver Miners ETF (SIL)

These funds may make more sense in a portfolio than the energy ETFs, but they aren't our preferred way of tapping into commodity-producing companies. For our preference, keep reading.

Materials or natural resources ETFs

For extra exposure to companies that mine for gold and silver, produce oil and gas, and either produce or distribute other commodities, we prefer broader natural resource funds. (We say "extra" because we already get exposure in our other stock funds.) If commodity prices pop, the broader natural resource funds generally do well, and you're not taking on too much risk by banking on any one commodity or commodity group. A natural resources fund may also be called a *materials* fund.

Options in this category include these ETFs:

- ✔ iShares S&P/TSX Capped Materials Index Fund (XMA)
- ✔ Materials Select Sector SPDR (XLB)
- ✔ iShares Dow Jones U.S. Basic Materials Sector Index Fund (IYM)
- ✔ Vanguard Materials ETF (VAW)
- ✔ iShares S&P North American Natural Resources Sector Index Fund (IGE)

One of Russell's favourites in this category is the SPDR S&P Global Natural Resources ETF (GNR). This fund has an expense ratio of 0.50 percent. About 45 percent of its holdings are in Canada or the United States, and the remaining 55 percent are spread out through both the developed world and emerging markets. It offers exposure to a good variety of commodity firms: oil and gas, 27 percent; fertilizers and agricultural chemicals, 19 percent; diversified metals and mining, 15 percent; and so on.

Tapping into commodity-rich countries

As commodity prices go, so (often) go the stock markets of countries that supply the world with much of its commodities. By and large, these are the emerging market nations. (Yes, developed nations, such as Canada, Australia, and the United States, also bring the world many commodities. But you already own Canadian companies, and because the other economies are larger and more diverse, commodity prices have a much lesser effect on their stock markets.)

Although country funds can be just as volatile as commodities themselves, you can invest, through iShares, in the stock markets of nations. For example, you can invest in these:

- ✔ Gold-rich South Africa via iShares MSCI South Africa (EZA)
- ✔ Timber giant Brazil through iShares MSCI Brazil (XBZ)
- ✔ Multi-mineral-laden Malaysia with iShares MSCI Malaysia (EWM)
- ✔ Top silver producers Chile and Peru through iShares MSCI Chile Investable Market (ECH) and iShares MSCI All Peru Capped (EPU)

We would suggest that, instead of needlessly taking on the risks associated with any single country, you diversify any investment in emerging markets through one of several ETFs that allow you to invest in a broad array of emerging market nations. These funds include the iShares MSCI Emerging Markets Index ETF (XEM), the BMO Emerging Markets Equity Index ETF (ZEM), and the Vanguard FTSE Emerging Markets Index ETF (VEE).

Chapter 15

Working Non-ETFs and Active ETFs into Your Investment Mix

*I*t wasn't that long ago that building an entire, optimally diversified portfolio out of ETFs was just about impossible — sort of like trying to paint a landscape with no blues or yellows. There were holes, and many of them. You could not, for example, buy an ETF that gave you exposure to international bonds. Only one ETF at that time allowed you to tap into international small cap stocks. And none allowed for investing in international REITs.

In 2006, when there were but 300 ETFs around North America from which to choose, many of those tracked the same kinds of investments (such as large cap stocks). You had to look elsewhere if you wished to invest in certain asset classes. Today, the landscape is quite different. Among the more than 1,300 available ETFs, you have blues, yellows, greens . . . an entire palette from which to compose a very well-diversified portfolio. In fact, you have more than enough. Now, not only can you track just about any conceivable stock, bond, or commodity index with passive ETFs, but you also have actively managed ETFs to consider.

In this chapter, we discuss those active ETFs. But first we identify some non-ETFs, such as certain mutual funds and even a few individual stocks, that still — despite the wide variety of ETFs — just might play a positive role in your portfolio. We also explain the differences between ETFs and exchange-traded notes (ETNs).

 This chapter serves as a reference if you already have a non-ETF portfolio in place and, for whatever reason, want to keep it more or less intact. Perhaps you have huge unrealized tax gains and don't care to donate to the CRA just yet. Or the investment options in your pension plan may not include ETFs. Or you may simply be happy with your indexed or active mutual funds, which (depending on which ones you own) may be fine.

For some of you — ah, yes, we know you're out there — no amount of cajoling will ever convince you to index or diversify your investments. You fervently believe that by picking a few individual stocks, and buying and selling at the right times, you can clobber the market. So be it. We fear you are going to lose your shirt, but we will simply have to agree to disagree. We can still urge you to consider investing in an ETF here and there — and we will!

So, without further ado, we now give you our take on how indexed ETFs, active ETFs, and non-ETFs can get along in peace, harmony, and profitability.

Tinkering with an Existing Stock or Mutual Fund Portfolio

Maybe you're intent on staying put with your existing portfolio. We understand that. But even you can benefit from an occasional ETF holding. (And we're sure you know that, or else you wouldn't be reading this page right now.)

Improving your diversification

We'll start by assuming that you are invested in individual stocks and bonds, saving mutual funds for the next section.

Unless you are really rich, like Warren Buffett rich, you simply cannot have a truly well-diversified portfolio of individual securities — not nearly as well-diversified as even the simplest ETF or mutual fund portfolio. Where would you even start? To have a portfolio as well diversified as even a simple ETF portfolio, you'd have to hold a bevy of large company stocks (both growth and value), small company stocks (again, both growth and value), foreign stocks (Asia and Europe and emerging markets, growth and value, large and small), and real estate investment trust (REIT) stocks. And that's just on the equity side!

On the fixed-income side of your portfolio, you would ideally have a mix of short-term and long-term bonds and government and corporate issues.

Get real. Examine your portfolio. If you, like so many Canadian investors, have the large majority of your equity holdings in large company Canadian stocks, you can diversify in a flash by adding a small cap ETF or two (refer to Chapters 7 and 8) and a couple of international ETFs (refer to Chapter 9).

If you, like so many investors who lost their shirts in 2008, are simply too heavily invested in stocks, you may want to tap into some of the more sedate bond ETFs (refer to Chapter 12).

Minimizing your investment costs

Now, let's assume you're basically a mutual fund kind of guy or gal. You've been reading *MoneySense* magazine for years. You believe that you have winnowed down the universe of mutual funds to a handful of winners, and goshdarnit, you're going to keep them in your portfolio.

You may or may not have heard the terms *core* and *satellite*. They refer to an investment strategy that has been very much in vogue lately. *Core* refers to a portfolio's foundation, which is basically invested in the entire market, or close to it. Then, you have your *satellites:* smaller investments designed to outdo the market. It isn't such a bad strategy.

Suppose you have four mutual funds that you love: one tech fund, one health care fund, one energy fund, and one international growth fund. Each charges you a yearly fee of 2 percent (about the mutual fund average in Canada). And suppose you have $250,000 invested in all four. You are paying a total of $5,000 ($250,000 × 2 percent) a year in management fees, and that's to say nothing of any taxes you're paying on dividends and capital gains.

Consider trimming those investments down and moving half the money into an ETF or two or three. Turn your present core into satellites, and create a new core using broad-market funds, such as the S&P/TSX Capped Composite Index Fund (XIC). It carries an expense ratio of 0.25 percent. Your total management fees are now ($125,000 × 2 percent) + ($125,000 × 0.25 percent), or $2,500 + $312.50, which totals $2,812.50. You've just saved yourself a very nifty $2,187.50 a year.

With the newer generation of actively managed ETFs, it's quite possible that the *MoneySense* picks of the month may include ETFs. If you are swapping actively managed mutual funds for actively managed ETFs, you may still save money too. More on actively managed ETFs later in this chapter.

Using ETFs to tax harvest

Regardless of whether you hold individual stocks or mutual funds, you should hope for nothing but good times ahead but be prepared for something less. Historically, the stock market takes something of a dip in one out of every three years. In the dip years, ETFs can help ease the pain.

Say it's a particularly bad year for financial stocks, and you happen to own a few of the most beaten down of the dogs. Come late December, you can sell your losing tech stocks or mutual funds. As long as you don't buy them back for 30 days, you can claim a tax loss for the year, and the Canada Revenue Agency, in a sense, helps foot the bill for your losses. Ah, but do you really want to be out of the market for the entire month of January (typically one of the best months for stocks)? You don't need to be.

Buy yourself a financial sector ETF, such as the iShares S&P/TSX Capped Financials Index Fund (XFN), and you're covered should the market suddenly take a jump. Although we'd much rather you simply hold onto your ETF as a permanent investment, if you wish, at the end of 30 days, you can always sell your ETF and buy back your beloved individual stocks or active mutual funds.

We believe that tax harvesting has its place, but it has been in the past a by-and-large overvalued and overdone strategy. After all, there are costs involved whenever you make a trade. With ETFs and stocks, you pay a commission when you buy or sell. With any security, there is a spread. You can't just buy and sell without some middleman somewhere taking a small cut. Still, many investors cling to tax harvesting religiously. All we're saying is please discuss the strategy with your tax advisor (or clergy) before proceeding next year, okay?

Looking Beyond the Well-Rounded ETF Portfolio

In this section, we address those of you who are convinced that ETFs are the best thing since the abolition of pay toilets. You're ready to build a portfolio of ETFs but are wondering if other investments may fit into the mix and, if so, what investments those might be. Let us provide you with a few possibilities.

If you are considering investing in mutual funds, we suggest that you read the latest edition of Andrew Bell's and Matthew Elder's *Mutual Fund Investing For Canadians For Dummies* (Wiley) and investigate mutual fund options on www.morningstar.ca. The options we discuss in the following sections are all *no load* (meaning you'll pay no commission), have reasonable management expenses, and are run by mutual fund companies with reputations for honesty and solid management. We include websites and telephone numbers in case you want to go directly to the fund provider. Please read the prospectus before purchasing any mutual fund.

Mutual funds nearly as cheap as ETFs

The main issue with keeping some of your money in active investments is those darn mutual fund fees. You'd better be sure your fund beats the market handily, or those costs will put you in the red. Although most companies charge higher-than-ETF fees, some fund operations have figured out that if they don't reduce their management expense ratios, people will stop buying their funds.

One of the leading low-fee mutual fund companies is Calgary's Mawer Investment Management. Its Mawer Balanced Fund — a fund that holds a diversified selection of stocks and bonds — costs 0.98 percent. Most of its other equity funds cost between 1.25 and 1.50 percent, which is pretty great for mutual funds.

RBC-owned PH&N is another company that charges below-average fees. You can pick up a short-term bond fund for 0.61 percent, or a Canadian equity fund for 1.18 percent. Other low-fee firms include Leith Wheeler, McLean Budden, and Beutel Goodman.

Of course, these investments still cost a lot more than ETFs, so you need to ask yourself whether you really need active management or not. Is a broad Canadian equity ETF better than a broad Canadian equity mutual fund? You know where we stand on that (if not, then you haven't been reading), but if you do want some of your money managed by an actual person, then at least invest with a company that has low mutual fund fees.

The lowest cost mutual fund is actually an "index fund." It's similar to an ETF in that it owns the equities that make up an index. For instance, the TD Canadian Index e-Series fund (TD's the leader in index mutual funds) mimics the S&P/TSX Composite Index. These funds are great for smaller investors because they're cheap — this particular TD index fund has a 0.33 percent management expense ratio — and, because they're mutual funds, you don't have to pay a commission to buy them. As we've discussed before, it doesn't make sense to put $100 in an ETF because of the $29.99 fee, but since that fee doesn't apply to index funds, you can invest any amount you'd like. For more information on TD e-Series funds, visit www.tdwaterhouse.ca/tdeseriesfunds.

Keep in mind the basic differences between ETFs and mutual funds:

✔ ETFs allow you to trade throughout the day, which can be a good thing or a bad thing, depending on whether you use or abuse that privilege. (Vanguard founder John Bogle has numerous times expressed dismay that ETFs encourage investors to trade frequently.)

- ✔ ETFs typically involve trading fees and small spreads, and they may be subject to some small tracking error (nothing to worry much about unless you are trading frequently).

- ✔ ETFs follow an index, and the stocks rarely change from day to day. Fund managers pick the stocks in mutual funds and can make changes to their holdings as they see fit. That can be good or bad, depending on the reasons why the fund manager sold a stock.

Where few investors have gone before: DFA funds

Perhaps you've never heard of the mutual fund company called Dimensional Fund Advisors, or DFA. For the ultimate in slicing and dicing a portfolio, no mutual fund company compares. Only through DFA can you, for example, find index funds that allow you to invest in emerging markets small cap, emerging markets value, and U.K. small company. All of DFA's funds are expertly managed funds with reasonable expense ratios (although a bit higher than most ETFs).

The only problem with DFA is that you can invest in their funds only if you are an institution with huge bucks, or if you go through a *fee-only* wealth manager (meaning he takes no commissions). The problem with that, of course, is that you have to pay the fee-only wealth manager. Because you're reading this book, you're probably a hands-on, do-it-yourself kind of investor, and you may not want to pay someone to manage your money.

If, however, you have a handsome portfolio, and if you can find a fee-only wealth manager who charges you a reasonable amount (try the Financial Planning Standards Council, www.fpsc.ca or the Portfolio Management Association of Canada, www.investmentcounsel.org), by all means, do consider DFA (www.dfaca.com). It would be nice if DFA would get into the ETF business, but we doubt that will happen; all those fee-only advisors would stand to lose clientele.

Timber REITs

Real estate comes in many forms, from shopping malls to condos to office buildings. As we explain in Chapter 13, you can invest in these properties through publicly listed real estate investment trusts (REITs), which are companies that buy and develop land and pay their investors largely in handsome dividends. A handful of REITs own timberland — gazillions of acres of trees.

The land on which the trees grow tends to rise and fall in value along with the going price for timber. Therefore, these special REITs behave largely as a separate asset class. There are days and weeks when most REITs go one way and timber REITs go another. For that reason, if we have a client with a fairly large portfolio, we may take a percentage of the U.S. REIT allocation and move it into timber.

Technically speaking, two timber REIT ETFs exist: the Guggenheim Timber ETF (CUT) and the iShares S&P Global Timber & Forestry Index ETF (WOOD). We're not big fans of either. They both charge fairly high fees (0.65 and 0.48 percent, respectively), but our bigger issue is that they invest only in a handful of timber REITs, simply because there *are* only a handful of them. Then, to fill their portfolios (because you can't have an ETF with two or three holdings), these ETFs also invest in companies that make toilet paper and cardboard boxes and stationery and such. These companies are not "timber" companies. They are simply related to timber . . . not the same thing.

For that reason, rather than buy a watered-down ETF, we recommend buying individual stocks to tap into this asset class. We'd rather not, but what's available is what's available. Two of the largest timber REITs (these two together make up about one-fifth of the holdings of WOOD) are the following:

- **Plum Creek Timber Company (PCL):** 800-254-4961; www.plumcreek.com
- **Rayonier Timber (RYN):** 904-357-9155; www.rayonier.com

Keep in mind that these are individual company stocks. Throughout this book we say that you really shouldn't invest in individual companies, but we're making a small exception here for timber. Individual stocks can be volatile and sometimes awfully capricious. We suggest limiting your allocation to absolutely no more than 6 percent of the equity side of your portfolio. Perhaps take that 6 percent and split it between PCL and RYN.

Just like all REITs, timber REITs must distribute 90 percent of their income as dividends. And those dividends will be taxed. Keep your timber REITs, if possible, in a tax-advantaged retirement account. In fact, if you don't have room for them in your tax-advantaged accounts, we'd suggest that you may want to pass. Timber is good to have in your portfolio for diversification purposes, and the stocks may — knock wood — perform very well moving forward, but these holdings are not essential.

Market-neutral mutual funds

Market-neutral funds use vastly different strategies to meet their ends. The goal of most is to produce long-term returns that are more similar to bonds than stocks (perhaps a tad higher than bonds) while having no correlation to either the bond or stock market.

Some market-neutral funds use a *long-short* strategy. That is, they buy stocks to enjoy the potential appreciation. They also *short* stocks (often stock ETFs) to make money when the market is going down. Others employ this strategy by buying one stock while simultaneously shorting another — whose prospects look poor by comparison — in the same sector. In general, the two stocks will move in the same direction as their sector and the market, but the hope is that the superior stock will ultimately provide superior returns, allowing fund investors to earn the difference. It's a tricky business, and you want to find an experienced manager who has been doing it for a while.

Another strategy involves investing very short term in companies that are just on the cusp of getting gobbled up by other companies. Such small-fish-about-to-be-eaten companies, if they can be identified, tend to be tasty investments.

Some of the newer actively managed ETFs may promote themselves as market neutral, but if there is any area of investing where you want to see some kind of track record, we'd say this is it.

Fixed immediate annuities

For older people especially, and almost definitely for those with no heirs, an annuity — either fixed or variable — can make enormous sense. With an annuity, you give up your principal, and in return you enjoy a yield typically far greater than you would likely get with any other fixed-income option.

Many horrible annuities are out there. Russell can't tell you how often a new client has walked into his office, thrown <u>her</u> annuity papers on the table, and said, "*Why* did I ever buy this stupid thing?" Most of the really bad ones are variable annuities, not the fixed kind that he prefers.

If you are interested in an annuity, contact the different insurance companies. It's a good idea to compare rates of return and product offerings, so call a few. For more information on annuities, visit the Canadian Life and Health Insurance Association website at www.clhia.ca.

Venturing into exchange-traded notes

Exchange-traded notes (ETNs) sure sound like exchange-traded funds, and the two do have some things in common. But they also have one or two big differences. The commonalities include not only their names but also the fact that both ETFs and ETNs trade throughout the day, they both tend to track indexes, and they both can be more tax efficient than mutual funds.

A few odd ducks

In this chapter, we discuss mutual funds, individual securities (stocks or bonds), and annuities as possible alternatives, or complements, to ETFs. But the investment world offers other options as well. Here are a few less commonly known investments, some of which may be worth considering for your portfolio:

✔ **Closed-end mutual funds:** Just as the word *burger* without any qualifiers is usually understood to mean *ham*burger — not veggie burger or turkey burger — so are the words *mutual fund* usually understood to mean *open-end* mutual fund. The vast majority of mutual funds are open ended. That means that the fund has no set limit of shares, which are purchased from the fund sponsor. As more investors buy into the fund, the fund grows, acquiring more securities and issuing more shares.

Closed-end funds, on the other hand, are created with a certain number of shares, and that number typically doesn't change. If any new investors want to buy in, they must buy shares from existing investors. For that reason, closed-end mutual funds, unlike open-end mutual funds, may sell shares at a premium or a discount. (ETFs may also trade at a premium or discount, but it tends to be negligible. Closed-end funds, in contrast, may sometimes be bought or sold for 50 percent more or less than the value of the underlying securities.) Closed-end mutual funds tend to be more volatile than open-end mutual funds, and the management fees tend to be higher.

✔ **Unit investment trusts:** Some ETFs, especially the older ones such as the QQQ (Qubes), SPDR S&P 500 (SPY), and SPDR S&P Mid Cap 400 (MDY), actually are unit investment trusts (UITs). However, not all UITs are ETFs.

A *UIT* is a fixed portfolio of stocks or bonds generally sold to investors by brokers. The UIT is usually sold through a one-time public offering. It has a termination date, which could be anywhere from several months to 50 years down the road. Upon termination, the UIT dissolves.

In the case of ETF/UITs, however, it's a slightly different story. When the first ETFs were created, there was an original termination date of 25 years hence. But as the ETFs grew in popularity, ETF providers petitioned regulators to make an exception, which they did.

✔ **Hedge funds/limited partnerships:** *Hedge funds* — funds that promise insurance against bad markets — come in many different flavours and use any number of strategies to achieve (or try to achieve) their objective. Most hedge funds are neither mutual funds nor ETFs; rather, they are organized as limited partnerships. Limited partnerships are largely unregulated, fees tend to be high, and *liquidity* (the ability to get your money out if you want or need to) can be very limited. Proceed with great caution.

Only a few Canadian ETNs exist, so if you want to buy this product, it's highly likely that you'll have to purchase ones listed on an American exchange.

Given these commonalities, the term *exchange-traded products,* or ETPs, has been used to describe both ETFs and ETNs, as well as closed-end funds, which we describe in the sidebar "A few odd ducks."

The big, big, BIG difference (are you listening?) between ETFs and ETNs is this: An ETN is a debt instrument. In other words, a firm like Barclays, which issues the iPath ETNs, promises to pay holders of its ETNs a rate of return commensurate with some index. For example, the iPath DJ-UBS Tin Subindex Total Return ETN (JJT) promises to pay you according to how much the price of tin goes up (or down), minus fund expenses.

Whether Barclays actually invests your money in tin, or in Treasuries, or in whatever the heck it wants, is up to Barclays. The company simply made you a promise to pay, just as if you held one of its bonds. An ETN is more like a bond, really, than an ETF. Instead of a fixed rate of interest, however, you get paid according to some other measure, often the change in price of a commodity or in a foreign currency relative to the dollar.

If all goes well (and the price of tin or the value of the euro goes up), you get your money. But if something should happen to Barclays, you could lose everything. Your capital is not guaranteed, regardless of what happens in the commodity or currency markets. So quite clearly, you should buy ETNs only from solid companies, and you should never hold too much of your portfolio in any one ETN or group of ETNs issued by any one company.

As for the currency ETNs, unless you know a whole lot more about currency exchanges than the average person, you're likely to take a bath. Steer clear of these funds. They are expensive. They are volatile. And they are unpredictable.

ETNs that are not speculating in currencies and not tracking commodity indexes are typically offering you the "opportunity" to double or triple your money in a hurry with leveraged strategies. Or they are employing leveraged "inverse" strategies, promising you big money in a bear market. Do yourself a big favour and stay away from these. (We explain why in Chapter 11.)

Going Active with ETFs

It was perhaps foreshadowing, and somewhat ironic, that the very first actively managed ETF was issued by Bear Stearns. That was in March 2008. Within several months, the financial collapse of the investment banking industry, led by Bear Stearns, was well on its way to creating the worst bear market (more irony) of our lifetimes. That first ETF died, folding (with money returned to investors) in October 2008, as Bear Stearns, after 85 years in business, collapsed and itself folded.

Since that time, we've seen the arrival of only about three dozen actively managed ETFs and ETNs. And even those active funds that have appeared have failed to accumulate a whole lot in assets. Here's why:

- **Most ETF buyers are indexers by nature.** They know that index funds, as a group, do much, much better over time than actively managed funds. (Read about this topic in Chapter 1, or for much more detail, see Russell's book *Index Investing For Dummies,* also published by Wiley.)

- **Most ETF buyers want transparency.** Active managers, reluctant to reveal their "secret sauce," have not been too keen to comply with the transparency rules of ETFs, and many would like the authorities to do away with those transparency rules.

- **Many of the active funds are just plain goofy.** Cases in point: the WisdomTree Dreyfus New Zealand Dollar (BNZ), the WisdomTree Dreyfus Indian Rupee ETF (ICN), and a dozen others that deal with currency flux. They are highly speculative and not the kinds of investments into which smarter investors (as most ETF investors tend to be) are going to plunk their money. (Explain to us again why the New Zealand dollar is a good investment? Does it have anything to do with wallabies?)

- **A few of the active funds have been issued by relatively unknown and not terribly well-funded companies.** An example is Columbia Management, which sponsors the Columbia Concentrated Large Cap Value Strategy Fund (GVT). Dent Tactical ETF (DENT), based on the strategies of best-selling author and crystal-ball gazer Harry S. Dent, entered the market in the summer of 2010 with a performance thud. In its first 13 months of existence, DENT showed a return of about 2 percent annualized, versus about 16 percent for the S&P 500. Oh, and in August the fund folded. More proof that you should be careful of actively managed ETFs.

Toronto-based Horizons ETF has made some inroads in Canada with actively managed products. It has a number of offerings, but even so, they should be used by savvier investors only.

One downside to actively managed ETFs is that they're expensive. Some of the Horizons funds have fees of around 0.8 percent.

You may be inclined to choose an actively managed fund. Heck, we may do so ourselves someday (maybe, possibly . . . but not likely). After all, if you're going to go active, there's no reason not to do it with an ETF. The active ETFs will probably wind up being less expensive and more tax efficient than their corresponding mutual funds.

But keep in mind that historically, actively managed funds as a group have not done nearly as well as index funds. That being said, active management may sometimes have an edge, especially in some areas of the investment world (such as commodities and non-Treasury bonds). And much of the advantage of index investing has been in its ultra-low costs — something that actively managed ETFs could possibly emulate. We will see.

If you want to go with an actively managed fund, we would ask you at least to keep in mind the lessons learned from indexing and what has made indexing so effective over time. Basically, you want certain index-like qualities in any actively managed fund you pick:

- **Choose a fund with low costs.** With so many ETFs allowing you to tap into stocks or bonds for less than one-quarter of a percentage point a year, you do not need or want any fund that charges much more. Any U.S. stock or bond fund that charges more than a percentage point, or any foreign fund or commodity fund that charges more than 1.5 percent, is asking too much, and the odds that such a fund will outperform are very, very slim. Go elsewhere.

- **Watch your style.** Make sure that any fund you choose fits into your overall portfolio. Studies show that index funds tend to do better than active funds in both large caps and small caps, but you have a better chance in small caps that your active fund will beat the indexes.

- **Check the manager's track record — carefully.** Make sure that the track record you're buying is long-term. (Any fool can beat the S&P/TSX Composite Index in a year. Doing so for ten years is immensely more difficult.) We'd look at performance in both bull and bear markets, but your emphasis should be on average annual returns over time compared with the performance of the fund's most representative market index over the same period.

- **Don't go overboard with active management.** Studies show *so* conclusively that index investing kicks butt that we would be very hesitant to build anything but a largely indexed portfolio, using the low-cost indexed ETFs that we suggest throughout this book.

Part IV
Putting It All Together

In this part . . .

Pick up your hammer and grab some nails: It's time now to get your hands dirty actually building an ETF portfolio. In the next four chapters, we walk you through the entire construction process. We then share some important maintenance tips, such as when to tweak your portfolio and when to keep your hands off. And finally, we take you into the world of retirement, to see how your ETF portfolio may someday provide you with a steady and secure income.

Chapter 16

Sample ETF Portfolio Menus

*I*f there is such a thing as a personal hell, and if, for whatever reason, we piss off the Big Guy before we die, we're fairly certain that we will spend eternity in either a Home Depot or a RONA. The only real question we have is whether His wrath will place us in plumbing supplies, home decor, or flooring.

Neither of us are the handyman type. Even the words "home renovation" are enough to send shivers up our spines. And yet, despite our failed relationships with power tools, we both love one kind of construction: portfolio construction.

We enjoy crafting portfolios not only because it involves multicoloured pie charts (Russell's always had a soft spot for multicoloured pie charts) but also because the process involves so much more than running a piece of wood through a table saw and hoping not to lose any fingers. Portfolio construction is — or should be — a highly individualized, creative exercise that takes into consideration many factors: economics, history, statistics, and psychology among them.

The ideal portfolio (if such a thing exists) for a 30-year-old who makes $75,000 a year is very different from the portfolio of a 75-year-old whose income is $30,000 a year. The optimal portfolio for a 40-year-old worrywart differs from the optimal portfolio for a 40-year-old devil-may-care type. The portfolio of dreams following a three-year bear market when interest rates are low may look a wee bit different from a prime portfolio following a ten-year bull run when interest rates are high.

Every financial professional we know goes about portfolio construction in a somewhat different way. In this chapter, we walk you through some of the steps that, we've found, work.

Needless to say (because this is, after all, a book about exchange-traded funds), our primary construction materials are ETFs, because we believe they're good for most, but not all, investors. Our portfolio-building tools involve some sophisticated Morningstar software, Russell's HP 12C financial calculator, a premise called *Modern Portfolio Theory,* a statistical phenomenon called *reversion to the mean,* and various measures of risk and return. But rest assured that this isn't brain surgery, or even elbow surgery. You can be a pretty good portfolio builder yourself by the time you finish this chapter.

So, How Much Risk Can You Handle and Still Sleep at Night?

The first questions anyone building a portfolio should ask themselves are these: *How much return does the portfolio-holder need to see? And how much volatility can the portfolio-holder stomach?* So few things in the world of investments are sure bets, but this one is: The amount of risk you take or don't take will have a great bearing on your long-term return. You simply are not going to get rich investing in a GIC. On the other hand, you aren't going to lose your nest egg in a single week, either. The same cannot be said of a tech stock — or even a bevy of tech stocks wrapped up in an ETF.

A well-built ETF portfolio can help to mitigate risks but not eliminate them. Before you build your portfolio, ask yourself how much risk you need to take to get your desired return . . . and take no more risk than that.

Please forget the dumb old rules about portfolio building and risk. How much risk you can or should take on depends on your wealth, your age, your income, your health, your financial responsibilities, your potential inheritances, and whether you're the kind of person who tosses and turns over life's upsets. If anyone gives you a pat formula — "Take your age, subtract it from 100, and that, dear friend, is the percentage of assets you should have in stocks" — please take it with a grain of salt. Things just aren't nearly that simple. (Although if you're going to go with *any* formula, the one we just provided is far better than most!)

A few things that just don't matter

Before we lay out what matters most in determining appropriate risk and appropriate allocations to stocks, bonds, and cash (or stock ETFs and bond ETFs), we want to throw out just a few things that really *shouldn't* enter into your thinking, even though they play into many people's portfolio decisions:

- ✔ The portfolio of your best friend, which has done great guns.

- ✔ Your personal feelings on the current government, where the Bank of Canada stands on the prime interest rate, and which way hemlines on women's dresses are moving this fall.

- ✔ The article you clipped out of *Lotsa Dough* magazine that tells you that you can earn 50 percent a year by investing in . . . whatever.

Listen: Your best friend may be in a completely different economic place than you are. Her well-polished ETF portfolio, laid out by a first-rate financial planner, may be just perfect for her and all wrong for you.

As far as the state of the nation and where the S&P/TSX is headed, you simply don't know. Neither do we.

The stock market over the course of the past century has returned an average of about 10 percent annually (7 percent or so after inflation). Bonds have returned about half as much. A well-diversified portfolio, by historical standards, has returned something in between stocks and bonds — maybe 7 to 8 percent (4 to 5 percent after inflation). Using some of the advice in this book, even though market performance in the future may fall a bit shy of the past, you can see personal returns roughly approximating these numbers. But don't take inordinate risk with any sizeable chunk of your portfolio in the hope that you are going to earn 50 percent a year after inflation — or even before inflation. It won't happen.

On the other hand, don't pooh-pooh a 7 to 8 percent return. Compound interest is a truly miraculous thing. Invest $20,000 today, add $2,000 each year, and within 20 years, with "only" a 7.5 percent return, you'll have $171,566. (If inflation is running in the 3 percent ballpark, that $171,566 will be worth about $110,000 in today's dollars.)

The irony of risk and return

In a few pages, we provide you with some sample portfolios appropriate for someone who should be taking minimal risk as opposed to someone who should be taking more risk. At this point, we want to digress for a moment to say that in a perfect world, those who need to take the most risk would be the most able to take it on. In the real world, sometimes sadly ironic, those who need to take the most risk really can't afford to.

Specifically, a poor person needs whatever financial cushion he has. He can't afford to risk the farm (not that he has a farm) on a portfolio of mostly stocks. A rich person, in contrast, can easily invest a chunk of discretionary money in the stock market, but she really doesn't need to because she's living comfortably without the potential high return. It just isn't fair. Yet no one is to blame, and nothing can be done about it. It is what it is.

Moving on. . . .

The 20× rule

Whatever your age, whatever your station in life, you probably wouldn't mind if your investments could support you. But how much do you need in order for your investments to support you? That's actually not very complicated and has been very well studied: You need at least 20 times whatever amount you expect to withdraw each year from your portfolio, assuming you want that portfolio to have a good chance of surviving at least 20 to 25 years.

That is, if you need $30,000 a year — in addition to Canada Pension Plan and Old Age Security payments and any other income — to live on, you should ideally have $600,000 in your portfolio when you retire, assuming you retire in your mid-60s. You can have less, but you may wind up eating into the principal if the market tumbles — in which case, you should be prepared to live on less, or get a part-time job.

(Factor in the value or partial value of your home only if it is paid up and if you foresee a day when you can downsize.)

The rationale behind the 20× Rule is this: It allows you to withdraw 5 percent from your portfolio the first year, and then adjust that amount upward each year to keep up with inflation. The studies show that a well-diversified portfolio from which you take such withdrawals has a good chance of lasting at least 20 years, which is how long you may need the cash flow if you retire in your 60s and live to your mid-80s.

If you think you may live beyond your mid-80s, or if you want to retire before your mid-60s, then having more than 20 times your anticipated expenses is an excellent idea. Another excellent idea is to limit your initial withdrawal, if you can, to 4 percent a year, just in case you live a long life.

In truth, we'd much rather see you have 25 times your anticipated expenses in your portfolio before you retire at any age. But for many Canadians who haven't seen a real pay increase in years, this is indeed a lofty goal. For that reason, we say go with 20 times but be prepared to tighten your belt if you need to.

If you're still far away from that 20 times mark, and you aren't in debt, and your income is secure, and you aren't burning out at work, and you have enough cash to live on for six months, then with the rest of your loot, you may think about tilting toward a riskier ETF portfolio (mostly stock ETFs). You need the return.

If you have your 20 times (or better yet, 25 times) annual cash needs already locked up, or close to it, and you're thinking of giving up your day job soon, you should probably tilt toward a less-risky ETF portfolio (more bond ETFs). After all, you have more to lose than you have to gain. (See the upcoming sidebar "The 'today and tomorrow' portfolio modelling technique" for more on our suggestion that you should have not one but two model portfolios: one for right now, and one for the future.) You do need to be careful, however, that your investments keep up with inflation. Savings accounts are unlikely to do that.

If you have way more than 25 times annual expenses, congratulations! You have many options, and how much risk you take will be a decision that's unrelated to your material needs. You may, for example, want to leave behind a grand legacy, in which case you may shoot for higher returns. Or you may not care what you leave behind, in which case leaving your money in a tired savings account, or "investing" in a high-performance but low-yielding Ferrari, wouldn't make much difference.

Other risk/return considerations

We doubt we can list everything you should consider when determining the proper amount of risk to take with your investments, but here are a few additional things to keep in mind:

- **What is your safety net?** If worse came to worst, do you have family or friends who would help you if you got in a real financial bind? If the answer is yes, you can add a tablespoon of risk.

- **What is your family health history? Do you lead a healthy lifestyle?** These are the two greatest predictors of your longevity. If Mom and Dad lived to 100, and you don't smoke and you do eat your vegetables, you may be looking at a long retirement. Add a dollop of risk — you'll need the return.

- **How secure is your job?** The less secure your employment, the more you should keep in nonvolatile investments (like short-term bonds or bond funds); you may need to draw from them if you get the pink slip next Friday afternoon.

- **Can you downsize?** Say you are close to retirement, and you live in a McMansion. If you think that sooner or later you will sell it and buy a smaller place, you have some financial cushion. You can afford to take a bit more risk.

The limitations of risk questionnaires

Russell, a financial advisor, gives his clients a risk questionnaire. And then he goes through it with them to help them interpret their answers. You can fill out an investment risk questionnaire yourself online, but instead of having anyone interpret the answers, a computer just spits out a few numbers: You should invest *x* in stocks and *y* in bonds. Yikes!

Please, please, don't allow a computer-generated questionnaire to determine your financial future! The answers can be wacky.

For example: One question that appears on many web questionnaires is this: *Please rate your previous investment experience and level of satisfaction with the following six asset classes.* And then they list money market funds, bonds, stocks, and so on.

Russell had a client named Jason who was a 38-year-old with a solid job and no kids. After taking an online questionnaire, he was told he should be invested almost entirely in money market funds and bonds based on his previous "very low" satisfaction with stocks and stock mutual funds. This young man definitely should not invest in any stocks or stock funds, the computer-generated program told him, because of his "very low" satisfaction with the funds he had invested in previously.

Oh, yeesh. The reason Jason had "very low" satisfaction with stocks and stock funds is that he got snookered by some stockbroker (posing as a "financial planner") into buying a handful of full-load, high-expense-ratio, actively managed mutual funds that (predictably) lost him money. That experience should have *no* bearing on the development of this young man's portfolio, which should have the lion's share invested in stock ETFs or mutual funds.

What we're saying is that after reading this book, if you aren't too certain where you belong on the risk/return continuum, perhaps you should hire an experienced and impartial financial advisor — if only for a couple of hours — to review your portfolio with you. We write more about seeking professional help in Chapter 20.

Keys to Optimal Investing

When you have a rough idea of where you should be in terms of risk, your attention can turn next to fun matters such as Modern Portfolio Theory, reversion to the mean, cost minimization, and tax efficiency. Please, allow us to explain.

Incorporating Modern Portfolio Theory into your investment decisions

The subject we're about to discuss is a theory much in the same way evolution is a theory: The people who don't believe it — and, yes, there are some — are those who decide to disregard all the science. *Modern Portfolio Theory* (MPT) says that if you diversify your portfolio — putting all kinds of eggs into all kinds of baskets — you reduce risk and optimize return.

REMEMBER

You get the most bang for your buck, according to MPT, when you mix and match investments that have little *correlation*. In other words, if you build your portfolio with different ETFs that tend to do well (and not so well) in different kinds of markets, you'll have a lean and mean portfolio.

Lately, MPT has been the source of a lot of controversy. It hasn't been working as well as it did in the past. At times in the past few years, there have been stretches of days, or even weeks and months, when different asset classes — Canadian stocks, foreign stocks, commodities, and real estate — have all moved up and down nearly in lockstep. This was the case, unfortunately, in 2008. Like a flock of geese, just about every investment you can imagine headed south at the same time.

While correlations can change over time — and lately the major asset classes have shown alarmingly high rates of correlation — you shouldn't simply scrap the idea that diversification and the quest for noncorrelation are crucial. However, you may want to be cautious of too much reliance on diversification. Yes, you can diversify away much risk. But you should also have certain low-risk investments in your portfolio, investments that hold their own in any kind of market. Low-risk investments include CDIC-insured savings accounts; money market funds; short-term, high-credit-quality bonds; and GICs.

Minimizing your costs

Most ETFs are cheap, which is one of the things we love about them. The difference between a typical mutual fund that charges 1.4 percent and a typical ETF that charges 0.2 percent adds up to a *lot* of money over time. One of our favourite financial websites, www.moneychimp.com, offers a fund-cost calculator. Invest $100,000 for 20 years at 8 percent, and deduct 0.2 for expenses; you're left with $449,133. Deduct 1.4 percent, and you're left with $359,041. That's a difference of about $90,000.

Because the vast majority of ETFs fall into the super-cheap to cheap range (generally 0.10 to 0.15 percent), the differences among ETFs won't be quite so huge. Still, in picking and choosing ETFs, cost should always be a factor.

Of course, with ETFs, you often pay a small trading fee every time you buy and sell. That, too, should be examined and minimized. Do all your trading online, and choose a brokerage house that gives you the best deal. If you're going to make frequent buys and sells, either choose ETFs that you can trade commission free or opt instead to build your portfolio with mostly low-cost, no-load index mutual funds. See Russell's book *Index Investing For Dummies* (Wiley) for more on index mutual funds.

Striving for tax efficiency

Keeping your investment dollars in your pocket and not lining the federal government's is one big reason to choose ETFs over mutual funds. ETFs are, by and large, much more tax efficient than active mutual funds. But some ETFs are going to be more tax efficient than others. We cover this issue in depth in Chapter 19, where we talk about tax-advantaged retirement accounts, such as RRSPs and TFSAs.

For now, let us say that you must choose wisely which ETFs get put into which baskets. In general, interest-paying ETFs (REIT ETFs, bond ETFs) are best kept in tax-advantaged accounts.

Timing your investments (just a touch)

If you've read much of this book already, by now you realize that we're largely *efficient market* kind of guys. We believe that the ups and downs of the stock and bond market — and of any individual security — are, in the absence of true inside information, unpredictable. (And trading on true inside information is illegal.) For that reason, among others, we prefer indexed ETFs and mutual funds over actively managed funds.

However, that being said, we also believe in something called *reversion to the mean.* This is a statistical phenomenon that colloquially translates to the following: What goes up must come down; what goes waaaay up, you need to be careful about investing too much money in.

At the time we're writing this, for example, gold and silver and Canadian REITs have been flying high for a while. Emerging market stocks and bonds have also been outperforming big time. These are good reasons that you may want to be just a wee bit cautious about overstocking your portfolio in these particular asset classes.

We're *not* suggesting that you go out and buy any ETF that has underperformed the market for years, or sell any ETF that has outperformed. But to a small degree, you should factor in reversion to the mean when constructing a portfolio.

For example, say you decide that your $100,000 portfolio should include a 15 percent allocation in the iShares S&P/TSX 60 Index Fund (XIU) and an equal allocation in the iShares S&P/TSX Small Cap Index Fund (XCS). And say you happen to be entering the market after an incredible several-year bull market in large cap stocks, with small caps falling far behind. If anything, we'd be inclined to slightly overweight small cap stocks, putting perhaps 16 or 17 percent in XCS and maybe 13 to 14 percent in XIU.

Please don't go overboard. We're suggesting that you use reversion to the mean to very gently tweak your portfolio percentages — not ignore them! This "going-against-the-crowd" investment style is popularly known as *contrarian investing*. In Chapter 18, we introduce one investment advisor, Neil Stoloff, who has developed a compelling twist on being a contrarian.

Finding the Perfect Portfolio Fit

On the following pages, you'll find some sample portfolios. Which one should you follow? Look for the client who you most resemble, and that example will give you a *rough* idea of the kind of advice an advisor may give you. For the sake of brevity, we provide you with only a thumbnail sketch of each client's financial situation.

Considering the simplest of the simple

The best part about ETFs is that you can create a portfolio using less than a handful of funds or you buy a whole bunch. Let's start with the most basic portfolio and we'll expand from there.

Bringing in balance

This is the most basic portfolio of the bunch, and it has a simple mix of stocks and bonds, but it still covers all the important bases.

	Allocation
Canadian Equity iShares S&P/TSX Capped Composite (XIC)	20%
U.S./International Equity iShares MSCI World (XWD)	40%
Canadian Bonds iShares DEX Universe Bond (XBB)	40%

A well-rounded portfolio

This strategy adds a little more into the mix. It also uses some U.S.-based ETFs for the nondomestic part of the portfolio.

	Allocation
Canadian Equity iShares S&P/TSX Capped Composite (XIC)	20%
U.S. Equity Vanguard Total Stock Market (VTI)	15%
International Equity Vanguard Total International Stock (VXUS)	15%
Real Estate Investment Trusts BMO Equal Weight REITs (ZRE)	10%
Real Return Bonds iShares DEX Real Return Bond (XRB)	10%
Canadian Bonds iShares DEX Universe Bond (XBB)	30%

Bring on the dividends

If you're an income-seeking investor — and who isn't these days — then consider following this portfolio. It's loaded with dividend-paying ETFs. Hold it in a non-registered account so you can take advantage of the attractive dividend tax credit.

	Allocation
Canadian Dividend Equity iShares S&P/TSX Canadian Dividend Aristocrats (CDZ)	20%
Canadian Dividend Equity iShares Dow Jones Canada Select Dividend (XDV)	20%
Global Dividend Equity iShares Global Monthly Advantaged Dividend (CYH)	10%
Real Estate Investment Trusts BMO Equal Weight REITs (ZRE)	10%
Preferred Shares iShares DEX Hybrid Bond (XHB)	5%
U.S. High-Yield Bonds iShares Advantaged U.S. High-Yield Bond (CHB)	5%
Canadian Bonds iShares Advantaged Canadian Bond (CAB)	30%

Get more aggressive

Want to add a little more spice to your portfolio? Consider this strategy, which is based on the idea that value and small cap stocks deliver higher returns over time. More ETFs are listed here than the average investor would probably want to hold, so take this approach only if you know what you're doing.

	Allocation
Canadian Equity iShares Canadian Fundamental (CRQ)	12%
Canadian Small Cap iShares S&P/TSX Small Cap (XCS)	6%
U.S. Equity Vanguard Total Stock Market (VTI)	12%
US Small Cap Value Vanguard Small Cap Value (VBR)	6%
International Equity iShares MSCI EAFE Value (EFV)	6%
International Small Cap iShares MSCI EAFE Small Cap (SCZ)	6%
Emerging Markets Equity Vanguard Emerging Markets (VWO)	6%
Global Real Estate SPDR Dow Jones Global Real Estate (RWO)	6%
Government Bonds BMO Mid Federal Bond (ZFM)	20%
Corporate Bonds BMO Short Corporate Bond (ZCS)	20%

Racing toward riches: A portfolio that may require a crash helmet

High-risk/high-return ETF portfolios are made up mostly of stock ETFs. After all, stocks have a very long history of clobbering most other investments — *if* you give them enough time. Any portfolio that is mostly stocks should have Canadian, U.S., and international stocks, large cap and small cap, and value and growth, for starters. If the portfolio is diversified into industry sectors (an acceptable strategy, as we discuss in Chapter 10), a high-risk/high-return strategy emphasizes fast-growing sectors such as technology.

Consider the case of Alana, a hypothetical single 33-year-old media buyer. Alana came to her advisor after getting burned badly by several high-cost, load mutual funds that performed miserably over the years. Still, given her steady income of $120,000 and her minimal living expenses (she rents a one-bedroom apartment in Winnipeg, Manitoba), Alana has managed to sock away $220,000. Her job is secure. She has good disability insurance. She anticipates saving $20,000 to $30,000 a year over the next several years. She enjoys his work and intends to work till normal retirement age. She plans to buy a new car (ballpark $30,000) in the next few months but otherwise has no major expenditures earmarked.

Alana can clearly take some risk. An ETF-based portfolio that would work for her is represented in Figure 16-1. Note that we think Alana should put four to six months' of emergency money, plus the $30,000 for the car, into a high-interest bank account, so that amount isn't factored into this portfolio.

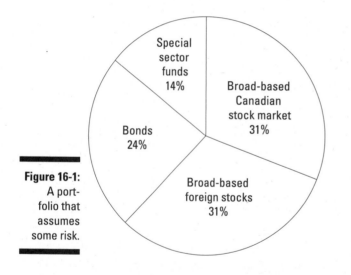

Figure 16-1:
A portfolio that assumes some risk.

Although this portfolio is technically 76 percent stocks and 24 percent bonds, we include a 4 percent position in emerging market bonds, which can be considerably more volatile than your everyday bond. As such, we don't really think of this as a 76/24 portfolio, but more like an 80/20 portfolio, which is just about as volatile a portfolio as we'd like to see.

Broad-based Canadian stock market: 31 percent

iShares S&P/TSX Capped Composite (XIC)	15 percent
iShares S&P/TSX Small Cap (XCS)	9 percent
iShares Dow Jones Canada Select Growth (XCG)	7 percent

Broad-based U.S. and foreign stocks: 31 percent

Vanguard Total Stock Market (VTI)	7 percent
Vanguard Small Cap Value (VBR)	6 percent
iShares MSCI EAFE Value Index (EFV)	5 percent
iShares MSCI EAFE Growth Index (EFG)	5 percent
iShares MSCI EAFE Small Cap Index (SCZ)	4 percent
Vanguard Emerging Markets ETF (VWO)	4 percent

Special sector funds: 14 percent

BMO Equal Weight REITs (ZRE)	4 percent
Vanguard REIT ETF (VNQ)	4 percent
iShares Global Infrastructure (CIF)	6 percent

Bonds: 24 percent

iShares DEX Universe Bond (XBB)	10 percent
iShares DEX Real Return Bond (XRB)	5 percent
iShares Advantaged U.S. High-Yield Bond (CHB)	5 percent
BMO Emerging Markets Bond (ZEF)	4 percent

Sticking to the middle of the road

Here, we present Jay and Racquel, who are ages 63 and 59, married, and have successful careers. Even though they are old enough to be Alana's parents, their economic situation actually warrants a quite similar high-risk/high-return portfolio. Both husband and wife, however, are risk-averse.

Jay is an independent businessman with several retail properties (valued at roughly $1.6 million); Racquel is a vice president at a major publishing house. Their portfolio: $800,000 and growing. Racquel also will receive a fixed pension annuity of about $30,000. The couple's goal is to retire within five to seven years, and they have no dreams of living too lavishly; they should have more than enough money. The fruits of their investments, by and large, should pass to their three grown children and any charities named in their wills.

Being risk-averse, Jay and Racquel keep 30 percent of their portfolio in high-quality government bonds. They want to know how to best invest the other 70 percent ($560,000), a small amount of which they wish to place in commodity ETFs. We feel that 30 percent high-quality bonds is quite enough ballast, so they don't need to add to their bond position by very much. We therefore favour a portfolio of largely domestic and foreign stock ETFs. The size of their portfolio (versus Alana's) warrants the addition of a few more asset classes, such as holdings in two large timber REITs.

The "today and tomorrow" portfolio modelling technique

Career coaches constantly tout the importance of having a career plan; we're going to tout the importance of having a portfolio plan. Times change; circumstances change. Your portfolio needs to keep up with the times. Suppose you are 45 years old and saving for retirement. Using the 20× rule we discuss in this chapter, you decide that your goal is someday to have a portfolio worth $1 million. Your current portfolio has $300,000, so you have a good ways to go.

To get where you want, you realize you need to take some risk, but when you start to approach your goal, you want to lower your risk. After all, at that point, you'll have more to lose than gain with any market swings. You should model your portfolio today but also have a picture of what your portfolio may look like when you reach, say, $700,000 . . . whenever that is.

Your picture may look something like this:

Today's $300,000 portfolio

iShares S&P/TSX 60 (XIU)	30 percent
iShares S&P/TSX Small Cap (XCS)	20 percent
Vanguard Total Stock Market (VTI)	15 percent
Vanguard Small Cap Value (VBR)	10 percent
iShares MSCI EAFE Value (EFV)	15 percent
iShares DEX Universe Bond (XBB)	10 percent

Tomorrow's $700,000 million portfolio

iShares S&P/TSX 60 (XIU)	20 percent
iShares S&P/TSX Small Cap (XCS)	10 percent
Vanguard Total Stock Market (VTI)	10 percent
Vanguard Small Cap Value (VBR)	5 percent
iShares MSCI EAFE Value (EFV)	10 percent
iShares DEX Universe Bond (XBB)	45 percent

By having your portfolio model for today and your picture of what it may look like tomorrow, you'll always know where you're heading. Trust us, it makes sense. Or trust Yogi Berra, who said, "If you don't know where you're going, you may wind up someplace else."

We don't suggest they buy any Canadian REITs other than the timber REITs, because so much of the couple's wealth is already tied up in commercial real estate. Figure 16-2 presents the portfolio breakdown.

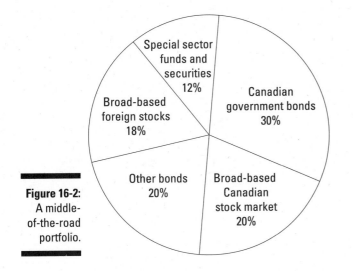

Figure 16-2:
A middle-
of-the-road
portfolio.

Broad-based Canadian stock market: 20 percent

iShares S&P/TSX Capped Composite (XIC)	12 percent
iShares S&P/TSX Small Cap (XCS)	5 percent
iShares Dow Jones Canada Select Growth (XCG)	3 percent

Broad-based foreign stocks: 18 percent

Vanguard Total Stock Market (VTI)	5 percent
Vanguard Small Cap Value (VBR)	4 percent
Vanguard Total International Stock (VXUS)	4 percent
iShares MSCI EAFE Small Cap Index (SCZ)	3 percent
Vanguard Emerging Markets ETF (VWO)	2 percent

Special sector funds and securities: 12 percent

Vanguard International Real Estate ETF (VNQI)	3.5 percent
SPDR S&P Global Natural Resources ETF (GNR)	3.5 percent
Plum Creek Timber Company (PCL)	2.5 percent
Rayonier Timber (RYN)	2.5 percent

Canadian government bonds: 30 percent

iShares DEX Universe Bond (XBB)	30 percent

Other bonds: 20 percent

BMO Short Corporate Bond (ZCS)	15 percent
BMO Emerging Market Bond (ZEF)	5 percent

Taking the safer road: Less oomph, less swing

Financial professional types hate to admit it, but no matter how much they tinker with their investment strategies, no matter how fancy their portfolio software is, they can't entirely remove the luck factor. When you invest in anything, a bit of a gamble is always involved. (Even when you decide *not* to invest, by, say, keeping all your money in cash, stuffed under the proverbial mattress, you're gambling that inflation won't eat it away or a house fire won't consume it.) Thus, the best investment advice ever given probably comes from Kenny Rogers:

> *You got to know when to hold 'em, know when to fold 'em*
>
> *Know when to walk away and know when to run.*

The time to hold 'em is when you have just enough — when you've pretty much met, or have come close to meeting, your financial goals.

We now present Richard and Maria, who are just about the same age as Jay and Racquel. They are 65 and 58, married, and nearing retirement. Richard is in a job he detests in the ever-changing (and not necessarily changing for the better) newspaper business. Maria is doing part-time public relations work. By adding up Richard's Canadian Pension Plan and Old Age Security payments, a small pension from the newspaper, Maria's part-time income, and income from their investments, we reckon Richard doesn't have to stay at a job he hates. The couple has enough money for Richard to retire, providing they agree to live somewhat frugally, and providing the investments — $700,000 — can keep up with inflation and not sag too badly in the next bear market.

We should add that the couple owns a home, completely paid for, worth approximately $350,000. They both agree that they can downsize, if necessary.

For a couple like Richard and Maria, portfolio construction is a tricky matter. Go too conservative, and the couple may run out of money before they die. Go too aggressive, and the couple may run out of money tomorrow. It's a delicate balancing act. In this case, we suggest Richard and Maria take the $700,000 and allocate 25 percent — $175,500 — to a fixed annuity. (The annuity should be put in one spouse's name, with 50 percent survivorship benefit for the other spouse. If the named spouse dies before Maria, the other could sell the home and buy or rent something more economical.) The rest of the money — $525,000 — we think should be allocated to a broadly diversified portfolio largely constructed using ETFs. Figure 16-3 shows the portfolio breakdown.

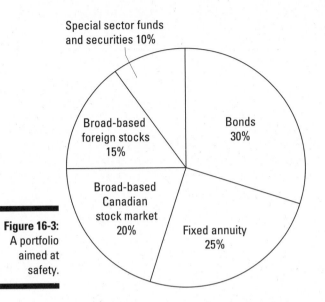

Special sector funds and securities 10%

Broad-based foreign stocks 15%

Bonds 30%

Broad-based Canadian stock market 20%

Fixed annuity 25%

Figure 16-3: A portfolio aimed at safety.

Broad-based Canadian stock market: 20 percent

iShares S&P/TSX Capped Composite (XIC)	13 percent
iShares S&P/TSX Small Cap (XCS)	7 percent

Broad-based foreign stocks: 15 percent

Vanguard Total Stock Market (VTI)	9 percent
Vanguard Total International Stock (VXUS)	6 percent

Special sector funds and securities: 10 percent

Vanguard International Real Estate ETF (VNQI)	3 percent
SPDR S&P Global Natural Resources ETF (GNR)	3 percent
Plum Creek Timber Company (PCL)	2 percent
Rayonier Timber (RYN)	2 percent

Bonds: 30 percent

iShares DEX Universe Bond (XBB)	15 percent
BMO Short Corporate Bond (ZCS)	15 percent

Fixed annuity: 25 percent

With 50 percent survivorship benefit

Chapter 17

Exercising Patience: The Key to Any Investment Success

In This Chapter

▶ Peeking into the world of day trading

▶ Examining "investment pornography"

▶ Treating time as your friend, not your enemy

*N*ow, dear reader, we get to the part of this book you've been waiting for: How to get rich quick using ETFs! The trick is understanding charting patterns.

Let us explain what we mean.

The chart in Figure 17-1 captures a hypothetical daily pricing pattern for a hypothetical ETF that we will give the hypothetical ticker symbol UGH. What you see at point A is a major reversal pattern known to technical analysts as the "Head and Shoulders." Notice that as the price dips below the "Neckline" and then rises with simultaneous "Increased Volume" that the "Reversal" of the "Trend" begins to manifest. Buy! Buy!! Within a short time, however, as you can clearly see at point B, a "Minor Top" forms, indicating an "Upward Trend" reinforced by the classic "Inverted Triangle." Sell! Sell!! Two minutes later, at point C, where volume increases yet again and the price again rises a point, we see a "Breakaway Gap." Buy! Buy! Buy!

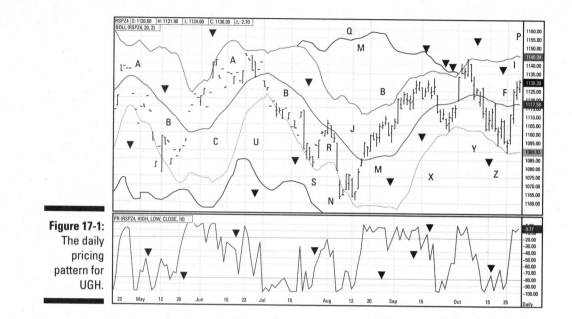

Figure 17-1:
The daily pricing pattern for UGH.

In the next chart (see Figure 17-2), we examine the daily pricing patterns of a hypothetical ETF that we will hypothetically call DUM. You can make millions overnight if you truly understand this charting pattern!

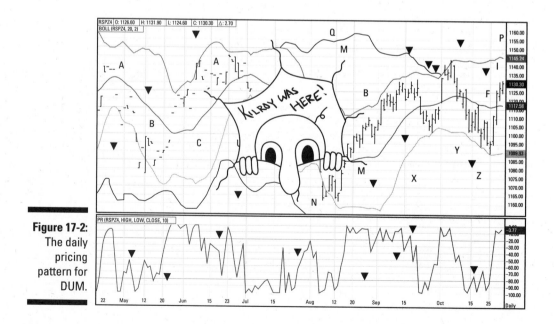

Figure 17-2:
The daily pricing pattern for DUM.

Unless you are totally humour challenged, by now you see that we're not being entirely serious. Many, if not most, day traders (who just *love* ETFs, especially the really kooky ones) believe in something called *technical analysis:* the use of charts and graphs to predict movements in securities. Much of the language we use to explain Figure 17-1, as well as the basic idea behind the charts, comes from a best-selling book on technical analysis.

Russell once had the honour of interviewing one of the biggest names in technical analysis. This guy writes books, gives seminars, and tells everyone that he makes oodles and oodles of money by following charting patterns and buying and selling securities accordingly. At the time Russell interviewed him, Russell had been a journalist for 20 years, writing for many of the top U.S. magazines, covering many topics. If you develop one thing being a journalist for two decades, it is a very well-honed hogwash radar. Russell can tell you after spending an hour on the phone with this so-called expert that he is perhaps making oodles and oodles of money with his books and seminars, but he is *not* making oodles and oodles of money with his charts.

And neither will you.

The key to success in investing isn't to do a lot of trading based on secret formulas every bit as fruitless as alchemy. The key is to keep your investment costs low (ETFs will do that for you), diversify your portfolio (ETFs can do that, too), lose as little as possible to taxes (ETFs can help there, too), and exercise patience (that part's up to you).

In this chapter, we present the evidence to back up our contention that buying and holding, more or less, with regular rebalancing, is the thing to do. Yes, that's true even in today's über-turbulent markets. You will see that the true champions of the investing world are those with the most patience. Here's a great quote that you may want to post next to your computer to look at the next time you contemplate swapping one ETF for another. It's from someone we admire quite a bit — someone who, we've heard, knows a little bit about investing.

> *The stock market is a method for transferring money from the impatient to the patient.*

> —Warren Buffett

In this chapter, you also discover the difference between hypothetical investing (the kind of investing where you allegedly get rich overnight) and investing in the real world in which Warren Buffett invests. The difference is huge.

The Tale of the Average Investor (A Tragicomedy in One Act)

We talk a bit in this book about *correlation,* the tendency for two things (such as two ETFs or other investments) to move in the same direction. A correlation of 1.0 indicates a *perfect* correlation: think Jimmy Fallon in the mirror imitating Jerry Seinfeld. Another perfect correlation is the correlation between stock prices and the public's willingness to purchase those stocks.

For some strange reason, the market for stocks (and stock funds, such as ETFs) does not work the same way as, say, the market for cars, shoes, or pineapples. With most products, if the seller drops the price, the public is likely to increase consumption. With stocks and stock funds, when the price *rises,* the public increases consumption.

For example, after tech stocks had their fabulous run in the 1990s, only then — in the latter part of the decade — did money start pouring into tech stocks. After the bubble had burst and tech stocks were selling cheaper than tarnished dirt, people were selling right and left, and no one was buying. As we write these words, the same kind of buying frenzy has been seen more recently with real estate investment trusts (REITs) and some dividend stocks. As soon as the bubble bursts on these, well, it'll be red-tag-sale day once again.

Returns that fall way short of the indexes

The investment research group Dalbar compares the returns of indexes to the returns that mutual fund investors see in the real world. In its 2010 study, the Dalbar research crew found that the average stock mutual fund investor for the 20 years prior to December 31, 2009, earned a little more than 3 percent a year. This compares to the more than 8 percent that someone would have earned by just plunking money in an S&P 500 index fund for those two decades and leaving it put. Bond fund investors did just as poorly in relation to the bond indexes.

How to explain such lacklustre investor returns? In part, the culprit is the average investor's inclination to invest in pricey and poor-performing mutual funds. Another problem is that the average investor jumps ship too often, constantly buying when the market is hot, selling when it chills, and hopping back on board when the market heats up again. He is forever buying high and selling low — not a winning strategy, by any means.

ETFs can solve the first part of the problem. They are, as long as you pick the right ones, not pricey. In fact, they cost very little. Most ETFs are also guaranteed not to underperform the major indexes because they mirror those indexes. As for the jumping-ship problem, however, we fear that ETFs can actually *exacerbate* the problem.

ETFs can make failure even easier!

ETFs were brought into being by marketing people from our very own Toronto Stock Exchange who saw a way to beef up trading volume. Unlike mutual funds, which can be bought and sold only at day's end, ETFs trade throughout the day. In a flash, you can plunk a million in the stock market. A few seconds later, you can sell it all.

Yippeee!

In other words, the next time Dalbar does a 20-year return study, after ETFs have really caught on with the average investor, we fear that its findings, if it includes ETFs, may be even more dismal. Remember: Just because ETFs can be traded throughout the day doesn't mean you *have* to or that you *should* trade them!

The vast majority of ETF trades are made by institutional investors: managers of mutual funds or hedge funds, multibillion-dollar endowments, pension funds, and investment banks. These are highly trained, incredibly well-paid professionals who do nothing all day but study the markets.

When you go to buy, say, the S&P/TSX Capped Financials Index Fund (XFN), which represents stocks in the Canadian financial sector, you're betting that the price is going to go up. If you're day trading, you're betting that the price will go up that day. If you're selling, you're betting that the price will fall that day. Someone — most likely a highly educated financial professional with an army of researchers and computers more powerful than the RCMP's, someone who does nothing but study financial stocks 80 hours a week (for which reason his wife is about to leave him) — is on the other end of your transaction. As you sell, he — we'll call him Doug — is buying. Or, as you buy, he is selling. Obviously, Doug's vision of the next few hours and days is different from yours. Doug may not know that his wife, Barbie, is about to leave him for a professional hockey player, but if either of you has any idea which way financial stocks are headed, well. . . . Do you really think that you know something Doug doesn't? Do you really think that you're going to get the better end of this deal?

Obviously, lots of ETF traders think they're pretty smart because ETFs are among the most frequently traded of all securities — see the sidebar "The ten Canadian ETFs that day traders love the most." Also see the sidebar "Russell's confession (and a few rules if you are going to day trade)" later in the chapter for an inside view of a repentant day trader's mind.

The lure of quick riches

If you jump on the Internet and type in the words "market timing success," you will see all kinds of websites and newsletters offering you all kinds of advice (much of it having to do with reading charts) that's sure to make you rich. Add the initials "ETF" to your search, and you'll quickly see that an entire cottage industry has formed to sell advice to wannabe ETF day traders.

According to these websites and newsletters, following their advice has yielded phenomenal returns in the past (and they'll give you specific BIG numbers proving it). And following their advice in the future (after you've paid your hefty subscription fee) will likewise yield phenomenal returns.

John Rekenthaler, a VP at Morningstar, once said, "Investment newsletter publishers have the same rights as tabloid publishers. There's nothing illegal about a headline that reads 'Martian Baby Born with Three Heads!' and there's nothing illegal about a headline that reads 'We Beat the Market Year In and Year Out!'" Both should be read with equal skepticism.

The ten Canadian ETFs that day traders love the most

They are volatile. They are *liquid* (meaning that they trade easily). And the following ten Canadian ETFs are flipped more often than all other Canadian ETFs:

✔ iShares S&P/TSX 60 Index Fund (XIU)

✔ Horizons BetaPro NYMEX Crude Oil Bull Plus (HOU)

✔ Horizons BetaPro NYMEX Natural Gas Bear Plus (HND)

✔ Horizons BetaPro NYMEX Natural Gas Bull Plus (HNU)

✔ Horizons BetaPro NYMEX Crude Oil Bear Plus (HOD)

✔ Horizons BetaPro S&P 500 VIX (HVU)

✔ Horizons BetaPro S&P/TSX Global Gold Bull Plus (HGU)

✔ iShares S&P/TSX Capped Energy Index Fund (XEG)

✔ iShares S&P/TSX Global Gold Index Fund (XGD)

✔ iShares S&P 500 Index Fund (CAD-Hedged) (XSP)

"Investment Pornography" in Your Mailbox

Investment websites and newsletters are part of a phenomenon that financial journalist Jane Bryant Quinn once called "investment pornography." Many newsletters, magazines, newspaper columns, books, and television shows exist to titillate and tease you with the promise of riches. Achieving those riches with ETFs is only the latest gimmick.

One glossy consumer finance magazine that arrived in Russell's mailbox caught his attention. A very attractive woman is walking along the beach. She holds a purse in her hand. (Why is she carrying a purse on the beach?) The caption under her left foot says that the attractive woman earned a 40 percent return in one year.

Russell turned to page 65 of the magazine, and there she is: a single woman! She earned her 40 percent by investing ("on the advice of a friend") in the Hodges mid cap mutual fund. Mid caps happened to have kicked serious butt in the 12 months prior to this issue's release. What the article doesn't tell you is that the Hodges fund has a fairly hefty expense ratio and — no big surprise here — a 15-year return that trails the S&P MidCap 400 index by 3.54 percent annually.

No wonder that poor woman carries her purse on the beach. She has determined that someone is out to steal her money.

In 1999, a very popular book entitled *Dow 36,000: The New Strategy for Profiting from the Coming Rise in the Stock Market* gave readers 300 pages of in-depth explanation why the Dow Jones Industrial Average, at that time riding around 10,000, was destined to more than triple in value. "The case is compelling that 36,000 is a fair value for the Dow today. And stocks should rise to such heights very quickly," wrote James K. Glassman and co-author Kevin A. Hassett. Of course, as soon as the book came out, advising people to pour money into stocks, the Dow proceeded to tumble to less than 8,000 in a three-year bear market.

Where do you suppose James K. Glassman is today? Why, he's writing an investment advice column, of course. And he's writing more books. And he's making more predictions.

Before Glassman, there were the Beardstown Ladies. In 1983, 16 women in Beardstown, Illinois, started an investment club. In 1994, claiming a 23.4 percent annualized ten-year return, they wrote a book called *The Beardstown Ladies' Common-Sense Investment Guide*. It became a huge bestseller. Oops.

It turns out, upon further inspection, that the Beardstown Ladies overstated their returns. Their actual return was 9.1 percent a year, considerably less than the stock market.

What happened to the good Ladies of Beardstown? Why, they went on to write five more investment books, of course.

Don't even get us started on Jim "Mad Money" Cramer. If you haven't taken his screaming advice and lost money on your own, simply search for his name on the Internet, along with the words "actual performance" or "flip of the coin," and you will be very disinclined ever to buy based on one of Mr. Mad Money's tips.

We share these investment horror stories of the past and present so that you won't wind up as a player in any future ones. One way to make sure you don't is to be on the lookout for ridiculous claims. Market timing services are popping up all over the Internet. Why not? ETFs are hot. They are in the news. They sound so impressive. And there is a sucker born every minute.

Please, please, don't fork over your money assuming that you're going to get the secrets to instant wealth by trading ETFs. It won't happen.

Patience Pays, Literally

The flip side of flipping ETFs is buying and holding them, which is almost certain, in the long run, to bring results far superior to market timing. It's the corollary to choosing ETFs over stocks. Study after study shows that the markets are, by and large, *efficient*. What does that mean? So many smart players are constantly buying and selling securities, always on the lookout for any good deals, that your chances of beating the indexes, whether by market timing or stock picking, are very slim.

One of but many studies on the subject, "The Difficulty of Selecting Superior Mutual Fund Performance" by Thomas P. McGuigan, appeared in the *Journal of Financial Planning.* McGuigan found that only 10 to 11 percent of actively managed mutual funds outperform index funds over a 20-year period. (*Active managers* are professionals who try to pick stocks and time the market.)

We can probably safely assume that the professionals do better than the amateurs, and even the professionals fail to beat the market 90 percent of the time.

Talk about unpredictability

Timing doesn't work because markets are largely random. The unpredictability of the stock market (and the bond market, for that matter) never ceases to amaze us. Just when things seem certain to take off, they sink. Just when they seem certain to sink, they fly.

Russell had one client, Tom, a 52-year-old allergist in Allentown, Pennsylvania, who several years ago read up on avian flu and became so concerned about what a pandemic might do to the stock market that he urged Russell to take his $500,000 portfolio and put everything in cash. A meeting was set up in Tom's office, and Russell was able to temper his desire to cash out. (However, Russell did move his portfolio to a somewhat more conservative position.)

Prior to the meeting, Russell sent the client the following e-mail, which he'd like to share with you:

> *Dear Tom,*
>
> *Since your initial e-mail on this topic, I've done a fair amount of reading, and you have reason to be concerned, for sure. I am, too.* (Russell's note: I was being truthful here, although my concern was more a health concern than a financial one.)
>
> *Holding some cash and gold wouldn't be a bad idea. (If we had a real economic crisis, you would want small gold coins . . . 1/10 ounce.)*
>
> *But don't assume that pandemics, or any other crises, necessarily result in stock market crashes.*
>
> *Keep in mind that 1918, the year of the worst pandemic in world history, was a good year for stocks:* `www.econ.yale.edu/~shiller/data/chapt26.html`.
>
> *1962 (Cuban Missile Crisis) was a very good year. 1942 (Japan attacked Pearl Harbor; Hitler marched across Europe) wasn't too bad, either.*
>
> *In contrast, let's look at the worst years for the stock market. In 1929, nothing catastrophic was going on. Ditto for 1987. Ditto for 2000.*
>
> *I can't explain the incredible unpredictability of the markets. I can only share these historical truths.*
>
> *Yours,*
>
> *Russell*

Since he wrote that note, we've been though yet another of history's worst years for the stock market. That was 2008. Although there was something of a banking crisis going on, we're not sure that the demise of Lehman Brothers compares to Hitler's blitzkrieg of Europe. But more on 2008 in just a moment.

A short history of the market's resiliency

As we write this chapter, in April 2013, no one's quite sure where the market is headed. While the S&P 500 is having another great year, the S&P/TSX Composite is down. There are still worries over slowing growth in China and Europe's not out of the headlines either. While there hasn't been a crash, the ride during the last while has been bumpy. Still, we've come a long way since the summer of 2012, when things in Europe looked even sicker than it does now, and we're doing much better than in August 2011, when the U.S. government-made crisis — the debt-ceiling debacle, as Bryan likes to call it — resulted in a downgrade of U.S. Treasuries by S&P and, then, a pullback in the market. It's easy to panic in volatile times like these, but do we? No.

When we look at the market's 2012 returns, U.S. stocks rose by an incredible 12 percent. Canadian stocks didn't fare as well, climbing by about 4 percent. However, that's a lot better than the 11 percent drop the S&P/TSX Composite Index experienced in 2011. As you can see, the market always seems to find a way to recover.

Remember September 11, 2001? Following the destruction of the World Trade Center towers, the Dow immediately dropped more than 7 percent. Six months later, the Dow was up by 10.5 percent. On September 24, 1955, President Eisenhower's heart attack led to a one-day drop of 6.5 percent. Six months later, the Dow was up 12.5 percent. We could give example after example.

In 2008, the market had its worst dip since the Great Depression; The S&P 500 tumbled nearly 37 percent for the year, while the S&P/TSX Composite fell nearly as much. But it came back, gaining 26 percent in 2009 and about 15 percent in 2010. The Canadian market jumped 55 percent in 2009 (from its March 9 low) and 13 percent in 2010. Had you rebalanced in 2008, shaving off bonds and buying up stock at rock-bottom prices, your portfolio (provided it was well-diversified) would likely have fully recovered in just two years.

That's not to say that the market will *always* come back. One of these days . . . well, even Rome eventually fell. But history shows that the stock market is a mighty resilient beast. We suggest that you build a portfolio of ETFs — including stock and bond ETFs — and hang tight. Sooner or later (barring some truly major economic upheaval), you will very likely be rewarded.

Russell's confession (and a few rules if you are going to day trade)

Um . . . er . . . I don't know quite how to say this, but, despite all of the talk in this chapter and throughout this book about buying and holding, and the futility of day trading, yes — YES! YES! — I've done it. I admit it! I've bought and sold ETFs within the same day in the hope of making a quick gain! I've done it with the QQQ (an ETF that tracks the NASDAQ) and with EEM (an emerging-markets ETF).

What can I say? Gambling (and that is what such short-term forays into the market are) can be fun. Not only that, but the odds of making money by gambling on an ETF are much greater than they are by, say, playing the horses, shooting craps, or standing in line at 7-11 on a Friday afternoon to buy lottery tickets. After all, the "house" takes only a small cut when you play the markets. And time is on your side.

Have I made any short-terms gains? Sure. I've also lost some money. On balance, over the years, I've probably just about broken even . . . or maybe earned ten cents an hour for all my efforts. But it has been fun!

I am sharing this with you because I know that some of you are going to occasionally have that feeling in your gut that you "know" some security is going to go up (or down, if you're into short selling), and you may take a stab.

Okay, go ahead if you must; I'll just ask you to play by a few rules.

Rule #1

Separate gambling from investing; have a (small) fixed amount of money to gamble with. Take it from cash. Don't sell your buy-and-hold investments to finance your gambling.

Rule #2

If you find that you are getting fixated on your wins and losses, quit. If it isn't fun, don't do it. If you find that you are spending an inordinate amount of time playing the markets, quit. There is more to life.

Rule #3

Don't buy on margin. If you are borrowing money from the brokerage house to trade, that could spell big trouble. Margin money usually costs much more than you think. I hold Fidelity Investments in high regard, but I really don't like the full-page magazine advertisements it's run in the past that offer low rates for margin borrowing. If you read the very small print at the bottom of the page, it explains that the advertised rate pertains only to margin loans over $500,000. Small players — like you and me — pay much more.

Rule #4

Ask yourself what you're going to do if you get stuck. Have an exit plan. What if you buy EEM on an exceptionally volatile day, and you expect it to rise 3 percent, but instead it falls 4 percent? Are you going to hold it until it climbs back up? Are you going to cash out and take the hit? Have a plan in place before you make the trade, and stick to it. Consider placing a stop-loss order going in, at a price that reflects how much you're willing to lose. That way, if the trade goes against you, your plan will be implemented automatically without requiring you to make a gut-wrenching decision in the heat of the moment.

Rule #5

If you think that you have a superhuman ability to time the markets, ask yourself if that is really what you want to do for a living. Day trading isn't exactly a career that benefits the community or grows your consciousness. I've known a good number of day traders; they tend not to be the happiest or most enlightened people on the planet.

To find out more about day trading, read *Day Trading For Canadians For Dummies*, co-authored by Bryan Borzykowski (Wiley).

Chapter 18

Exceptions to the Rule (Ain't There Always)

*I*nvesting in the '90s was a snap. You'd buy a few mutual funds, or if you were a bit savvier than the average investor, you'd create your own basket of stocks. Then you'd hang on. For much of that decade, the market went up, up, and up and everyone made a lot of money on their investments. It was the days of buy-and-hold investing — buy a security, and hold on forever. Making money was easy.

Of course, buying and holding works only if the market doesn't crash, and it did, twice, last decade. Although it's still reasonable to think that over the long term the market will continue to rise, the economic crisis taught us that you have to be a little more active when it comes to your portfolio. That doesn't mean you need to be a day trader, but rather, if you want to keep that portfolio climbing you may need to make some adjustments here and there.

In this chapter, we discuss certain circumstances where trading ETFs rather than buying and holding them makes sense. For example, you need to rebalance your portfolio, typically on an annual basis, to keep risk in check, and on occasion you may want to swap ETFs to harvest taxes at year end. We also discuss the ways in which life changes may warrant tweaking a portfolio. And finally, we introduce you to the world of ETF options, where frequent trading is a way of life.

Rebalancing to Keep Your Portfolio Fit

Few investors walked away from 2008 smelling like a rose. But those who were slammed, truly slammed, were those who had more on the stock side of their portfolios than they should have. It happens, and it happens especially after bull markets, such as we saw in the several years prior to 2008.

Take the case of Samantha. In 2003, when she was 50 years old, she sat down and looked at her financial situation and goals. She determined that she warranted a 60/40 (60 percent stock/40 percent bond) portfolio and duly crafted a darned good one. But then she got lazy. She held that portfolio without touching it through the stock market boom years of 2003 through 2007. As a result, her portfolio morphed from a 60/40 mix to a 70/30 mix by the start of 2008.

Uh-oh.

In other words, just when the market tanked, just when she could have really used the ballast that bonds provide, her lopsided portfolio, because of neglect, was primed for disaster. The stock market fell by about 40 percent, and her 70 percent stock portfolio fell by about a quarter. That's a big fall. And to add insult to injury, just when stocks hit rock bottom, she had no "dry powder" (cash) with which to reload her stock portfolio.

It is in large part to prevent such big falls, and lack of "dry powder," that you need to rebalance. That is, on a regular basis, you need to do exactly the opposite of what most investors do: You need to sell off some of your winners and buy up the losers.

By doing so, not only do you cap your risk, but studies show that you will also juice your returns. By systematically buying low and selling high, you may, over the long run, increase your average annual returns by as much as 1.5 percent. That's not a bad return at all for an exercise that shouldn't take you more than a couple hours! (*Note:* We say "as much as 1.5 percent" because the profitability of rebalancing will depend on how many asset classes you own and the correlations they have to each other.)

How rebalancing works

Samantha actually hurt herself in two ways. In 2008, she was 55 years old: five years closer to retirement than she was when she established her "ideal" 60/40 portfolio. It would have been reasonable at that point for Samantha to adjust her mix to, say, 50/50 to reflect the need for a bit more protection against market losses as retirement neared. Had Samantha started off 2008 with a proper portfolio, whether it was 60/40 after rebalancing or 50/50 after reassessing and then rebalancing, she would have been in a much better position to weather the storm that was coming.

Prepare yourself for the next market storm! How? The answer is fairly simple: Don't allow any one slice of your portfolio to overtake the rest. Periodically pull your portfolio back into balance.

To illustrate, we'll use the simple middle-of-the-road ETF portfolio that we introduce in Chapter 16. At the start of the year, the portfolio is just where you want it to be: 60 percent diversified stocks, 40 percent bonds. But it turns out to be a banner year for stocks, and especially for Canadian real estate investment trusts (REITs). At the end of the year, as you can see in Table 18-1, the portfolio looks quite different.

Table 18-1	A Shifting Portfolio Balance
Beginning of Year One (In Balance)	
ETF	**Percent of Portfolio**
Canadian Equity iShares S&P/TSX Capped Composite (XIC)	20 percent
U.S. Equity Vanguard Total Stock Market (VTI)	15 percent
International Equity Vanguard Total International Stock (VXUS)	15 percent
Real Estate Investment Trusts BMO Equal Weight REITs (ZRE)	10 percent
Real Return Bonds iShares DEX Real Return Bond (XRB)	10 percent
Canadian Bonds iShares DEX Universe Bond (XBB)	30 percent
End of Year One (Out of Balance)	
ETF	**Percent of Portfolio**
Canadian Equity iShares S&P/TSX Capped Composite (XIC)	23 percent
U.S. Equity Vanguard Total Stock Market (VTI)	16 percent
International Equity Vanguard Total International Stock (VXUS)	16 percent
Real Estate Investment Trusts BMO Equal Weight REITs (ZRE)	14 percent
Real Return Bonds iShares DEX Real Return Bond (XRB)	6 percent
Canadian Bonds iShares DEX Universe Bond (XBB)	25 percent

What to do? Bring things back into balance, starting with the bond position. That's because the split between stocks and bonds has the greatest impact on portfolio risk. In this example, you need to increase the bond allocation from 31 percent back up to 40 percent. If you have a year-end portfolio of $100,000, that means you'll buy $9,000 of XRB and XBB to bring up your bond allocation by 9 percentage points.

Where will the $9,000 come from? That depends. You could sell off part of your stock position, which may be necessary given that things are pretty seriously out of balance. But do keep in mind that selling off winning positions in a taxable account will require you to pay capital gains — and possibly a small commission on the ETF trades. So to the extent possible, try to rebalance by shoring up your losing positions with fresh deposits or with dividends and interest earned on your portfolio.

How often to rebalance

The question of how often to rebalance has been studied and restudied, and most financial professionals agree that once a year is a good time frame, at least for those still in the accumulation phase of their investing careers. Anything less frequent than that increases your risk as positions get more and more out of whack. Anything more frequent than annually, and you may lower your returns by interrupting rallies too often and increasing your *friction costs* (trading commissions, spreads, and possible taxes).

Keep these costs in mind as you rebalance. Tweaking a portfolio by a few dollars here and there to achieve "perfect" balance may not make financial sense.

Never pay more than one-half of 1 percent to make a trade for rebalancing purposes. In the example in the preceding section, if a trade of $8,000 for XBB will cost you $10, you are forking out only 0.125 percent to make the trade . . . so, by all means, make the trade.

If, however, to get your portfolio in perfect balance, you were faced with making a $1,000 trade that would cost you $10 (1 percent of the amount you're trading), we don't think we'd opt to spend the $10. We'd rather wait another year (or perhaps less, if we sensed that a major shift had occurred) before acting.

Another way to approach rebalancing is to seek to address any allocations that are off by more than 10 percent, and don't sweat anything that's off by less. In other words, if XBB is given an allocation in the portfolio of 30 percent, we wouldn't worry too much about rebalancing unless that percentage falls to 27 percent, or rises to 33 percent.

Rebalancing for retirees

If you are in the *decumulation* phase of your investing career (that's a fancy way of saying that you are living off of your savings), you may want to rebalance every 6 months instead of 12. The reason: Rebalancing has a third purpose for you, in addition to risk reduction and performance juicing. For you, rebalancing is a good time to raise whatever cash you anticipate needing in the upcoming months. In times of super-low interest rates on money market and saving accounts, such as we've seen in recent years, it can be profitable to rebalance more often so that you don't need to keep as much cash sitting around earning squat. We provide more information on raising cash for living expenses in retirement in Chapter 19.

Contemplating Tactical Asset Allocation

Astute readers — such as you — now may be wondering this: If you can juice your returns by rebalancing (systematically buying low and selling high), can you perhaps juice your returns even more by *over*-rebalancing? In other words, suppose you design a 60/40 portfolio, and suddenly stocks tank. Now you have a 50/50 portfolio. Might you consider not only buying enough stock to get yourself back to a 60/40 portfolio but also (because stocks are so apparently cheap) buying even *more* stocks than you need for simple rebalancing purposes?

Investment professionals call this kind of manoeuvre *tactical asset allocation.* It is the art of tilting a portfolio given certain economic conditions. Tactical asset allocation is different than market timing only in the degree to which action is required. With tactical asset allocation, you make a gentle and unhurried shift in one direction or another, whereas market timing entails a more radical and swift shifting of assets. While tactical asset allocation, done right, may add to your bottom line, market timing will almost always cost you. The division between the two can be a fine line, so proceed with caution.

Understanding the all-important P/E ratio

We talk about reversion to the mean in Chapter 16. If a certain asset class has been seeing returns much, much lower than its historical average, you may want to very slightly overweight that asset class. If, for example, you are considering overweighting Canadian stocks, it makes more sense to do it when Canadian stocks are selling relatively cheaply. Typically, but not always, an asset class may be "selling cheap" after several years of underperforming its historical returns.

But is there any way to find a more objective measure of "selling cheap"? Investment legend Benjamin Graham liked to use something called the P/E ratio. The *P* stands for price. The *E* stands for earnings. When the market price of a stock (or all stocks) is high, and the earnings (or profits for a company or companies) are low, then you have a high P/E ratio; conversely, when the market price is down but earnings are up, you have a low P/E ratio. Graham, as well as his student Warren Buffett, preferred to buy when the P/E ratio was low.

Throughout Part I of this book, we urge you to consider tilting your entire stock portfolio, on a permanent basis, toward lower P/E stocks, otherwise known as *value stocks*. Here, we're talking not about a permanent tilt but a mild, temporary one. It stands to reason that if value stocks outperform other stocks — and historically they have done just that — if the entire stock market appears to be a value market, then that market may outperform in the foreseeable future.

Recent work by Yale University economist Robert J. Shiller has lent credence to the notion that buying when the P/E ratio is low raises your expected returns. In fact, Shiller has tinkered with the way the P/E ratio is defined so that the earnings part of the equation looks back over a decade (rather than the typical one year) and then factors in inflation. Shiller's research, based on tracking market returns with varying P/E ratios over the decades, indicates that when his adjusted P/E ratio is low, the stock market is more likely to produce gains over the following decade. When the P/E ratio is high (it reached an all-time high of about 44 in 1999, for example), you may be looking forward to a decade of very low (or no) returns.

Applying the ratio to your portfolio

Although Shiller's theories have been hotly debated, it stands to reason that, if they are applied carefully, you may just do yourself a favour to slightly overweight all stocks when the P/E ratio is low and to underweight all stocks when the P/E ratio is high. But against the probability that Shiller's formula holds, you need to weigh the very real transaction costs involved in shifting your portfolio. On balance, we wouldn't suggest engaging in tactical asset allocation very often . . . and then only if the numbers seem to be shouting at you to act.

One very quick way to check the P/E ratio for the entire stock market would be to look up an ETF that tracks the entire market, such as the S&P/TSX Capped Composite Index (XIC) in Canada and the Vanguard Total Stock Market ETF (VTI) for the U.S. market. You can also check just about any financial website (such as www.morningstar.ca). Or, to see Shiller's newfangled P/E calculations, go to www.multpl.com. (The P/E ratio is sometimes called the "multiple.")

The historical average for Shiller's adjusted P/E over the past 50 years is 19.5. As we're writing these words, the P/E for the U.S. market is lower, at around 15 times earnings. The Canadian market is at a similar P/E too. Tactical asset allocation may work in certain situations, but the market has been much cheaper over the last few years. So be careful, because the P/E is now trending upward. If stock prices should race ahead of or fall way behind earnings, though, and you start to see an adjusted P/E of, say, 30 or more, or 10 or less, you may want to gently — very gently — tweak your portfolio in one direction or another.

Did we remember to say *gently*?

If, all things being equal, you determine that you should have a portfolio of 60 percent stocks, and if the adjusted P/E falls to the low teens, consider adding 2 to 3 percentage points to your stock allocation, and that's all. If the market P/E falls to 10, then maybe, provided you can stomach the volatility, consider adding yet another percentage point or two, or even three, to your "neutral" allocation. If the adjusted P/E rises to 30 or so, you may want to lighten up on stocks by a few points. Please, keep to these parameters. Tilting more than a few percentage points — particularly on the up side (more stocks than before) — increases your risks beyond the value of any potential gain.

Buying unloved assets

Ever notice how weeds grow so much faster than the plants that you *want* to see grow? For years, Morningstar has advocated, and continues to advocate with varying levels of enthusiasm, something called "Buy the Unloved." It calls not for overweighting asset classes that sport low P/E ratios, but for overweighting asset classes that investors (being the lemmings that they are) have abandoned in droves. In other words, you are encouraged to buy "weeds."

If you shift from the "loved" to the "unloved" (in other words, you allocate tactically) and hold the "unloved" for three to five years, you'll tend to outperform the market per Morningstar. "From the beginning of 1994 to the end of 2010, the unloved earned 308% cumulatively or 9% annualized. That's far better than the loved, which earned 157% cumulatively or 6.1% annualized," says the company. During this time, the S&P 500 returned 8 percent annualized.

Investing the SweetSpot way

No matter how well you may tend to the weeds in your garden, they will never win an award at the county fair. The weeds that you buy as an investor, on the other hand, are actually more likely to blossom into big winners than the most highly prized — and high-priced — petunias that tend to wither at the first sign of bad weather.

About a year ago, Russell encountered a man named Neil Stoloff, a wealth manager outside Detroit, Michigan, who calls his shop SweetSpot Investments LLC. Just as Robert Shiller crunched historical data to come up with a new and improved way of measuring P/E, Stoloff crunched historical data and came up with a new and improved way of defining "unloved."

Each January, Stoloff examines more than 500 ETFs and mutual funds that track about 100 different U.S. and global industry sectors (from energy to financials to health care), as well as entire foreign markets (such as France, South Africa, and Malaysia). He calculates the flow of money into and out of each sector and market over the year that just ended, looking for the greatest outflows. And that's where he invests: in the areas that most investors have decided they wouldn't touch with the proverbial ten-foot pole. These are the weediest weeds Stoloff can find. A year later he repeats the process, and while he's at it he sells whatever was bought three years prior.

Given that he tinkers just once a year, we would classify Stoloff as a professional tactical asset allocator rather than a market timer. You can find out more about what he does and why he does it in a paper published in April 2011: http://sweetspotinvestments.com/wp-content/uploads/paper.pdf.

How has SweetSpot performed? Exceptionally well, and far better than Morningstar. For the latest performance figures, go to Stoloff's website, www.sweetspotinvestments.com. (Disclosure time: Neil and Russell have become good friends. At Russell's urging, Neil had his return figures audited by an independent accounting firm, and Russell believes he's being objective in saying that this guy may be on to something.)

Stoloff's strategy is not one that do-it-yourselfers can easily employ. Finding and making sense of the data on flows for each of 500 funds isn't nearly as easy as finding market-sector P/E ratios. Stoloff is a money manager whose fee is a percentage of assets under management, but he began his career as a do-it-yourself investor.

Even if SweetSpot isn't your cup of tea, you can still benefit from the wisdom of investing contrarily. Often you can get a sense of the direction in which the herd is running simply by keeping your ears open at cocktail parties. Just move opposite the crowd — slowly — and you'll likely outperform over time. As with any other kind of tactical asset allocation, we urge you to always consider your total allocation and make certain that you remain well diversified.

Harvesting Tax Losses, and the CRA's Oh-So-Tricky "Superficial Loss Rule"

So you had a bad year on a particular investment? You had a bad year on *many* of your investments? Allow the Canada Revenue Agency to share your pain. You only need to sell the investment(s) by December 31, and you can use the loss to offset any capital gains that have occurred in the prior three years. Don't have any gains to offset? No problem. You can carry the loss forward indefinitely.

But keep this in mind: Because of the CRA's "superficial loss rule," you can't sell an investment on December 31 and claim a loss if you buy back that same investment or any "substantially identical" investment within 30 days of the sale. You may simply want to leave the sale proceeds in cash. That way, you save on any transaction costs and avoid the hassle of trading.

On the other hand, January is historically a very good time for stocks. You may not want to be out of the market that month. What to do?

ETFs to the rescue!

What the heck is "substantially identical" anyway?

The CRA rules are a bit hazy when it comes to identifying "substantially identical" investments. Clearly, you can't sell and then buy back the same stock. But if you sell $10,000 of Suncor Energy (SU) stock, you *can* buy $10,000 of an ETF that covers the energy industry, such as the iShares S&P/TSX Capped Energy Index Fund (XEG). They're not the same thing, for sure, but either one can be expected to perform in line with SU (and its competitors as well) for the 30 days that you must live without your stock. And rest assured, no ETF could reasonably be deemed to be "substantially identical" to any individual stock.

We, of course, would prefer that you keep most of your portfolio in ETFs in the first place. Even then, if you follow our advice, and one year turns out to be especially bad for, say, large cap value stocks, no problem. If you are holding the iShares S&P/TSX Capped Composite Index Fund (XIC) and you sell it at a loss, you can buy the BMO S&P/TSX Capped Composite Index ETF (ZCN), hold it for a month, and then switch back if you wish.

Two ETFs that track similar indexes are going to be very, very similar but not "substantially identical." At least the CRA *so far* has not deemed them substantially identical. But the CRA changes its rules often, and what constitutes "substantially identical" could change tomorrow or the next day. It's usually a good idea to consult with a tax professional (which we are not) before proceeding with any tax harvesting plans.

As always, consider cost

We'll remind you again that trading an ETF may require you to pay a trading commission to a brokerage house. Harvesting a tax loss generally requires four trades. (Sell the original holding, buy the replacement, sell the replacement, buy back the original holding.) If you're paying $10 per trade, that adds up to $40. Plus, you lose a bit of money on each trade with the *spread* (the difference between the ask and bid prices on a security). So keep that in mind before making those trades.

Revamping Your Portfolio with Life Changes: Marriage, Divorce, and Babies

Rebalancing to bring your portfolio back to its original allocations, making tactical adjustments, and harvesting losses for tax purposes aren't the only times it may make sense to trade ETFs. Just as you may need a new suit if you lose or gain weight, sometimes you need to tailor your portfolio in response to changes in your life.

As we discuss in Chapter 16, the prime consideration in portfolio construction is whether you can and should take risks in the hope of garnering high returns or whether you must limit your risk with the understanding that your returns will likely be modest. (Diversification can certainly help to reduce investment risk, but it can't eliminate it.) Certain events may occur in your life that warrant a reassessment of where you belong on the risk/return continuum.

If a single person of marrying age walks into his advisor's office and asks for help in building a portfolio, the advisor will want to know if wedding bells will be ringing in the near future. If a married couple walks into the same office, one of the first things the advisor may take note of is how close they sit together. And if the woman has a swollen belly, the advisor should really take notice.

No, the advisor isn't being nosy. Marriage, divorce, and the arrival of babies are major life changes and need to be weighed heavily in any investment decisions. So too are the death of a spouse or parent (especially if that parent has left a hefty portfolio to the adult child); a child's decision to attend college; any major career changes; or the imminent purchase of a new house, new car, or Fabergé egg.

Betsy and Mark: A fairly typical couple

Betsy and Mark are engaged to be married. They don't have a lot of money. But both are young (early 30s), in good health, gainfully employed, and without debt. They plan to merge their savings of roughly $38,500 and want to invest it for the long haul.

The first thing they need to do is to decide how much money to take out to cover emergencies. Given their monthly expenses of roughly $3,500, they decide to earmark five months' of living expenses — $17,500 — and plunk that into an online savings account. That leaves them with $21,000 to invest.

If we were advising them, we usually wouldn't consider an ETF portfolio for $20,000, but this is money they claim they aren't going to touch until retirement. We'd urge them both to open a Tax-Free Savings Account. . (Any money you put into a TFSA grows tax free for as long as you wish, and withdrawals are likewise tax free; more on retirement accounts in Chapter 19.) We'd ask them to divide the $21,000 between the two accounts. Because each of them can contribute $5,500 in 2013 (the rules changed this year) and $5,000 in 2012 we'd have them both make double contributions — one for the past year and one for the current year.

To save on transaction costs and keep things simple for now, we'd limit the number of investments and give each partner a "partial" portfolio. Neither account alone is well-diversified, but together, they are.

Betsy's TFSA

iShares S&P/TSX Capped Composite (XIC)	$4,500
Vanguard FTSE All-World ex-US Small Cap Index ETF (VSS)	$3,000
iShares DEX Universe Bond (XBB)	$3,000

Mark's TFSA

Vanguard S&P 500 Index ETF (CAD-Hedged) (VSP)	$4,500
Vanguard Small Cap ETF (VB)	$3,000
iShares DEX Universe Bond (XBB)	$3,000

As Betsy and Mark's portfolio grows, we would plan to add other asset classes (real estate investment trusts, emerging market stocks, inflation-protected securities, and so on) and other accounts.

One year later

Betsy is pregnant with twins! The couple is saving up for their first home, with a goal of making that purchase within 18 months. If they had saved money in an RRSP, which isn't normally to be touched (without paying tax) before retirement, an exception would be made for first-time home purchases. Betsy and Mark could take out as much as $25,000 without penalty.

They're using a TFSA, though. We'd rather that they leave that money untouched, but the couple thinks the money may need to be tapped. At this point, the money in the TFSA has grown from $21,000 to $22,000 (for illustration purposes, we're pretending that each investment grew by an equal amount), and Betsy and Mark can each contribute another $5,500 in fresh money, bringing the total of both accounts to $33,000. Because there is a possibility that $10,000 will need to be yanked in one year, we'd advise them to earmark any fresh money to a fairly nonvolatile short-term bond ETF.

Betsy's TFSA

iShares S&P/TSX Capped Composite (XIC)	$4,900
Vanguard FTSE All-World ex-US Small Cap Index ETF (VSS)	$3,300
iShares DEX Universe Bond (XBB)	$3,300
iShares 1–5 Year Laddered Corporate Bond Index Fund (CBO)	$5,000

Mark's TFSA

Vanguard S&P 500 Index ETF (CAD-Hedged) (VSP)	$4,900
Vanguard Small Cap ETF (VB)	$3,300
iShares DEX Universe Bond (XBB)	$3,300
iShares 1–5 Year Laddered Corporate Bond Index Fund (CBO)	$5,000

Yet one year later

The twins (Bob and Doug) have arrived! Much to their surprise, Betsy's parents have gifted the couple $10,000 for the purchase of the home. The TFSA money needn't be touched. At this point, we would tell them to sell the short-term bond fund and add to their other positions. Also, provided the couple has another $5,500 each to contribute, we'd suggest they begin adding asset classes to the mix, perhaps starting with the iShares MSCI Emerging Markets Index Fund (XEM), the iShares S&P/TSX Capped REIT Index Fund (XRE), the Vanguard S&P 500 Index ETF (VFV), or Vanguard MSCI EAFE Index ETF (CAD-Hedged) (VEF). Hopefully, Betsy and Mark (and Bob and Doug) will have many happy years together. And with each major life event, we would urge them to adjust their portfolio appropriately.

Are Options an Option for You?

Beyond the world of exchange-traded funds, an entirely different universe is filled with things called *exchange-traded derivatives*. A *derivative* is a financial instrument that has no real value in and of itself; rather, its value is directly tied to some underlying item of value, be it a commodity, a stock, a currency, or an ETF.

The most popular derivative is called an *option*. Let's explain it in a way we can all understand: through movies! You can't do this in real life, but for our purposes pretend that Hollywood is now letting your reserve movie tickets in advance for a fraction of the ticket's actual price. When you reserve the ticket you pay $1.99 rather than the full $12.99. Only if you go to the movie do you have to cough up the difference. If you decide to stay home and watch DVDs instead you only lose the $1.99. It's more complicated than that, but in other words buying an option gives you the option of purchasing a security at a later date.

Most options in the investment world give you the right either to buy or sell a security at a certain price (*the strike price*) up to a certain specified date (*the expiration date*). Options are a prime example of a *leveraged* investment. In other words, if you buy an option, you're leveraging the little bit of money that you pay for the option — the *premium* — in hopes of winning big money. If you're an option seller, you stand to make the amount of the small premium, but you risk losing big money. For the system to work, the sellers have to win much more often than the buyers . . . and they do.

Lately, options on ETFs have been hot, hot, hot — especially on American names — and growing hotter. Options on certain ETFs, most notably the SPY (which represents the S&P 500) and the QQQ (which represents the 100 largest company stocks traded on the NASDAQ), typically trade just as many shares on an average day as the ETFs themselves. (See the sidebar "SPY, QQQ, and SPX are the options champs.") On most days, options on ETFs like the QQQ and SPY trade more shares than any other kind of options, including options on individual stocks, commodities, and currencies.

You see, ETFs provide traders with the opportunity to trade the entire stock market, or large pieces of it, rather than merely individual securities. In the past, this was doable but difficult. You cannot trade a mutual fund on the options market as you can an ETF.

Much of this often- renetic trading in ETF options, at least on the buying side, is being done by speculators, not investors. If you have an itch to gamble in the hopes of hitting it big, options may be for you. In that case, we'll refer you to *Futures & Options For Dummies* by Joe Duarte, M.D. (Wiley). Dr. Duarte will warn you, as we are warning you, that successful option trading takes an iron gut, a lot of capital, and a lot of expertise. And even if you have all that, you may still end up getting hurt.

SPY, QQQ, and SPX are the options champs

ETFs are a *huge* part of the options market. The most commonly traded options include many individual stocks, but the most active of the active are all ETFs. The five most frequently traded, of late, are these:

ETF	Ticker Symbol
SPDR S&P 500	SPY
PowerShares QQQ Trust Series 1	QQQ
iShares Russell 2000	IWM
ProShares VIX Mid-Term Futures	VIXM

Understanding puts and calls

All kinds of options exist, including options on options (sort of). The derivatives market almost seems infinite — as does the number of ways you can play it. But the two most basic kinds of options, and the two most popular by far, are *put options* and *call options,* otherwise known simply as *puts* and *calls.* We're going to take just a moment to describe how these babies work.

Calls: Options to buy

With a call option in hand, you have bought yourself the right to buy, for example, 100 shares of the PowerShares QQQ Trust (currently trading at $50) at $55 (the strike price) a share at any point between now and, say, December 18 (the expiration date). If QQQ rises above $55, you would, of course, take the option and buy the 100 shares at $55. After all, you can then turn around and sell them immediately on the open market for a nifty profit. If, however, the price of QQQ does not rise to $55 or above, you are not going to exercise your option. Why in the world would you? You can buy the stock cheaper on the market. In that case, your option expires worthless.

Puts: Options to sell

With a put option in hand, you have bought yourself the right to sell, for example, 100 shares of QQQ (currently trading at $40) at $35 (the strike price) a share at any point between now and, say, December 15 (the expiration date). By December 15, if QQQ has fallen to any price under $35, you will likely choose to sell. If QQQ is trading above $35, you'd be a fool to sell. In the latter case, your option will simply expire, unused.

Using options to make gains without risk

Those people who use calls as an investment (as opposed to gambling) strategy are assuming (as do most investors) that the market is going to continue its historical upward trajectory. But instead of banking perhaps 60 or 70 percent of their portfolio on stocks, as many of us do, they take a much smaller percentage of their money and buy calls. If the stock market goes up, they may collect many times what they invested. If the stock market doesn't go up, they lose it all — but only a modest amount. Meanwhile, the bulk of their money can be invested in something much less volatile than the stock market, such as bonds.

Zvi Bodie, Professor of Finance and Economics at Boston University School of Management, wrote a book with Michael J. Clowes entitled *Worry-Free Investing: A Safe Approach to Achieving Your Lifetime Financial Goals* (Prentice Hall) in which he suggests an investment strategy using long-term stock options and Treasury Inflation-Protected Securities (TIPS) (or Real Return Bonds, as they're called in Canada). If you have $100,000 to invest, says Bodie, you might consider putting roughly 90 percent of it into TIPS. (A very convenient way to do that would be to purchase the iShares Barclays TIPS Bond Fund ETF. Or, if you want a Canadian option, the iShares DEX Real Return Bond Index Fund.) That way, he asserts, your principal is protected.

To shoot for growth, says Bodie, take the other 10 percent or so and invest it in long-term call options (otherwise known as *Long-Term Anticipation Securities,* or *LEAPS*), going about three years out. If the market soars, you take home the bacon. If, however, the market sinks, your call options merely expire, and you still have your TIPS, which by this point, three years later, have grown to match your original $100,000.

It's an intriguing strategy that just may make sense, especially for older investors tapping into their savings who can't wait for the stock market to come back after a serious bear market.

Interestingly, a similar kind of "worry-free investing" may be achieved by owning *all* stocks (or close to it) but using put options to protect yourself from the downside. Certain "inverse" ETFs exist that should, in theory, allow you to achieve the same end. As we discuss in Chapter 11, these funds haven't worked so well in the real world.

Insuring yourself against big, bad bears

The put option is an option to sell. This investment strategy allows you to have money in the stock market (all of it, if you so desire), but you carry insurance in the form of puts. If the market tumbles, you're covered.

Suppose you want to invest everything in the NASDAQ index through the QQQ. Normally, an investor would have to be insane to bet everything on such a volatile asset. But with the right put options in place, you can actually enjoy explosive growth but limit your losses to whatever you wish: 5 percent, 10 percent, 15 percent.

With a pocketful of puts, you can laugh a bear market in the face. If the QQQ drops by, say, 50 percent in the next week, you will have checked out long before, smiling as you hold your cash.

Seeming almost too good to be true

So options allow you to capture the gains of the stock market with very limited risk. They allow you to invest in the market and not have to worry about downturns. What's not to love about options?

Whoaaa. Not so fast! You need to know a couple little things about options:

- **They are expensive.** Every time you buy either a put or a call, you pay. The price can vary enormously depending on the strike price, the expiration date you choose, and the volatility of the ETF the option is based on. But in no case are options cheap. And the *vast majority* of options reach their expiration date and simply expire.

  So, yes, options can save you in a bear market, and they can help you to capture a bull market, but either way, you're going to pay. Free lunches are very hard to come by!

- **Taxes are tricky!** Generally, gains and losses from options are taxed as capital gains. It's complicated, though, because there's more to trading options than buying and selling like you would a stock. Talk to a tax professional before jumping into the options market.

Weighing options strategies against the diversified ETF portfolio

Don't misunderstand us. We're not saying that the price you pay for options isn't worth it — even after taxes are considered. Options do provide investors with a variety of viable strategies. The real question, though, is whether using puts and calls makes any more sense than investing in a well-diversified portfolio of low-cost ETFs. Most financial professionals are skeptical.

How to profit with ETF options in a stagnant market

Selling covered calls is a traditional way that many people get started in the world of options, says Jim Bittman, an instructor with the Chicago Board Options Exchange's Options Institute. "You can take a nondividend paying ETF and turn it into an income-generating asset," he says. Here is how selling a covered call, otherwise known as a *buy-write strategy,* works:

You buy, say, 1,000 shares of the PowerShares QQQ Trust Series 1 ETF (QQQ). Let's assume that the current price is $50 a share. You've just invested $50,000 (plus a small trading commission of perhaps $10 or so, which, for simplicity's sake, we'll ignore for the moment).

Now you sell a covered call. This means that, through a brokerage house, you offer someone else the right to purchase your shares at a certain price in the future. You may, for example, offer the right to purchase your 1,000 shares at $52 (the strike price) within 90 days (the expiration date). You get paid for selling this right. In this scenario, you may be paid something in the ballpark of 75 cents a share for a total of $750 (roughly 2 percent of your original investment).

If, in the next 90 days, the QQQ stays between $50 and $52 (the market is relatively flat), your covered call expires worthless. You walk away with your $750, and life is good. (However, you will have to pay the IRS a short-term capital gains tax on that money. The short-term capital gains tax is usually the same as your marginal income tax rate. In many cases, that will be about twice as high as the tax you would pay after cashing out a long-term investment.)

But now suppose that the market tanks: You are left holding 1,000 shares of the QQQ that may be worth much less than $50,000, the only offset being the $750 (before taxes) that you received.

And suppose the market soars: You just lost out, too. The QQQ may be selling at $60 a share, but the guy who bought your contract can buy your shares from you (and certainly *will* buy them from you, or will sell the option to someone else who will buy them from you) at the agreed-upon price of $52 a share. In the end you will lose the difference between the actual value of your QQQ shares and their value at the strike price, again offset only by the $750 that you received when you sold the option.

And there's the catch. We've known a good number of investors who *rave* about their experiences with covered calls . . . as long as the markets are relatively stagnant. As soon as there is major movement either up or down — which has been known to happen — they stop raving and start ranting.

In the past few years, we've seen the introduction of several exchange-traded products that allow you to buy a basket of covered calls. These include the BMO Covered Call Canadian Banks ETF (ZWB) and the Horizons Enhanced Income International Equity ETF (HEJ). (Horizons has several covered call ETFs for sale.) Both have expense ratios of 0.65 percent. Both were introduced in 2011. Both have lost money. Will funds like these ever make money? Yes . . . if we see several years of a flat market. What are the chances of that?

To be sure, if we knew a bear market was coming, we would definitely buy ourselves a slew of put options. If we knew a bull market was in the offing, we would certainly buy a fistful of call options. But here's the problem: We don't know which way the market is going, and neither do you. And if we buy both puts and calls on a regular basis, we're going to be forever bleeding cash.

Not only that, but if the market stagnates, then both our puts and calls will expire worthless. In that case, we're really going to be unhappy.

So here's the way we look at it. The chances of success with a steady call strategy are one in three: We win if there's a bull market; we lose if there's a bear market; we lose if the market stagnates. Ditto for a put option strategy: We win if there's a bear market; we lose if there's a bull market; we lose if the market stagnates. It's hard to like those odds.

With a well-diversified portfolio of low-cost ETFs — stock, bond, REIT, and commodity ETFs — we reckon our chances of success are more like two in three: We lose if there's a bear market; we win if there's a bull market; in the case of a stagnant stock market, *something* in our portfolios will likely continue to make money for us anyway.

You may recall us saying earlier in this chapter that the derivatives market almost seems infinite, as does the number of ways you can play it. If you wish, ETF options strategies exist that allow you to make money in a stagnant market, too. The most common such strategy is called a *buy-write strategy* or *selling a covered call*. We explain how that strategy works (but don't necessarily advocate it) in the sidebar "How to profit with ETF options in a stagnant market."

Factoring in time and hassle

One final (but fairly major) consideration: Options trading generally requires much more time and effort than does buy-and-hold investing in a diversified portfolio. Let us ask you this: Would you rather spend your spare time at your computer tinkering with your investments, or would you rather do just about anything *but* that?

Chapter 19

Using ETFs to Fund Your Golden Years

In This Chapter

▶ Differentiating various retirement account options

▶ Knowing which ETFs to sock into which accounts

▶ Calculating how much money you need to retire

▶ Planning your cash flow needs after the paycheque stops

*I*magine if someone made a movie about RRSP planning. No doubt, there'd be a scene that would go something like this:

Financial advisor: Our clients invest a lot of money with us, and we really don't ever want to lose them.

Advisor's boss: No problemo! We'll suggest a retirement plan that's so incredibly bad that our clients will *never* be able to retire and spend their money! Just take a look at this array of some of the most expensive and poorly performing mutual funds available on the market today. That's what we offer!

Financial advisor: Good. And what about portfolio diversification?

Advisor's boss: None. Four of the nine mutual funds under our umbrella are large Canadian equity funds. We offer no small caps. No international anything. Just large domestic stocks, a few ridiculously expensive and volatile bond funds, and an overpriced lifestyle fund with wholly inappropriate allocations for people of all ages.

Financial advisor: Excellent! Will the fees wipe out any potential gains?

Advisor's boss: Absolutely! Each mutual fund in the plan charges at least a 5 percent load and a good chunk of cash each year beyond that in operating fees, and then we slap on yet *another* high "wrap" fee on top of it all! We can almost guarantee you that your clients' investments won't earn squat, and we'll be working for them forever.

Okay, maybe this is a paranoid fantasy on our part, but sometimes we wonder. Many RRSP plans are so manifestly terrible, so ridiculously designed and priced, and so poorly managed that you can't help but imagine that someone set out to make them that way.

And that makes us sad. The traditional company pension — Grandpa's retirement plan that provided him with a steady paycheque from the day he retired till the day he died — is disappearing from the land. The Canadian Pension Plan (CPP) and Old Age Security (OAS) typically provide a modest income, and no more, and even that is at risk. That leaves the omnipresent RRSP as many working people's last hope for a comfortable retirement.

Our advice: Read this chapter. It's about the use of ETFs in retirement plans — potential financial knights in shining armour.

ETFs alone are not going to allow everyone to retire to the golf course. But they can take you a very long way in that direction. In this chapter, we discuss how you should be using your ETFs in tax-advantaged retirement accounts to get the most bang for your investment buck, and we explain the differences between an RRSP and a TFSA. We also escort you into your retirement years to see how an ETF portfolio may provide you with the income you need to replace your current paycheque.

Aiming for Economic Self-Sufficiency

I've got all the money I'll ever need — if I die by four o'clock this afternoon.

— Henny Youngman

How much you need in your portfolio to call yourself economically self-sufficient ("retired," if you prefer) starts off with a very simple formula: $A \times B = \$\$\$\$$. A is the amount of money you need to live on for one year. B is the number of years you plan to live without a paycheque. $\$\$\$\$$ is the amount you should have before bidding the boss adieu. There you have it.

Of course, that formula is waaay oversimplified. You also need to factor in such things as return on your future portfolio, inflation, CPP and OAS, and (for the very lucky) potential inheritances. For a more detailed reckoning of how much money you should be looking to save, we refer you to some fairly decent online retirement calculators; see the sidebar "How much is enough?"

How much is enough?

A reasonable accumulation goal for most couples is 20 times the amount you spend in a year. To reach that goal, you may have to set aside a minimum of 15 percent of your salaries for a minimum of two to three decades. For more accurate (but still ballpark) numbers, we can refer you to a number of online retirement calculators. Note that none of these is perfect; we recommend that you use several. Take note that you'll get different — in some cases, vastly different — numbers. Consider each a ballpark figure. Average them for another ballpark-of-ballparks figure.

✔ Good (and quick!): CIBC at www.cibc.com/ca/retirement/article tools/rrsp-calc-intro.html

✔ Better: The "How Much Should You Be Saving for Retirement" calculator at www.fiscalagents.com/toolbox/index.shtml#tb2

✔ Best (but still not perfect): Canadian Retirement Income Calculator at www.servicecanada.gc.ca/eng/isp/common/cricinfo.shtml

Note: Be realistic about your expected rate of return.

Taking the basic steps

Whatever amount you set as your goal, you need to do three basic things to achieve it:

✔ Perhaps obvious, although most people prefer to ignore it: You have to *save*. A retirement portfolio doesn't just pop up from out of nowhere and grow like Jack's beanstalk. You need to feed it. Regularly.

✔ You need to invest your money wisely. That's where a well-diversified portfolio of ETFs comes in.

✔ It behooves you to take maximum advantage of retirement plans such as your company's pension plan — even if it's subpar — RRSPs, and the relatively new tax-free savings account (TFSA).

Choosing the right vessels

If you will, try to think of your retirement plans — your RRSP, your TFSA — as separate vessels of money. How much your nest egg grows depends not just on how much you put into it and which investments you choose, but also which vessels you have.

There are three types of investment savings accounts:

✔ Canada's main retirement savings account is the Registered Retirement Savings Plan. This is a *tax-deferred* vessel: You don't pay taxes on the money in the year you earn it; rather, you pay taxes at whatever point you withdraw money from your account, typically only after you retire.

✔ The second option (but becoming the first for many people) is the Tax-Free Savings Account, which became available in January 2009. This is a *tax-free* vessel: As long as you play by certain rules (discuss them with your accountant), anything you plunk into a TFSA (money on which you've generally already paid taxes) can double, triple, or (oh please!) quadruple, and you'll never owe the CRA a cent.

✔ Finally, you can also invest in a non-registered account. All the holdings in this account are taxable, but some investments have more favourable tax rates than others. Most people recommend using the registered accounts for retirement purposes and this type of vessel if you have money left over.

Why your choice of vessels matters — a whole lot

How much can your choice of vessels affect the ultimate condition of your nest egg? *Lots.* Even in a portfolio of all ETFs.

When it comes to taxes and investment accounts, think of an ETF like a mutual fund. If you hold a fund in a non-registered account, you'll have to pay capital gains on the money you make when you sell, but you may also be taxed on the interest and dividend income that the fund gives off.

With mutual funds, you often have to pay some capital gains even if you don't sell. If the fund manager sells a fund, some of the distribution you receive may be in the form of a gain, which you'll be taxed on. A big benefit to ETFs is that, in most cases, ETFs have far less turnover than mutual funds, so you won't be on the hook for these types of forced capital gains.

Still, it's usually better to put money away into a TFSA or RRSP because you won't be taxed on dividend or interest income or anything else. The downside, though, is that the amount of money that you can put into retirement accounts is limited. You're allowed to put 18 percent of your annual income into an RRSP and $5,500 per year into a TFSA. (However, the room accumulates in both, so if you've never contributed you'll have a lot more space to work with.)

What should go where?

If you want to use all of your available options, you may be asking yourself which ETFs (and other investments) should get dibs on becoming retirement assets, and which are best deployed elsewhere? Follow these five primary principles, and you can't go too wrong:

- ✔ **Any investment that generates a lot of (otherwise taxable) income belongs in your retirement account.** Any of the bond ETFs and REIT ETFs are probably best held in your retirement account because these pay distributions that are taxed as income.

- ✔ **Keep your emergency funds out of your RRSP.** Any money that you think you may need to withdraw in a hurry should be kept out of your retirement accounts. Withdrawing money from a retirement account can often be tricky, and it will usually trigger taxation. You don't want to have to worry about such things when you need money by noon tomorrow because your teenage son just totalled the family car.

  Note: You can move money in and out of the TFSA without worrying about a tax hit. But the TFSA is supposed to be for retirement savings, so it's not a good idea to use it as a personal ATM. Plus, the recontribution process is complicated (you can't just put back in what you've taken out) and may get you in trouble with the CRA if it's not done correctly.

- ✔ **House investments with the greatest potential for growth in your TFSA.** This may include your small cap value ETF, your technology stock fund, or your emerging markets ETF. TFSA money won't ever be taxed (presuming there are no changes in the law), so why not try to get the most bang for your ETF buck?

- ✔ **Dividend ETFs can be kept in a non-registered account.** It's debatable as to whether you should put yielding stocks and ETFs in your RRSP, TFSA, or non-registered account, but dividends are taxed at a much more favourable rate than other income. Compounding the dividend interest tax-free in a retirement vehicle is a big plus, but if you do have some extra money to save, then you should take advantage of the attractive dividend tax rate.

- ✔ **Foreign ETFs should be held in your RRSP.** It's actually much more complicated than that, but for simplicity's sake we say to hold non-Canadian funds in your RRSP. The reason is that foreign dividends are subject to a withholding tax, usually about 15 percent. You can get that money back on U.S. investments, but not on stocks based in other countries. The withholding tax doesn't apply on investments held inside an RRSP.

Before you decide where to plunk your investments, refer to the following two sections for the basic rules.

Retirement accounts

Here are ETFs and other investments generally best kept in a retirement account:

- ✔ **Taxable bond ETFs:** Examples include
  - iShares DEX Universe Bond (XBB)
  - BMO Short Corporate Bond (ZCS)
  - iShares DEX Real Return Bond (XRB)

- ✔ **ETFs that invest in real estate investment trusts (REITs):** Examples include

    - BMO Equal Weight REITs (ZRE)

    - iShares S&P/TSX Capped REIT Index Fund (XRE)

- ✔ **High-dividend Canadian-based ETFs that hold U.S. stocks:** Examples include

    - BMO High Yield U.S. Corporate Bond Hedged to CAD Index (ZHY)

    - iShares U.S. High Yield Bond Index Fund (CAD-Hedged) (XHY)

- ✔ **Foreign-stock ETFs:** Examples include

    - Vanguard Total Stock Market ETF (VTI)

    - iShares Core S&P 500 ETF (IVV)

    - iShares MSCI World Index Fund (XWD)

- ✔ **Actively managed funds, whether mutual funds or ETFs**

Taxable accounts

Here are ETFs and other investments that can be kept in a taxable account:

- ✔ **Cash reserve for emergencies**

- ✔ **Stock ETFs:** Examples include

    - iShares S&P/TSX 60 Index Fund (XIU)

    - iShares S&P/TSX Capped Composite Index Fund (XIC)

    - Vanguard MSCI Canada Index ETF (VCE)

- ✔ **Dividend-paying ETFs holding Canadian stocks:** Examples include

    - Vanguard FTSE Canadian High Dividend Yield Index (VDY)

    - iShares S&P/TSX Canadian Dividend Aristocrats Index Fund (CDZ)

    - BMO Canadian Dividend ETF (ZDV)

TFSAs versus RRSPs

It wasn't long ago that Canadians had one retirement savings option (outside of a company pension plan). But now that we can save two ways, in an RRSP or a TFSA, we all should be asking ourselves which account is best for our investments. Here, we compare the two options.

The RRSP

RRSPs became popular because it allows people to grow their savings tax free until they take it out. As well, most Canadians receive a tax refund — the amount you contribute is deducted from your taxable income, so you get taxes you already paid through work back — which you can then use for whatever you please. (We suggest reinvesting, but we won't judge you if you really need to go somewhere warm next winter.) The idea is that you contribute in your working years, when you're in a higher tax bracket, and then you withdraw in retirement, when you're in a lower tax bracket. (It's lower because you're not working.) Keep in mind that you will be taxed at your marginal rate when you take out the money. You can also contribute about 18 percent of your annual income each year, and that unused room accumulates from year to year.

The TFSA

The Tax-Free Savings Account also lets you grow your savings tax free (hence the name), but one major difference exists: You don't get taxed when you withdraw the funds. That's because you've already paid tax on the money you're contributing. A lot of people like that feature because it's a lot less complicated. What goes in can come right out, though hopefully you'll have more, thanks to dividends and capital gains. The one main downside is that you can contribute only a certain amount every year (at present, the limit is $5,500), though unused room does accumulate year after year.

Taxes Now or Taxes Later? (Or, What's Better?)

It really depends on one thing: Will you be in a lower tax bracket when you retire than when you contribute? If yes, then use an RRSP. If no, then use a TFSA. Unfortunately, a lot of people don't know what their tax status will be in 20 or 30 years. More people are working well into retirement, which could keep the person in a higher tax bracket. Others have been such diligent savers all their lives that when it comes time to withdraw at age 72 (more technically, the year you turn 72), they'll be taking out so much that they'll be in the highest tax bracket. You must consider two factors: How much do you want to save, and do you make less than $40,000 a year? If you want to save more than $5,500 a year, use an RRSP. If you make less than $40,000, there's no tax benefit to investing in an RRSP. We have heard rumours that the government will up the yearly TFSA limit to $10,000. If that happens, you can probably kiss the RRSP goodbye.

Ushering Your Portfolio into Retirement Readiness

A fee-only financial planner named William P. Bengen, CFP, wrote a book for financial planners called *Conserving Client Portfolios During Retirement* (FPA Press). Bengen did an enormous amount of number crunching, reviewing historical return figures going back to 1926. He and his computer played out scenario after scenario: If you retired in year *X,* and you took out $Y for *Z* years . . . that sort of fun analysis. His conclusion: The conventional wisdom is both right and wrong. Right, stocks drive a portfolio. Wrong, once you retire, you should live off bonds.

15+ years and counting

If you have 15 years or longer until retirement, the money in your retirement account — if history is our guide — should be pretty close to fully invested in stocks. If it is, and we look back over many years, your odds of coming out ahead in any 15-year period seem to be pretty close to a certainty. Forget the bonds. But, but, but . . . the future may *not* be like the past, which is why we never advocate a portfolio that isn't invested at least 20 percent in bonds or cash or some other kind of hedge against a potential stock market tumble.

Less than 15 years to retirement

Every year, starting 15 years from retirement, says Bengen, you may want to tilt your asset mix a bit more conservatively. When you retire, assuming you're looking at a life expectancy of 30 or so years at that point, you should be thinking not about the conventional mostly bonds retirement portfolio but, rather, about something closer to 60 percent stocks and 40 percent bonds. With that mix, your portfolio has the best chance of being around as long as you are.

Throughout his book (as we do throughout this book), Bengen urges investors not to be "wooden" and not to adhere to any strict formulas. The percentages suggested here can, and should, vary with your individual circumstances.

Given the incredible volatility in stocks of late, and some rather serious economic issues facing the United States and other nations, many advisors have been leaning their portfolios a bit toward the more conservative side. For a retired or soon-to-be-retired client who may have warranted a 60/40 (stocks/bonds) portfolio several years ago, we might now suggest a 60/40 portfolio only if that portfolio is very, very well-diversified with different kinds of stocks and bonds, and the client has at least two years of living expenses in cash and near-cash (short-term GICs, high-quality and very short-term bonds). But in most cases, we'd prefer to see a 50/50 portfolio.

We also urge you to think of *stocks* and *bonds* in the broadest sense of "growth investments" and "security investments." Growth investments may include commodities or real estate, as well as stocks. Security investments may include a fixed annuity or a market-neutral mutual fund (with a proven track record), as well as government and corporate bonds. Of course, both your stock and bond positions can — and likely should — be held in ETFs.

Withdrawing Funds to Replace Your Paycheque

How much can you withdraw from your retirement funds each year and have a good chance of not running out of money? That, of course, is one of the biggest financial questions retirees have. According to Bengen, the answer, at least for people in their 60s, is somewhere around 4 to 5 percent, depending on your health, your investment choices, market conditions, the rate of inflation, how much you'll pay in taxes, and how much you want to leave behind for those rotten children of yours who never come to visit anymore.

We say, go with Bengen's rough estimate of 4 to 5 percent and use some of the retirement calculators we mention in the sidebar "How much is enough?" to smooth out the estimate a bit, but do plan to sit down with a financial planner at least once to get a better idea of where you stand. You don't want to run out of money!

Know that Bengen's work has been hotly, hotly disputed in financial-planning circles, with some researchers claiming that 4 to 5 percent is way too high (and you risk running out of money by withdrawing so much), while others claim it is too low (and you risk not enjoying your money as much as you could). But we think the fact that both camps feel so strongly about the issue means that 4 to 5 percent is probably about right . . . although we highly recommend regular monitoring and some flexibility in your spending. Did the market boom last year? Take that vacation to Maui. Did it bust? Sorry — no new car for you this year (sigh).

As far as withdrawing funds from your ETF portfolio, in the following sections we offer a few special words of advice that may make life easier.

Don't obsess over maintaining principal or drawing from dividends

We're not quite sure where this absurd division of the nest egg into *principal* and *interest* got started. It's seemingly some form of mass hysteria that began many years ago and continues to delude the populace.

Listen: If you have an account with, say, $100,000, and you withdraw $5,000, how much do you have left? The answer is $95,000. Got it? The answer will *always* be $95,000. It doesn't matter in the slightest whether that $5,000 came from principal or you took it out of recently received dividends or interest. (There may be a tax difference in a non-retirement brokerage account, but in a retirement account, there is absolutely no difference.)

So what does this mean in terms of withdrawing funds to live on in retirement?

The best way to achieve that end is to rebalance your portfolio with some regularity (perhaps every six months), tapping into whichever funds have performed the best and effectively create your own "artificial dividend." For example, say that you have an RRSP with a balance of $100,000. The money is invested (for simplicity's sake) in three ETFs thusly:

- ✔ iShares S&P/TSX 60 Index Fund (XIU): $25,000 (25 percent)
- ✔ iShares MSCI World Index Fund (XWD): $25,000 (25 percent)
- ✔ BMO Aggregate Bond Index ETF (ZAG): $50,000 (50 percent)

You determine that you need to withdraw $7,500. Your portfolio master plan calls for only 45 percent bonds, but after a horrible year for stocks and a good one for bonds, your bond allocation is now 50 percent. The source of your $7,500 withdrawal is clear: Take it out of the bond ETF. Doing so will not only generate the cash you need but will also bring your portfolio into alignment with your target allocations.

(Because your new portfolio balance after withdrawing the $7,500 will be $92,500, your bond fund, now with $42,500, will represent 45.9 percent of the portfolio. That's close enough in our book. Literally.)

Fast-forward six months . . .

Stocks have been on a recent tear, and the "principal" you now have invested in stocks has grown considerably relative to your bonds. Your ZAG bond fund has also grown (from its starting position of $42,500), due mostly to earned interest, which has been reinvested in the ETF. Your bond fund is now worth $45,000.

Your portfolio, even though you withdrew $7,500 in cash during the year, is now worth $115,000. It now looks like this:

- ✔ iShares S&P/TSX 60 Index Fund (XIU): $34,500 (30 percent)
- ✔ iShares MSCI World Index Fund (XWD): $34,500 (30 percent)
- ✔ BMO Aggregate Bond Index ETF (ZAG): $46,000 (40 percent)

Nothing has really changed in your life (except that you are now a bit older and greyer), so you determine that you don't need to shake up your original target portfolio allocation: 45 percent ZAG, 27.5 percent XIU, and 27.5 percent XWD. You now figure that you are going to need yet another $10,000. Do you take it out of the bond fund because its growth was due to interest, and not the stock funds because their growth was in principal? Many people would say yes. Mass hysteria, we say! That makes no sense.

In this case, we would have you take $5,000 each from your two stock ETFs. That leaves you with a portfolio of $105,000, invested as follows:

- ✔ iShares S&P/TSX 60 Index Fund (XIU): $29,500 (28 percent)
- ✔ iShares MSCI World Index Fund (XWD): $29,500 (28 percent)
- ✔ BMO Aggregate Bond Index ETF (ZAG): $46,000 (44 percent)

You have provided yourself with the $10,000 you need, *and* you've brought your portfolio back into near-perfect balance. And near-perfect is good enough, because . . .

As always, watch the fees

In the scenario presented in the preceding section, to bring your portfolio into pitch-perfect balance would require shaving a few hundred dollars from each stock fund to move into the bond fund. That would require you to pay commissions on three trades, at a cost (if you trade online, which you certainly should) of perhaps $30. (If you're paying much more than that, you are with the wrong brokerage house.) And on top of that, there will be minor other transaction costs. That money spends. Why give it away for no good reason? Given the volatility of the markets, your portfolio will be out of perfect balance the day after you get it into perfect balance, so let it be!

In general, we'd say that you never want to spend more than one-half of 1 percent on a trade, and — unless you have a teensy-weensy portfolio, this second part shouldn't hinder you in complying with the first part — you never want to let your portfolio get too out of balance. Let's express this in percentages: If your biggest allocation factor — stocks versus bonds — is out of whack by more than 5 percentage points (bonds should be 40 percent, but instead they've dipped to less than 35 percent or risen to more than 45 percent), you need to make a move.

Take your minimum required distributions

During the year you turn age 72, you *must* start taking money out of your RRSP — by then it's converted into a Registered Retirement Income Fund — and you have to take out at least the minimum required distribution. The minimum payout is a percentage that's based on your age, and it goes up the older you get. To find out how much you'll owe, search for a calculator by Googling the words "RRIF calculator," and you'll have many to choose from. Unlike some other calculators, these are all essentially the same.

RRSP, TFSA, or regular (taxable) brokerage account: Which to tap first?

For those of you older than 71, your cash needs will come first from government cheques, any pension you may have, and the minimum required distribution on your RRIF. After that, you can draw additional cash from any available source. For those of you between 60 and 71, the choices are all yours. You decide when to begin receiving government benefits; whether and when to take distributions from your retirement account(s); and whether or when to start tapping your taxable account(s). Most money managers suggest pulling money from your taxable accounts first and holding off on drawing down your tax-advantaged accounts. We're not so sure.

Sure, leaving a tax-deferred account untouched will keep this year's taxes to a minimum. But those taxes will be paid eventually, if not by you then by your heirs. If you care about what you'll be leaving behind, you should know that a large taxable inheritance can create real headaches with the CRA. In the end, for many families it may make the most sense to take needed cash from both types of accounts — taxable and tax deferred — more or less equally. But there are many factors involved. It would be worth your while to discuss the matter with your financial planner, accountant, and, if you have a sizeable estate, an estate attorney.

Caveat: From our experience, accountants sometimes tend to focus a wee bit too much on your present taxes, while estate attorneys can focus a tad too much on your legacy. Let their counsel, as well as ours, guide you. But ultimately, you need to be the judge.

Part V

The Part of Tens

The 5th Wave   By Rich Tennant

"We believe in all-Canadian investments. Take a look at this Grandma's tourtiere pie chart..."

In this part . . .

Time now to wrap up this book with some practical tips (just in case we haven't provided you with enough in previous chapters). We begin by answering the ten most common ETF questions. That is followed by a discussion of the ten mistakes that most investors — yes, even smart ETF investors — often make. And finally, we could hardly call ourselves financial writers unless we (like seemingly all other financial writers) made some predictions! And so, we end Part V by pulling out our crystal ball and making ten forecasts about the future of ETFs. Only time will tell if we're right.

Chapter 20

Ten FAQs about ETFs

In This Chapter

▶ Assessing risk

▶ Considering professional help

▶ Figuring out which ETFs make sense for you

*O*h, writing a book about exchange-traded funds has been fun! Often when someone asks us what we're working on and we say, *"Exchange-Traded Funds For Canadians For Dummies,"* eyes glaze over. And then, if the topic isn't immediately steered in a new direction, we're inevitably asked what the heck an exchange-traded fund is. And so we explain (essentially quoting, from memory, a few lines from this book's Introduction). The *next* question that's asked is invariably one of the following.

Are ETFs Appropriate for Individual Investors?

You bet they are. Although the name *exchange-traded funds* sounds highly technical and maybe a little bit scary, ETFs are essentially friendly index mutual funds with a few spicy perks. They are *more* than appropriate for individual investors. In fact, given the low expense ratios of most ETFs, as well as the ease with which you can use them to construct a diversified portfolio, these babies can be the perfect building blocks for just about any individual investor's portfolio.

Are ETFs Risky?

That all depends.

Some ETFs are way riskier than others. It's a question of what kind of ETF we're talking about. Most ETFs track stock indexes, and some of those stock indexes can be extremely volatile, such as individual sectors of the Canadian economy (oil and gas, mining, technology, and so on) or the stock markets of emerging-market nations. Other ETFs track broader segments of the Canadian stock market, such as the S&P/TSX Composite Index, or of the U.S. stock market, such as the S&P 500. Those can be volatile, too, but less so. Commodity ETFs can be more jumpy than stocks.

Other ETFs track bond indexes. Those tend to be considerably less volatile (and less potentially rewarding) than stock ETFs. One ETF (ticker symbol XGB) tracks mostly short-term Government of Canada bonds, and as such is only a little bit more volatile than a money market fund.

Many of the newer generation ETFs are *leveraged,* using borrowed money or financial derivatives to increase volatility (and potential performance). Those leveraged ETFs can be so wildly volatile that you are taking on risk of Las Vegas proportions.

When putting together a portfolio, a diversity of investments can temper risk. Although it seems freakily paradoxical, you can sometimes add a risky ETF (such as an ETF that tracks the price of a basket of commodities, or the stocks of foreign small companies) to a portfolio and lower your overall risk! How so? If the value of your newly added ETF tends to rise as your other investments fall, that addition will lower the volatility of your entire portfolio. (Financial professionals refer to this strange but sweet phenomenon as *Modern Portfolio Theory.*)

Do I Need a Financial Professional to Set Up and Monitor an ETF Portfolio?

Do you need an auto mechanic to service your car? It's hard to say. The answer depends on both your particular skills and your inclination to spend a Sunday afternoon getting greasy under the hood. Setting up a decent ETF portfolio, with the aid of this book, is very doable. You can certainly monitor such a portfolio, as well. A professional, however, has special tools and (hopefully) objectivity to help you understand investment risk and construct a portfolio that fits you like a glove, or at least a sock. A financial planner can also help you properly estimate your retirement needs and plan your savings accordingly.

Do be aware that many so-called investment advisors out there are nothing more than salespeople in disguise. Don't be at all surprised if you bump into a few who express their disgust of ETFs! ETFs don't make money for those salespeople, who make their living hawking expensive (and often inferior) investment products. Your best bet for good advice is to find a *fee-only* financial planner (one who doesn't take commissions). If you're more or less a do-it-yourselfer but simply want a little guidance, try to find a fee-only planner who will work with you on an hourly basis.

How Much Money Do I Need to Invest in ETFs?

You can buy one share of any number of ETFs for as low as the price of a share. But because you usually pay a commission to trade (sometimes as much as $29.99), buying one $20 share would hardly make good sense. Starting at about $10,000 perhaps, investing in ETFs may be worth your while, but only if you plan to keep that money invested for at least several years. Smaller amounts are best invested in mutual funds (preferably low-cost index mutual funds), money markets, or other instruments that incur no trading costs.

If you wish to invest in an ETF at a brokerage house that doesn't charge trading commissions for that particular ETF (Scotia iTrade, for example, doesn't charge you for buying certain ETFs), then you can buy one share at a time with impunity.

Hundreds of ETFs Exist to Choose from, So Where Do I Start?

The answer depends on your objective. If you're looking to round out an existing portfolio of stocks or mutual funds, your ETF should complement that. Your goal is always to have a well-diversified collection of investments. If you're starting to build a portfolio, you want to make sure to include stocks and bonds and to diversify within those two broad asset classes.

Not much in the world of stocks, bonds, and commodities can't be satisfied with ETFs. Try to have Canadian, U.S., and international stock ETFs. And within the stock arena, aim to have large cap growth, small cap growth, large cap value, and small cap value. (We explain these terms in Chapters 5 through 8.) You can also diversify your stock ETFs by industry sector: consumer staples, energy, financials, and so on. (Refer to Chapter 10 for a discussion of sector diversification.) Generally, we wouldn't attempt to use separate ETFs to accomplish both grid diversification and sector diversification; doing so would require an unwieldy number of holdings.

On the bond side of your portfolio, you want both government-issued bonds and corporate bonds. For more conservative portfolios in which bonds play a major role, foreign bonds may offer added diversification.

Although most ETFs are somewhat reasonably priced, some are more reasonably priced than others. If you're going to pay 0.50 percent a year in operating expenses for a certain ETF, you should have a good reason for doing so. Many ETFs are available for less than 0.30 percent, and some for even less than 0.10 percent.

There are other things to consider as well when buying, such as liquidity of the ETF and its underlying holdings, the fund's assets under management, and the risk characteristics of the ETF. Much of this covered throughout the book.

Where Is the Best Place for Me to Buy ETFs?

Setting up an account with financial institutions such as TD Waterhouse, Scotia iTrade, or BMO InvestorLine, or online brokerages like Qtrade or Questrade, is a good idea. Each of these allows you to hold ETFs, along with other investments — such as mutual funds or individual stocks and bonds — in one account.

Different financial firms offer different services and charge different prices depending on how much you have to invest, how often you trade, and whether you do everything online or by phone. You need to do some shopping around to find the brokerage house that works best for you. We provide more suggestions for shopping for online brokerage firms in Chapter 3, where you can also find contact information, and website addresses are listed in Appendix A.

Is There an Especially Good or Bad Time to Buy ETFs?

Nope, not really, at least not a time that can be determined in advance. Studies show rather conclusively that the stock and bond markets (or any segment of the stock or bond markets) are just about as likely to go up after a good day as they are after a bad day (week, month, year, or any other piece of the calendar). Trying to time the market tends to be a fool's game — or, just as often, a game that some like to play with other people's money.

Do ETFs Have Any Disadvantages?

Because most ETFs follow an index, you probably won't see your ETF (or any of your index mutual funds) winding up as number one on *MoneySense* magazine's list of top Canadian funds. (But you probably won't find any of your ETFs at the bottom of such a list, either.) The bigger disadvantage of ETFs — compared with mutual funds — is the cost of trading them, although that cost should be minimal.

Building a well-diversified portfolio of ETFs — stocks, bonds, large cap, small cap, U.S., international — may also seem to have the disadvantage that in any given year some of your ETFs are going to do poorly. Just remember that next year those particular investments, the ones that look so disgustingly dull (or worse) right now, may be the shiniest things in your portfolio.

Does It Matter Which Exchange My ETF Is Traded On?

No. Most ETFs are traded on the Toronto Stock Exchange; U.S. ones trade on the NYSE Arca (Archipelago) exchange. Others are traded on the NASDAQ. It doesn't matter in the slightest to you, the individual investor. The cost of your trade is determined by the brokerage house you use. The *spread* (the difference between the price a buyer pays and the price the seller receives) is determined in large part by the share volume of the ETF being traded. Regardless of the exchange, if the volume is small (such as would be the case for, say, the Global X Nigeria ETF), you may want to place a *limit order* rather than a *market order*. We explain the different kinds of orders in a sidebar in Chapter 2.

Which ETFs Are Best in My RRSP, and Which Are Best in a Non-registered Account?

Generally, investments that are taxed as income are best kept in a tax-advantaged retirement account, such as your Registered Retirement Savings Plan (RRSP) or Tax-Free Savings Account (TFSA), including any bond, real estate investment trust (REIT), or guaranteed investment certificate (GIC). You'll eventually need to pay income tax on any money you withdraw from your RRSP, but paying later rather than sooner is usually better. In the case of a TFSA, you will never have to pay taxes on anything — not the earnings or principal — when you withdraw. Dividend income and capital gains are taxed at a favourable rate, so many people recommend putting these investments in a non-registered account. Putting your investments in an RRSP first is always a good idea, but consider putting some dividend-paying ETFs, or risky funds with big capital gains potential, outside your retirement accounts.

Because you have to pay tax on anything you remove from your RRSP, putting any emergency money in either a TFSA or a non-retirement account is a good idea.

Chapter 21

Ten Mistakes Most Investors (Even Smart Ones) Make

. . . .

In This Chapter

▶ Paying and risking too much

▶ Trading too frequently

▶ Saving too little and expecting too much from the market

▶ Ignoring inflation and RRSP rules

. . . .

Remember that personal investing course you took in high school? Of course you don't! Your high school never offered such a course. Chances are that you've never taken such a course. Few of us have. And that lack of education — combined with a surfeit of cheesy and oft-advertised investment industry products — leads many investors to make some very costly mistakes.

Paying Too Much for an Investment

Most investors pay way, way too much to middlemen who suck the lifeblood out of portfolios, leaving too many folks with too little to show for their investments. By investing primarily in ETFs, you can spare yourself and your family this tragic fate. The typical ETF costs a fraction of what you'd typically pay in yearly management fees to a mutual fund company. You never pay any *loads* (high commissions). And trading fees, as long as you're not dealing in dribs and drabs, and being charged for each drib and drab, should be minimal.

Failing to Properly Diversify

"Thou shalt not put all thy eggs in one basket" is perhaps the first commandment of investing, but it is astonishing how many sinners there are among us. ETFs allow for easy and effective diversification. By investing in ETFs rather than individual securities, you have already taken a step in the right direction.

Don't blow it by pouring all your money into one ETF in a single hot sector! You want to invest in both stock and bond ETFs, and in Canadian, U.S., and international securities. You want diversification on all sides. Invest, to the extent possible, mostly in *broad* markets: value, growth, small cap, large cap. On the international side of your portfolio, aim to invest more in regions than in individual countries (refer to Part II). ETFs make such diversification easy.

Taking On Inappropriate Risks

Some people take on way too much risk, perhaps investing everything in highly volatile technology or biotech stocks. But many people don't take enough risk, leaving their money to sit in secure but low-yielding money market funds or, worse, in the vault of their local bank branch. If you want your money to grow, you may have to stomach some volatility. In general, the longer you can tie up your money, and the less likely you are to need to tap into your portfolio anytime soon, the more volatile your portfolio can be. A portfolio of ETFs can be amazingly fine-tuned to achieve the levels of risk and return that are appropriate for you.

Selling Out When the Going Gets Tough

It can be a scary thing, for sure, when your portfolio's value drops 10 or 20 percent . . . never mind the 40 percent that an all-stock portfolio would have lost in 2008 (demonstrating graphically why you shouldn't have an all-stock portfolio). Keep in mind that if you invest in stock ETFs, that scenario is going to happen. It has happened many times in the past; it will happen many times in the future. That's just the nature of the beast. If you sell when the going gets tough (as many investors do), you lose the game. The stock market is resilient. Hang tough. Bears are followed by bulls (think about 2009 and 2010). Your portfolio — as long as you're well diversified — will almost surely bounce back, given enough time.

Paying Too Much Attention to Recent Performance

Many investors make a habit of bailing out of whatever market segment has recently taken a dive. Conversely, they often look for whatever market segment has recently shot through the roof, and that's the one they buy. Then, when *that* market segment tanks, they sell once again. By forever buying high and selling low, their portfolios dwindle over time to nothing.

When you build your portfolio, don't overload it with last year's ETF super-stars. You don't know what will happen next year. Stay cool. You may notice that in this book we don't include performance figures for any of the ETFs discussed (except in one or two circumstances to make a specific point). That omission is intentional. Many of the ETFs we discuss are only a few years old, and a few years' returns tell you nothing. On the other hand, the indexes tracked by certain ETFs go back decades. In those cases, we often do provide performance figures.

Not Saving Enough for Retirement

Compared to spending, saving doesn't offer a whole lot of joy. But you can't build a portfolio out of thin air. If your goal is one day to be financially inde-pendent, to retire with dignity, you probably need to build a nest egg equal to about 20 times your yearly budget (more on that subject in Chapter 19). Doing so won't be easy; it may mean saving 15 percent of your paycheque for several decades. The earlier you start, the easier it will be.

Savings come from the difference between what you earn and what you spend. Remember that both are adjustable figures. One great way to save is to con-tribute at least enough to your pension plan at work to get your employer's full match, if any. Do it! Another is to remember that material goodies, above and beyond the basics, don't buy happiness and fulfillment. Honest. Psychologists have studied the matter, and their findings are rather conclusive.

Having Unrealistic Expectations of Market Returns

One reason many people don't save enough is that they have unrealistic expectations; they believe fervently that they are going to win the lottery or (next best thing) earn 25 percent a year on their investments. The truth: The stock market, over the past 80 years, has returned nearly 10 percent a year before inflation and 7 percent a year after inflation. Bonds have returned about 5 percent before inflation and 2 to 3 percent after inflation. A well-bal-anced portfolio, therefore, may have returned 7 or 8 percent before inflation and maybe 5 percent or so after inflation.

Five percent growth after inflation — with interest compounded every year — isn't too shabby. In 20 years' time, an investment of $10,000 growing at 5 per-cent will turn into $26,530 in constant dollars. Most of us in the investment field expect future returns to be more modest. But with a very well-diversi-fied, ultra-low-cost portfolio, leaning toward higher-yielding asset classes (refer to Part II), you may be able to do just as well as Mom and Dad did. If you want to earn 25 percent a year, however, you're going to have to take on inordinate risk. And even then, we wouldn't bank on it.

Discounting the Damaging Effect of Inflation

No, a dollar certainly doesn't buy what it used to. Think of what a candy bar cost when you were a kid. Think of what you earned on your first job. Are you old enough to remember when gas was 32 cents a litre? Now look into the future, and realize that your nest egg, unless it's wisely invested, will shrivel and shrink. Historically, certain investments do a better job of keeping up with inflation than others. Those investments, which include stocks, tend to be somewhat volatile. It's a price you need to pay, however, to keep the inflation monster at bay. The world of ETFs includes many ways to invest in stocks, but if you find the volatility hard to take, you may temper it with a position in Government of Canada bonds.

Not Following the RRSP Rules

A lot of people who need money withdraw cash from their RRSPs. Doing that, though, triggers a tax hit. If you make more money at the time of withdrawal than when you invested, you'll actually lose money, not to mention immediately lose the great benefit of tax deferral. You really need to play by the rules, or you can wind up worse off than if you had never invested in the first place.

People older than 71 must take a minimum amount out of their Registered Retirement Income Fund (an RRSP turns into a RRIF the year someone turns 72). To find out how much you'll need to remove, simply type "RRIF withdrawal calculator" into your favourite search engine and you'll get your answer.

Failing to Incorporate Investments into a Broader Financial Plan

Have you paid off all your high-interest credit card debt? Do you have proper disability insurance? Do you have enough life insurance so that, if necessary, your co-parent and children can survive without you? A finely manicured investment portfolio is only part of a larger picture that includes issues such as debt management, insurance, and estate planning. Don't spend too much time tinkering with your ETF portfolio and ignore these other very important financial issues.

Chapter 22

Ten Forecasts about the Future of ETFs and Personal Investing

*W*atching investment shows on television is sometimes difficult. So-called Stock Expert Number One gives his prediction of the future. Then Expert Number Two gives her (often contradictory) opinion. Viewers may be amused by the heated debate, but they never know what to do in the end.

Making predictions about the future is often a foolish endeavour, but in this chapter we give it a shot anyway! We can't resist. It just seems like so much fun!

Here are our predictions, for whatever they are worth, about the world of ETFs.

ETF Assets Will Continue to Grow . . . for Better or for Worse

Most people should be investing most of their money in index mutual funds or ETFs, but that probably won't happen — not now, not ever. The initial popularity of ETFs was due largely to the interest of educated institutional investors and savvy individual investors, like you, who loved ETFs for their low-cost indexing and diversification power.

During the past few years, educated and savvy investors have continued to invest in ETFs, but there has also been a huge inflow of money from investors who have little if any idea of what they're getting into. Some, though fortunately not most, of this recent inflow is going into leveraged and inverse leveraged

ETFs and other pricey, complex, and largely pointless if not outright dangerous ETFs. We warn you about these products throughout this book.

While it may take years for ETF assets to catch up to mutual funds — if ever — more people will look for low fee assets that produce index-like returns. Some will look for those risky plays, but most will, hopefully, stick with the reliable funds that produce market returns.

More Players May Enter the Field, but Only a Few

The Canadian ETF market isn't nearly as developed as America's. Likely, more companies will start offering ETFs — perhaps other U.S. operations will follow Vanguard's lead and set up shop in the Great White North — but you won't see as many providers selling ETFs as you see selling mutual funds. Unlike in the world of mutual funds, the profit margin on ETFs is fairly modest. Some players, such as Horizons Exchange Traded Funds, have started offering actively managed funds, which may do well. But the exponential growth we've seen in the number of ETFs and ETF providers will certainly start to slow.

Investors Will Get Suckered into Buying Packaged Products

Alas, even good ETFs can be turned into bad financial products; this is happening in the U.S. with some of the ETF offerings in 401(k) plans. Perfectly good ETFs are packaged in such a way that the investor (trapped like a fly in a bowl of milk in his or her company's plan) is paying much higher management fees. These funds don't track a simple index. They're designed to hold a "package" of indexes and other investments. The SPDR SSgA Income Allocation ETF (INKM), for instance, holds preferred shares ETFs, dividend ETFs, high yield bond ETFs, and more. The expense ratio on this is 0.70 percent, which is much higher than what you'd get owning one or two of these funds on their own.

Good ETFs are similarly popping up in crappy annuity plans and other investments where someone somewhere stands to make big bucks off the small investor. PowerShares several years back tried to slap loads on ETFs, but it didn't work. Canadians haven't been gouged as badly as some Americans, but as the market develops, and institutions try to figure out new ways to make money, bad products may hit the market.

ETF Investors Will Have More, and Better, Options

Despite all the questionable recent offerings in the ETF world, some of the newer ETFs have been quite pleasant surprises, and we discuss those in every chapter of this book. We anticipate the introduction of a number of *market-neutral* ETFs (which, like hedge funds, have little to no correlation to the broad stock market, even though they may invest in stocks). Thus, the advantages (and, alas, the perils) of hedge fund investing — once limited to institutions and high-net-worth individuals — will be available to the retail investor. We will also see ETFs that represent certain asset classes that don't even exist yet, and some of those may make excellent investments. (Shuttlecraft and warp-drive production ETFs, perhaps?)

(Unfortunately) See Greater Correlation than in the Past

As the world continues to become a smaller place, and the economies of nations become yet more interdependent, so too will stock and bond markets around the world tend to move up and down in unison. This is not a good thing for investors because it lessens the power of diversification to moderate risk.

However, that diversification is not dead! Although world markets in 2008 were distressingly correlated (in other words, they took a collective swan dive), some markets recovered much faster than others. And the next market swoon may not see such correlation; we simply don't know. But it is fairly safe to say that investors will find a growing need to tap into new ways to diversify a portfolio. An expanded menu of ETFs will make implementing such a strategy much easier for everyone.

Asset Class Returns Will Revert toward Their Historic Means

Astronomical rises in the prices of certain commodities (silver and gold in particular) may continue for a while, but not forever. We can also expect an end to the seemingly permanent sag of the U.S. housing market. (That's a good thing for Canada — our economy improves when the United States' economy improves.) When commodity prices fall, they may fall hard. And when housing prices rise, they may rise swiftly. At some point in the distant future, commodity prices will rise again, and housing will fall. And so on and so forth. All asset class returns tend to revert to their historical norms.

The price of gold, for example, has just about kept up with inflation over the past 100 years. The double-digit returns of the past few years are an anomaly. Anomalies are, by definition, temporary.

In terms of an ETF portfolio, this may be a good time to slightly underweight commodities and overweight those asset classes that have lagged their historical returns over the past several years. (Tilt your portfolio oh so slightly, because these are just our predictions! Moreover, by the time you have this book in your hands, new information may have caused us to revise these predictions.)

We'll Have to Cut Back Our Spending

Thanks to low interest rates, Canadians have gotten used to borrowing cash for next to nothing. Mortgage rates have been ridiculously low — some five-year fixed rates were being offered for 2.99 percent — while financial institutions have kept interest on lines of credit and some credit cards dirt cheap too.

Wait, why are we complaining about inexpensive borrowing costs? Because some Canadians have been spending like they've won the lottery. At the end of 2012, non-mortgage debt climbed to its highest level in almost a decade. The average Canadian owed a whopping $27,485 in debt. Again, that doesn't include housing balances.

At the time of writing, rates are still low. By the time you're reading this, the Bank of Canada may have raised rates, and if it hasn't, , it will soon. When that happens, interest rates on lines of credit, some credit cards, and variable rate mortgages will rise. If you don't prepare for those rising costs, then you may be in trouble. So what should you do? Pay down your debt now and cut your spending.

Inflation Will Remain Tame

Although we're certainly concerned about inflation and recognize that it can devastate a paycheque or a portfolio, we're not too worried about a return to the double-digit inflation of the 1970s and '80s. Back then, two major oil shocks resulted in high unemployment and inflation. Although that can happen again, monetary policy has changed and the policy-makers, we hope, have learned from past mistakes.

While there are forces at play today that argue for greater inflation, we also have forces at play working in the other direction. We anticipate that inflation in the next decade or two will be similar to what it has been in the past decade or two: somewhere in the ballpark of 3 percent.

Whether we're right about the 3 percent, or whether inflation runs higher, you can protect yourself with a good helping of stock ETFs (stocks have a very good track record of keeping up with inflation) and a position in the iShares DEX Real Return Bond Index, which has its interest payments linked to the consumer price index (CPI) inflation rate.

Private Pensions (of Sorts) May Emerge from the Rubble

One kind of risk exists against which all the good saving and wise investing in the world can only go so far to protect you. That is "longevity risk." In order to live a life of comfort post-retirement, you need to save and invest as if you may live to be 105 . . . because you just may. But, in point of fact, you probably won't live nearly that long. Wouldn't it be nice if we could all save just enough to get us through to the average life expectancy (mid 80s), and the money from those who die sooner could help support those who live longer? Alas, that seems unlikely.

But private industry may offer us better old-age insurance in the form of reasonably priced annuities instead of the horribly overpriced, confusing, restrictive, inflexible, locked-in, complicated, and tricky annuities that have come to dominate the insurance market. One day we'd like to see annuities, just like ETFs, become simple, transparent, inexpensive, and sensible. Perhaps ETFs themselves may evolve into such instruments. We can dream.

Hype Will Prevail

Of all our predictions, this is the one to put your money on.

We'll be seeing more magazine articles, websites, blogs, television clips, and advertisements with headings and leads such as "Build Instant Wealth and Retire Early with ETFs!" And books will be published with titles such as *Beat the Market with ETFs!* and *You Can Make a Killing in ETFs!* Some of them may become bestsellers, which means they'll make a lot of money for some people — but not for the people who read them.

Bull markets are followed by bear markets, which are followed by bull markets. Trading floors are replaced by electronic trading platforms. Mutual funds are challenged by ETFs. The world of investing keeps changing, morphing into something hardly recognizable from the days when just about all investors were men who wore funny hats, smoked cigars, and spent hours reading tickertapes.

But one thing will remain constant: The financial industry will continue to produce hype in the hope that you'll buy its new products — and sell, and buy, and sell, and buy — regardless of how ridiculously complex and expensive whatever products it pushes happen to be.

If you've read through this book, you now know better. Put your knowledge to good use. Build a diversified portfolio of low-cost, transparent ETFs. Keep an eye on your nest egg, but don't make changes very often. Just be sure to rebalance at regular intervals. Sit back and relax. Let the hype pass over you like a summer breeze.

Part VI
Appendixes

The 5th Wave   By Rich Tennant

"I'm not familiar with investment terms. What does that mean?"

In this part . . .

In this part, you get some handy reference info: We start with a list of websites to check whenever you're craving even more ETF or general investment info. We follow with a glossary that can help you navigate this book and any other ETF or finance resource.

Appendix A

Great Web Resources to Help You Invest in ETFs

You can find anything online: gobs and gobs of information — and misinformation. And in the world of finance, more misinformation than information is out there. If pressed, we'd put the ratio at 7:2. Here are some websites you can trust to keep you informed about ETFs and other investment issues.

Independent, ETF-Specific Websites

www.archerETF.com: A discretionary portfolio management firm that offers independent analysis of ETFs that are selected for quality and relevance to individual and high net-worth investors.

canadiancouchpotato.com: This blog, written by Toronto-based personal finance writer Dan Bortolotti, is a stellar source for Canadian ETF news and commentary.

etfdb.com: Boasts daily ETF news, educational articles, analysis, and an ETF screener. Find out which ETFs represent what asset classes for the lowest fees.

www.etfguide.com: A good, quick summary of the entire ETF world. Contains a complete listing of all ETFs available, along with ticker symbols.

www.etftrends.com: A gossip column of sorts for U.S. ETF enthusiasts. You can find chit-chat about new ETFs on the market, ETFs pending approval of the SEC, behind-the-scenes industry workings, and rumours.

finance.yahoo.com/etf: Features a search function with intimate details on individual funds, an ETF glossary, and regularly updated news and commentary.

`www.theglobeandmail.com/globe-investor/funds-and-etfs/etfs`: Globe Investor's ETF page offers useful news and performance information. Find out which funds are making money or losing big.

`www.indexuniverse.com`: See the News link under the Sections heading for the most up-to-date information on ETFs and index mutual funds. See the Data section to help screen for ETFs of your liking.

`www.moneysense.ca`: Canada's premier personal finance magazine is a big proponent of ETFs. The site is filled with plenty of must-read info on ETFs, but you can also find insightful stories on other investing and finance issues.

`www2.morningstar.ca`: Click the ETF icon at top of screen to find thorough information on individual funds, along with Morningstar's trademarked rating system. (One star is bad, five stars is grand.)

`seekingalpha.com/dashboard/etfs`: Features some the smartest commentary on fund investing you'll find anywhere.

Websites of ETF Providers

About 63 percent of all the money that goes into Canadian ETFs is spent on iShares products (22.3 percent of all assets are in the company's S&P/TSX 60 Index Fund). The rest is split among six other players.

The biggies

`ca.ishares.com`: BlackRock's iShares are the biggest in the business.

`www.etfs.bmo.com`: The Bank of Montreal is at the top of the ETF heap among the big five banks.

`www.vanguardcanada.ca`: This U.S. ETF behemoth came to Canada in June 2011.

Some of the other players

`www.firstasset.com`: First Asset offers a variety of ETFs, including some innovative — and unique to Canada — bond funds.

`www.horizonsetfs.com`: Horizons Exchange Traded Funds has the most ETF products on the market.

`www.invescopowershares.com`: The country's fourth-largest ETF provider offers some unusual funds, for better or for worse.

`funds.rbcgam.com/etfs`: The second bank to offer ETFs. RBC offers only eight fixed income funds, but that'll likely change soon.

The U.S. market

Canadians with an online brokerage account can buy most American ETFs. Here are some U.S. providers, listed in alphabetical order, for you to check out.

`www.direxionshares.com`: Leveraging is their game.

`www.elementsetn.com`: Exchange-traded notes that track commodities and stocks.

`www.globalxfunds.com`: They seem to be issuing a new ETF every day.

`www.guggenheimfunds.com`: Features narrow segments of markets.

`www.ipathetn.com`: The Barclays lineup of exchange-traded notes.

`usishares.com`: Not only is this company the leading ETF provider in Canada, but it's huge in the U.S. too.

`www.pimcoetfs.com`: Bond people. Purely bond people.

`www.proshares.com`: ETFs for a wild ride.

`www.spdrs.com`: SPDRs are issued by State Street Global Advisors (SSgA).

`www.wisdomtree.com`: You say you like dividends?

Retirement Calculators

How large a portfolio are you going to need to retire in style? How much are you going to have to sock away, and what kind of rate of return do you need to get there? None of the online calculators is perfect, so we suggest you use a few and average the answers. Start with this one:

www.servicecanada.gc.ca: Visit Service Canada's Retirement Planning page, and click on the link for the Canadian Retirement Income Calculator. Book some time off before you use this calculator. You'll spend about 30 minutes to get through a variety of questions, but at the end you'll get a comprehensive look at your savings. Find out how much money you'll need in your golden years, and calculate your OAS and CPP benefits. Also see what will happen to your savings if you sock away more every month. (Yes, saving more is possible.) Everyone should try this calculator out at least once.

Don't have 30 minutes to spare? Try these calculators:

- www.retirementadvisor.ca: Click on the Tools tab, and then choose the Standard Retirement Calculator.
- www.getsmarteraboutmoney.ca: Click on the Tools & Calculators tab, click on the Calculators link, and then choose the RRSP Savings Calculator.
- www.hsbc.ca/1/2/personal/borrowing/loans/rrsp-loan/calculator

Financial Supermarkets

Otherwise known as large brokerage houses, here are some places where you can buy, sell, and house your ETFs — as well as other investments, such as mutual funds and individual stocks and bonds.

www.tdwaterhouse.ca: Or telephone TD Waterhouse at 1-866-222-3456.

www.scotiabank.com/itrade: Or telephone Scotia iTrade at 1-888-872-3388.

www.bmoinvestorline.com: Or telephone BMO InvestorLine at 1-888-776-6886.

www.rbcdirectinvesting.com: Or telephone RBC Direct Investing at 1-800-769-2560.

www.investorsedge.cibc.com: Or telephone CIBC Investor's Edge at 1-800-661-7494.

www.qtrade.ca: Or telephone Qtrade Financial Group at 1-877-787-2330.

www.virtualbrokers.com: Or telephone Virtual Brokers at 1-877-310-1088.

www.interactivebrokers.ca: Or telephone Interactive Brokers at 1-877-745-4222

Stock Exchanges

`www.tmx.com`: Every Canadian ETF is listed on the Toronto Stock Exchange, which is run by the TMX Group. Investors can find a lot of great ETF info on the TMX website.

`nyse.nyx.com`: Most American ETFs are traded on the NYSE platforms. Surprisingly, the website doesn't have a lot of ETF information, but it does have a wealth of general information about the world of finance.

`www.nasdaq.com`: Despite the fact that not many ETFs are listed on the NASDAQ, the website has some very cool ETF-related things. Check out the ETF Dynamic Heatmap, found by clicking on Market Activity and then on ETFs.

Specialty Websites

`www.canadianmoneyforum.com`: A personal finance and investing forum with lots of insightful discussions about ETF and index investing.

`www.m-x.ca`: The Montreal Exchange — if options trading is your kind of thing.

`www.investopedia.com`: Maybe the most comprehensive investing website on the planet. And it's Canadian based!

`www.canadianmoneysaver.ca`: It's a magazine, it's a website, it's an investment advisory! Interesting info you won't find anywhere else.

`www.multpl.com`: Robert Shiller's modified P/E index for tactical asset allocators (refer to Chapter 18).

`www.theglobeandmail.com/globe-investor`: Type "online broker rankings" into the search bar, and Globe Investor's annual broker survey pops up. The survey is a must-read for DIY investors.

`sweetspotinvestments.com`: Provides an interesting twist on contrarian investing.

Where to Find a Financial Planner

`www.fpsc.ca`: The Financial Planning Standards Council website has a great search tool to help you find a local CFP professional.

`www.moneysense.ca`: *MoneySense* magazine has a comprehensive list of fee-only financial planners that's updated each year. In the search bar, type "Where to find a fee-only financial planner."

`www.kyfa.com`: An independent website that tries to pair people with planners.

`www.advocis.ca`: The website for the Financial Advisors Association of Canada includes a useful advisor-finding form.

`www.investmentcounsel.org`: The Portfolio Management Association of Canada has a website that lists many discretionary portfolio managers who generally serve high net-worth individuals.

Regulatory Agencies

`www.iiroc.ca`: IIROC may sound like a new Apple product, but the acronym stands for the Investment Industry Regulatory Organization of Canada. It oversees Canadian investment dealers that trade stocks, bonds, mutual funds, options, forex, and other securities. The site offers tips on how to find an advisor and has lots of great information about regulation and investment industry news.

`www.osc.gov.on.ca`: Each province has a securities commission that's responsible for making sure markets work efficiently and for keeping fraudsters away from your money. Perusing your province's securities commission site is a good idea, but the Ontario one is worth looking at too, because it's the biggest commission. You can find information on investor protection initiatives and updates to securities law.

The People Who Create the Indexes

Dow Jones, Russell, Standard & Poor's, and others create the indexes that ETFs track. Just in case you're interested:

- `www.standardandpoors.com`
- `www.canadianbondindices.com`
- `www.morningstar.com`
- `www.djindexes.com`
- `www.ftse.com`
- `www.msci.com`
- `www.russell.com`
- `www.wilshire.com`

Good Places to Go for General Financial News, Advice, and Education

finance.yahoo.com: Extensive information and analysis, all for free.

www.bloomberg.com: Hardcore financial data.

www.canadianbusiness.com: Canadian business news and high-level investing content written by one of this book's authors.

www.moneysense.ca: Personal finance site loaded with investing content and other personal finance information.

www.theglobeandmail.com/globe-investor: In-depth reporting on ETFs, stocks, mutual funds, and more.

www.financialpost.com: Long-time business newspaper is filled with a plethora of investing and business content.

www.advisor.ca: A different take on business news — it's the site most Canadian financial advisors read.

www.moneychimp.com: For the more advanced investor.

www.morningstar.com and www.morningstar.ca: Anything and everything about stocks, mutual funds, and ETFs. (The U.S. and Canadian site have different content.)

www.seekingalpha.com: Brilliant website loaded with investing ideas. Be sure to click on the ETF tab.

Yours Truly

www.bryanborzykowski.com and twitter.com/bborzyko: The first URL takes you to the Canadian author's website, and the second lets you follow him on Twitter. Say hello with an e-mail or an @reply.

www.globalportfolios.net or www.russellwild.com: Both URLs take you to the same place: the American author's own website. Feel free to visit him anytime.

Appendix B

Glossary

....

*I*f you're going to be an ETF investor, you need to know the lingo. If you're not going to be an ETF investor, you can still use the following phrases to impress people at cocktail parties. Please note that any word or phrase in **boldface and italics** (except for the phrase **boldface and italics**) appears as its own entry elsewhere in the glossary.

active investing: Ah, to beat the market. Isn't that every investor's dream? Through stock picking or market timing, or both strategies, active investing offers hope of market-beating returns. Alas, it sounds a lot easier than it really is. Compare to **passive investing.**

alpha: Given a certain level of **risk,** you can expect a certain rate of return. If your stock, fund, or portfolio return exceeds that expectation, congratulations! You've just achieved what people in the finance world call *positive alpha.* Pass the caviar. If your stock, fund, or portfolio return falls shy of that expectation, you're in the dark and depressing land of *negative alpha.* Pass the herring.

ask price: The rock-bottom price that any stock or ETF seller is willing to accept. If any buyer is willing to fork over that amount, a sale is made. If no buyers are willing to match the ask price, gravity will eventually start to drag down the price of the stock. Compare to **bid price** and **spread.**

asset class: To build a diversified portfolio (meaning not having all your eggs in one flimsy straw basket), you want to have your investments spread out among different asset classes. An asset class is any group of similar investments. Examples may include small value stocks, utility stocks, high-yield bonds, Japanese small company stocks, or Rembrandts (the paintings).

beta: A common measurement of the **volatility** of an investment. If your ETF has a beta of 1.5, it tends to move up one and a half times as much as the market (usually represented by the S&P 500 Index or, in Canada, the S&P/TSX Composite Index). So, if the market as a whole goes down 10 percent, your ETF will fall 15 percent. Note that beta is a relative measure of **risk,** while **standard deviation** (a generally more useful tool) is an absolute measure of risk.

bid price: The highest price that any buyer is willing to spend to purchase shares of a stock or ETF. Compare to *ask price* and *spread.*

black swan: A term popularized by mathematician Nassim Taleb. It refers to a rare and extreme event (like the Russian government debt default that sunk Long-Term Capital Management in 1998) that has the potential to throw financial markets into turmoil. Many alternative investments (including Taleb's own hedge fund) advertise that they protect investors against such events.

cap size: A less-fancy way of saying *market capitalization.* The term refers to the size of a company as measured by the total number of stock outstanding times the market price of each share. In general, in Canada, stocks are classified as *large cap* (more than $5 billion), *small cap* (less than $1 billion), or *mid cap* (anything in between).

closed-end fund: Like a mutual fund or an exchange-traded fund, a closed-end fund pools securities, but it differs from its open-ended cousins in that it rarely creates or redeems new shares. Because of the fixed supply of shares, eager investors who want into the fund may wind up paying a significant premium over the market value of the pooled securities. On the other hand, if investor demand lags, the shares of a closed-end fund can sell for a hefty discount.

closet index fund: A mutual fund may call itself actively managed and may charge you a boatload of money, but it may be, in essence, an index fund. Shh. . . . The manager doesn't want to come out of the closet, lest he lose his excuse for charging you what he charges you and be forced to surrender the keys to the Mercedes.

correlation: The degree to which two investments — such as two ETFs — move up and down at the same time. A correlation of 1 means that the two investments move up and down together, like the Rockettes. A correlation of –1 means that when one goes up, the other goes down, like two pistons. A correlation of 0 means that no correlation between the two exists, like the price of bananas and the Philadelphia Eagles.

diversification: This means dividing your investments into different *asset classes* with limited *correlation.* Diversification is good. Very good. ETFs make it easy. Did we already mention that diversification is good?

emerging markets: This is a common euphemism for people who live in developing nations. People who invest in emerging markets hope that these countries (mostly in Africa, South America, and Asia) are, in fact, emerging. No one knows. The fortunes of emerging market stocks are closely tied to the markets for natural resources. Emerging market ETFs tend to be rather volatile but offer excellent return possibilities.

expense ratio: Sometimes referred to as the *management fee,* this is a yearly bill you pay to a mutual fund or ETF. The money is taken directly out of the fund's account, which then reduces the unit value of the fund. The expense ratio for ETFs is usually much, much less than that of mutual funds. If the expense ratio for your entire portfolio is more than 1 percent, you're paying too much.

fundamental analysis: If you're going to be picking stocks, doing some fundamental analysis — an analysis of a company's profitability, both present and future — makes sense. Just know that fundamental analysis is an awfully fuzzy science. And, ironically, the strongest, fastest-growing companies don't always make for the most profitable stocks. See also ***value premium.***

growth fund: A fund that invests in stocks of companies that have been fast-growing and are expected (by fundamental analysts) to continue to be fast-growing. In its day, Enron was a growth stock. You never know. . . .

hedging: If you expect that Asset A may zig, and you purchase Asset B in the hope that it will simultaneously zag, you've just hedged your position. A common hedging strategy is to use *short* positions (selling stock shares you don't own, but borrow) to offset any potential loss you may suffer by holding a *long* (buy and hold) position. Hedging reduces ***risk,*** but it also tends to mute returns. The term *inflation hedge* refers to any asset or type of asset, such as commodities, expected to appreciate in value in a climate of rising prices.

indexing: This term is synonymous with ***passive investing.*** Index investing has been around for a good while; ETFs simply make it easier, less expensive, and more tax efficient.

iShares: This is the brand name for ETFs issued by BlackRock, the largest purveyor of ETFs in the world.

leverage: An investment made with borrowed funds is said to be leveraged. A common type of leveraged investment, although usually not thought of as such, is a home purchased with little money down and a big mortgage. Leveraged investments, which include some ETFs, offer great potential for profit or — as many homeowners have found out the hard way in recent years — risk of loss.

liquidity: A liquid asset can readily be turned into cash. Examples include money market funds and very short-term bond funds. *Illiquid assets* are trickier to turn into cash. The classic example of an illiquid asset is the family home.

load: A wad of cash that you need to fork over in order to purchase certain mutual funds. Study after study shows that load funds perform no better than no-load funds, yet people are willing to pay rather huge loads. Go figure. ETFs never charge loads. Gotta love that about them.

Modern Portfolio Theory: This theory says that a portfolio doesn't have to be excessively risky, even if its separate components are riskier than skydiving without a parachute. The trick is to fill your portfolio with investments that have low *correlation* to one another. When one crashes, another soars — or at least hovers.

MSCI EAFE index: EAFE stands for Europe, Australia, and Far East, and MSCI stands for Morgan Stanley Capital International. This index is often used (incorrectly) to represent foreign stocks. What it really tracks are large cap stocks of developed foreign nations.

passive investing: You buy an index of stocks (preferably through an ETF), and you hold them. And you hold them. And you hold them. It's as boring as a game of bingo in which none of the letters called are the ones you need. And yet passive investors beat the pants off most active investors, year in and year out.

price/earnings ratio (P/E): Take a company's total earnings over the past 12 months and divide that by the number of shares of stock outstanding. The resulting number represents earnings, the lower number in the equation. Price, the upper number, refers to the market price of the stock. The P/E is the most common way in which stocks are identified as either value stocks or growth stocks. High P/E = growth. Low P/E = value.

Qubes: A nickname for the QQQ, an index that tracks the top 100 companies listed on the NASDAQ stock exchange. QQQ is also the ticker for the most popular ETF that tracks the QQQ. For years, the ticker was QQQQ and not QQQ. Why? We don't knowww.

real estate investment trust (REIT) stock/fund. A stock or fund that invests in a company or companies that make their money in real estate — most often commercial real estate, such as office buildings and shopping malls. REIT funds tend to be interest-rate sensitive and often have limited *correlation* to other funds.

risk: When we investment types talk of risk, we generally mean just one thing: *volatility,* or the unpredictability of an investment. The higher the risk, the greater the potential return.

R-squared: This measurement shows how tightly an investment hugs a certain index. An R-squared of 0.90 means that 90 percent of a fund's movement is attributable to movement in the index to which it's most similar. For an index fund or ETF, an R-squared of 1.00 is usually the goal. For a supposedly actively managed fund, an R-squared of 1.00 (or anything higher than 0.85 or so) means that you have a *closet index fund* — and you are being ripped off.

sector investing: If you break up your stock portfolio into different industry sectors — energy, consumer staples, financials — then you're a sector investor. Another option is *style investing.*

Sharpe ratio: A *risk*-adjusted measure of fund performance. In other words, it measures a fund's average historical return per unit of risk. The higher the number, the happier you should be.

sophisticated investor: Often mistaken for someone who trades every day and is constantly checking his account balance, or someone who uses charts and graphs and tries to time the markets. In the real world, such supposedly sophisticated investors rarely do as well as the so-called dummies who build well-diversified portfolios of low-cost index funds (such as ETFs) and let them sit undisturbed.

SPDR: This is the name of the brand line for ETFs issued by State Street Global Advisors (SSgA), the second-largest purveyor of ETFs after BlackRock.

spread: The difference between the *ask price* and *bid price* for a stock, ETF and other types of securities, such as bonds, currencies, and more.

standard deviation: The most used measure of *volatility* in the world of investments. The formula is long and complicated with lots of Greek symbols. Suffice it to say this: A standard deviation of 5 means that roughly two-thirds of the time, your investment returns will fall within 5 percentage points of the mean. So if your ETF has an historical mean return of 10 percent, two-thirds of the time you can expect to see your returns fall somewhere between 5 percent and 15 percent. If your ETF has an historical mean return of 5 percent, two-thirds of the time you can expect your return to be somewhere between 0 percent and 10 percent.

style investing: If you divvy up your stock investments into large, small, value, and growth, you are a style investor, as opposed to a sector investor. Which is better? Hard to say. See also *sector investing.*

style drift: It's 11 p.m. Do you know where your investments are? A manager of an active mutual fund tells you that her fund is, say, a large-growth fund.

And perhaps it was in the past. But lately, she has been loading up on large-value companies. Is she a growth investor or a value investor? Only she knows for sure. Investors, meanwhile, get stuck with her style drift and aren't sure exactly what they're holding. See also *transparency.*

tax-loss harvesting: Late in the year (most often), you can sell off a losing investment in order to claim a loss on your taxes. You can usually use tax losses — also called *capital losses* — to wipe out capital gains of the same amount. What if your loss exceeds your gain? Use what's left over to offset gains you made in the prior three years, or carry it forward indefinitely into the future.

technical analysis: The use of charts and graphs to try to predict the stock market. Some people take technical analysis very, very seriously — despite a lack of any evidence that it works.

ticker: The two- to five-letter symbol used for a stock, mutual fund, or ETF. Examples include RIM, BCE, and TAP; the latter is the clever NYSE ticker for the former Canadian beer company Molson Coors Brewing. Some ETF tickers are quite cute, too. One, for example, is called DOG (but none exists yet with the ticker GOD), which allows you to bet that DOW is going down. Another, called MOO, invests in agribusiness.

transparency: ETFs are beautifully transparent, which means that you know exactly what stocks or bonds your ETF holds, and how many of each. The same is not always true of mutual funds, hedge funds, or your spouse's safety deposit box.

turnover: The degree to which a fund changes its investments during the course of a year. A turnover rate of 100 means that the fund starts and ends the year with a completely different set of stocks. Turnover generally creates unpleasant tax liabilities for investors. Turnover, almost always, also involves hidden trading costs.

value fund: A mutual fund or ETF that invests in companies whose recent growth may be less than eye-popping but whose stock prices are believed to be cheap in comparison to the prices of stocks of other like companies.

value premium: During the past century or so, ever since the birth of organized stock markets, value stocks have performed much better than growth stocks, with relatively the same degree of *risk.* Theories abound, but to date, economists can't seem to agree on why this apparent value premium exists or whether it is likely to continue.

volatility: Whoooeee! What goes up fast often comes down just as fast. A stock or ETF that gained 40 percent last year can lose 40 percent this year. The market is volatile. It is risky. It can bring you great joy or great misery. Hope for the former, but be prepared for the latter.

yield: This term is most often used to mean the income derived from an investment over the past 12 months, as a percentage of the total investment. Income may come from dividends (most often the case with stocks or stock ETFs) or interest (from a bond or bond ETF). If you sink $10,000 into an ETF and it generates $500 in yearly income, your yield is 5 percent. If it generates $600, your yield is 6 percent, and so on.

YTD: Year-to-date return, or the total return (dividends plus any rise in the price of the stock or ETF) from the market's close on December 31 to the market's close on December 31 of the next year.

Index

• *D* •

About the Authors

Russell Wild is a NAPFA-certified financial advisor and principal of Global Portfolios, an investment advisory firm based in Allentown, Pennsylvania. He is one of only a handful of wealth managers in the nation who is both fee-only (takes no commissions) and welcomes clients of both substantial *and* modest means. He calls his firm Global Portfolios to reflect his ardent belief in international diversification — using exchange-traded funds to build well-diversified, low-expense, tax-efficient portfolios.

Wild, in addition to the fun he has with his financial calculator, is also an accomplished writer who helps readers understand and make wise choices about their money. His articles have appeared in many national publications, including *AARP The Magazine, Consumer Reports, Details, Maxim, Men's Health, Men's Journal, Cosmopolitan, Reader's Digest,* and *Real Simple.* He writes a regular finance column for *The Saturday Evening Post.* And he has also contributed to numerous professional journals, such as *Financial Planning, Financial Advisor,* and the *NAPFA Advisor.*

The author or coauthor of two dozen nonfiction books, Wild's last work (prior to the one you're holding in your hand) was *One Year to an Organized Financial Life,* coauthored with professional organizer Regina Leeds, published by Da Capo Press. He also wrote two other *For Dummies* titles in addition to this one: *Bond Investing For Dummies* and *Index Investing For Dummies.* No stranger to the mass media, Wild has shared his wit and wisdom on such shows as *Oprah, The View, CBS Morning News,* and *Good Day New York,* and in hundreds of radio interviews.

Wild holds a Master of Business Administration (MBA) degree with a concentration in finance from The Thunderbird School of Global Management, in Glendale, Arizona (consistently ranked the number-one school for international business by both *U.S. News and World Report* and *The Wall Street Journal*); a Bachelor of Science (BS) degree in business/economics *magna cum laude* from American University in Washington, D.C.; and a graduate certificate in personal financial planning from Moravian College in Bethlehem, Pennsylvania (America's sixth-oldest college). A member of the National Association of Personal Financial Advisors (NAPFA) since 2002, Wild is also a longtime member and past president of the American Society of Journalists and Authors (ASJA).

The author grew up on Long Island and now lives in Allentown, Pennsylvania. His son, Clayton, attends George Washington University in Washington, D.C. His daughter, Adrienne, is in high school. His dog, Norman, a standard poodle, protects their home from killer squirrels. His website is www.global portfolios.net.

Bryan Borzykowski is a Toronto-based financial journalist. He writes about investing and personal finance for *Canadian Business* magazine, *MoneySense,* the *Toronto Star,* and other publications. He also contributes small business stories to *The New York Times* and *The Globe and Mail,* and he's written for Time Inc., Forbes Media, and Bloomberg L.P. Bryan's talked about the markets and personal finance on several television and radio stations, including BNN, CTV News Channel, CHCH, and Citytv. Borzykowski is also the coauthor of two other *For Dummies* books: *Day Trading For Canadians For Dummies* and *Building Wealth All-in-One For Canadians For Dummies.* He's also the contributing editor and lead writer for *Canadian Business* magazine's annual *Investor's Guide* issue.

Borzykowski grew up in Winnipeg but now lives in Toronto with his wife and kids. Find out more at www.bryanborzykowski.com and at www.twitter.com/bborzyko.

Russell's Dedication

To the small investor, who has been bamboozled, bullied, and beaten up long enough.

Bryan's Dedication

To my parents, Brenda and Abe, who taught me how to make responsible choices in life and that actions have consequences. While their words of wisdom weren't directly about finances, those two lessons in particular have made me smarter about money.

Russell's Acknowledgments

Although I've written many books, the first edition of this book was my first *For Dummies* book, and writing a first *For Dummies* book is a bit like learning to ride a bicycle — on a very windy day. If it weren't for Joan Friedman, project editor, who kept a steady hand on the back of my seat, I would surely have fallen off a curb and been run over by a pickup truck flying a Confederate flag. Joan, hands down, is one of the best editors I've ever worked with. She's a very nice person, too. For those reasons, I was absolutely thrilled when I learned that Joan would be project editor on the second edition, as well. If there's ever a third edition . . . Joan?

Other nice people that I'd also like to tip my bicycle helmet to include Marilyn Allen of Allen O'Shea Literary Agency (she calls me "babe," just like agents do in movies; I love that) and Stacy Kennedy, acquisitions editor at Wiley. If these two gals hadn't gotten together, I wouldn't have had a bicycle to ride.

Thanks, too, to Paul Justice, CFA, editor of Morningstar's ETFInvestor newsletter. Paul, who knows a heck of a lot about ETFs, was the official technical editor on the U.S. version of this book, and he checked every chapter to make certain that this remained strictly a work of nonfiction. Fellow fee-only financial advisor and good friend Neil Stoloff then double-checked. You da man, Neil.

I'd like to thank Morningstar — all the folks there aside from Paul — for extreme generosity in providing fund industry data and analysis. Additional good data came from the various ETF providers, such as Vanguard, State Street, BlackRock, and T. Rowe Price, as well as a few non-ETF providers, such as Dimensional and the U.S. Treasury. Thanks, all.

I'd also like to thank Donald Bowles, my old professor of economics at American University, for showing me that supply and demand curves can be fun. Sorry we lost touch, but I haven't forgotten you.

And finally, I'd like to thank my old man, attorney Lawrence R. Wild, both my most beloved and most difficult client, who, if he told me once, told me a thousand times: "Rich or poor, it's good to have money." It took me years, Dad, to discover the profound wisdom in that statement.

Bryan's Acknowledgments

Behind every good writer is a great editor, and there's no doubt that I have one of the best editors around in Anam Ahmed. If it weren't for her, it's not certain this book would have gotten done. She kept the process moving smoothly, helpfully reminded me of deadlines, and asked insightful questions when things weren't clear. She's always a pleasure to work with and should receive a lot of the credit for getting this on the shelves. Give her a big high-five if you ever meet her.

I'd also like to thank Vikash Jain, the technical editor of the Canadian version of this book and the vice president and chief investment officer at Morguard Financial Corp. He's an ETF savant and helped make sure this book is accurate and the advice is sound.

Dan Bortolotti deserves a shout-out too. He's the author of the Canadian Couch Potato blog, which has tons of useful ETF information, including product reviews, portfolio examples, and more. Visit his website at canadian couchpotato.com.

A head nod goes out to all the web developers who've made finding information on the various ETF websites easy. One of the reasons why I like ETF investing so much is that finding out what's in an investment and how much it will cost is simple. Every website has detailed information on each ETF, so you have no excuse not to know what you're getting into.

Finally, I'd like to thank the entire Wiley Canada team for having me back again and again and for doing such a fantastic job in putting these books together. Investors of all skill levels can find out a lot in the *For Dummies* books. The Wiley crew makes sure these tomes are packed with information to not just help get you started but also to get you a few steps closer to a healthy and wealthy retirement.

Publisher's Acknowledgments

Acquisitions Editor: Anam Ahmed

Copy Editor: Andrea Douglas

Technical Editor: Vikash Jain

Senior Project Coordinator: Kristie Rees

Production Editor: Pamela Vokey

Cover Image: ©iStockphoto.com/Björn Meyer

EDUCATION, HISTORY & REFERENCE

978-0-7645-2498-1

978-0-470-46244-7

Also available:
- Algebra For Dummies 978-0-7645-5325-7
- Art History For Dummies 978-0-470-09910-0
- Chemistry For Dummies 978-0-7645-5430-8
- English Grammar For Dummies 978-0-470-54664-2
- French All-in-One For Dummies 978-1-118-22815-9
- Statistics For Dummies 978-0-7645-5423-0
- World History For Dummies 978-0-470-44654-6

FOOD, HOME, & MUSIC

978-1-118-11554-1

978-1-118-28872-6

Also available:
- 30-Minute Meals For Dummies 978-0-7645-2589-6
- Bartending For Dummies 978-0-470-63312-0
- Brain Games For Dummies 978-0-470-37378-1
- Cheese For Dummies 978-1-118-09939-1
- Cooking Basics For Dummies 978-0-470-91388-8
- Gluten-Free Cooking For Dummies 978-1-118-39644-5
- Home Improvement All-in-One Desk Reference For Dummies 978-0-7645-5680-7
- Home Winemaking For Dummies 978-0-470-67895-4
- Ukulele For Dummies 978-0-470-97799-6

GARDENING

978-0-470-58161-2

978-0-470-57705-9

Also available:
- Gardening Basics For Dummies 978-0-470-03749-2
- Organic Gardening For Dummies 978-0-470-43067-5
- Sustainable Landscaping For Dummies 978-0-470-41149-0
- Vegetable Gardening For Dummies 978-0-470-49870-5

WILEY

GREEN/SUSTAINABLE

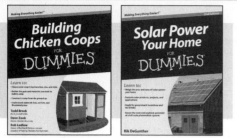

978-0-470-59896-2   978-0-470-59678-4

Also available:
- Alternative Energy For Dummies 978-0-470-43062-0
- Energy Efficient Homes For Dummies 978-0-470-37602-7
- Global Warming For Dummies 978-0-470-84098-6
- Green Building & Remodeling For Dummies 978-0-470-17559-0
- Green Cleaning For Dummies 978-0-470-39106-8
- Green Your Home All-in-One For Dummies 978-0-470-59678-4
- Wind Power Your Home For Dummies 978-0-470-49637-4

HEALTH & SELF-HELP

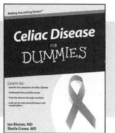

978-0-471-77383-2   978-0-470-16036-7

Also available:
- Body Language For Dummies 978-0-470-51291-3
- Borderline Personality Disorder For Dummies 978-0-470-46653-7
- Breast Cancer For Dummies 978-0-7645-2482-0
- Cognitive Behavioural Therapy For Dummies 978-0-470-66541-1
- Emotional Intelligence For Dummies 978-0-470-15732-9
- Healthy Aging For Dummies 978-0-470-14975-1
- Neuro-linguistic Programming For Dummies 978-0-470-66543-5
- Understanding Autism For Dummies 978-0-7645-2547-6

HOBBIES & CRAFTS

978-0-470-28747-7   978-1-118-01695-4

Also available:
- Bridge For Dummies 978-1-118-20574-7
- Crochet Patterns For Dummies 97-0-470-04555-8
- Digital Photography For Dummies 978-1-118-09203-3
- Jewelry Making & Beading Designs For Dummies 978-0-470-29112-2
- Knitting Patterns For Dummies 978-0-470-04556-5
- Oil Painting For Dummies 978-0-470-18230-7
- Quilting For Dummies 978-0-7645-9799-2
- Sewing For Dummies 978-0-7645-6847-3
- Word Searches For Dummies 978-0-470-45366-7

HOME & BUSINESS COMPUTER BASICS

978-1-118-13461-0

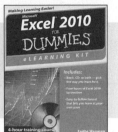

978-1-118-11079-9

Also available:
- Office 2010 All-in-One Desk Reference For Dummies 978-0-470-49748-7
- Pay Per Click Search Engine Marketing For Dummies 978-0-471-75494-7
- Search Engine Marketing For Dummies 978-0-471-97998-2
- Web Analytics For Dummies 978-0-470-09824-0
- Word 2010 For Dummies 978-0-470-48772-3

INTERNET & DIGITAL MEDIA

978-1-118-32800-2

978-1-118-38318-6

Also available:
- Blogging For Dummies 978-1-118-15194-5
- Digital Photography For Seniors For Dummies 978-0-470-44417-7
- Facebook For Dummies 978-1-118-09562-1
- LinkedIn For Dummies 978-0-470-94854-5
- Mom Blogging For Dummies 978-1-118-03843-7
- The Internet For Dummies 978-0-470-12174-0
- Twitter For Dummies 978-0-470-76879-2
- YouTube For Dummies 978-0-470-14925-6

MACINTOSH

978-0-470-87868-2

978-1118-49823-1

Also available:
- iMac For Dummies 978-0-470-20271-5
- iPod Touch For Dummies 978-1-118-12960-9
- iPod & iTunes For Dummies 978-1-118-50864-0
- MacBook For Dummies 978-1-11820920-2
- Macs For Seniors For Dummies 978-1-11819684-7
- Mac OS X Lion All-in-One For Dummies 978-1-118-02206-1

PETS

978-0-470-60029-0

978-0-7645-5267-0

Also available:
- Cats For Dummies 978-0-7645-5275-5
- Ferrets For Dummies 978-0-470-13943-1
- Horses For Dummies 978-0-7645-9797-8
- Kittens For Dummies 978-0-7645-4150-6
- Puppies For Dummies 978-1-118-11755-2

SPORTS & FITNESS

978-0-470-88279-5

978-1-118-01261-1

Also available:
- Exercise Balls For Dummies 978-0-7645-5623-4
- Coaching Volleyball For Dummies 978-0-470-46469-4
- Curling For Dummies 978-0-470-83828-0
- Fitness For Dummies 978-0-7645-7851-9
- Lacrosse For Dummies 978-0-470-73855-9
- Mixed Martial Arts For Dummies 978-0-470-39071-9
- Sports Psychology For Dummies 978-0-470-67659-2
- Ten Minute Tone-Ups For Dummies 978-0-7645-7207-4
- Wilderness Survival For Dummies 978-0-470-45306-3
- Wrestling For Dummies 978-1-118-11797-2
- Yoga with Weights For Dummies 978-0-471-74937-0